THE PSYCHOLOGY OF WISDOM

The Psychology of Wisdom: An Introduction is the first comprehensive coursebook on wisdom, offering an engaging, balanced, and expert introduction to the psychology of wisdom. It provides a comprehensive and up-to-date account of the psychological science of wisdom, covering wide-ranging perspectives. The extensive pedagogical features in each chapter include a glossary, bolded key terms, discussion questions, a brief description of the authors' research interests, and practical applications. The topics covered include: philosophical foundations, folk conceptions, and psychological theories of wisdom; the relationship of wisdom to morality and ethics, to personality and well-being, and to emotion; wisdom and leadership; and wisdom and social policy. These topics are presented in a non-technical, bias-free, and student-friendly manner. Written by the most eminent experts in the field, this is the definitive coursebook for undergraduate and graduate students, as well as for interested professionals and researchers.

ROBERT J. STERNBERG is Professor of Psychology at Cornell University and Honorary Professor of Psychology at the University of Heidelberg, Germany. His PhD is from Stanford University, and he holds 13 honorary doctorates. He was awarded the Grawemeyer Award in Psychology, and the APS William James and James McKeen Cattell Awards. He is former president of the American Psychological Association, the Federation of Associations in Behavioral and Brain Sciences, and the International Association for Cognitive Education and Psychology.

JUDITH GLÜCK is Professor of Developmental Psychology at the University of Klagenfurt, Austria. Her research focuses on how wisdom develops, how it can be measured, how it manifests itself in real life, and how it can be fostered in individuals as well as communities. She has held several grants from the Austrian Science Fund, and has published in journals including the *Annual Review of Psychology, Developmental Psychology,* and *The Journals of Gerontology: Psychological Sciences*.

T0381888

THE PSYCHOLOGY OF WISDOM

An Introduction

EDITED BY

ROBERT J. STERNBERG

Cornell University

JUDITH GLÜCK

University of Klagenfurt

CAMBRIDGE
UNIVERSITY PRESS

CAMBRIDGE
UNIVERSITY PRESS

University Printing House, Cambridge CB2 8BS, United Kingdom

One Liberty Plaza, 20th Floor, New York, NY 10006, USA

477 Williamstown Road, Port Melbourne, VIC 3207, Australia

314–321, 3rd Floor, Plot 3, Splendor Forum, Jasola District Centre, New Delhi – 110025, India

103 Penang Road, #05–06/07, Visioncrest Commercial, Singapore 238467

Cambridge University Press is part of the University of Cambridge.

It furthers the University's mission by disseminating knowledge in the pursuit of education, learning, and research at the highest international levels of excellence.

www.cambridge.org
Information on this title: www.cambridge.org/9781316514634
DOI: 10.1017/9781009085724

© Cambridge University Press 2022

First published 2022

A catalogue record for this publication is available from the British Library.

Library of Congress Cataloging-in-Publication Data
NAMES: Sternberg, Robert J., editor. | Glück, Judith, editor.
TITLE: The psychology of wisdom : an introduction / edited by Robert J. Sternberg, Cornell University, Judith Glück, University of Klagenfurt.
DESCRIPTION: Cambridge, United Kingdom ; New York, NY : Cambridge University Press, 2022. | Includes bibliographical references and index.
IDENTIFIERS: LCCN 2021057206 (print) | LCCN 2021057207 (ebook) | ISBN 9781316514634 (hardback) | ISBN 9781009088008 (paperback) | ISBN 9781009085724 (epub)
SUBJECTS: LCSH: Thought and thinking. | Wisdom–Psychological aspects. | Intellect. | BISAC: PSYCHOLOGY / Applied Psychology
CLASSIFICATION: LCC BF441 .P834 2022 (print) | LCC BF441 (ebook) | DDC 153.4/2–DC23/eng/20220208
LC record available at https://lccn.loc.gov/2021057206
LC ebook record available at https://lccn.loc.gov/2021057207

ISBN 978-1-316-51463-4 Hardback
ISBN 978-1-009-08800-8 Paperback

Contents

Figures

vii

Tables

Contributors

DON AMBROSE, Rider University

MONIKA ARDELT, University of Florida

SUSAN BLUCK, University of Florida

DOWON CHOI, Florida State University

MICHEL FERRARI, University of Toronto

JUDITH GLÜCK, University of Klagenfurt

IGOR GROSSMANN, University of Waterloo

SAREH KARAMI, Mississippi State University

JAMES C. KAUFMAN, University of Connecticut

JUENSUNG J. KIM, University of Toronto

UTE KUNZMANN, University of Leipzig

SARAH F. LYNCH, Boston University

BERNARD MCKENNA, University of Queensland

STEPHANIE MORRIS, University of Toronto

STEPHEN PRIDGEN, Concord University

DAVID ROONEY, Macquarie University

BARRY SCHWARTZ, University of California Berkeley

KENNETH E. SHARPE, Swarthmore College and Dartmouth College

ROBERT J. STERNBERG, Cornell University

JASON D. SWARTWOOD, Saint Paul College

NIC M. WESTSTRATE, University of Illinois at Chicago

Preface

During the twentieth century, IQs around the world increased by 30 points. Yet this steep rise in IQ seems to have achieved little in helping humanity to address and successfully cope with the enormous challenges that face the world today – global climate change, air and water pollution, pandemics, hunger, political instability, global inequality, and weapons of mass destruction, to name just a few. Something beyond IQ, and the education that is based on it, is needed to successfully confront these major problems. We suggest that this "something" is wisdom.

Throughout human history, wisdom has been defined in many different ways, and there is still no one universally accepted definition. However, most scholars of wisdom would agree that wise people are concerned not just for their own interests and those of their friends and family, but also for those of humanity at large. They seek to create a better world by making a positive, meaningful, and potentially enduring difference, whether at the level of family, community, country, world, or some other level.

Not long ago, the field of wisdom research was moribund, at least among psychologists. Among philosophers and theologians, of course, the study of wisdom has long been a major pursuit. Their methods are not empirical, and it was not clear to empirical researchers just how to study or even to think about wisdom.

Perhaps the scholars who turned the field around most were Paul Baltes, Director of the Max Planck Institute for Human Development in Berlin, and Vivian Clayton, who started off as a graduate student at the University of Southern California. In the latter half of the twentieth century, Baltes proposed a theory and conducted empirical tests of it that still figure prominently in the field of wisdom research today. Clayton wrote an impressive theoretical and empirical doctoral dissertation on wisdom that also led to one of the earliest theories. The field was ready to take off – and it did.

In 1990, Cambridge University Press published a volume titled *Wisdom: Its Nature, Origins, and Development*, edited by Robert J. Sternberg. The volume contained essays by many of the major figures in the field who were studying wisdom at that time. According to Google Scholar, the book has been cited over 1000 times, but the individual essays in the book have been cited far more often. Much of the work was still theoretical, but it was clear that psychologists were converging on what they believed to be an important but neglected construct in psychology. The work of Baltes and Clayton helped enormously, because it provided measurement tools. However, the field was still in its infancy and, for some time, Baltes's research group was by far the best known one studying wisdom empirically.

By the beginning of the twenty-first century, the field had begun to diversify, and research on wisdom was making real progress. This work was captured in the *Handbook of Wisdom: Psychological Perspectives,* edited by Robert J. Sternberg and Jennifer Jordan, and published in

2005. The book represented the state of the field at the turn of the twenty-first century, and according to Google Scholar it has been cited around 400 times, but again the individual chapters have been cited far more often.

In 2011, Barry Schwartz and Kenneth Sharpe published *Practical Wisdom: The Right Way to Do the Right Thing*, a fine and well-regarded exposition of the importance of wisdom in everyday life. In 2014, Michel Ferrari and Nic Weststrate published *The Scientific Study of Personal Wisdom: From Contemplative Traditions to Neuroscience*, an edited volume that provided a good summary of the state of the field.

The field was now growing exponentially. The handbook was out of date within less than a decade, and in 2019, Cambridge University Press published the *Cambridge Handbook of Wisdom*, edited by Robert J. Sternberg and Judith Glück.

Whereas the first Cambridge volume, *Wisdom* (Sternberg, 1990), ran to 352 fairly small pages, and *A Handbook of Wisdom* (Sternberg & Jordan, 2005) had 406 pages, *The Cambridge Handbook of Wisdom* (Sternberg & Glück, 2019) ran to 828 pages. It is probably fair to say that not only the book length but also the amount of theory and research roughly doubled between 2005 and 2019.

Motivation for Writing This Book

At the time of writing, the topic of wisdom is producing 3.5 million hits in Google Scholar and 388 million hits in Google. However, until now there has been no widely available textbook on the subject of psychological approaches to wisdom, despite the importance of the field not only to psychology, but also to the world.

Our motivation for editing this book has therefore been to produce the first and, at the time of publication, the only widely available textbook on the psychology of wisdom. Our goal is to facilitate the teaching of a course on the topic by faculty in psychology, human development, and related disciplines.

The Target Readership for the Book

The primary audience for the book is upper-division undergraduates and graduate students who are studying wisdom in the context of psychology and related social-science disciplines. In addition, there may be laypeople who are interested in educating themselves on the topic, but who would find the full *Cambridge Handbook of Wisdom* too forbidding.

The Concept of a Multi-Contributor Textbook

This is an edited textbook containing contributions from multiple authors. The concept underlying an edited textbook is different from that underlying a textbook written by one or just a few authors. There are two obvious potential drawbacks – that the book will not have a single coherent point of view, and that there will be differences in the writing styles among the various chapters.

First, let us consider the fact that, instead of representing a single coherent point of view, the book will offer multiple viewpoints. This actually reflects the state of the field of wisdom today, and is likely to be the state of the field for a long time to come. In contrast to, say, the fields of physics or chemistry, there is no single unified consensus point of view on major issues. An edited textbook represents the diversity of the field. The book can and should be reflective of the current state of the field, showing the various viewpoints that exist, and the strengths and weaknesses of the different approaches. One of us is currently using a textbook in one of his courses that takes a single position in a field where there are diverse points of view. The downside to this textbook is that the professor constantly has to be reminding students that the author has a strong point of view that does not represent a consensus in the field. The author also often fails to adequately address other points of view, the reasons why his scholarly competitors hold those views, and the evidence supporting them.

Second, with regard to writing style, we have found that careful editing can achieve a largely unified sense of writing style within a multi-contributor book. For example, *Human Intelligence: An Introduction,* edited by Robert J. Sternberg and published by Cambridge University Press, has multiple authors, but the combined work of the book's editor and the editing team at Cambridge University Press has provided a strong sense of a unified volume.

An edited textbook also has three additional advantages.

First, the involvement of multiple authors ensures that various well thought out points of view will be adequately represented and defended. In the field of wisdom there are few, if any, final answers. It is a field that, historically, has invited many different perspectives, some of which, such as the philosophical one, lie outside of psychology proper. Having multiple authors ensures that the different points of view will be properly characterized, and their strengths and weaknesses elucidated.

Second, the field of wisdom has quickly expanded from what it was in earlier times. Researchers have specialized in different topics within the field, which now represents an almost astonishing array of different approaches and kinds of expertise. One of the advantages of an edited textbook is that it draws on diverse types of expertise that are unlikely to be found together in any one person.

Third, an edited textbook can present the viewpoints of the authors at first hand, ensuring that they are correctly represented and that the current research is being described by the people who are actually conducting much of that research.

On balance, we believe that an edited textbook has advantages over one written by one or just a few authors. These advantages have been shown in *Human Intelligence: An Introduction* and in another textbook, namely *Creativity: An Introduction,* edited by James Kaufman and Robert Sternberg. Both are published by Cambridge University Press.

The present textbook is divided into 15 chapters in order to provide coverage of all the main topics currently being investigated in the field. At this length, the book fits conveniently into a one-semester course. The content of the chapters is briefly summarized below.

Part I   Introduction to Wisdom Theory and Research

1   Introduction: What Is Wisdom and Why Is It Important?
This chapter introduces the concept of wisdom, defines it, and describes why it is so important in today's world.

2   Philosophical Foundations for the Study of Wisdom
This chapter covers the philosophical literature that has served as the core for the psychological study of wisdom, from the time of Plato and Aristotle up to the present day.

Part III   The Modifiability of Wisdom

11   The Development of Wisdom

This chapter describes how wisdom develops, from childhood through old age. It also considers the longstanding debate as to whether, in adulthood, wisdom increases or decreases with age, or whether it remains largely unchanged.

12   Interventions for Developing Wisdom

This chapter describes how schools and parents can teach children in a way that enhances the wisdom of young people.

Part IV   Wisdom in the World

13   Wisdom in the Professions

This chapter describes wisdom as it is manifested in various professions, and how it can be developed through those professions.

14   Wisdom and Leadership

This chapter describes the characteristics of wise leadership, and why wise leadership is so important for the world today. It also discusses why people often fear wise leaders and instead choose "toxic" leaders.

15   Wisdom and Social Policy

This chapter describes how wisdom can and should be incorporated into social-policy decisions. How can wisdom help the world to address the problems that it is currently facing, such as global climate change, air and water pollution, resource shortages, severe economic inequality, and global pandemics?

Pedagogy

This textbook includes the following pedagogical features to enhance learning and make it easier for students to understand the material that is presented in each chapter:

(1) **Comprehension and discussion questions.** These questions challenge students to actively and reflectively think about the material in the chapter.
(2) **Key terms.** Bold print identifies those terms that the authors of the chapters believe are most important for students to learn.
(3) **Glossary.** The glossary defines the bolded terms for students, so that they do not have to spend valuable time looking them up.
(4) **Investigations.** This section of the chapter gives a brief description of the authors' research programs on wisdom. The investigations acquaint students with cutting-edge research in the field.
(5) **Practical applications.** This section of the chapter describes how contemporary research can be applied in real-world practice in order to improve people's lives.

REFERENCES

Ferrari, M. and Weststrate, N. M., eds. (2014). *The Scientific Study of Personal Wisdom: From Contemplative Traditions to Neuroscience.* Springer.

Schwartz, B. and Sharpe, K. E. (2010). *Practical Wisdom: The Right Way to Do the Right Thing.* Riverhead Books.

Sternberg, R. J., ed. (1990). *Wisdom: Its Nature, Origins, and Development.* Cambridge University Press.

Sternberg, R. J. and Glück, J., eds. (2019). *The Cambridge Handbook of Wisdom.* Cambridge University Press.

Sternberg, R. J. and Jordan, J., eds. (2005). *A Handbook of Wisdom: Psychological Perspectives.* Cambridge University Press.

PART I

Introduction to Wisdom Theory and Research

CHAPTER I

Introduction
What Is Wisdom and Why Is It Important?[1]
Robert J. Sternberg and Judith Glück

1.1 Introduction

There are many tales in great works of literature, including religious literature, of people who, by any standard, would be considered exceptionally wise. For example, King Solomon, in the Old Testament, allegedly discovered which of two women was the true mother of a child by suggesting that the child be cut in half, and each woman be given half. He believed that the woman who rejected the offer would be, for sure, the true mother of the child. In the New Testament, Jesus is alleged to have told the story of the Good Samaritan, who helps a Jew who has been robbed and beaten, despite the fact that, at the time, the Jews and the Samaritans detested each other. And the Buddha is quoted as having said that the best ornament is humility, and the greatest wealth, **wisdom**. The wisdom shown by King Solomon in his dealings with the alleged mothers, by Jesus in his story of the Good Samaritan, and by the Buddha in his recognition of the importance of wisdom, is the topic of this chapter and of this book.

Stories of wisdom are not limited to the murky past. In modern times, Nelson Mandela transformed himself from a violent revolutionary into one of the greatest and wisest leaders that the world has seen in a long time, bringing peace to a country, South Africa, that had been torn by dissension and violence. Martin Luther King, Jr., of the USA, defied enormous societal pressure and imprisonment to become one of the foremost leaders advocating civil rights and equality for all. In recent times, Malala Yousafzai fought for rights for women in Pakistan and got shot in the face for doing so. Even after the shooting, she continued to campaign for human rights. And Alexei Navalny fought for human rights in Russia, was poisoned, in all likelihood at the direction of the Russian government, and almost died as a result. Upon miraculously recovering, he returned to Russia again to fight for human rights, only to be imprisoned. Wisdom and the courage that goes with it are not stories just from the past. They are stories of current times as well.

If one thing has become abundantly clear in modern times, it is the importance and, indeed, the indispensable nature of wisdom to societies around the world (Sternberg, 2019a). We sometimes refer to the world today as a "knowledge society," to distinguish it from earlier industrial society, where the role of industry was king, and from pre-industrial societies, where industry had not yet taken over the means of production. A knowledge society is one in which knowledge – what you know and what you know how to do – drives society and its development. The importance attached to knowledge in today's world is shown by the importance attached to

[1] This chapter draws in part on ideas earlier presented in Sternberg, R. J. (2019a). Race to Samarra: the critical importance of wisdom in the world today. In R. J. Sternberg and J. Glück, eds., *The Cambridge Handbook of Wisdom*. Cambridge University Press, pp. 3–9.

education – to college and university degrees attesting to one's level of, and success in, becoming educated.

This chapter, and many of the chapters to follow, will argue that we may need to shift our emphasis – that what matters most to the world today is not knowledge, but rather how we use the knowledge we have. And what matters especially is not just any use of that knowledge, but rather, especially, the wise use of that knowledge.

1.2   What Is Wisdom?

What, exactly, is wisdom? In this textbook you will find many definitions of wisdom. We shall not attempt an exact definition, because the field does not yet have a consensus. However, there are some characteristics that most researchers and experts on wisdom would agree are characteristics of the wise person (see, e.g., Grossmann et al., 2019; Jeste et al., 2010; Sternberg & Glück, 2019; Sternberg et al., 2019). Here, we first discuss some general points about what wisdom is and what it is not, with the intention of illustrating why today's world urgently needs more wisdom.

1.2.1   Wise People Seek a Common Good

Wise people have in common that they are not focused only on their own benefit, or on the benefit of those who are in some way like them – their metaphorical "tribe." In making judgments and decisions, in general, they think beyond themselves and those who are somehow like them – family, friends, colleagues, or people of the same nationality, ethnicity, or other group.

It is too easy, in making our decisions, just to consider our own interests and those of others like us, especially in an age in which self-preoccupation and narcissism seem to be on the rise. Often, success in individualistic societies is about one's own outcomes, without considering also how those outcomes affect others. As a result, people no longer work together as harmoniously as they sometimes did in the past.

In the USA, in the third decade of the twenty-first century, the two major political parties, the Republicans and the Democrats, have become practically incapable of working together and cooperating toward the achievement of a **common good**. In many other countries, political polarization is increasing as well. In every country, strict guidelines have been set with regard to priority levels for people receiving a COVID-19 vaccine, but this has not stopped many individuals from relentlessly trying to push ahead of others in higher-priority categories. In some cases, the violations of protocol have been ridiculous, as in the case of a multi-millionaire couple who flew to Canada's remote Yukon Territory and pretended to be local motel workers in order to become eligible for the vaccine, which they did indeed receive (Farzan, 2021).

Why is a common good so very important? In a less connected world, it actually probably was less important. It mattered for communities, then states or provinces, then perhaps nearby countries that might go to war with each other. But today the entire world is highly interconnected. What people do in one country can affect countries halfway around the world. In case there are any doubters, perhaps nothing showed this interconnectedness better than the worldwide spread of COVID-19. Although the origin of the particular novel coronavirus is unknown, it appears likely to have started in or near some kind of animal market, probably in or near Wuhan, China (Centers for Disease Control and Prevention, 2020). The world would soon discover how an isolated event in China – or anywhere – could become a worldwide problem that would cost millions of people their lives, and sicken many millions more.

It appears clear that local Chinese government officials initially hid the existence and certainly the severity of the outbreak from national officials (Wong et al., 2020). But then, other nations did not realize the severity of the outbreak. Today, that is all history. An event that once would have remained a problem in a very localized part of the world had caused a catastrophic global mess.

Society is more fractured recently than it has been in many years. Competition rather than cooperation with respect to COVID-19 vaccines is one example, but there are so many others. One obvious example is the unprecedented incursion into the US Capitol Building that occurred on January 6, 2021. Many of the raiders appear to have believed they were acting like patriots in invading the Capitol Building, trashing part of it, and causing the death of five people. Some planned to take hostages, or worse (Biesecker et al., 2021). Many of these people were well educated. What has gone wrong? How could such events take place in the twenty-first century?

1.3 Why Intelligence Is Not Enough

Intelligence – the ability to learn, reason, and adapt to the environment – is often viewed as multipartite. Modern models of intelligence divide the construct into many factors and hierarchically arranged subfactors (Carroll, 1993; McGrew, 2005). Many of the commonly used models derive from the work of Cattell (1971), who distinguished between crystallized and fluid intelligence.

1.3.1 *Crystallized Intelligence*

Crystallized intelligence is basically knowledge base. It is what you know. When we talk about a "knowledge society," we are talking about the build-up of crystallized intelligence. Crystallized intelligence and the knowledge that represents it are clearly needed, in some degree, for wisdom. One cannot make recommendations about a field or about the world, in general, if one's knowledge base about the field or the world is severely limited. One great advantage of the Internet is that knowledge has been made much more accessible to people around the world. Unfortunately, this has also meant that falsehoods – so-called "alternative facts" – which are sometimes hard to distinguish from actual facts, have become much more widespread. In addition, maybe the concept of a knowledge society itself is not as good an idea as it might first seem to be.

First, having knowledge provides no guarantee that the knowledge will be used wisely. Many of the US congresspeople who are at each other's throats have degrees – in some cases, advanced degrees – from prestigious colleges and universities. Their well-developed knowledge bases have not helped them to work together effectively. Similarly, government officials around the world had been warned for years – decades, in fact – that a pandemic of some kind was just over the horizon. Yet almost all of them were ill-prepared when the pandemic finally arrived in 2020.

It gets worse. Nazi doctors had medical degrees and others among the Nazis had other kinds of advanced degrees. Not only did their knowledge not stop them from slaughtering people, but that knowledge was actually used by many of them in the service of the creation of a spurious ideology of racial superiority. Going back a bit further, during the US Civil War, many educated, even highly educated White people in the South supported slavery, while many in the North opposed it. A deadly war was fought in part over whether slavery should be allowed to exist.

Knowledge is important, but, in the end, what matters most is how that knowledge is deployed. People can know a lot and have all kinds of advanced degrees attesting to that knowledge, but possessing knowledge is, at best, necessary but not sufficient for wise thinking. And it is even worse than that, because there is quite general agreement that the kind of knowledge that most matters for wisdom is not academic or formal knowledge, but rather informal knowledge about people and about life. This kind of knowledge is sometimes also called tacit knowledge (Polanyi, 1976; Sternberg et al., 2000). It is what one needs to know in order to succeed in everyday life that is not formally taught, and that may not even be verbalized. Wisdom is built primarily, although not exclusively, on a foundation of informal knowledge (Baltes & Staudinger, 1993, 2000; Sternberg, 1998, 2019b; Webster, 2003, 2007; Weststrate & Glück, 2017). People can have a lot of academic knowledge but lack informal knowledge about the world, or simply not know how to use that knowledge.

1.3.2   Fluid Intelligence

Fluid intelligence is one's ability to solve relatively novel problems or more familiar problems that are nevertheless presented in relatively novel contexts. According to Cattell's theory, fluid intelligence gives rise to crystallized intelligence (Cattell, 1971).

Fluid intelligence is measured by tests such as number series (e.g., 2, 5, 8, 11?) and word classification (e.g., Which word does not belong? BOAT, SHIP, SAIL, VESSEL). Fluid intelligence, like crystallized intelligence, is needed for wisdom. Wise people are always confronting novel tasks and situations largely unlike any they have encountered before. And yet . . .

Fluid intelligence, like crystallized intelligence, may not be all it is cracked up to be. James Flynn (1987, 2012) discovered that, during the twentieth century, the IQs of adults around the world increased by roughly 30 points between 1900 and 2000. That's about 3 points every 10 years. A difference of 30 points roughly represents the difference between a person who is identified as borderline mentally challenged and someone identified as intellectually average, or between a person who is identified as intellectually average and someone identified as borderline intellectually gifted. Clearly, that is a huge difference. The average IQ remained 100 only because test publishers re-normed the tests. That is, they kept resetting the average to 100, regardless of the number of correct answers that test-takers supplied. Most of this gain – really, almost all of it – was in fluid intelligence.

Flynn (2012) has explained this difference as reflecting the increased cognitive demands of the modern world. Part of the difference may also be the result of more intelligence-oriented parenting and early education. In any case, IQs are not fixed generationally. Rather, they respond to the demands of the environment. However, Flynn and many others have recognized that, even with all those IQ points, people do not seem to be doing such a great job in responding to all the challenges the world presents. The initial response to the pandemic of COVID-19 was a mess. Governments all over the world bungled the response –first in being unprepared, then in stopping the spread of the disease, and then in equitably distributing the vaccine. Governments have also failed to rise to the challenge of global climate change, which has been getting worse and worse as governments, at best, talk the talk without walking the walk. And then there is the absurd overuse of antibiotics, which has resulted in many harmful bacteria being enabled to develop mutations that would allow them to resist the effects of the antibiotics. Experts have been warning about all these dangers for a long time, but despite all their collective intelligence, many governments do not seem to be heeding the warnings.

As Flynn (2012) recognized, the greatest challenges of the twenty-first century are not in our levels of intelligence, but rather in how our intelligence is deployed. Sternberg (2021a) has even defined a construct of *adaptive intelligence*, or the intelligence that is needed to make the world a better place. And a key part of this adaptive intelligence is wisdom – seeking a common good rather than using our own intelligence only for our own exclusive benefit. So, intelligence seems to be up to today's challenges only if it includes a wisdom component.

1.4 Why Creativity Is Not Enough

Creativity offers possibilities for innovation that intelligence, at least as traditionally defined, does not offer. Creativity is usually defined as the making of a contribution – an idea or a product – that is both novel and useful or effective in some way (Kaufman & Sternberg, 2019). Intelligence tests measure primarily your knowledge (crystallized intelligence) and your analytical thinking with that knowledge (fluid intelligence), but creativity goes beyond this in requiring one, somehow, to go beyond the given in a meaningful way.

Many of the greatest ideas and inventions have been a result of human creativity. Leonardo da Vinci's *Mona Lisa,* Plato's *Republic,* Toni Morrison's *Beloved,* Mozart's *Requiem,* Marie Curie's explorations of radium, and, in a different domain, Jacinda Ardern's plan to keep New Zealand almost free of COVID-19, all required creativity. Without creativity, we would not have computers, cell phones, TVs, or flush toilets, for that matter. Creativity has made possible a world that would scarcely have been imaginable in the past, except in science fiction (itself a product of creativity).

However, creativity has not yet been adequate to solve many of the world's greatest problems. Oddly enough, creativity has been, in part, responsible for many of these problems. For example, global climate change is due in large part to human-caused innovations, such as internal-combustion engines, industrial farming, and various kinds of pollutants emitted by factories. Antibiotics were a wonderful creative innovation that was undermined by humans when they decided to overuse them. Nuclear technology could have been, and still is and can be, a tremendous innovation with regard to production of energy, but it also has been used to produce weapons of mass destruction. And human errors in nuclear plants can be catastrophic, as they were at Chernobyl.

Because creativity has been used for negative as well as positive purposes, much as intelligence has been, some investigators of creativity distinguish between positive and negative creativity. Positive creativity is the production of ideas, products, and any innovations at all that are novel and useful, as per the definition of creativity, but that are also beneficial in some way to humanity at any level (Clark & James, 1999; James et al., 1999; James & Taylor, 2010; Sternberg, 2021b, in press). *Transformational creativity* goes beyond positive creativity, in that it seeks transformational change that makes the world a better place (Sternberg, 2021c). Positive creativity can be distinguished from negative creativity, which is creativity that is in some way, and at some level, harmful to humanity. At its extreme, negative creativity is sometimes referred to as *malevolent creativity* (Cropley et al., 2008, 2010, 2014), which is creativity that is intended to be harmful. Scams and hacking of people's computer accounts are examples of malevolent creativity.

Positive creativity can be viewed in different ways, but our way of viewing it is as creativity tempered by wisdom. It is the utilization of creativity to attain some kind of common good, even if at a very basic level, such as the well-being of people close to one, whereby that well-being does not come at other people's expense.

Clearly, the judgment of something as either positive or negative is, to some extent, in the eye of the beholder. However, believers in the value of wisdom as a psychological construct generally agree that there is some sense of common good that rises above people's mere personal opinions or ideologies. For example, the so-called golden rule – to act toward others as you would have them act toward you – is a principle of wisdom that seems to transcend boundaries of personal taste. Similarly, acting so as to minimize harm to others, so far as is possible, is a precept of wisdom that would seem to transcend personal idiosyncratic judgments.

Thus, both intelligence and creativity in themselves are not sufficient for negotiating the serious problems that face the world today, unless they draw upon wisdom.

1.5 Why Wisdom Is So Hard to Find

Why is it so much easier to find intelligence and creativity in the real world than to find wisdom? One can fairly easily think of intelligent leaders, relatively easily think of creative leaders, but only with difficulty call to mind wise leaders. We make some suggestions here regarding the paucity of wisdom, building upon Sternberg (2019a). Basically, the reasons amount to there being so many other options besides wisdom, many of which are rewarded more, in the short term at least, than is wisdom.

1.5.1 Kinds of Wisdom

Wisdom can apply, outside oneself, across domains of inquiry and within specific domains of inquiry, or it can apply to oneself. For example, Staudinger (2019) has suggested that wisdom is quite different when it is applied outside oneself to others, and Grossmann et al. (2019) have suggested that wisdom can be quite domain-specific.

Table 1.1 lists the kinds of wisdom that might be relevant to dealing with a wide variety of situations (domain-general wisdom), specific kinds of situations (domain-specific wisdom), and

Table 1.1 *Kinds of wisdom*

Depth of wisdom: Domain application of wisdom:	Deep (D)	Shallow (S)
Domain general (G)	**GD** Deeply insightful advice across domains	**GS** Modestly insightful advice across domains
Domain specific (S)	**SD** Deeply insightful advice in a single domain	**SS** Modestly insightful advice in a single domain
Personal (P)	**PD** Deeply insightful realization regarding oneself	**PS** Modestly insightful realization regarding oneself

Rows (first letter in acronym): G = domain general; S = domain specific; P = personal.
Columns (second letter in acronym): D = deep; S = shallow.

oneself (personal wisdom) (Sternberg, 2019a). An example of domain-general wisdom would be acting toward others as you would have them act toward you. An example of domain-specific wise advice would be to ensure that you cite relevant previous scholarship upon which you base your new arguments in a scholarly paper. An example of personal wisdom would be to recognize that if you study wisdom but tend to be arrogant or selfish, you must try to control those tendencies because they will undermine your credibility if your audience finds out about them. People may be generally wise but not wise when it comes to matters concerning themselves.

The problem with regard to wisdom being displayed in the world is twofold. If, indeed, much of wisdom is specific to particular kinds of domains and situations, wisdom across all of these domains and situations might be hard to attain, given the amount of tacit knowledge that one would need in order to be wise across such a wide range of human endeavors. As with creativity, which tends to be largely domain-specific (Baer, 2015) – in part because of the domain-specific knowledge needed within a given domain in order to be creative – people might exhaust their domain-specific wisdom pretty quickly outside domains in which they possess high levels of world knowledge. Furthermore, if personal wisdom is indeed a relatively distinct construct, in the manner of interpersonal and intrapersonal intelligences in Gardner's (2011) theory of multiple intelligences, then people might be wise with respect to either certain domains or personal situations, but not both. In other words, wisdom might be out there, but just be very limited in how widely it can be applied.

The second issue highlighted in Table 1.1 is that wisdom can be either deep or shallow. When wisdom is shallow, it analyzes a problem but at a superficial level. Superficial wisdom is probably not sufficient to solve challenging real-world problems. The result may be that the solution just is not wise enough to provide a basis for dealing adequately with the problem at hand. Some scholars do not even view shallow wisdom as actual wisdom, but rather as an attempt at wisdom.

1.5.2   Non-Wisdom

A second class or problem in the manifestation of wisdom in the real world is that so much of what appears to be wisdom is not in fact wisdom (Sternberg, 2019a). Table 1.2 lists six kinds of non-wisdom that might appear, at first glance, to be wisdom, but that in fact are not.

The first kind of non-wisdom is *quasi-wisdom*, in which there is a limited definition of the common good. Someone may believe that they are being wise, but they apply their quasi-wisdom only to people like themselves or to people whom they perceive as being members of the same

Table 1.2 *Kinds of non-wisdom*

Kind of non-wisdom	Manifestation
Quasi-wisdom: limited definition of common good	Incomplete specification of affected stakeholders
Quasi-wisdom: limited balancing of interests	Imbalance of interests to favor one group over another
Veneer of wisdom	False appearance of wisdom as a result of position of power or authority
Egocentric pseudo-wisdom	False appearance of wisdom motivated by self-interest
Dark pseudo-wisdom	False appearance of wisdom motivated by evil intentions
Unrealized wisdom	Wisdom in words but not deeds

tribe as them, such as people from their family or extended family, or of their race, ethnicity, nationality, religion, or whatever.

The second kind of non-wisdom is *quasi-wisdom*, in which there is a failure to adequately **balance** – to weigh fairly against each other – different and often competing interests. Rather, the quasi-wise person favors the interests of one group or some groups over others, whether deliberately or inadvertently, or simply balances the scale heavily in their own favor.

The third kind of non-wisdom is the *veneer of wisdom,* in which the individual is labeled by some in authority or by some followers as wise, merely by dint of their position of power or authority or their charismatic leadership. They may have no wisdom at all, but their followers act, either voluntarily (as in a voluntary cult) or involuntarily (as in a dictatorship, often disguised as a democracy), as though the individual is wise.

The fourth kind of non-wisdom is *egocentric pseudo-wisdom,* which is the false appearance of wisdom that is really motivated by self-interest. The individual acts as though they are helping others, although they are only interested in benefiting themselves.

The fifth kind of non-wisdom is *dark pseudo-wisdom,* in which the false appearance of wisdom is motivated by evil intentions, such as to harm others.

The sixth kind of non-wisdom is *unrealized wisdom,* which is the production of a wise course of action that is not then followed through with action. It is not easy to generate wise ideas, but it is far easier to generate a wise idea than to enact it, as there is often serious opposition to the enactment of wise ideas.

In summary, there are at least six kinds of ideas that can appear at first to be wise but which, upon closer examination, turn out not to be.

1.5.3   Foolishness

People also fail to be wise because they succumb to **foolishness**. Intelligence is no guarantee against foolishness. Rather, people who are intelligent may actually be more susceptible to foolishness because they believe they are immune to it. Table 1.3 lists eight kinds of foolishness, although there are certainly others (Sternberg, 2005, 2019a).

First, people are unrealistically optimistic when they believe that, because an idea is theirs, it must be good. Second, people are egocentric when they believe that, in the end, everything is about them. Third, people are falsely omniscient when they mistakenly believe they know everything, or at least everything that is needed to solve a complex problem. Fourth, people are

Table 1.3 *Kinds of foolishness*

Fallacy	Manifestation
Unrealistic optimism	"If it's my idea, it must be good"
Egocentrism	"It's all about me"
False omniscience	"I know everything I need to know"
False omnipotence	"I am all-powerful"
False invulnerability	"No one can get back at me"
Ethical disengagement	"Ethics are important for other people"
Myside (confirmation) bias	"So many others just don't see things as clearly as I do"
Sunk cost fallacy	"I've already invested so much in this way of doing things"

falsely omnipotent when they believe they are all-powerful. Fifth, people are falsely invulnerable when they believe that, no matter what they do, they can get away with it. Sixth, people are ethically disengaged when they believe that ethical principles apply to others but not to them. Seventh, people engage in myside (confirmation) bias when they believe that they see things clearly, but others don't, so they favor their own interests. Finally, people commit the sunk-cost fallacy when they fail to let go of a losing strategy for solving a problem – they metaphorically "throw good money after bad."

1.5.4 Toxicity

The last impediment to wisdom is **toxicity** (Lipman-Blumen, 2006; Sternberg, 2018), which occurs when people, often leaders, have few or no moral boundaries and, as a result, act in ways that benefit themselves without regard to whether their actions harm others. Some politicians around the world have always been toxic, claiming to look out for others while only looking out for themselves. Regrettably, there will always be people with authoritarian or destructive impulses who will follow such leaders out of belief, fear, collusion, or a desire to stay out of the spotlight.

1.6 Conclusion

Perhaps no attribute is more important to human well-being and even survival than wisdom. However, wisdom has not received the attention it deserves, whether in the home, in education, or in society. We have had no lack of intelligent and even creative leaders. What we have lacked are wise leaders. We hope that those of you who learn about wisdom through this textbook will become the wise leaders of the emerging generation, and will work to solve the problems that your predecessors have often not addressed as wisely as they might have done. However, learning about wisdom from a book is not enough. Try to act wisely in your own life whenever possible.

1.7 Comprehension and Discussion Questions

(1) Based on what you have read so far, and based on your own intuitions, what do you believe wisdom to be?
(2) How do you believe intelligence is related to wisdom?
(3) How do you believe creativity is related to wisdom?
(4) Why is wisdom emphasized so little in education?
(5) What do you see as the major impediments to wisdom being implemented in everyday life?

1.8 Investigations

Robert J. Sternberg's research is focused on attempting to incorporate wisdom into people's notions of what it means to be "intelligent." Historically, wisdom has been seen as related to, but distinct from, intelligence. And certainly there are aspects of human intelligence that are distinct from wisdom. However, our "raw" intelligence is destroying the world as we know it. We humans are creating problems for ourselves that, in the long run, may become insurmountable, such as climate change, pollution, weapons of mass destruction, and pandemics resulting from ever greater proximity of humans to wildlife that used to have its own preserve. If we do not think of intelligence *adaptively,* as involving wisdom as well as sheer brainpower to solve complex but abstract problems removed from everyday life, future generations of humans that would have been may never come to be, as a result of our own short-sightedness in applying our intelligence to our individual needs rather than to our collective well-being.

Judith Glück's research is focused on how wisdom develops. Why are so few people very wise, and how did the wise ones acquire their wisdom? Wisdom is probably not acquired by life experience in itself, but by a special way of learning from experiences. Judith is also interested in how wisdom can best be measured. A quality that typically manifests itself in rare, difficult, uncertain situations is hard to study in psychologists' labs. Finally, she studies how people from different cultures perceive wisdom.

1.9 Practical Applications

Wisdom is sorely lacking in the world. If we are to see more of it at a time when it is so important, we need to understand what it is. Furthermore, we need to understand why it is important, and why intelligence and creativity have proven inadequate to solving the problems of the world. This chapter has discussed these issues and also why wisdom is so rare in the world. Schools need to teach students not only to be smart and knowledgeable, but also to be wise.

Glossary

balance weigh different aspects of the self, such as cognitive, affective, and reflective processes, or different interests, such as those of oneself and others

common good a good that benefits all stakeholders, not just a limited selection of them

creativity acting in ways that exhibit novelty and usefulness or effectiveness

foolishness lack of wisdom – acting in ways that prioritize oneself over others, or that prioritize the short term over the long term

intelligence narrowly defined, knowledge and analytical skills – ability to learn, reason, and adapt to the environment

toxicity acting in ways that are harmful to others, usually in order to maximize one's own self-interest

wisdom the seeking of a common good, by achieving some balance within the person and also some balance of interests external to the person

REFERENCES

Baer, J. (2015). *Domain Specificity of Creativity.* Academic Press.

Baltes, P. B. and Staudinger, U. M. (1993). The search for a psychology of wisdom. *Current Directions in Psychological Science,* 2(3), 75–80.

   (2000). A metaheuristic (pragmatic) to orchestrate mind and virtue toward excellence. *American Psychologist,* 55(1), 122–36.

Biesecker, M., Bleiberg, J., and Laporta, J. (2021). Capitol rioters included highly trained ex-military and cops. *AP News,* January 15; https://apnews.com/article/ex-military-cops-us-capitol-riot-a1cb17201dfddc98291edead5badc257

Carroll, J. B. (1993). *Human Cognitive Abilities: A Survey of Factor-Analytic Studies.* Cambridge University Press.

Cattell, R. B. (1971). *Abilities: Their Structure, Growth, and Action.* Houghton Mifflin.

Centers for Disease Control and Prevention (2020). Identifying the source of the outbreak. *COVID-19*, July 1; https://www.cdc.gov/coronavirus/2019-ncov/cases-updates/about-epidemiology/identifying-source-outbreak.html

Clark, K. and James, K. (1999). Justice and positive and negative creativity. *Creativity Research Journal*, 12(4), 311–20.

Cropley, D. H., Kaufman, J. C., and Cropley, A. J. (2008). Malevolent creativity: A functional model of creativity in terrorism and crime. *Creativity Research Journal*, 20(2), 105–15.

Cropley, D. H., Cropley, A. J., Kaufman, J. C., and Runco, M. A., eds. (2010). *The Dark Side of Creativity.* Cambridge University Press.

Cropley, D. H., Kaufman, J. C., White, A.E., and Chiera, B. A. (2014). Layperson perceptions of malevolent creativity: The good, the bad, and the ambiguous. *Psychology of Aesthetics, Creativity, and the Arts*, 8(4), 400–12.

Farzan, A. N. (2021). Wealthy couple chartered a plane to the Yukon, took vaccines doses meant for Indigenous elders, authorities said. *Washington Post*, January 26; https://www.washingtonpost.com/nation/2021/01/26/yukon-vaccine-couple-ekaterina-baker/

Flynn, J. R. (1987). Massive IQ gains in 14 nations. *Psychological Bulletin*, 101(2), 171–91.
    (2012). *Are We Getting Smarter?* Cambridge University Press.

Gardner, H. (2011). *Frames of Mind: The Theory of Multiple Intelligences* (rev. ed.). Basic Books.

Grossmann, I., Kung, F. Y. H., and Santos, H. C. (2019). Wisdom as state versus trait. In R. J.Sternberg and J.Glück, eds., *The Cambridge Handbook of Wisdom.* Cambridge University Press, pp. 249–73.

Grossmann, I. Weststrate, N. M., Ardelt, M. et al. (2020). The science of wisdom in a polarized world: Knowns and unknowns. *Psychological Inquiry*, 31(2), 1–31. doi: 10.1080/1047840X.2020.1750917

James, K. and Taylor, A. (2010). Positive creativity and negative creativity (and unintended consequences). In D. H. Cropley, A. J. Cropley, J. C. Kaufman, and M. A. Runco, eds., *The Dark Side of Creativity.* Cambridge University Press, pp. 33–56.

James, K., Clark, K., and Cropanzano, R. (1999). Positive and negative creativity in groups, institutions, and organizations: A model and theoretical extension. *Creativity Research Journal*, 12(3), 211–26.

Jeste, D. V., Ardelt, M., BlazerD. et al. (2010). Expert consensus on characteristics of wisdom: A Delphi method study. *The Gerontologist*, 50(5), 668–80.

Kaufman, J. C. and Sternberg, R. J., eds. (2019). *The Cambridge Handbook of Creativity.* Cambridge University Press.

Lipman-Blumen, J. (2006). *The Allure of Toxic Leaders: Why We follow Destructive Bosses and Corrupt Politicians – And How We Can Survive Them.* Oxford University Press.

McGrew, K. S. (2005). The Cattell-Horn-Carroll theory of cognitive abilities: Past, present, and future. In D. P. Flanagan and P. L. Harrison, eds., *Contemporary Intellectual Assessment: Theories, Tests, Issues,* 2nd ed. Guilford Press, pp. 136–81.

Polanyi, M. (1976). Tacit knowledge. In M. Marx and F. Goodson, eds., *Theories in Contemporary Psychology.* Macmillan, pp. 330–44.

Staudinger, U. (2019). The distinction between personal and general wisdom: How far have we come? In R. J. Sternberg and J. Glück, eds., *The Cambridge Handbook of Wisdom.* Cambridge University Press, pp. 182–201.

Sternberg, R. J. (1998) A balance theory of wisdom. *Review of General Psychology*, 2(4), 347–65.
    (2005). Foolishness. In R. J. Sternberg and J. Jordan, eds., *Handbook of Wisdom: Psychological Perspectives.* Cambridge University Press, pp. 331–52.
    (2018). Wisdom, foolishness, and toxicity in human development. *Research in Human Development*, 15(3–4), 200–10.
    (2019a). Race to Samarra: the critical importance of wisdom in the world today. In R. J. Sternberg and J. Glück, eds., *The Cambridge Handbook of Wisdom.* Cambridge University Press, pp. 3–9.
    (2019b). Why people often prefer wise guys to guys who are wise: An augmented balance theory of the production and reception of wisdom. In R. J. Sternberg and J. Glueck, eds., *The Cambridge Handbook of Wisdom.* Cambridge University Press, pp. 162–81.

(2021a). *Adaptive Intelligence: Surviving and Thriving in Times of Uncertainty*. Cambridge University Press.

(2021b). Positive creativity. In A. Kostic and D. Chadee, eds., *Current Research in Positive Psychology*. Palgrave Macmillan.

(2021c). Transformational creativity: the link between creativity, wisdom, and the solution of global problems. *Philosophies* 6(3), 75.

(in press). Positive creativity as the intersection between creativity, intelligence, and wisdom. In H.Kapoor and J. C.Kaufman, eds., *Creativity and Morality*. Academic Press.

Sternberg, R. J., and Glück, J., eds. (2019). *The Cambridge Handbook of Wisdom*. Cambridge University Press.

Sternberg, R. J., Nusbaum, H. C., and Glück, J., eds. (2019). *Applying Wisdom to Contemporary World Problems*. Palgrave Macmillan.

Sternberg, R. J., Forsythe, G. B., Hedlund, J. et al. (2000). *Practical Intelligence in Everyday Life*. Cambridge University Press.

Webster, J. D. (2003). An exploratory analysis of a self-assessed wisdom scale. *Journal of Adult Development*, 10(1), 13–22.

(2007). Measuring the character strength of wisdom. *International Journal of Aging and Human Development*, 65(2), 163–83.

Weststrate, N. M. and Glück, J. (2017). Hard-earned wisdom: exploratory processing of difficult life experience is positively associated with wisdom. *Developmental Psychology*, 53(4), 800–14.

Wong, E., Barnes, J. E., and Kanno-Youngs, Z. (2020). Local officials in China hid coronavirus dangers from Beijing, U.S. agencies find. *New York Times*, August 19; www.nytimes.com/2020/08/19/world/asia/china-coronavirus-beijing-trump.html

CHAPTER 2

Philosophical Foundations for the Study of Wisdom

Jason D. Swartwood

2.1 Why Wisdom Matters

Tough decisions about how to live are an inescapable feature of our existence. We have to grapple, for instance, with situations in which it is unclear what is best for ourselves or others. (Should I take that dream job that pays more but that would have a longer commute time?) We have to weigh values such as truth telling against considerations of loyalty, concern for others' **well-being**, or social justice. (What should I do if I learn that a friend has been unfaithful to their partner or has cheated in an exam?) Sometimes we don't even notice important questions when they are right in front of us. (Should I view my colleague's disability as something to pity or as a difference to be celebrated and accommodated?) Pressing questions about how one ought to live are as ubiquitous as they are varied and complex.

If identifying and grappling effectively with questions about how we ought to live is the problem, then what is the solution? In many philosophical traditions, the answer is that we need wisdom. But what is wisdom, and how can we get it? How should we study wisdom? Is doing so the province of science, philosophy, or something else? This chapter will give you a taste of some prominent philosophical puzzles, ideas, and arguments about the nature and study of wisdom, along with references that you can use to examine them in more depth.

2.2 Three Types of Wisdom

If we were going to study cats, it would be helpful to specify whether we were interested in the common housecat (*Felis catus*) or in all members of the family Felidae (which includes wild cats such as lynx and tigers). Similarly, studying wisdom requires us to determine whether there are distinct types of wisdom that we might be interested in. Philosophers have distinguished between at least three types.[1]

The life of the ancient Greek philosopher Socrates illustrates two senses in which a person can be wise. Socrates spent his time finding people who claimed to be wise and then subjecting their views about the most important things – "wisdom or truth or the best possible state of your soul" (*Apology* 29e–30a) – to intense scrutiny. Socrates insisted that he did not have a deep grasp of how one ought to live, so he was not wise in that sense. However, he believed that he did have a kind of "human wisdom," because he was aware that he knew nothing about these most important things (*Apology* 20d).

---

[1] Parts of Sections 2.2–2.5 are adapted from Swartwood and Tiberius (2019).

On Socrates' view, his "human wisdom" is a form of **epistemic humility** – an awareness of one's ignorance of the most important things, such as the nature of a good and virtuous life. (The word "epistemic" is derived from the Greek word for "knowledge," so epistemic humility is humility about one's own knowledge.) Socrates thought that this kind of wisdom was important insofar as it helped people to pursue a further kind of wisdom, which, following Aristotle, we can call **practical wisdom** (corresponding to the Greek term *phronesis*) – a deep and comprehensive grasp of how we ought to live. To illustrate this, suppose that Carmen knows the limits of her knowledge about how to cope well with tough decisions in her life. She is in a sense wiser than Donald, who is blissfully unaware of his own ignorance. Carmen has wisdom as epistemic humility, whereas Donald does not. However, if Carmen is content to wallow in her ignorance and abandon the search for a deep grasp of how she ought to live, then there is another sense in which she is not wise – she lacks practical wisdom (and the desire to achieve it).

Following Aristotle (1999, bk. VI, chapter 7), we should distinguish between practical wisdom and theoretical wisdom. Whereas **theoretical wisdom** (corresponding to the Greek term *sophia*) is a deep and comprehensive grasp of how things *are* (how the world and the creatures and things in it tend to be or behave), practical wisdom is a deep and comprehensive grasp of how things *ought* to be (how we ought to live, or what is good, bad, virtuous, vicious, right, or wrong). To illustrate this, suppose that Glenda is a polymath scientist who has a masterful grasp of chemistry, psychology, physics, biology, and mathematics. Nevertheless, she is clueless about how to cope with interpersonal conflicts, she is casually cruel and thoughtless, and she always values even the most minor academic achievements above all else. Glenda has a deep grasp of **descriptive truths** (truths about how the world *is* and how the things in it actually *are* or tend to be), but she does not have a deep grasp of **prescriptive reasons and truths** (truths about how we *ought* to conduct ourselves, or about what *matters*, or reasons why we *ought* to conduct ourselves in certain ways but not others).[2] Glenda, we could say, has theoretical wisdom but lacks practical wisdom.

Although people sometimes use the word "wisdom" to refer to (among other things) theoretical wisdom or epistemic humility, the frequency with which wisdom is offered as a solution to challenging questions about how to live indicates that practical wisdom is of primary importance.[3]

2.3   Why the Study of Practical Wisdom Is an Interdisciplinary Project

Philosophers and wisdom scientists (such as psychologists and sociologists) are interested in examining some central questions about practical wisdom (hereafter simply referred to as "wisdom"). For example:

- *What is wisdom, and who has it?* What attitudes, motivations, knowledge, dispositions, and decision-making processes (for instance) are part of being practically wise? How would wise people think, feel, or conduct themselves? How is wisdom related (or not) to other important concepts, states, or traits, such as wellbeing, happiness, goodness, virtues, or right action?
- *How can we get wisdom?* Is it something that some people are born with? If not, how can it be acquired? Can it be obtained through, for example, reflection, experience, or teaching?

---

[2] Philosophers usually use the term "normative" instead of "prescriptive," but I have avoided doing that here, because "normative" means something different in psychology and the sciences.

[3] For more on Socrates' view of wisdom, see Plato's dialogues, starting with the *Euthyphro, Apology, Crito,* and *Phaedo.* For more on the distinction between practical and theoretical wisdom, see Baehr (2012), Grimm (2015), and Ryan (1999).

You might wonder why philosophers are even part of this project. Wisdom, after all, is a psychological concept – it deals with the mind and behavior of human beings. Psychologists get by just fine without philosophers when studying introversion and other personality traits. So why should philosophers be part of wisdom research?

To understand why philosophers need to be part of the project, we have to look at how wisdom differs from other psychological constructs, such as introversion.

Wisdom is what philosophers call **a prescriptive ideal** – it is supposed to tell us how we *ought* to be, not simply to describe how anyone actually *is*. Imagine someone saying, "My mother is wise – she has a really great grasp of how she ought to conduct herself, even in tough situations – but I don't think being wise like that is good or valuable or something anyone ought to aspire to." If mother's "wisdom" is not necessarily something that we ought to aspire to, then it is unclear if we are actually talking about wisdom at all. If we describe a way of being and conducting ourselves, but it is *not* capturing how we *ought* to be or how we *ought* to conduct ourselves, then our account of wisdom has missed the mark. The *ought-to-be-done-ness*, we might say, is baked into the very idea of wisdom, which explains why we value it.

Many other psychological constructs, such as introversion, are different. "Introversion" is an idea that we use to describe a general difference between some human beings. To put it simply, some people are energized by solitude (introverts), whereas others are energized by socializing (extroverts). To decide whether this conception of introversion is plausible, we don't need to assume that people *ought* to be introverted – that it is desirable, valuable, and something we should aspire to. A good account of introversion just needs to accurately describe features of people as they actually are. We may or may not later find some reason to believe that introversion is good or bad, but whether our account of introversion is plausible does not hinge on that. Unlike wisdom, introversion is not a prescriptive ideal.

This distinction matters because prescriptive ideals such as wisdom are supposed to tell us how things ought to be, and science alone cannot imply or validate claims about how things ought to be.

Suppose you want to convince a friend that "you ought to recycle" (a prescriptive claim). You might think that you can show that this prescriptive claim is true simply by noting some empirical findings: Recycling helps to preserve natural resources for future generations (a descriptive claim). You might hope that your descriptive claim about the effects of recycling could serve as a premise that entails your prescriptive conclusion:

(1)   Recycling helps to preserve natural resources for future generations.

     Therefore, you ought to recycle.

The problem is that this argument is incomplete. Even if Premise 1 (your descriptive claim about the effects of recycling) is true, that does not by itself mean that the conclusion is true. To complete the argument, you would need to add a prescriptive premise, like this:

(1)   Recycling helps to preserve natural resources for future generations.
(2)   You ought to help preserve natural resources for future generations.

     Therefore, you ought to recycle.

Your argument now has the premises it needs – if the premises are true, that fact means that the conclusion is also true. But notice that your argument no longer relies on descriptive claims alone.

It needed a prescriptive premise in order to establish its prescriptive conclusion. Importantly, this holds for all other similar arguments. To establish a prescriptive conclusion about how things ought to be, descriptive premises alone will not be enough; we need at least one prescriptive premise in the mix. Put simply, you will never validly infer an *ought* from *is* alone.

Since science is focused on how the world *is*, the upshot is that science alone cannot help us to test and evaluate prescriptive ideals such as wisdom. Science provides an excellent method for testing the descriptive assumptions that underlie our accounts of wisdom, but we need additional tools to develop and test the prescriptive components of those accounts. Fortunately, philosophy can help to fill this gap.[4]

2.4   A Core Philosophical Conception of Practical Wisdom

Philosophers develop and test prescriptive ideals such as wisdom by first identifying the implications and puzzles that arise from our basic starting beliefs about wisdom, and then subjecting them to rational scrutiny. To illustrate this, the rest of this chapter describes a core philosophical conception of wisdom that systematizes some important beliefs about wisdom, and then discusses various philosophical puzzles that arise from this conception.[5]

2.4.1   *Wisdom as a Grasp of How One Ought to Live*

Based on the definition we started with, practical wisdom is a grasp of how one *ought* to live and conduct oneself. Because it is a prescriptive ideal, wisdom does not involve merely grasping how we want to act, how people tend to act, or even how people think we should act. The mere fact that people want to cheat, or that they tend to cheat, or that they think cheating is justified, does not show that we actually ought to cheat. Wisdom is valuable and worth aspiring to because possessing it gives us a handle on how we *ought* to conduct ourselves.

2.4.2   *Wisdom as an All-Things-Considered Grasp*

Suppose your friend in a college class tells you that they cheated on a paper assignment – they bought a copy off the Internet and handed it in as their own. Now that you have this information, what should you do? We could approach this question with a particular goal in mind: What should you do *if you are to avoid making your friend angry*? Grasping the answer to this question does not necessarily make you practically wise, because a wise person grasps how to evaluate and balance all the various (and sometimes competing) goals they might pursue in the situation. Is it really important to avoid making your friend angry here? How does that goal weigh against considerations of fairness, protecting your own wellbeing, or helping your friend to be a good person? A wise person navigates these complexities because they have a grasp of what they should do not just given one specific goal, but *all things considered.*

---

[4] For more on the argument that *is* doesn't imply *ought*, see David Hume, *A Treatise of Human Nature*, Bk III, Pt. I, Section II. See also Tiberius (2015) for an accessible introduction to this argument and related issues.
[5] Parts of Section 2.4 are adapted from the account of the "minimal philosophical conception" of wisdom discussed in Swartwood (2020, pp. 77–80).

2.4.3 *Wisdom as a Grasp of What One Ought to Do in Particular Situations*

Our interest in wisdom is not abstract. Our hope is that it can help us with concrete situations and choices. Consider the following examples:[6]

Gloria: A Mexican mother in her forties, Gloria struggles to make enough money to provide food and shelter for her family, including her two young children. As a result of local economic stagnation and government corruption there are very few job opportunities; this situation, coupled with the threat of violence by organized crime groups, leaves her worried about her children's future. Several other women she knows have addressed this challenge by illegally entering the USA to work and send back money. Gloria wonders if she should pursue a similar solution, either leaving her kids with their grandparents or attempting to take them on the potentially perilous border crossing. Which option would be best for the kids, or for her? Gloria struggles to decide what to do.

Maryam: Although she is not a psychologist, Maryam has grown familiar with ASD (autism spectrum disorder) through her work as a teacher. This familiarity has led to a difficult decision. Maryam's friend Jules has recently shared a number of challenges that she has encountered with her three-year-old son. He is very rigid and has tantrums when things are not just so, he will only eat four different foods, he does not seem interested in engaging with other people socially in the expected ways, and he is obsessively focused on airplanes. Jules is clearly distressed by her son's behavior, which is causing stress at home between herself and her husband. Maryam knows that Jules and her husband have expressed skepticism about psychologists, who they think are responsible for pathologizing kids. "Why can't they just let kids be kids?," they often say. Jules has made it clear that she is not interested in Maryam's views about what is happening with her son, even though she is very aware that Maryam has experience of helping children with all kinds of challenges. Maryam wonders if she should tell Jules to have her son assessed for ASD, since getting help early could lead to great gains for her son. Still, she worries about how Jules will react if she mentions this. What should she do?

Raheem: Raheem is a student at a small liberal arts college in the Midwestern USA. He and his friends have been frustrated by the lack of productive discussions about racism in the community, which is predominantly white, but includes a sizable number of racial and ethnic minorities. A recent incident has inflamed the tensions but seems to be bringing the issue to the forefront in a productive way. A racist note was found placed on someone's car in a college parking lot, and this has sparked an investigation by the college administration. Members of the college and the community at large are having more discussions about the problem of racism. Raheem has felt hopeful that these conversations, although challenging and painful, could lead to progress. To his surprise, he has found out that one of his acquaintances at school, who also shares his frustration with the lack of progress, actually forged the racist note to try to start a conversation about racism. Raheem sees that this deceit may result in some good for the community, but there are also some potential downsides for

---

[6] Gloria's case is adapted from a real-life situation described at https://immigrationtalk.org/2012/09/28/immigrant-mothers-making-tough-choices-for-their-families/ Maryam's and Raheem's cases are adapted from Swartwood (2020). Raheem's case is based upon a real-life incident (Brooks & Walsh, 2017).

the individuals who are being investigated. In addition, the cause would potentially be harmed if the deceit is revealed. What should Raheem do with this information?

Even if you haven't faced any situations exactly like these, you will surely have faced situations that require balancing competing values (honesty vs. compassion, loyalty vs. justice, etc.), or where it is unclear how best to achieve a particular value. If a wise person grasps anything, we would hope that it would be what to do in situations like these. Imagine someone who could reliably spout general platitudes that others often found inspiring or compelling to think about, but who was routinely blundering and befuddled when trying to figure out how to address situations in their own life. Perhaps this could be described as wisdom of a sort (the wisdom of the advice guru). This person nevertheless lacks wisdom in an important sense – they lack practical wisdom, because their grasp of what they ought to do is not conducive to living a good human life. Just as a chess "expert" would not deserve the title if they in fact never win any games, a person deserves the appellation "practically wise" only to the extent that they have a good grasp of how they ought to live, all things considered, in particular situations that they face.

2.4.4   *Wisdom as a Master Virtue*

Often, wisdom is listed as a **virtue** (an excellent character trait) alongside a variety of other virtues, such as compassion, generosity, self-respect, loyalty, justice, honesty, bravery, and so on. But how is wisdom related to these other virtues? Is it just one desirable trait among many?

In many traditions, wisdom is characterized as a **master virtue** that controls or guides the other virtues. Viewing wisdom as a master virtue helps to make sense of how the **character virtues** fit together in a well-lived life.

Living well requires responding well to the many and varied valuable ends and goals that are part of human existence. We have to determine, for instance, when and how to tell the truth, be loyal, use humor in social situations, promote justice, and balance promoting others' well-being with protecting our own. In other words, we need to have character virtues such as honesty, loyalty, wittiness, justice, compassion, and self-respect.

But how should we describe character virtues such as honesty? Some might think that honesty is a disposition always to tell the truth. Yet this cannot be right (Hursthouse & Pettigrove, 2016). For one thing, there are times when you should *not* share what you believe to be the truth, such as when an acquaintance is seeking gossip about a friend's private and painful secrets, or when an angry mob seeks your assistance in finding a would-be victim. In addition, there are often good and bad ways to tell the truth as you see it, even when truth-telling is the thing to do. (Anyone who has read any comment forums on the Internet can probably understand this point!) Being honest also requires having the right motivations. A teacher who tells a student the painful truth about the quality of their essay in order to help them improve may be acting in accordance with the virtue of honesty; however, a teacher who does so in order to delight in their student's humiliation and misery is not. Finally, having the virtue of honesty requires one to respond well across a variety of situations. An inveterate liar who deals honestly only with one close confidant does not have the virtue of honesty.

Similar points hold for the other character virtues. Following Aristotle, we can say that each character virtue is a deep disposition to respond to an important value, end, or goal in the right ways, at the right times, and for the right reasons (Aristotle, 1999, l. 1109a25; Hursthouse &

Pettigrove, 2016). Having the virtue of compassion requires the disposition to respond to threats to others' well-being in the right ways, at the right times, and for the right reasons. Having the virtue of wittiness requires the disposition to use humor in social situations in the right ways, at the right times, and for the right reasons. Having the virtue of loyalty requires the disposition to be partial to others' interests in the right ways, at the right times, and for the right reasons. And so on.[7]

Being **a virtuous person** – someone with all the virtues – is thus a lofty achievement that requires a good grasp of how the many valuable commitments of a good human life fit together. This is why many philosophers – including Aristotle and the ancient Chinese philosopher Mengzi (also known as Mencius) – think wisdom is an intellectual virtue (a virtue of mind) that is necessary for being a virtuous person. A wise person grasps what matters and how to achieve it across the variety of situations that make up a life. A non-virtuous person facing Raheem's choice might feel that justice and honesty are pulling them in different directions, whereas a wise person's grasp of what matters allows them to identify the course of action that resolves the apparent conflict. A non-virtuous person facing Gloria's choice might be unsure what compassion requires her to do for her children, whereas a wise person grasps how best to promote the children's well-being. Wisdom is an essential part of a virtuous life because it is essential for possessing and integrating the other important traits required for living well.

2.5   Philosophical Puzzles about Practical Wisdom

According to the core philosophical conception that we have been examining, wisdom is a grasp of how one ought to conduct oneself all things considered in particular situations; it is an intellectual virtue that guides and controls the character virtues.[8]

This core philosophical conception of wisdom is certainly not the only conception on offer. Nevertheless, many philosophers think that it provides an ideal worth aspiring to, because it systematizes many of the elements that people associate with wisdom into a coherent and rationally defensible whole. The philosophical work of continuing to test, develop, and apply this conception requires grappling with the resulting puzzles about wisdom. This section will give brief overviews of some of those puzzles and the ideas and arguments to which they have given rise.

2.5.1   *What Character Virtues Does Wisdom Guide or Promote?*

In the 1982 movie *Conan the Barbarian*, a warlord asks the eponymous hero "What is best in life?" He replies: "To crush your enemies, see them driven before you, and hear the lamentations of their women." Conan, it seems, would have a very different idea than many of us about which character traits are virtues, and so would also have a very different view about what goals, commitments, and values a wise person has. Indeed, real-world disagreements about virtue are easy to come by. Is it a virtue to be ruggedly self-reliant and individualistic, or would a person of

---

[7] For more on specific virtues and special questions about virtues, see Bell (2009), Blum (2007), Cherry (2021), Gambrel and Cafaro (2010), Gyekye (2011), Hursthouse (2007), McBride (2017), and Tessman (2005).

[8] For some different takes on the core philosophical conception of wisdom (and some views that deviate from it in interesting ways), see Annas (2011), Broadie (1993), Brouwer (2014), Grimm (2015), Marshall (2002), Mengzi (2008), Ryan (2016), and Tiberius (2008).

good character subordinate their needs to those of their community? People disagree. So how can we decide which character traits are virtues and which are not?

There are a variety of options here. For instance, some philosophers think that we should start by finding people who are admirable (some have suggested Confucius or Jesus) and then identify what character traits they have (Olberding, 2008; Zagzebski, 2010). According to this view, we can determine which traits are virtues by seeing which traits are part of what makes those admirable people admirable.

Other philosophers think that we should work to specify the idea that the virtues are the traits that contribute to flourishing or living well (the Greek term is **eudaimonia**). Some define virtues as traits that promote a specific list of goods. One influential account (Nussbaum, 1988, 2001) suggests goods such as life, bodily health, bodily integrity, senses, imagination, and thought, emotions, play, practical reason, and control over one's environment. The Confucian philosopher Mengzi thought that the three cardinal virtues (compassion, righteousness, and propriety, all controlled by wisdom) are extensions of different aspects of an innately good human nature (Mengzi, 2008). Philosophers in some Southern African traditions define the virtues as the traits that contribute to *ubuntu* (meaning "humanness") – a prescriptive ideal according to which flourishing is a matter of living engaged in community (Metz, 2012). Still others elaborate on the Aristotelian idea that flourishing means developing and exercising well the rational and social capacities that are characteristic of human beings (Kraut, 2009).

These are just a few of the options, briefly described. By examining which account is most rationally compelling, we can specify the values and commitments that are part of wisdom.

2.5.2   *Is Wisdom the Same for Everyone?*

A related puzzle concerns whether wisdom would look the same in everyone who has it. In what ways (if any) would a wise eleventh-century Persian's grasp of what they ought to do be similar to or different from that of (for instance) a seventeenth-century Cherokee, an Ashanti in twentieth-century Ghana, or a twenty-first-century Korean-American? Could individuals with different temperaments, abilities, or personal interests manifest the same level of wisdom in different ways?

Some might suggest that what is actually wise for a person depends solely on their culture. This is implausible, because it would imply that whatever one's culture views as wise is therefore actually wise, even if that culture endorses oppressively autocratic, theocratic, racist, misogynistic, or genocidal attitudes. Some might try instead to make wisdom relative to the individual – what is wise for a person is living up to their own commitments and values. This, however, is not any more plausible – the vindictive authoritarian autocrat and the serial killer are not virtuous just because they live up to their own warped commitments.

This is why Aristotle distinguished between wisdom and mere **cleverness** (Aristotle, 1999, ll. 1144a9–10; 1144a25–36). The wise person and the merely clever person both grasp how to achieve their ends and successfully pursue their commitments, but, unlike the wise person, the merely clever person is committed to the wrong things. When it comes to the values and goals that are part of wisdom, not just anything goes.

Still, there is reason to avoid going too far in the other direction. There has to be *some* variation in the ways in which wise lives can be lived, at least in certain details. Surely a person's level of wisdom is not contingent solely on having a specific occupation or set of hobbies, for instance. There are probably also times when there are multiple equally virtuous ways to respond to a situation – the introvert's more private consolation of a friend may do the trick just as well as the extrovert's more socially ambitious approach.

So how do we thread the needle between these extremes of total variation and no variation? One option would be to say that all wise people will live by the same general principles but conduct themselves differently due to their differences in circumstances. According to this view, a commitment to avoiding causing unnecessary suffering to animals might lead a wise Lakota person to practice sustainable hunting, while the same principles might lead a person with abundant plant-based options to swear off meat altogether. A related approach is to argue that there are general ends or values that are universally part of well-lived human lives, but that allow for variation due to contingencies of culture and context (Kekes, 1995, p. 19; Nussbaum, 1988). Examining these options further will tell us more about the variety we can expect in wise lives.[9]

2.5.3 Does Having One Virtue Require One to Possess All the Others?

Suppose that Jasmine has the virtue of honesty. Must she therefore have all the other virtues as well, or is it possible that she lacks compassion, justice, and the like? Aristotle (1999, ll. 1144b30–1145a1) argued that having one virtue requires possession of them all, and this argument for the **unity of the virtues** has important implications for our understanding of wisdom.

The argument can be quickly sketched. If Jasmine has the virtue of honesty, then she tells the truth at the right times, in the right ways, and for the right reasons. To do this, she must grasp when telling the truth is what matters and when, alternatively, it is less relevant than other commitments. For instance, she grasps what to do in situations such as those described in Section 2.4. Should Maryam tell Jules that she should have her son assessed for ASD, or is it more important to avoid upsetting and distancing her? Should Raheem reveal that the incident is a fraud, or is it more important to preserve the community's focus on addressing the reality of racism? If a virtuous person grasps when and how to tell the truth, they will also need to have a grasp of when and how to promote others' well-being (the virtue of compassion), how to give people what is fair or what they are due (the virtue of justice), and so on. Grasping the reasons that are relevant to one virtue requires grasping the reasons that are relevant to the others. Thus, having one character virtue requires possession of all the others, and wisdom (the cross-situational grasp of what virtue requires) is necessary for possession of the virtues.

Despite its apparent plausibility, some think that this argument leads to a puzzle (Wolf, 2007). In our everyday life, it is tempting to say that we come across people who have one virtue but lack others. A soldier might strike us as brave but lacking compassion, or a friend might strike us as loyal but lacking self-respect. Our everyday judgments seem to conflict with the unity of the virtues thesis. How should we respond to this apparent contradiction?

One response to the puzzle would be to reject the unity of the virtues thesis and say that having one virtue does not require one to have all the others (Badhwar, 1996, pp. 306–7). This response rejects the idea that wisdom is a master virtue, because it implies that there is not one

---

[9] For more sophisticated ways to argue that wisdom (and morality and virtue) are somewhat relative to culture or group, see Gowans (2016), Prinz (2007), and Wong (2002).

unified set of knowledge or understanding that ties all the virtues together. Responding to the puzzle in this way is feasible if we have more reason to be more confident in our everyday judgments (that people sometimes have one virtue but lack others) than we have to be confident in the reasoning that supports the unity of the virtues thesis. But *do* we have reason to be confident about that?

If the answer to that last question is 'No,' then that provides a different response to the puzzle. According to this view, which some see as Aristotle's (Pakaluk, 2005, p. 232), our everyday judgments do not actually show that people sometimes have one virtue but lack others. When we say, in our everyday judgments, that someone is brave, we are not really ascribing to them the *virtue* of bravery – the disposition to respond to fear in the right ways, at the right times, and for the right reasons. Perhaps we are only saying they have the *psychological trait* of bravery – a tendency to do things despite fear. This response seeks to resolve the puzzle by showing that our everyday judgments are consistent with the prescriptive ideal embodied in the unity of the virtues thesis.

Many philosophers respond to the puzzle by modifying the unity of the virtues thesis so that it is compatible with our everyday judgments. Some argue that having one virtue requires having the rest to some degree, but not necessarily fully (Hursthouse, 1999, p. 156). Others suggest that the unity of the virtues claim applies within each domain in our lives, but not between those domains – a person cannot be an honest parent without being a compassionate parent, but being an honest parent does not require one to be a compassionate coworker (Badhwar, 1996). Yet another argument is that having one virtue requires having a knowledge of what all the other virtues require, but not necessarily the motivation to act on it – an honest person knows, for example, what compassion requires but does not always act accordingly (Wolf, 2007). Determining how best to respond to the puzzle about the unity of the virtues has important implications with regard to the value and nature of wisdom.

2.5.4   *Can You Be Wise without Being Virtuous?*

Suppose Athena is wise and therefore has a good grasp of how she ought to conduct herself, but she finds herself facing a tough situation. She knows that she should help her friend to get to a doctor's appointment, because her friend would prefer not to take a cab, the appointment is important and stressful, and Athena has promised to help. However, Athena could easily beg off and complain of a tough week or unanticipated conflict, thereby ensuring a pleasant night of reading and relaxation. If Athena is indeed wise, is it possible that she could fail to do the virtuous thing?

If resolving the puzzle of the unity of the virtues requires that having one virtue implies having the knowledge of what all the virtues require but not necessarily the motivation to act on them, then perhaps Athena could be wise but fail to do the compassionate thing for her friend. Wisdom, according to this view, would be necessary but not sufficient for being virtuous. Athena has succumbed to weakness of the will (the Greek term is *akrasia*) – she knows what she ought to do but lacks the motivation to actually do it.

Some philosophers think that this is implausible. Being wise, according to their view, guarantees that a person will conduct themselves virtuously. A distinction from Aristotle could help to show why this is so (McDowell, 1979; Peters, 2013). A virtuous person is different from a **continent** person – both end up doing the right thing, but the latter only does so after struggling against the temptation to do otherwise. Athena would be admirable if she virtuously saw her friend's need as a reason to help and was not even tempted by the warm bed and the novel. But she would be less admirable and lacking in virtue if she only got around to helping after struggling desperately with those temptations. After all, if she really saw it as the thing she ought to do, all things considered, then how could she even be tempted? According to this view, a wise person's grasp of what they ought to do includes the motivation to do it.

Determining which view is plausible will tell us important things about how wisdom is related to virtuous motivation and action.

2.5.5   *Can We Codify Wise Understanding?*

According to the core philosophical conception, a wise person's reliably good grasp of what they ought to do is what distinguishes them from others. Those of us who would like more wisdom might wonder whether there is a way to distill the wise person's understanding into a set of principles that a less wise person could use to decide what they ought to do.

Many philosophers think that such a project could not succeed, because the wise person's grasp is *uncodifiable* – the factors that govern good decision making are too many and complex to capture in a set of principles that a non-virtuous person could understand and use to derive good guidance in all the concrete circumstances of their lives (Aristotle, 1999, ll. 1094b15–1095a1; 1104a1–4; Hursthouse, 1999, pp. 39–40; McDowell, 1979). This does not mean that particular decisions cannot be justified with arguments, principles, or reasons. Julia Annas (Annas, 2004) makes the point with a comparison. We can't expect to model the wise person's understanding on a computer manual in which you can just input a description of any situation you're facing and it points you to the answer. Even once we find plausible principles (such as "You should sacrifice to promote others' well-being if . . ."), it will often take experience and reflection to decide which ones apply to a particular situation and what they imply we should do.

One reason for believing that the wise person's grasp is uncodifiable is straightforward. Although age does not guarantee wisdom, experience and reflection seem to be necessary in order to fully grasp what matters and how you ought to live. That is why we would not expect even a really clever teenager to be wise (Annas, 2004; Hursthouse & Pettigrove, 2016).

However, a more forceful argument for **uncodifiability** is simply that attempts to codify virtuous action in comprehensive principles that could be applied by the non-virtuous have failed. Suppose someone offered the principle that "An action is virtuous and right if it produces the most good for society." This principle would obviously give bad guidance in some situations. For example, if you could help to pass a new labor law (one that would help to reduce income inequality) by falsely accusing one of the law's opponents of a crime, wouldn't that still be wrong even if it benefited society overall? How might we revise the principle to avoid these problems? Moral philosophers have developed a variety of competing moral theories that do a much better job of capturing what is right and virtuous, but the most plausible are much more complicated than our pet example. More importantly, the most plausible theories could not be applied mechanically – it would take experience and reflection to determine what they say we ought to do.

Despite these arguments, some authors have attempted to defend the idea that wisdom and virtue could be codified (Tsu, 2017). Determining who is right will tell us important things about the content of wise understanding, and could have implications for how we should (or should not) approach the study of wisdom.

2.5.6   What Kind of Reflection Helps Us to Develop Wisdom?

Development of wisdom requires that we refine the attitudes that we have absorbed from our family, culture, and environment into a reliable grasp of what matters and how to achieve it. This is why many think reflection is necessary for wisdom. But what kind of reflection is needed?

Aristotle believed that reflection conducive to virtue would have to focus both on the universal and on the particulars of situations (Aristotle, 1999, ll. 1141b10–15; 1142a14). It would have to focus on the particulars because whether a particular act of truth-telling, for instance, is honest will depend on the details of when, how, and why it takes place. It would have to focus on the universal because examining what shared features of actions make them virtuous is the way to ensure that one is living out all of one's commitments in a coherent manner.

Reasoning by analogy is one way to reflect on the particulars of the situation. Mengzi argued that we develop the virtues by "extending" the "sprouts" of good character that are part of our innately good human nature. The virtue of compassion, for instance, is developed by reflecting on the nearly universal feeling of concern for others' well-being. Even the most hard-hearted person will experience situations where they feel concern for others. Mencius thought that we could develop virtue by reflecting on whether other situations are similar in the ways that matter (Wong, 2002). To adapt an argument by Peter Singer (1972), suppose that you come across a child drowning in a shallow pool, and you could save them at the mere cost of your time and the sullying of your new shoes. Most of us will feel an obligation to help. However, if standing by and letting the child drown would be lacking in compassion, then why is it any better to stand by while people (including children) starve or die of preventable illnesses across the globe? If sullying your shoes does not justify refusing to save the drowning child, then why would having to give up buying luxuries and entertainment justify refusing to donate to proven poverty relief efforts? By examining analogies such as this, we can develop our grasp of how to show concern for others in the right ways, at the right times, and for the right reasons.

While analogies help us to focus on the particulars, other forms of reasoning could help us to reflect on the universals. Some philosophers think that by reflecting on particular cases (for example, particular compassionate acts) we can identify general principles that help us to better grasp what virtue requires (Annas, 1995, 2011; Hursthouse, 1999, p. 37). Think of situations where someone is clearly exhibiting the virtue of compassion. Can you think of a general principle that explains these ("Conduct is compassionate when . . .")? Perhaps this kind of reflection can help us to develop a principled grasp of what we ought to do, albeit one that (due to uncodifiability) would often require additional experience and reflection to apply well.

Philosophers disagree about the extent to which either of these types of reflection is necessary, with those who reject most or all principled reasoning (**particularists**) at one end of the spectrum, and those who emphasize the importance of grasping general principles at the other. Examining which view is most compelling could tell us more about how we can develop wisdom.

2.5.7   Can a Wise Person Explain or Justify What They Do?

Suppose Raheem is wise and grasps what to do after finding out that the racist note was a forgery. Will he be able to explain his reasons and justify his actions to others? Or does being wise just require "seeing" what to do without necessarily being able to articulate one's wisdom?

Alison Hills (2015) notes that a variety of answers are possible, ranging from **intellectualism** (the view that a fully wise and virtuous person can always explicitly grasp and explain the reasons why their action is right) to **naivety** (the view that a fully wise and virtuous person need not have this explicit grasp or ability to explain), or something in between. Which view is most plausible?

Following Hills (2015, pp. 15–27), we can identify a variety of opposing arguments. One argument for naivety is that grasping what one ought to do all things considered does not conceptually require an ability to explain oneself (Arpaly, 2002; McDowell, 1979, p. 332). The fully virtuous person's judgment that they ought to help the person stranded at the side of the road even though they are in a hurry just requires seeing the other person's need as a reason to stop and assist. Being able to explain why this course of action is virtuous, or why it is superior to the alternatives, seems superfluous. Julia Driver makes the point with an analogy to language mastery. Just as a native speaker can be fluent in a language without being able to justify themselves with rules of grammar, a wise and virtuous person need not be able to explain why their choice is the right one (Driver, 2013, p. 286).[10]

On the other hand, intellectualism seems more plausible when we think about the nature of moral development. A person's intuition (their ability to see quickly, immediately, and without conscious deliberation what they ought to do) is likely to be reliable only if it has been formed and validated through experience and reflection (Swartwood, 2013a, chapters 3 and 4). (Many people used to have the intuition that interracial relationships were "unnatural" and wrong, but these intuitions do not survive scrutiny. It is not hard to find cases like this where untutored intuitions lead people astray.) We need to do some reflection (of the sort previously described) to see whether our intuitions are worth listening to. If the wise person's understanding is honed through this kind of reflection, then perhaps we can expect that the wise will usually be able to justify and explain their intuitions.

Hills (2015, pp. 27–33) argues that more decisive evidence for intellectualism comes from the fact that justifying oneself is often a requirement for being virtuous. Being compassionate and just, for instance, often requires being able to justify oneself to others or to give advice. For Raheem to display the virtue of justice, he would not only need to grasp how he should respond to his knowledge of the false accusation, but also be able to justify that response to those parties he might upset. In general, being virtuous requires that all parts of our self – cognitive, affective, motivational, etc. – respond in the right ways, at the right times, and for the right reasons. Thus an ability to explain oneself is a component of a wise person's grasp of what they ought to do, not an unnecessary add-on.

Examining which of these alternatives – intellectualism, naivety, or something in between – is most defensible will give us a better sense of what the wisdom we strive for will look like.

2.5.8 Can We Measure Practical Wisdom?

Psychologists have developed ways to measure cognitive capacities such as intelligence, and personality traits such as introversion. Can we find a way to measure wisdom, too? If so, that would help us not only to identify who has it but also to find out what wisdom is like and how we can get it.

---

[10] For empirically informed philosophical discussions of the role of intuition in wisdom and virtue, see Annas (2011), Hills (2015), Stichter (2007), and Swartwood (2013b, 2013a, chapters 2–4).

Wisdom scientists have proposed a variety of measures of wisdom, described in Chapter 6 of this book, that rely upon a variety of different definitions of wisdom and means for operationalizing them. Jason Swartwood (2020) argues that none of these succeed in measuring wisdom, at least as it is defined according to the core philosophical conception, because they do not distinguish those who reliably succeed in making good all-things-considered decisions about how to conduct oneself in particular situations from those who do not.

Suppose that you wanted to measure expert performance (or the capacity for it) of some complex task, such as chess playing, crossword solving, or medical diagnosis. To measure whether someone is an expert – that is, if they reliably and successfully grasp how to do the task well – we need to be able to define what would count as success in performing the task. We can do this with things like chess playing, crossword solving, and medical diagnosis, because we have clear enough ways to tell if someone has won a chess game, correctly filled in the crossword, or accurately identified the cause of an illness. And to measure expertise, it is not enough just to be able to tell if someone *sometimes* succeeds. We need to be able to tell if they reliably succeed across a variety of situations, including challenging ones.

The problem with measuring wisdom is that we do not have clear success conditions in the way that we do for other areas. Succeeding at wisdom means making reliably good decisions about how one ought to live, all things considered, especially in challenging cases that befuddle those of us with a comparative lack of wisdom. Swartwood argues that existing attempts to operationalize wisdom are not informed by an account of these kinds of success conditions.

For instance, according to one prominent view (Ardelt, 2003, 2004), wisdom is a personality trait that we can measure by asking people to rate how much they agree with 39 general statements, such as "Things often go wrong for me by no fault of my own" or "I often have not comforted another when he or she needed it." These kinds of questions may tell us whether people care about the right general things, but we do not have reason to believe that they will tell us whether a person reliably makes good decisions about what virtue requires, all things considered, across particular situations (for example, those faced by Gloria, Maryam, and Raheem).

Another prominent approach (Oakes et al., 2019) attempts to measure wise reasoning by having participants recall a challenging interpersonal conflict and then answer questions that elicit their understanding of the situation and their reasoning about how to address it. Their responses are then rated according to the degree to which they exhibit an awareness of the limits of their own knowledge, examination of other perspectives, acknowledgement of the likelihood of change, predictions about what will happen given various contingencies, and the search for conflict resolution and compromise. However, it is easy to imagine people using these same general reasoning strategies to the same degree while coming to different – and not necessarily equally good – conclusions about what they ought to do, all things considered, in particular situations. Imagine two people considering whether to have an abortion, both of whom use the same general reasoning strategies. If both come to opposing conclusions (one that the abortion is wrong, and the other that it is – all things considered – for the best), surely the fact that they were both considering other perspectives and searching for compromise (for example) does not show that they are both equally wise.

These are just a few examples, briefly described, but Swartwood argues that other existing attempts to measure wisdom fail for similar reasons. Just as a measure of chess expertise would not be useful if we did not know whether it distinguished those who reliably won games from those who did not, measures of wisdom will not be useful unless we have reason to believe that they distinguish those who make reliably good all-things-considered decisions about how they ought to approach particular situations from those who do not. There are a variety of other empirical frameworks and models of wisdom (Darnell et al., 2019; Glück, 2020; Grossmann et al., 2020; Sternberg & Glück, 2019; Sternberg & Karami, 2021). Could any of these be used to develop a measure that avoids this obstacle?

2.6 Conclusion: The Need for More Interdisciplinary Wisdom Research

By critically examining different responses to these puzzles, philosophers aim to develop a plausible prescriptive ideal of wisdom. However, these prescriptive ideals sometimes make empirical assumptions about what people are capable of, and we cannot determine from the armchair how they would manifest in real people. How can we more plausibly combine the philosophical and empirical methods into a productive, interdisciplinary research program?

Perhaps philosophers and psychologists can develop an account of wisdom that both survives philosophical scrutiny and can be operationalized. Another alternative approach is to compare wisdom to more familiar and easily studied achievements that are similar in the ways that matter. A number of philosophers have argued that we can learn important things about the nature and development of wisdom and virtue by comparing them to expert skill at tasks such as tennis, piano playing, chess, or firefighting (Annas, 2011; Stichter, 2018; Swartwood, 2013b). If it could be shown through reliable empirical study that certain characteristics (such as principled reflection, inarticulate intuition, etc.) are part of the relevant type of expert skill, and through philosophical argument that wisdom is similar in the ways that matter to that type of skill, then this could provide us with a useful interdisciplinary method of studying wisdom even if wisdom is not directly measurable. Do any of these analogies stand up to scrutiny? Philosophers continue to discuss this question.

This chapter has described a few of the wide variety of important philosophical accounts of what wisdom is like, how we can obtain it, and how we can study it. Engaging with philosophical conceptions of wisdom and the puzzles to which they give rise is an essential part of the interdisciplinary study of this important concept. Indeed, engaging in philosophical reflection about wisdom is not just for researchers – it will also help the rest of us to better grasp an ideal that we have good reason to aspire to.[11]

2.7 Comprehension and Discussion Questions

(1) Suppose that Chelsea is an expert coder – she understands how to achieve whatever computer programming task you put in front of her. She can tell quickly after looking at some code what it will do or why it is not doing what someone wants. Using the definition of theoretical wisdom given in this chapter, explain why Chelsea does not necessarily have theoretical wisdom.

(2) Some psychologists study the "need for cognition," which could be described as the inclination or desire to engage in challenging cognitive tasks (such as studying philosophy!). Is the need for cognition a prescriptive ideal? Why or why not?

[11] I am grateful to Judith Glück, Robert Sternberg, Ian Stoner, and Ruth Swartwood for feedback on drafts of this chapter.

(3) Suppose that someone offers the following descriptive claim as evidence for a prescriptive conclusion:

> Driving while drunk puts you and others at increased risk of injury (descriptive premise). Therefore, you should not drive while drunk (prescriptive conclusion).

What *prescriptive* premise would you have to add to this argument to make it complete, such that if the premises are true the conclusion has to be true, too?

(4) According to the account described in this chapter, a virtue is a stable and admirable disposition to respond in the right ways, at the right times, and for the right reasons in some important area of human choice. Compassion, for instance, can be described as the disposition to respond to threats to others' well-being in the right ways, at the right times, and for the right reasons. Identify two other character virtues that you think are important, and define them by filling in the blanks: __ *[name of the virtue]* __ *is a disposition to* _____ *at the right times, in the right ways, and for the right reasons.* Then, for each virtue, give specific (real or hypothetical) examples where someone is clearly exhibiting this virtue, and cases where they are not.

(5) Suppose that someone defines the virtue of loyalty as the tendency to be partial to people, groups, or causes that one cares about. Using what you have learned in this chapter, give examples that help to explain why this is *not* a good definition of the *virtue* of loyalty.

(6) Below is a quote from the ancient Chinese philosopher Mengzi. Read the quote and then explain how Mengzi's archery analogy illustrates the ways in which wisdom is a master virtue. (Hint: suppose that by the term "sagacity" Mengzi means having the character virtues.)

> Wisdom may be compared to skillfulness. Sagacity may be compared to strength. It is like shooting an arrow from beyond a hundred paces: its making it there is due to your strength, but its hitting the bull's-eye is not due to your strength. (*Mengzi* 5B1.7)

(7) This chapter described at least two reasons why wisdom is necessary for virtue. First, wisdom helps a person to grasp what a particular virtue (such as compassion) requires in situations where a person with less wisdom would be befuddled (for example, the case of Gloria in Section 2.4.3). Second, wisdom helps a person to grasp what to do when virtues appear to be in conflict (for example, when honesty seems to require telling your dad that you think his haircut is ugly, but compassion seems to require a white lie). Pick a few virtues other than compassion, and give your own examples to illustrate each of these two types of cases. How do they illustrate why having wisdom is necessary for being a virtuous person?

(8) Is theoretical wisdom a prescriptive ideal in the same sense that practical wisdom is? Why or why not?

(9) Section 2.2 of this chapter uses the case of Glenda to illustrate why having theoretical wisdom is not sufficient for having practical wisdom – you can be theoretically wise without being practically wise. But is having theoretical wisdom necessary for having practical wisdom? In other words, can you be practically wise without being theoretically wise? Discuss and try to support your answer with specific examples.

(10) Some wisdom scientists study people's conceptions of wisdom (sometimes called implicit theories of wisdom). They study non-scientists' views about who is wise and what wisdom is like (Weststrate et al., 2019). See Chapter 3 of this book for an overview of that research. Given what you have learned from this chapter, do you think studying

people's conceptions of wisdom could be useful for figuring out what practical wisdom is actually like? Why or why not?

(11) Think about someone whom you believe is wise. Explain some specific reasons why you think they are wise. Does the core philosophical conception described in Section 2.4 of this chapter do a good job of explaining the sense in which they are wise? Why or why not?

(12) Section 2.5 of this chapter describes a puzzle concerning how to tell which character traits are virtues and which are not. Suppose that someone offered this answer: virtues are the character traits that would contribute to a human being reproducing and passing on their genetic material. Would that be a plausible way to distinguish virtues from vices? Why or why not?

(13) Select one of the puzzles described in Section 2.5 of this chapter. Write down (clearly, precisely, and in your own words) the question that the puzzle raises. If there are others with whom you can have a discussion, divide into debate groups, each of which defends a different answer to the puzzle. (If you are by yourself, identify what you think is the best answer to the puzzle. What objections might someone raise to that answer? Is there a way to defend your answer against the objections?)

2.9 Investigations

I am interested in combining the methods of philosophy and findings from empirical psychology to learn more about what wisdom is like and how we can get it. I ask questions such as the following: Are wisdom scientists measuring the kind of wisdom that philosophers are interested in? Exploring this question led me to conclude that wisdom scientists are not measuring wisdom as it is conceived according to the core philosophical account described in Section 2.4 of this chapter (Swartwood, 2020). By discussing this argument, I hope we can better understand the prospects for measuring the sort of wisdom we have good reason to care about. Since I am skeptical about the possibility of directly measuring wisdom, I have looked for other ways in which we can combine philosophy and empirical science to learn more about what wisdom will look like in real people and how we can obtain it. For instance, my mentor Valerie Tiberius and I have outlined a method for using philosophical reflection to refine people's conceptions of wisdom (Tiberius & Swartwood, 2011), and in my own work I have argued that we can learn more about wisdom by examining the ways in which it is analogous to expert skill in areas such as firefighting (Swartwood, 2013a, b).

2.10 Practical Applications

If my argument (Swartwood, 2013b, 2013a) for the expert skill model of wisdom is correct, then developing wisdom takes deliberate practice, in the same way that expertise in other complex decision-making skills does. Firefighters develop expert skill in figuring out how to fight fires by getting feedback on their decisions through experience and reflection. However, while firefighters can often get feedback on the quality of their decisions just through repeated observation (for example, seeing if the roof caves in after spraying in one place instead of another), we cannot obtain feedback on our decisions about how we *ought* to conduct ourselves all things considered through observation alone (for reasons discussed in Section 2.3 of this chapter). Therefore, we can expect that the development of wisdom requires engaging in reflection that could help us to get feedback on our decisions and judgments. I have co-authored a textbook (Stoner & Swartwood, 2021) that helps people to develop some of the reasoning skills – thinking about analogies, and identifying and applying principles – that I think would help us to do this.

Glossary

character virtue a deep disposition to respond well in a particular area of human choice. For example, compassion is the disposition to show concern for others' well-being in the right ways, at the right times, and for the right reasons.

cleverness according to Aristotle, a merely clever person is someone who reliably grasps how to achieve their goals, although, unlike a person with practical wisdom, they are aiming at the wrong goals or commitments.

continent term used to describe a person who does the right thing for the right reasons but, unlike the fully virtuous person, only after struggling against the desire to do otherwise.

descriptive truths truths about how the world *is* (or was or will be) and how the things in it actually *are* or tend to be.

epistemic humility account of wisdom an awareness of one's ignorance of the most important things, such as the nature of a good and virtuous life.

eudaimonia a Greek word that could be translated as "flourishing" or "living well."

intellectualism the claim that a wise and virtuous person could, to some significant degree, explain or justify their decisions to others.

master virtue a virtue (such as practical wisdom) that controls or guides other virtues.

naivety the claim that being able to explain or justify one's decisions to others is not necessary for a person to be fully wise or virtuous.

particularist a person who holds the view that moral reflection and decision making should focus (either solely or to a significant extent) on examining the particulars of a situation rather than applying general moral principles.

practical wisdom (Greek: *phronesis*) a deep and comprehensive grasp of how one ought to live.

prescriptive ideal a construct, concept, or account that is supposed to tell us how we *ought* to be, and not simply to describe how anyone actually *is*.

prescriptive reasons and truths truths about how we *ought* to conduct ourselves, truths about what *matters*, or reasons why we *ought* to conduct ourselves in certain ways but not others. In philosophy, these are often called "normative" reasons.

theoretical wisdom (Greek: *sophia*) a deep and comprehensive grasp of how things *are* (how the world and the creatures and things in it tend to be or behave).

uncodifiability thesis the claim that what is virtuous and wise cannot be captured in a set of principles that could be used by a non-virtuous person to reliably identify the right action in every situation that they face.

unity of the virtues thesis the claim that having one of the character virtues requires possession of them all.

virtue an excellent character trait.

virtuous person a person with all the virtues.

well-being what is good for someone; you have well-being to the extent that your life is going well for you rather than poorly.

REFERENCES

Annas, J. (1995). Virtue as a skill. *International Journal of Philosophical Studies*, 3(2), 227–43.

(2004). Being virtuous and doing the right thing. *Proceedings and Addresses of the American Philosophical Association*, 78, 61–75.

(2011). *Intelligent Virtue*. Oxford University Press.

Ardelt, M. (2003). Empirical assessment of a three-dimensional wisdom scale. *Research on Aging*, 25(3), 275–324.

(2004). Wisdom as expert knowledge system: A critical review of a contemporary operationalization of an ancient concept. *Human Development*, 47(5), 257–85.

Aristotle. (1999). *Nicomachean Ethics* (T. Irwin, trans.). Hackett Publishing Company.

Arpaly, N. (2002). *Unprincipled Virtue: An Inquiry into Moral Agency*. Oxford University Press.

Badhwar, N. (1996). The limited unity of virtue. *Nous*, 30(3), 306–29.

Baehr, J. (2012). Two types of wisdom. *Acta Analytica*, 27(2), 81–97.

Bell, M. (2009). Anger, virtue, and oppression. In L. Tessman, ed. *Feminist Ethics and Social and Political Philosophy: Theorizing the Non-Ideal*. Springer, pp. 165–83.

Blum, L. (2007). Racial virtues. In R. L. Walker and P. J. Ivanhoe, eds., *Working Virtues*. Oxford University Press, pp. 225–50.

Broadie, S. (1993). *Ethics with Aristotle*. Oxford University Press.

Brooks, J. and Walsh, P. (2017). St. Olaf: Report of racist note on black student's windshield was "fabricated." *Star Tribune*, May 11; http://www.startribune.com/st-olaf-report-of-racist-note-on-black-student-s-windshield-was-fabricated/421912763/

Brouwer, R. (2014). *The Stoic Sage: The Early Stoics on Wisdom, Sagehood and Socrates*. Cambridge University Press.

Cherry, M. (2021). *The Case for Rage: Why Anger is Essential to Anti-Racist Struggle*. Oxford University Press.

Darnell, C., Gulliford, L., Kristjánsson, K., and Paris, P. (2019). Phronesis and the knowledge-action gap in moral psychology and moral education: a new synthesis? *Human Development*, 62(3), 101–29.

Driver, J. (2013). Moral expertise: judgment, practice, and analysis. *Social Philosophy & Policy*, 30(1–2), 280–96.

Gambrel, J. C. and Cafaro, P. (2010). The virtue of simplicity. *Journal of Agricultural and Environmental Ethics*, 23(1–2), 85–108.

Glück, J. (2020). The important difference between psychologists' labs and real life: evaluating the validity of models of wisdom. *Psychological Inquiry*, 31(2), 144–50.

Gowans, C. (2016). Moral relativism. In *Stanford Encyclopedia of Philosophy* (Winter 2016). https://plato.stanford.edu/archives/win2016/entries/moral-relativism/

Grimm, S. R. (2015). Wisdom. *Australasian Journal of Philosophy*, 93(1), 139–54.

Grossmann, I., Weststrate, N. M., Ardelt, M. et al. (2020). The science of wisdom in a polarized world: knowns and unknowns. *Psychological Inquiry*, 31(2), 103–33.

Gyekye, K. (2011). African ethics. In *Stanford Encyclopedia of Philosophy*. https://plato.stanford.edu/entries/african-ethics/

Hills, A. (2015). The intellectuals and the virtues. *Ethics*, 126(1), 7–36.

Hursthouse, R. (1999). *On Virtue Ethics*. Oxford University Press.

(2007). Environmental virtue ethics. In R. Walker and P. J. Ivanhoe, eds. *Working Virtue: Virtue Ethics and Contemporary Moral Problems*. Oxford University Press, pp. 155–71.

Hursthouse, R. and Pettigrove, G. (2016). Virtue ethics. In *Stanford Encyclopedia of Philosophy* (Winter 2016). https://plato.stanford.edu/entries/ethics-virtue/

Kekes, J. (1995). *Moral Wisdom and Good Lives*. Cornell University Press.

Kraut, R. (2009). *What is Good and Why: The Ethics of Well-Being*. Harvard University Press.

McDowell, J. (1979). Virtue and reason. *Monist*, 62(3), 331–50.

Marshall, J. (2002). *The Lakota Way: Stories and Lessons for Living*. Penguin.

Mengzi. (2008). *Mengzi: With Selections from Traditional Commentaries* (B. W. Van Norden, trans.). Hackett Publishing Company.

Metz, T. (2012). Ethics in Africa and in Aristotle: some points of contrast. *Phronimon*, 13(2), 99–117.

Nussbaum, M. C. (1988). Non-relative virtues: an Aristotelian approach. *Midwest Studies in Philosophy*, 13(1), 32–53.

    (2001). *Women and Human Development: The Capabilities Approach*, Vol. 3. Cambridge University Press.

Oakes, H., Brienza, J., Elnakouri, A., and Grossmann, I. (2019). Wise reasoning: converging evidence for the psychology of sound judgment. In R. J. Sternberg and J. Glück, eds., *The Cambridge Handbook of Wisdom*. Cambridge University Press, pp. 202–25.

Olberding, A. (2008). Dreaming of the Duke of Zhou: exemplarism and the Analects. *Journal of Chinese Philosophy*, 35(4), 625–39.

Pakaluk, M. (2005). *Aristotle's Nichomachean Ethics: An Introduction*. Cambridge University Press.

Peters, J. (2013). Virtue, personal good, and the silencing of reasons. *Aristotelian Ethics in Contemporary Perspective*, 21, 69.

Prinz, J. (2007). *The Emotional Construction of Morals*. Oxford University Press.

Ryan, S. (1999). What is wisdom? *Philosophical Studies*, 93(2), 119–39.

    (2016). Wisdom: understanding and the good life. *Acta Analytica*, 31(3), 235–51.

Singer, P. (1972). Famine, affluence, and morality. *Philosophy & Public Affairs*, 1(3), 229–43.

Sternberg, R. J. and Glück, J. (2019). *The Cambridge Handbook of Wisdom*. Cambridge University Press.

Sternberg, R. J. and Karami, S. (2021). What is wisdom? A unified 6P framework. *Review of General Psychology*, 25(2), 134–51.

Stichter, M. (2007). Ethical expertise: the skill model of virtue. *Ethical Theory and Moral Practice*, 10(2), 183–94.

    (2018). *The Skillfulness of Virtue: Improving our Moral and Epistemic Lives*. Cambridge University Press.

Stoner, I. and Swartwood, J. (2021). *Doing Practical Ethics*. Oxford University Press.

Swartwood, J. (2013a). *Cultivating Practical Wisdom* Ph.D. Dissertation, University of Minnesota; http://conservancy.umn.edu/bitstream/154543/1/Swartwood_umn_0130E_13707.pdf

    (2013b). Wisdom as an expert skill. *Ethical Theory and Moral Practice*, 16(3), 511–28. https://doi.org/10.1007/s10677-012-9367-2

    (2020). Can we measure practical wisdom? *Journal of Moral Education*, 49(1), 71–97.

Swartwood, J. and Tiberius, V. (2019). Philosophical foundations of wisdom. In R. J. Sternberg and J. Glück, eds., *The Cambridge Handbook of Wisdom*. Cambridge University Press, pp. 10–39.

Tessman, L. (2005). *Burdened Virtues: Virtue Ethics for Liberatory Struggles*. Oxford University Press.

Tiberius, V. (2008). *The Reflective Life: Living Wisely With Our Limits*. Oxford University Press.

    (2015). *Moral Psychology: A Contemporary Introduction*. Routledge.

Tiberius, V. and Swartwood, J. (2011). Wisdom revisited: a case study in normative theorizing. *Philosophical Explorations*, 14(3), 277–95.

Tsu, P. S.-H. (2017). Can virtue be codified? *Virtue's Reasons: New Essays on Virtue, Character, and Reasons*, 37, 65.

Weststrate, N. M., Bluck, S., and Glück, J. (2019). Wisdom of the crowd: exploring people's conceptions of wisdom. In R. J. Sternberg and J. Glück, eds., *The Cambridge Handbook of Wisdom*. Cambridge University Press, pp. 97–121.

Wolf, S. (2007). Moral psychology and the unity of the virtues. *Ratio*, 20(2), 145–67.

Wong, D. (2002). Reasons and analogical reasoning in Mengzi. In X. Liu and P. J. Ivanhoe, eds., *Essays on the Moral Philosophy of Mengzi*. Hackett Publishing Company, pp. 187–220.

Zagzebski, L. T. (2010). Exemplarist virtue theory. *Metaphilosophy*, 41(1), 41–57.

CHAPTER 3

Folk Conceptions of Wisdom around the World

Nic M. Weststrate and Susan Bluck

3.1 Introduction

In the last few decades, the psychological science of wisdom has flourished, but where did it all begin? Before there were fancy expert theories of wisdom, the very first investigations of wisdom started by modestly asking everyday people for their ideas about what wisdom is. The doctoral research of Vivian Clayton in the late 1970s is often credited with stimulating contemporary interest in people's conceptions of wisdom. In her seminal study, Clayton inspected the perceptions of wisdom in three age cohorts of people, with the goal of identifying the underlying structure of wisdom (Clayton & Birren, 1980). From that pioneering study, Clayton concluded that wisdom is a multidimensional construct that integrates cognitive, affective, and reflective qualities. This initial investigation paved the way for an entire field of inquiry within the psychological science of wisdom, the goal of which has been to elucidate what laypeople think about wisdom (see also Holliday & Chandler, 1986; Sternberg, 1985).

Defining wisdom presents somewhat of a paradox. On the one hand, the construct of wisdom has been described as a rare, elusive, and even divine quality that may be hard for the average person to fully comprehend. On the other hand, wisdom is a highly relatable concept that concerns fundamental aspects of human life. After all, the name of our own species, *Homo sapiens*, translates from the Latin as meaning "wise person." Although this name descends from Western scientists, wisdom has a rich cultural heritage in virtually every corner of the world, enshrined in religious and philosophical texts and teachings (Assmann, 1994). Wisdom may very well be the ultimate expression of humanity across cultures – a quality that sets us apart from other species, past and present. As it turns out, when asked, people can fairly easily identify and describe particular attributes of wisdom, nominate certain people as wise, and recall instances of wisdom in their own lives, and all of this information has helped psychologists and other scholars to understand wisdom.

Thus people have conceptions of what it means to be wise, and these understandings have been the subject of systematic investigations for over four decades. The goal of this chapter is to summarize the literature on how people who are not experts on wisdom conceive of it. We shall begin by defining essential terms and situating this research tradition within the broader science of wisdom. Next, we shall discuss three distinct methodological approaches to the investigation of conceptions of wisdom. We shall then highlight key aspects of folk conceptions by answering the following core questions at the center of this field of inquiry:

(1) What is wisdom?
(2) Who is wise?
(3) In which situations is wisdom expressed?
(4) How does wisdom develop?
(5) How do conceptions of wisdom differ across people, places, and cultures?

In fact, before you read any further, we'd like you to take a moment to reflect on the five questions that we have just posed. Grab a pen and paper and jot down some quick thoughts in response to each of these questions. It will be interesting for you to compare your own reflections with the findings in the research literature, which we shall review throughout this chapter. We wonder if these questions were easy or difficult for you to answer. Is wisdom something that you've given much thought to in your life? Where did you learn about wisdom? These are all good questions to keep in mind as you continue reading.

3.1.1 Defining Terms

There is a growing vocabulary to describe what we refer to here as **folk conceptions** of wisdom. Researchers have used the adjectives *internal, implicit, subjective, layperson,* and *folk* to refer to people's informal *theories* or *conceptions* of wisdom. Any one of these labels is just fine to use, and distinctions between them are probably quite negligible and a matter of taste, although we have pointed out that some labels, such as "lay theories," might create an unnecessary divide that privileges the opinions of scholars above all other people (Weststrate et al., 2019). We would prefer to think that researchers interested in people's understandings of wisdom would view people's perspectives and opinions as valuable in their own right and as important sources of information. Of the menu of options provided above, for our present purposes, we most commonly use the word "folk," which carries a similar meaning in many languages, and is meant to convey that something is traditional or common to people or culture. Because people come to understand concepts such as wisdom through participation in culture, this seems appropriate. However, our usage of the word "folk" is not intended to imply that the concepts people hold of wisdom are old-fashioned, superstitious, or primitive in any way. Finally, we use the word "conception" rather than "theory" because people are likely to have beliefs about wisdom, but most are unlikely to carry full-blown theories in their mind.

People's folk conceptions of wisdom are sometimes contrasted with expert, explicit, or formal theories of wisdom devised by scholars. In fact, many expert wisdom theories were based on earlier investigations of people's folk conceptions (e.g., Ardelt, 2003; Jason et al., 2001), often in consultation with the historical and philosophical wisdom literatures. Unsurprisingly then, people's conceptions and expert theories generally converge on similar meanings of wisdom. As expert theories are based on explicit consideration of various relevant sources, they are usually more complex and comprehensive, but in some cases, research on people's conceptions exposes new information that experts may have ignored or did not think to examine. In fact, it sometimes seems that people have even better ideas than the so-called experts! Experts can use these insights as a foundation for future research and theorizing. However, the research methods used to study folk conceptions and expert theories are quite different. In the next section we shall review methods for capturing people's conceptions of wisdom.

3.2 Methods for Investigating Folk Conceptions of Wisdom

Researchers have gone about studying people's conceptions of wisdom in diverse and creative ways. On the one hand, most researchers have explored people's abstract schemas of what wisdom is, focusing on traits, characteristics, and abilities. On the other hand, some other researchers have taken a more contextual approach, suggesting that individuals' conceptions are strongly connected to real-world exemplars of wisdom, or to memories of real-life events involving wisdom (e.g., Bluck & Glück, 2004; Weststrate et al., 2018). Before turning to the findings from this research, in this section we shall first review some common methods used by researchers, highlighting their relative strengths and limitations.

3.2.1 *Descriptor Studies*

The most typical approach to studying people's conceptions of wisdom is to ask people to judge a list of single-word descriptors or short phrases (e.g., traits, abilities, characteristics, behaviors) for their relevance to wisdom. **Descriptor approaches** typically proceed in three stages, which we shall describe shortly, but first we would like you to take a moment to imagine that we presented you with the following list of 12 words. We would like you to do three things with this list. First, we want you to mentally sort them into two piles – those relevant to wisdom and those not relevant to wisdom. Next, we want you to mentally rank the items from most relevant to wisdom to least relevant to wisdom. Finally, we would like you to rate every word for how relevant it is to wisdom on a 5-point scale from "not important" (1) to "very important" (5) to wisdom.

Empathetic	Knowledgable
Experienced	Observant
Gentle	Peaceful
Intelligent	Pragmatic
Introspective	Sense of humor
Intuitive	Understanding

(1) **Generating.** In the first stage, a list of potential descriptors is generated, either by the researchers on a theoretical basis (e.g., Glück & Bluck, 2011), by designated experts (e.g., Sternberg, 1985), or by research participants (Hu et al., 2018). In many cases, pilot studies are conducted to generate the list of descriptors. The list of 12 words that we provided above came from a pilot study that Vivian Clayton conducted prior to her pioneering publication (Clayton & Birren, 1980). Sometimes it is necessary to reduce the list according to a specified decision-making criterion – for example, systematically removing synonyms or redundancies (e.g., Holliday & Chandler, 1986). Some studies end after having generated a comprehensive list that encapsulates how individuals conceive of wisdom (e.g., Hu et al., 2018).

(2) **Rating, ranking, or sorting.** Most studies move forward with the second stage, in which a new sample of people rates, ranks, or sorts the descriptors, just as you did in the opening exercise (Glück & Bluck, 2011; Hershey & Farrell, 1997; Holliday & Chandler, 1986; Jason et al., 2001). In some cases, comparator words are added that are neutral or negatively related to wisdom, to discriminate wisdom from other constructs (e.g., Glück et al., 2012; König & Glück, 2013). In the above case, all 12 of the words were selected because they were believed to be related to

wisdom to some degree. However, Clayton and Birren (1980) added three extra words to the list – *aged*, *wise*, and *myself*. They then asked participants to rate each possible pair of descriptors for their similarity to each other, which demonstrates yet another creative way to gather information about conceptions of wisdom.

(3) **Analyzing and describing.** Depending on the data produced in the second stage, in the third stage researchers mostly use statistical techniques to make sense of the information provided. Typically, multidimensional scaling, factor analysis, or cluster analysis is used to identify subcomponents of wisdom (e.g., Clayton & Birren, 1980; Glück & Bluck, 2011; Holliday & Chandler, 1986; König & Glück, 2013; Sternberg, 1985; Weststrate et al., 2016). Each of these techniques reduces the data in some way, so that they are more interpretable. The purpose is to identify underlying dimensions that organize people's conceptions. Often, when interpreting the results, consideration is given to how they overlap with existing formal theories of wisdom.

An advantage of the descriptor approach is that it is fairly easy to administer and analyze. A limitation is that it assumes that people understand the meaning of the adjectives presented by the researchers, which might make it an especially challenging method to use with children (Glück et al., 2012) or with people who have had little formal education. Another limitation is that the success of the second and third steps is highly dependent on the first step. If the list of adjectives used in the second step fails to cover all relevant aspects of wisdom, there is no way to identify this later in the research process. A final limitation of this approach is that it is quite disconnected from real life, as we shall see next.

3.2.2   Real-Life Approaches

The next group of methods assesses conceptions of wisdom in more contextualized ways. **Real-life approaches** range from simply asking people to nominate exemplars of wisdom to in-depth explorations of wisdom as it manifests in real-life experiences. We review three real-life approaches, presented in order of increasing complexity. First, however, we'd like you to give this method a try by responding to the following questions:

(1)   Who is the wisest person that you know? This could be someone that you know personally or someone you have never met. They could be alive or dead, fictional or real. Who is this person and what makes them so wise? Can you think of a specific memory or episode that demonstrates their wisdom? Tell us a story that brings their wisdom to life. Finally, how do you think this person got to be so wise?

(2)   Let us shift the lens and talk about *you* for a minute. Can you think of a time when you did, said, or thought something wise? If so, say a little about when, where, and what happened in that situation. Why did you think that situation required wisdom and not some other quality or ability? Finally, what specifically was it about what you did, said, or thought that was wise?

(3)   Reflecting on your responses to the above two questions, what might a researcher learn about your conception of wisdom? What if, instead, we had just asked you to define wisdom? To what extent would your definition align with your previous responses? By asking you to recall wisdom within a real-life context, did we learn something new or different about how you think of wisdom?

3.2.2.1 Nomination Procedures

As you saw above, the first real-life approach investigates conceptions of wisdom by asking participants to nominate people who embody or demonstrate wisdom, which is taken to be a reflection of their internal concept of wisdom. Typically, people are asked to nominate an exemplar of wisdom (i.e., the wisest person they can think of), either someone they know personally or a public figure (e.g., Glück et al., 2012; Jason et al., 2001). In some cases, they also explain why they have nominated a particular person or share a short story about that person's wisdom (e.g., Ardelt, 2008; Hu et al., 2018; König & Glück, 2012; Weststrate et al., 2016). Wisdom nominees are categorized in relation to demographic characteristics such as age, gender, and education level. This approach is based on exemplar theory, in which real-life exemplars act as reference points for individuals when it comes to understanding abstract concepts such as wisdom. Although exemplars vary in their representativeness of wisdom, shared characteristics across exemplars are likely to reflect an underlying wisdom prototype.

3.2.2.2 Autobiographical Narratives

The second real-life approach goes deeper into a research participant's specific life experiences. In two articles, Bluck and Glück (2004) and Glück et al. (2005) advanced an approach called the "wisdom of experience" method. This approach focuses on people's memories of real-life experiences involving wisdom –participants are asked to recall a time when they did, said, or thought something wise (Bluck & Glück, 2004; Glück et al., 2005; König & Glück, 2012) or felt that they had gained wisdom in their own life (Weststrate et al., 2018). The narratives provided are transcribed, if necessary, and then content-analyzed for significant themes. Such coding has, for example, looked at types of life situations, aspects of wise behavior, forms of wisdom, or the content of lessons learned.

3.2.2.3 In-Depth Qualitative Interviews

Somewhat recently, purely qualitative approaches have gained traction in this field. For example, researchers have examined manifestations of wisdom through in-depth interviews with relatively small samples of judges (Levitt & Dunnavant, 2015), Tibetan monks (Levitt, 1999), educators (Chen et al., 2014), and older adults (Montgomery et al., 2002). These approaches are well suited to developing knowledge about highly complex forms of wisdom (e.g., judicial wisdom; Levitt & Dunnavant, 2015). This research aims to richly describe the phenomenon of wisdom in a specific context, rather than make generalizable claims.

3.2.3 Experimental Designs

Researchers have also used **experimental approaches** to studying folk conceptions of wisdom. For example, Sternberg (1985) asked participants to rate different versions of a letter of recommendation that described hypothetical people, each differing in the extent to which intelligent, wise, and creative traits and abilities were emphasized. Hira and Faulkender (1997) manipulated the age of the target individuals in written or videotaped vignettes, and asked participants to rate them for wisdom. Finally, Glück et al. (2009) manipulated the gender of the target person in a descriptor study (i.e., "Paul" or "Paula"). Such formats help us to understand how conceptions of wisdom are related to particular demographic characteristics, such as age and gender. In all of these studies, characteristics of a target person are manipulated in order to examine what impact those features might have on judgments about wisdom. However, we do not know whether these hypothetical individuals would actually be considered wise in the real world.

3.3 Summarizing Folk Conceptions of Wisdom

Now that we have reviewed how researchers go about studying folk conceptions of wisdom, this section will summarize what we have learned so far about people's views on what wisdom is, what types of people are wise, how wisdom manifests in situations, and how wisdom develops. Unfortunately, most of the research that we shall review in this section comes from Western samples in Europe and North America. We shall review what is known about cross-cultural differences in conceptions of wisdom later in the chapter. Hopefully more and more research will examine folk conceptions in other cultures and regions of the world.

3.3.1   What Is Wisdom?

Recently, with Judith Glück, we reviewed folk conceptions of wisdom in a chapter that appeared in *The Cambridge Handbook of Wisdom* (Weststrate et al., 2019). In that chapter, we argued that the best way to classify the results of research on conceptions of wisdom is through three broad components, each with unique sub-facets. Specifically, we argued that, consistent with the very first research by Vivian Clayton (Clayton & Birren, 1980), wisdom conceptions continue to include exceptional personal qualities in the cognitive, reflective, and affective domains, as well as the underlying ability to translate these qualities into real-world action. Virtually all of the available studies, which have now asked thousands of people about their conceptions of wisdom, find evidence for some variation of these three components (e.g., Glück & Bluck, 2011; Weststrate et al., 2016). The three-component framework is used here to organize and integrate the literature, and is not intended to imply that the components are entirely independent of each other. In fact, the components are overlapping and interrelated in many ways. Still, we find this to be a useful framework for summarizing the literature (see Figure 3.1). We review each component in turn.

3.3.1.1   Cognitive Component

Without exception, researchers have found that people view wisdom as involving cognitive abilities. The **cognitive component** is composed of two sub-facets: (1) life knowledge and experience, and (2) reasoning ability and judgment. First, wise people are considered to be exceptional at learning through experience, and have therefore accumulated a broad and deep base of life knowledge (Clayton & Birren, 1980; König & Glück, 2013). Second, when complex and uncertain life challenges arise, wise people are able to reason through the problem, taking into consideration what is both known and unknown, in order to find a solution that balances the interests of multiple stakeholders (Sternberg, 1985; Yang, 2001). Thus the cognitive component of wisdom contains both accumulated knowledge and the ability to process that complex information. In open-ended studies, cognitive abilities tend to be the most frequently reported of all characteristics (Glück et al., 2012; König & Glück, 2013).

3.3.1.2   Reflective Component

The **reflective component** consists of three sub-facets: (1) deep insight, (2) critical self-reflection, and (3) humility. First, people believe that wise people are motivated to see beyond the simple

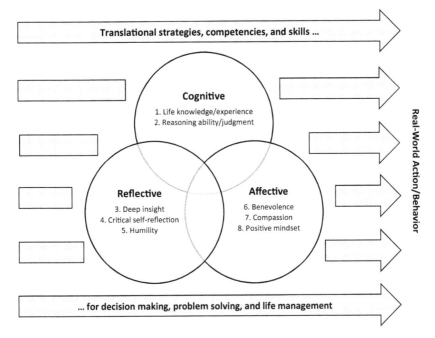

Figure 3.1   Visual representation of people's folk conceptions of wisdom, involving cognitive, reflective, and affective components each with sub-facets, as well as translational processes and abilities that enable wisdom to be translated into real-world action.

surface of complex problems, to look for deeper meanings, and to take different perspectives in order to see a situation from all sides (Holliday & Chandler, 1986; Sternberg, 1985; Yang, 2001). This entails maintaining a clear and unbiased view across situations. Second, wise people are believed to engage in critical self-reflection that is aimed at generating a deep self-understanding, such as questioning their own behaviors, thoughts, emotions, and motivations, and trying to identify blind spots and defense mechanisms (Chen et al., 2014; Hu et al., 2018). In general, wise people are thought to have a profound motivation to learn (König & Glück, 2013), and are believed to be receptive and open to new ways of thinking, feeling, and doing (Sternberg, 1985). Thus critical self-reflection is expected to be one of the practices through which wise people learn from life experience. Resulting from deep insight and critical self-reflection, the third reflective sub-facet involves humility (König & Glück, 2013), which has two aspects. First, wise people are thought to be intellectually humble – they acknowledge the limits of their own knowledge and control, the possibility of alternative perspectives, and the relativism of people's values and beliefs. Second, wise people are interpersonally humble – they are subtle, modest, and socially unobtrusive (Holliday & Chandler, 1986), and lack arrogance or pomp (Hershey & Farrell, 1997; Yang, 2001).

3.3.1.3   *Affective Component*

The third component that researchers consistently find in people's conceptions of wisdom is socio-emotional. The sub-facets of the **affective component** include (1) benevolence, (2) compassion, and (3) a positive mindset. First, wise people are viewed as benevolent, meaning that they have a deep concern for the welfare of others and for the common human good. This is expressed in characteristics such as warmth, respect, kindheartedness, love, generativity, and helpfulness (Glück et al., 2012; Yang, 2001). These attributes explain why wise people are seen as morally virtuous and good (Kałużna-Wielobób, 2014). Second, wise people are viewed as compassionate toward individuals in need. Through mature interpersonal skills (Holliday & Chandler, 1986), they empathically understand the suffering of people around them, and aim to ameliorate these concerns (Hu et al., 2018; Jason et al., 2001). Both benevolence and compassion require a degree of self-transcendence (i.e., seeing beyond oneself to the greater whole; Jason et al., 2001; König & Glück, 2013). Third, and finally, wise people are seen as having a positive mindset. They are viewed as calm, serene, cheerful, animated, and optimistic (Hu et al., 2018; König & Glück, 2013). Their positive mindset extends to a broader contentment, gratitude, and joy in life, involving self-acceptance and a sense of peace (Yang, 2001).

3.3.1.4   Translating the Components into Real-World Action

So far, this review has demonstrated that wise people are believed to possess exceptional qualities in the cognitive, reflective, and affective domains. Yet wisdom involves more than the mere possession of these qualities – wise people are able to *translate* these qualities into real-world behaviors. In studies of wisdom conceptions, people have consistently associated wisdom with a repertoire of practical strategies, competencies, and skills that are judiciously applied in problem-solving, decision-making, and life-management contexts (e.g., Chen et al., 2014; Holliday & Chandler, 1986). Some studies have aligned this procedural life knowledge with the cognitive component (König & Glück, 2013); however, wise people possess behavioural competencies that relate to the affective and reflective domains as well. For example, communication skills are required to give effective advice to people in need, and emotion regulation skills are required to productively engage in critical self-reflection. In summary, wisdom is associated with extraordinary personal qualities in three domains, and with the ability to translate these qualities into real-world action.

Before we move on to the next section, let us pause for a moment to critically reflect on this three-component model. Do you agree that it captures the essence of wisdom? Is anything missing from the list of traits, characteristics, or abilities just reviewed? What did you agree or disagree with, and what would you change?

3.3.2   Who Is Wise?

As we mentioned earlier, a number of investigations have asked people to nominate personally known or public figures of wisdom, providing an alternative view into people's folk conceptions of wisdom. You had the chance to do this when we asked you about the wisest person you know. The assumption is that an inspection of the characteristics of **wisdom exemplars** can tell us something about how people think about wisdom.

3.3.2.1   Personally Known Wisdom Exemplars

Researchers have asked participants to nominate wise individuals of whom they have personal, first-hand experience, such as friends, colleagues, or relatives. In these studies, wisdom nominees have tended to be highly educated middle- to old-aged men, a finding that has now been replicated on a number of occasions despite the gender, age, and culture of the nominator

(Ardelt, 2008; Glück et al., 2012; Jason et al., 2001; Yang, 2008). These studies, from a cultural–historical perspective, suggest that individuals may continue to draw on the iconic image of the "old wise man" when making nominations. This classic literary wizard figure, who appears in stories, myths, and fairy tales, is stereotyped as sitting calmly with his long white beard, dispensing sage advice and knowledge. People's conceptions of the connection between wisdom and age have also been well documented in descriptor studies, using both open-ended (König & Glück, 2013) and adjective-rating (e.g., Clayton & Birren, 1980; Heckhausen et al., 1989) methods.

3.3.2.2 *Publicly Known Wisdom Exemplars*

A less commonly used approach to studying conceptions of wisdom has asked people to nominate publicly known figures who exemplify wisdom (e.g., Jason et al., 2001; Paulhus et al., 2002). For example, Weststrate et al. (2016) focused specifically on cultural–historical exemplars of wisdom in a series of studies. In the first study, 180 participants collectively nominated 303 wisdom exemplars, spanning 106 different public figures and fictional characters. In descending order, the nominees most frequently came from the domains of politics, social activism, spirituality and religion, philosophy, art and culture, science, and business. Over 75 percent of the exemplars were men, although in this sample they were quite diverse with respect to race and nationality. This highlights the fact that although there is considerable overlap in some aspects of folk conceptions of wisdom, there are also important divergences.

Despite the range of exemplars nominated in this study, the 13 highest-frequency exemplars accounted for 56 percent of the nominations. In descending order of frequency, the exemplars were Mahatma Gandhi, Jesus Christ, Abraham Lincoln, Martin Luther King Jr., Winston Churchill, Thomas Jefferson, Socrates, Albert Einstein, Mother Teresa, Barack Obama, King Solomon, Benjamin Franklin, and Nelson Mandela. Pause for a moment to digest this list. What do you make of it? Are there any important public figures missing from this list of wisdom exemplars? When you look through these names, what makes these figures similar or different? What can we learn about people's conceptions of wisdom from this list?

In a second study, using a cluster analysis technique, these exemplars were reduced to three underlying wisdom prototypes, labelled practical, philosophical, and benevolent wisdom. Exemplars of the practical wisdom prototype were primarily political leaders (e.g., Churchill, Jefferson), who were well known for solving difficult societal problems (e.g., ending wars, changing oppressive laws) and thus greatly improving the lives of many people. Exemplars of the philosophical prototype were scientists and philosophers (e.g., Socrates, Einstein), who were concerned with answering fundamental questions about human nature and the physical world, investigated through deep contemplation and scientific methods. Finally, exemplars from the benevolent prototype were spiritual leaders and social activists (e.g., Mother Teresa, Jesus Christ), who dedicated their lives to helping others, often at great personal sacrifice. In fact, 41 percent of participants nominated someone as wise who had died for a cause that would ultimately embolden and benefit humanity on a large or a small scale.

Using the same procedure, other researchers (Hu et al., 2018) collected cultural–historical exemplars of wisdom from Han Chinese adults living in Mainland China, rather than the typical North American samples. They found evidence for the practical prototypes (political and military leaders, e.g., Chairman Mao) and the philosophical prototypes (scholars, e.g., Confucius), but no evidence of the benevolent prototype (no information was provided about nominee gender). These findings imply the role of culture in the shaping of people's conceptions of wisdom.

3.4   In Which Situations Is Wisdom Expressed?

A small collection of studies have asked participants to provide autobiographical memories of times when they did, said, or thought something that was wise (Bluck & Glück, 2004; Glück et al., 2005; König & Glück, 2012; Yang, 2008). These memories were analyzed for the types of situations in which wisdom was expressed by the participant or wisdom nominee. Among adults, the researchers found that wisdom was expressed in relation to *fundamental* situations that were typically about (1) important life decisions, (2) reactions to negative events, and (3) life management (Bluck & Glück, 2004; Glück et al., 2005), or some combination of these issues (Yang, 2008). Fundamental events have a significant influence on one's current and further life or the life of someone else. This suggests that wisdom is not typically expressed in everyday, trivial, or mundane events, but rather in events that involve significant life challenges. Within memories of life challenges, Glück et al. (2005) found that wisdom tended to be expressed in three general forms – as empathy and support (theme: "putting yourself in someone else's shoes"), as knowledge and flexibility (theme: "experience is the best teacher"), or as self-determination and assertion (theme: "standing up for one's values"). Interestingly, the form of wisdom expressed was somewhat dependent on the type of life situation reported and the age of the participant. These results open up potential lines of research into the ways in which characteristics of life events facilitate or constrain the expression of certain forms of wisdom.

3.4.1   How Does Wisdom Develop?

People's folk conceptions of how wisdom develops have provided an exciting new thread of research in the past decade or so. People almost invariably report that wisdom is developed through life experience, and, in particular, through challenging life events (e.g., Ardelt, 2008; Glück & Bluck, 2011; Montgomery et al., 2002). For example, in an early study on this topic, Ardelt (2008) asked 39 students in an undergraduate sociology class a variety of questions about intellectual knowledge and wisdom. Her students reported that intellectual knowledge is gained through formal learning, such as books (72 percent of respondents), whereas wisdom is gained through personal experience (87 percent of respondents). In another study, also using a university sample, young adults were asked to answer the open-ended question "How can a person achieve wisdom?" (König & Glück, 2013). Over half of the participants included life experience in their answer, and many further articulated that the *accumulation* of life experience is essential to wisdom. An interesting question, therefore, is what type of life experience people consider to be most conducive to the development of wisdom. The folk notion that individuals become "sadder but wiser" through personal hardship seems to be fairly pervasive, but it is an empirical question whether or not people associate wisdom development with adversity, which we shall examine next.

3.4.1.1   Beliefs about Experiences that Foster Wisdom
Probing the life-experience hypothesis further, Glück and Bluck (2011) asked a sample of adults the question "How does one become wise?" Participants rated nine statements describing

experiential factors that diverse literatures suggest may be important to the development of wisdom. In this study, the most highly endorsed response was "Through a broad spectrum of positive and negative experiences." The top four most highly endorsed statements also included "Through enduring and overcoming highly negative events" and "Through confronting human mortality." The latter two statements convey emotionally challenging situations; however, note that the most highly endorsed item referred to a diverse range of negative *and positive* experiences. Indeed, wisdom researchers have been re-thinking the assumed relationship between wisdom and adversity, arguing instead that the defining feature of a wisdom-fostering situation is the extent to which it challenges one's basic beliefs about life, rather than its emotional valence. What do you think? Have you had any extremely positive experiences that have led to learning important life lessons that you might consider wise?

The relationship between life experience and the development of wisdom has also been investigated autobiographically. This approach assumes that people are able to identify moments in their own life that have made them wiser, or, more modestly, have helped them to learn lessons or gain insight that could be considered wise. In one study (Weststrate et al., 2018), 502 middle-aged adults provided an autobiographical memory of a wisdom-fostering life event, which was rated by trained coders for three life-event characteristics theoretically relevant to wisdom (fundamentality, emotional valence, and cultural normativity), as well as the specific event type reported. The researchers found that people generally reported gaining wisdom from highly fundamental, emotionally negative, and culturally non-normative events (e.g., divorce, premature death of a loved one, job loss). It is unclear whether these events actually led to growth in wisdom or simply reflect stereotypical ideas about wisdom development.

3.4.1.2 Beliefs about Social Interactions that Foster Wisdom

Beyond the perceived importance of these relatively momentous life events, another notable theme that has emerged across studies is the role of social interactions, such as informal mentorship and advice giving, in the development of wisdom. For example, the participants in the study by Glück and Bluck (2011) rated "learning from wise individuals" as the second strongest determinant of wisdom development. Interestingly, people believe that both the mentor and the mentee stand to gain wisdom from these relationships. Weststrate et al. (2018) found that formal and informal learning experiences were the fourth most frequent type of wisdom-fostering event reported by middle-aged adults, with the most frequent sub-category involving advice giving and mentorship, often in occupational, spiritual, or family settings. Igarashi, Levenson, and Aldwin (2018) found that "social transactions" (e.g., seeking expert advice, receiving emotional support, making new social connections) were viewed as important sources of growth in wisdom through difficult life events. Do you have a wise mentor in your life? Who was that person and what have you learned from them?

These findings suggest that people perceive the development of wisdom as socially situated – that is, mentors, colleagues, and people in general are a social resource that supports the development of wisdom. Somewhat surprisingly, the influence of social interactions on actual wisdom development has been understudied by experts, although research has shown that even *imagining* a conversation with a person whose advice is typically found to be helpful can enhance wisdom in specific situations (Staudinger & Baltes, 1996). So next time you confront a life challenge, you might consider pausing for a moment to have an internal dialogue with one of the wise mentors in your life to imagine what advice they might give you.

Up to this point in the chapter, we have focused on beliefs about general characteristics of wisdom, its manifestation, and its development that are endorsed by *most people* in a particular milieu. The extent to which these beliefs are endorsed by individual people differs greatly, although sometimes in systemic and predictable ways. This variation is the subject of the next section. As you will see, beyond general cultural influences, individual conceptions of wisdom seem to be shaped by personal and professional experiences as well.

3.5   Individual and Cross-Cultural Differences in Folk Conceptions of Wisdom

Over the past decade, there has been increasing interest among researchers in how folk conceptions of wisdom differ across people and cultures. What do you think? Do you think conceptions of wisdom are more or less universal, or do you expect differences to emerge across genders, professional contexts, and cultures? If so, what might those differences look like and where do you think they come from? Let us take a look at what the research shows.

3.5.1   *Folk Conceptions across Gender*

Across three studies, each using different methods, Glück et al. (2009) reported small gender differences in conceptions of wisdom. First, in a descriptor-rating study, they found that men were somewhat more likely to view "intelligence" as important to wisdom, whereas women more frequently rated "love for humanity" and "acceptance of others" as important. In line with this, men rated "studying philosophy" as more important to wisdom development than did women, whereas women viewed "dealing with negative events," "confronting mortality," and "religious and spiritual experiences" as slightly more relevant. In a second, autobiographical study, men were more likely to report having thought, said, or done something wise within the context of their professional life, whereas women referred to a range of life domains, including family and events involving death and illness. Finally, in an experimental study, participants rated one of two fictitious characters, "Paul" or "Paula," for 80 wisdom-related characteristics. The only aspect that differed across the two questionnaires was the gender of the target individual. Male and female participants did not differ in their ratings of Paul and Paula. However, both male and female participants rated Paula slightly higher on a component of wisdom that reflected concern for others (e.g., "wants the best for others," "tries to help others"). Consistent with these findings, using a real-life approach, Weststrate et al. (2016) found that men were more likely to nominate exemplars who embodied the philosophical wisdom prototype (e.g., Einstein, Socrates).

Together, these results suggest that men have a slightly more cognitively oriented view of wisdom, whereas women also tend to include emotional and communal aspects of wisdom as important to its definition and development (see also Glück & Bluck, 2011). It seems that, like many other things, conceptions of wisdom reflect socially prescribed gender roles and should not be interpreted as representing essential differences in how men and women think. Please note that not all research has observed significant gender differences in folk conceptions of wisdom (e.g., König & Glück, 2013), and therefore any real difference is probably quite small.

3.5.2   Folk Conceptions across Professional Contexts

Early research by Sternberg (1985) suggested that the professions which people pursue may reflect and nurture particular worldviews that influence how they think about psychological character-istics such as wisdom. Sternberg (1985) found that, despite considerable overlap, professors of art, business, philosophy, and physics each emphasized unique aspects of wisdom that were consistent with their academic specializations. For example, art professors saw "sensitivity" as related to wisdom, whereas business professors felt that taking a "long-term perspective" on matters was indicative of wisdom.

Although not comparative, qualitative research has probed the meaning of wisdom in profes-sional contexts, with studies including in-service educators (e.g., teachers, principals, administra-tors; Chen et al., 2014), psychotherapists (Levitt & Piazza-Bonin, 2014), and judges (Levitt & Dunnavant, 2015). These rich explorations bring to light how wisdom is shaped by the demands of an occupation and applied on a contextual basis so as to achieve a specific goal, such as teaching others, helping others, or making a legal decision, respectively.

3.5.3   Folk Conceptions across Cultures

From ancient times until today, cultures around the world can be said to have had a wisdom tradition of some kind – that is, systems of belief and associated teachings that outline both the meaning of life and how to lead a meaningful life, which in turn shape the dominant values and goals of a particular society (Assmann, 1994; Clayton & Birren, 1980). How might folk conceptions of wisdom differ across time and context? Since people come to understand the meaning of wisdom through cultural engagement (e.g., in schools, families, spiritual communi-ties), their conceptions of wisdom should reflect the dominant sociocultural, religious, and philosophical traditions of a given milieu. The meaning of wisdom in Western nations, for example, is heavily influenced by ancient Greek philosophy (e.g., Artistotle, Plato, Stoics) and the Judeo-Christian religious traditions. Eastern traditions, on other the hand, have an impressive array of influences, including the spiritual teachings of Buddhism, Sufism, and Hinduism, as well as the philosophical influences of Taoism and Confucianism. Although seemingly expansive, we are sure that this list does little justice to the rich cultural origins of wisdom in each of these areas (for a more comprehensive treatment, see Edmondson & Woerner, 2019; Ferrari & Alhosseini, 2019; Swartwood & Tiberius, 2019; Yang & Intezari, 2019).

With this in mind, folk conceptions of wisdom *should* differ across cultures, but this is not entirely borne out in the empirical literature. Before reviewing what has been observed, a couple caveats are in order. First, there have been very few cross-cultural studies on conceptions of wisdom. Second, as Yang and Intezari (2019) point out, this research has almost entirely ignored Persia, Africa, Oceania, and Latin America, which are home to some of the oldest wisdom traditions in the world. Thus the findings presented here should, at best, be viewed as preliminary.

The majority of cross-cultural studies have made broad comparisons of Western (e.g., Canada, USA, Australia) and Eastern (e.g., Japan, Taiwan, India) conceptions of wisdom. Based on this research, Takahashi and colleagues (Takahashi, 2000; Takahashi & Bordia, 2000) have argued that Western conceptions of wisdom emphasize analytical dimensions (e.g., knowledge, reasoning), whereas Eastern conceptions integrate both cognitive and affective features (e.g., discretion, empathy) in a so-called "synthetic" understanding of wisdom, reflecting dominant philosophical traditions in each of those areas.

However, this distinction between analytical and synthetic conceptions of wisdom might be something of an oversimplification. Studies of folk conceptions in Western contexts have also observed similar affective characteristics (e.g., empathy, love for humanity; Glück & Bluck, 2011). Moreover, a study of wisdom exemplars in Mainland China found basically no evidence for the benevolent wisdom prototype (Hu et al., 2018), compared with a study in Canada and the USA (Weststrate et al., 2016), where one-third of the nominated exemplars demonstrated benevolence and compassion. Thus within-culture variability should not be underestimated, especially in highly diverse cultures. Until more research has been conducted, the safest conclusion to draw is that there is cross-cultural consensus on the major features of wisdom; however, cultures may differ in the degree to which they emphasize particular aspects over others.

3.6 Conclusion

As this review has shown, research into folk conceptions of wisdom is a rich and diverse field. Many of the first psychological investigations into wisdom focused on understanding everyday people's conceptions, and this line of inquiry continues to thrive today. New threads of research include studies on conceptions of how wisdom develops, and studies of individual and cross-cultural differences in the content of folk conceptions. Now, as always, research into folk conceptions is necessary for a full science of wisdom, and investigations into people's understanding of wisdom continue to move the field forward in exciting ways.

3.7 Comprehension and Discussion Questions

(1) In your own words, how would you define wisdom? What characteristics, qualities, abilities, or skills do you think are essential to wisdom? How does wisdom differ from intelligence, creativity, and morality?

(2) If you were asked to nominate both a person from your life and a public figure as exemplars of wisdom, whom would you choose and why? What might these nominations tell you about your own conception of wisdom?

(3) Thinking about your own life, how did you come to understand the concept of wisdom? What factors shaped your understanding of wisdom? Were there particular influences that now stand out as you look back?

(4) What is the difference between folk conceptions of wisdom and formal theories of wisdom? What are the possible relationships between these two approaches to the study of wisdom?

(5) How would you summarize the research literature on folk conceptions of wisdom? What are some of the major themes emerging from this literature? To what degree do the folk conceptions reviewed in this chapter align with your own understanding of wisdom? How are they different?

(6) Describe the three main approaches to studying folk conceptions of wisdom. What are the strengths and limitations of each approach? If you were going to design a study on folk conceptions of wisdom, which approach would you choose and why?

(7) Think for a moment about the cultures or communities to which you belong. Are there understandings of wisdom that are specific to those communities? How might these conceptions differ from those of other cultures or communities?

(8) What would you recommend to wisdom scientists as future directions for research on folk conceptions? Are there specific gaps in the literature that should be filled? Why would it be important to research those topics?

3.8 Investigations

Nic Weststrate's research program investigates the development, manifestation, and transmission of wisdom. Grounding his research in narrative theory and methods, he explores the role of storymaking and storytelling in how people learn fundamental lessons from and about life, and how they share those lessons with others in social contexts. His research on storymaking examines the characteristic ways in which people reflectively narrate both positive and negative life challenges. His research on storytelling examines the intergenerational transmission of wisdom within the context of families and communities. He is interested in what life lessons elders want to share with younger people, and also in the conditions that optimize such transmission. Recently, he has been investigating the process, content, and outcome of intergenerational storytelling in the LGBTQIA+ community.

Susan Bluck's program of research is grounded in taking a functional approach to autobiographical remembering. That is, she aims to understand how people use memories of past life experiences to serve them at the present time in their life. This approach has influenced her investigations of wisdom – her focus has been on how people remember and tell stories of times in their life when they acted wisely. This includes the kinds of events that they nominate and the forms that wisdom takes as they recall and narrate their lived experience, particularly in the face of challenge. As such, Susan studies everyday wisdom as it manifests in individual lives. Individuals describe how past events direct their current thinking through lessons learned and insights gained. Her work focuses on individuals across the adult lifespan, including those nearing death. In terms of theoretical work on wisdom, together with Judith Glück she developed the MORE Life Experience Model, which describes how wisdom develops, including life reflection as a necessary component for transforming life experiences into opportunities for wisdom.

3.9 Practical Applications

Nic Weststrate's research program has implications for real-world practice in educational, healthcare, and community settings. First, his research suggests that it is important for teachers to cultivate reflective thinking abilities in students, starting them on the path toward wisdom early on. Second, his research could have implications for how psychotherapists scaffold the meaning-making processes of their clients. Third, his research suggests that practitioners in the aging services sector should create meaningful opportunities for intergenerational social connection that centers on storytelling.

As a lifespan developmentalist, Susan Bluck has examined how individuals narrate stories of wisdom at different points across the lifespan. This includes a translational aspect – understanding how people recall and narrate experiences of losing a loved one or of facing their own death.

As such, she has collaborated with colleagues in nursing and other health professions that focus on palliative care and aim to improve the quality of life at the end of life. Being able to tell one's story in a meaningful and potentially wise way is important not only for the dying person, but also for the bereaved loved ones who carry the story of the death forward with them and attempt to integrate it into their life story.

Glossary

affective component one of three main components of people's folk conceptions of wisdom observed across methods and contexts. The affective component encompasses three facets: (1) benevolence, (2) compassion, and (3) positive mindset.

cognitive component one of three main components of people's folk conceptions of wisdom observed across methods and contexts. The cognitive components refer to exceptional ability in two areas: (1) life experience/knowledge, and (2) reasoning/judgment.

descriptor approach one of three common approaches to the investigation of folk conceptions. Participants are asked to generate, rate, or rank adjectives or short descriptors for their relevance to wisdom.

experimental approach one of three common approaches to the investigation of folk conceptions. Characteristics of a hypothetical person or situation are manipulated in order to study the impact of such factors on judgments about wisdom.

folk conception a non-expert's concept or theory of a psychological phenomenon – in this case, of wisdom. Folk conceptions are also referred to as implicit, internal, layperson, or subjective theories.

real-life approach one of three common approaches to the investigation of folk conceptions. Participants are asked to share instances of wisdom from their real-life experience or from the experience of another person deemed to be an exemplar of wisdom.

reflective component one of three main components of people's folk conceptions of wisdom observed across methods and contexts. The reflective component encompasses three facets: (1) deep insight, (2) critical self-reflection, and (3) humility.

wisdom exemplar a real-life person who demonstrates or embodies wisdom. Exemplars are ideal representations or paragons of wisdom.

REFERENCES

Ardelt, M. (2003). Empirical assessment of a three-dimensional wisdom scale. *Research on Aging,* 25(3), 275–324.
  (2008). Being wise at any age. In S. J. Lopez, ed., *Positive Psychology: Exploring the Best in People* (Vol. 1: *Discovering Human Strengths*). Praeger, pp. 81–108.
Assmann, A. (1994). Wholesome knowledge: concepts of wisdom in a historical and cross-cultural perspective. In D. L. Featherman, R. M. Lerner and M. Perlmutter, eds., *Life-Span Development and Behavior.* Vol. 12. Lawrence Erlbaum Associates, Inc., pp. 187–224.
Bluck, S. and Glück, J. (2004). Making things better and learning a lesson: experiencing wisdom across the lifespan. *Journal of Personality,* 72(3), 543–72.
Chen, L.-M., Cheng, Y.-Y., Wu, P.-J., and Hsueh, H.-I. (2014). Educators' implicit perspectives on wisdom: a comparison between interpersonal and intrapersonal perspectives. *International Journal of Psychology,* 49(6), 425–33.

Clayton, V. P. and Birren, J. E. (1980). The development of wisdom across the life span: a re-examination of an ancient topic. In P. B. Baltes and O. G. Brim, eds., *Life-Span Development and Behavior*. Vol. 3. Academic Press, pp. 103–35.

Edmondson, R. and Woerner, M. H. (2019). Sociocultural foundations of wisdom. In R. Sternberg and J. Glück, J., eds., *The Cambridge Handbook of Wisdom*. Cambridge University Press, pp. 40–68.

Ferrari, M. and Alhosseini, F. (2019). Cultural differences in wisdom and conceptions of wisdom. In R. J. Sternberg and J. Glück, eds., *The Cambridge Handbook of Wisdom*. Cambridge University Press, pp. 409–28.

Glück, J. and Bluck, S. (2011). Laypeople's conceptions of wisdom and its development: cognitive and integrative views. *The Journals of Gerontology: Series B: Psychological Sciences and Social Sciences*, 66B(3), 321–24.

Glück, J., Bluck, S., Baron, J., and McAdams, D. P. (2005). The wisdom of experience: autobiographical narratives across adulthood. *International Journal of Behavioral Development*, 29(3), 197–208.

Glück, J., Strasser, I., and Bluck, S. (2009). Gender differences in implicit theories of wisdom. *Research in Human Development*, 6(1), 27–44.

Glück, J., Bischof, B., and Siebenhüner, L. (2012). "Knows what is good and bad", "Can teach you things", "Does lots of crosswords": children's knowledge about wisdom. *European Journal of Developmental Psychology*, 9(5), 582–98.

Heckhausen, J., Dixon, R., and Baltes, P. (1989). Gains and losses in development throughout adulthood as perceived by different adult age groups. *Developmental Psychology*, 25(1), 109–21.

Hershey, D. A. and Farrell, A. H. (1997). Perceptions of wisdom associated with selected occupations and personality characteristics. *Current Psychology: Developmental, Learning, Personality, Social*, 16, 115–30.

Hira, F. and Faulkender, P. (1997). Perceiving wisdom: do age and gender play a part? *International Journal of Aging and Human Development*, 44(2), 85–101.

Holliday, S. G. and Chandler, M. J. (1986). *Wisdom: Explorations in Adult Competence*. Karger.

Hu, C. S., Ferrari, M., Liu, R.-D., Gao, Q., and Weare, E. (2018). Mainland Chinese implicit theory of wisdom: generational and cultural differences. *The Journals of Gerontology: Series B: Psychological Sciences and Social Sciences*, 73(8), 1416–24.

Igarashi, H., Levenson, M. R., and Aldwin, C. M. (2018). The development of wisdom: a social ecological approach. *The Journals of Gerontology, Series B: Psychological Sciences and Social Sciences*, 73(8), 1350–58.

Jason, L. A., Reichler, A., King, C. et al. (2001). The measurement of wisdom: a preliminary effort. *Journal of Community Psychology*, 29(5), 585–98.

Kałużna-Wielobób, A. (2014). Do individual wisdom concepts depend on value? *Polish Psychological Bulletin*, 45(2), 112–27.

König, S. and Glück, J. (2012). Situations in which I was wise: autobiographical wisdom memories of children and adolescents. *Journal of Research on Adolescence*, 22(3), 512–25.

(2013). Individual differences in wisdom conceptions: relationships to gratitude and wisdom. *The International Journal of Aging and Human Development*, 77(2), 127–47.

Levitt, H. M. (1999). The development of wisdom: an analysis of Tibetan Buddhist experience. *Journal of Humanistic Psychology*, 39(2), 86–105.

Levitt, H. M. and Dunnavant, B. R. (2015). Judicial wisdom: the process of constructing wise decisions. *Journal of Constructivist Psychology*, 28(3), 243–63.

Levitt, H. M. and Piazza-Bonin, E. (2014). Wisdom and psychotherapy: studying expert therapists' clinical wisdom to explicate common processes. *Psychotherapy Research*, 26(1), 31–47.

Montgomery, A., Barber, C., and McKee, P. (2002). A phenomenological study of wisdom in later life. *The International Journal of Aging and Human Development*, 54(2), 139–57.

Paulhus, D. L., Wehr, P., Harms, P. D., and Strausser, D. I. (2002). Use of exemplar surveys to reveal implicit types of intelligence. *Personality and Social Psychology Bulletin*, 28(8), 1051–62.

Staudinger, U. M. and Baltes, P. B. (1996). Interactive minds: a facilitative setting for wisdom-related performance? *Journal of Personality and Social Psychology*, 71, 746–62.

Sternberg, R. J. (1985). Implicit theories of intelligence, creativity,·and wisdom. *Journal of Personality and Social Psychology*, 49(3), 607–27.

Swartwood, J. and Tiberius, V. (2019). Philosophical foundations of wisdom. In R. J. Sternberg and J. Glück, eds., *The Cambridge Handbook of Wisdom*. Cambridge University Press, pp. 10–39.

Takahashi, M. (2000). Toward a culturally inclusive understanding of wisdom: historical roots in the east and west. *International Journal of Aging and Human Development*, 51(3), 217–30.

Takahashi, M. and Bordia, P. (2000). The concept of wisdom: a cross-cultural comparison. *International Journal of Psychology*, 35(1), 1–9.

Weststrate, N. M., Ferrari, M., and Ardelt, M. (2016). The many faces of wisdom: an investigation of cultural-historical wisdom exemplars reveals practical, philosophical, and benevolent prototypes. *Personality and Social Psychology Bulletin*, 42(5), 662–76.

Weststrate, N. M., Ferrari, M., Fournier, M. A., and McLean, K. C. (2018). "It was the best worst day of my life": narrative content, structure, and process in wisdom-fostering life event memories. *The Journals of Gerontology: Series B: Psychological Sciences and Social Sciences*, 73(8), 1359–73.

Weststrate, N. M., Bluck, S., and Glück, J. (2019). Wisdom of the crowd: exploring people's conceptions of wisdom. In R. J. Sternberg and J. Glück, eds., *The Cambridge Handbook of Wisdom*. Cambridge University Press, pp. 97–121.

Yang, S.-Y. (2001). Conceptions of wisdom among Taiwanese Chinese. *Journal of Cross-Cultural Psychology*, 32(6), 662–80.

  (2008). Real-life contextual manifestations of wisdom. *The International Journal of Aging and Human Development*, 67(4), 273–303.

Yang, S. Y. and Intezari, A. (2019). Cultural differences in wisdom and conceptions of wisdom. In R. J. Sternberg and J. Glück, eds., *The Cambridge Handbook of Wisdom*. Cambridge University Press, pp. 429–52.

CHAPTER 4

Psychological Theories of Wisdom[1]

Robert J. Sternberg, Judith Glück, and Sareh Karami

4.1 Introduction

Max is an English teacher and headteacher of a twelfth-grade class. He has a good relationship with his students. One day, the members of the class tell him that they are having a problem with their new math teacher. She does not seem to be particularly good at explaining things, and her answers to students' questions are not very helpful. The students have less than a year until their final exams, and they are very worried about failing the math exams. Max talks to the math teacher, but she is quite defensive. She tells him that she does not think there is a problem, and says that she is happy to let him teach the math classes if he thinks he can do better. Obviously, she is very angry at the students for complaining about her. What should Max do?

Many people might say that the math teacher is just a bad teacher and that Max should talk to the headmaster and ask to have her replaced. But is that a wise answer? What would be a wise answer? How would one know what a wise answer is?

This chapter is about psychologists' theories of wisdom – about what makes some people wise and what makes other people, however intelligent and creative they might be, unwise. There are several psychological theories of what wisdom is. They are intended to describe the underlying nature of wisdom and, as far as is possible, to explain it. A good theory also provides predictions – it produces a specific hypothesis, which in turn predicts what empirical results should follow from research if the theory is correct. Psychological theories of wisdom are useful because they help us to understand what wisdom is and what it is not, they make predictions about what should come to pass if the theory is true, they suggest how wisdom might be measured, they help us to understand why people differ in their levels of measured wisdom, and they suggest ways in which wisdom might be developed in people, including future leaders.

4.2 Major Psychological Theories of Wisdom

Several major psychological theories of wisdom have been proposed (see Glück et al., 2019; Sternberg & Glück, 2022; Sternberg & Karami, 2021a). This list is by no means comprehensive, but rather it serves to illustrate the range of psychological theories of wisdom that have been proposed.

---

[1] Portions of this chapter draw from ideas expressed in Sternberg, R. J. and Glück, J. (2022). *Wisdom: The Psychology of Wise Thoughts, Words, and Deeds*. Cambridge University Press, and Sternberg, R. J. and Karami, S. (2021a). What is wisdom? A unified 6P framework. *Review of General Psychology*, 25(2), 134–51.

4.2.1   *Origins of Contemporary Psychological Theories in Early Psychological Research*

Early psychological theorizing was of the "implicit" variety, whereby psychologists, instead of proposing their own theories, asked participants in psychological studies what they meant by "wisdom" (see overview in Chapter 3). Often, such implicit theorizing precedes explicit theorizing, whereby psychologists (or other professionals) reflect on the conceptions of laypeople or professionals and then try to systematize some of those thoughts and add their own, producing more formal explicit theories of the psychological construct of interest.

Much of contemporary theorizing about wisdom can be traced to the doctoral dissertation of Vivian Clayton, showing how students, sometimes inadvertently, can become thought leaders (Clayton, 1976, 1982; Clayton & Birren, 1980). Clayton asked people with no particular sets of expertise to list descriptors of a wise person. From these lists she identified the following set of 12 commonly listed descriptors: (1) experienced, (2) intuitive, (3) introspective, (4) pragmatic, (5) understanding, (6) gentle, (7) empathetic, (8) intelligent, (9) peaceful, (10) knowledgeable, (11) sense of humor, and (12) observant. After analyzing these data, Clayton concluded that individuals view wisdom as comprising three dimensions: cognitive, reflective, and affective. The cognitive dimension pertains to how people think – for example, do they seek deep understanding? The reflective dimension pertains to how people observe and think about their thinking – for example, do they try to understand things not only from their own point of view, but also from the point of view of others? And the affective dimension pertains to how people feel – for example, are they gentle, empathetic, and peaceful? As you will see in this chapter, these three dimensions still seem to capture many important aspects of wisdom.

Early studies that looked at people's folk conceptions of wisdom served as precursors of the explicit psychological theories that were to follow. The first of these was the Berlin Wisdom Model.

4.2.2   *The Berlin Wisdom Model*

The first major explicit theory of wisdom was proposed by the late Paul Baltes and his colleagues (Baltes & Kunzmann, 2003; Baltes & Staudinger, 1993, 2000; Baltes & Smith, 1990, 2008). According to the **Berlin Wisdom Model**, wisdom is an expert knowledge system. Experts are people who have gained extraordinary knowledge in a field through years of training and practice. The field of wisdom, according to the Berlin group, is concerned with the important and difficult matters of life. Wisdom-related expert knowledge involves five facets: rich factual knowledge, rich procedural knowledge, lifespan contextualism, relativism of values, and awareness and management of uncertainty. Rich factual knowledge includes knowledge about human nature, about the life course, and about the various kinds of challenges that people confront in their lives. Rich procedural knowledge involves the strategies that one can follow when dealing with life challenges and when giving advice on how to confront those challenges. Lifespan contextualism involves knowledge of how the cultural, societal, temporal, and other contexts that one encounters in life affect the kinds of decisions that one needs to make. Relativism of values means that wise people know that the values people hold can differ across people and cultures, with different people sometimes quite certain that their values somehow represent the ones that people "truly" should hold. Recognition and management of uncertainty refers to one's understanding that life is uncertain and unpredictable, and that one needs to find ways of dealing with this uncertainty, such that any strategy one ever develops may have to be changed in response to unexpected yet sometimes inalterable changes.

What does the Berlin model say about Max's problem with the math teacher? To find a wise solution, Max will need a lot of relevant factual knowledge – perhaps not about math, but about teaching, about young teachers and their fears of failure, and about his students. He should also have procedural knowledge about how to listen, in order to figure out what exactly the problem is, and how to talk to both sides. He should consider the influence of situations and contexts on behavior – for example, perhaps it is very important for the math teacher to gain a permanent position, or maybe the students are overreacting because the government has announced changes to the final-exam system. Max should also consider the fact that the goals and values of the new teacher may not be the same as his own or those of the students. Finally, he should consider that things might work out in many different ways, and make some alternative plans.

4.2.3 *The Balance Theory of Wisdom*

Around the same time that the Berlin model was developed, Sternberg (1998, 2003, 2019a, 2019b) proposed a **balance theory of wisdom**. The balance theory differs somewhat from other models in that its emphasis is not on personal traits per se, but rather on how these personal traits are deployed in the world. That is, a wise person is someone who uses whatever personal characteristics they have in order to accomplish certain ends. Thus it is a functional theory rather than a trait-based one.

According to Sternberg, a person is wise to the extent that they use their skills and knowledge to (1) achieve a common good, by (2) balancing intrapersonal (their own), interpersonal (others'), and extrapersonal (larger) interests over (3) the long term as well as the short term, through (4) the utilization of positive ethical values, by (5) adapting to, shaping, and selecting environments.

Achieving a common good means attaining a goal that benefits all of the parties who are affected by a judgment or decision, including people who have interests different from one's own. One achieves the common good by balancing one's own interests with the interests of others and of large entities, such as the community, a state or province, a country, the world, or even entities beyond the world, such as the universe (e.g., when one is concerned about polluting not only the Earth, but outer space as well, where tons of space junk sent up from Earth are a major source of pollution). Too often, people define the common good as a tribal good, viewing people different from themselves as unworthy of being considered as part of the common good. For example, the USA was founded on the principle of equality of all, but that equality excluded members of many groups, including women, people of color, and people of many religions other than mainstream Protestantism.

One of the reasons why it is hard for people to be wise in their lives is because they are so susceptible to viewing short-term effects at the expense of long-term effects. Antibiotics, for example, were a great innovation until they were overused, at which point their greatness began to diminish. Eventually, they started to become ineffective as mutant strains of bacteria gained resistance to them.

Wisdom also involves the infusion of positive ethical values, such as the golden rule of acting toward others as one would have them act toward oneself, or of communicating sincerely and honestly because once one party starts lying, this encourages others to begin doing so as well. And finally, wise action can be of three kinds. One can decide to adapt to the environment as it exists, sometimes accepting that what the environment offers is imperfect but that nothing better is to be had. Or one can decide to shape the environment, changing it to be better not only for oneself but also for others. Or one can decide that one cannot find a true common good in the environment in which one finds oneself, and then seek out a new environment. Sometimes environments are just not modifiable, and one has to decide whether to accept them or leave.

What would a balanced solution to Max's problem look like? It would have to be a solution that balances everyone's interests – those of the students, the new teacher, the school, perhaps even the interests of the students' parents and, possibly, of Max as well. The solution would also have to be viable in the long term as well as in the short term. If the teacher gets transferred to a different, lower-grade class, Max's students will pass their final exam, but the younger students in the other class might get a bad math education. Max's approach would have to be ethical – he would need to be honest with everyone and treat everyone with respect. Finally, he would want to teach his students that they did the right thing by trying to change their environment – the math class. However, he might also want to point out to them that in other, similar situations, it might be necessary for them to find a way to adapt to the new situation.

4.2.4   Ardelt's Three-Dimensional Model

Monika Ardelt (2003–2005, 2019) suggested that the Berlin Wisdom Model is incomplete in several respects. First, she argued that the model is too cognitive – it does not take into account emotional and motivational aspects of wisdom. Second, wisdom is not acquired through the accumulation of theoretical knowledge, but rather through reflection on one's own personal life experience. Ardelt suggested instead that wisdom involves three personality dimensions –based on the work of Clayton and Birren (1980) mentioned earlier, she labeled them as cognitive, affective, and reflective. This is the so-called **three-dimensional model of wisdom**.

The cognitive dimension is most similar to the Berlin model. It involves a desire to explore life and its vagaries. Some people are just curious about the complex questions of our existence, and these individuals are more likely to acquire wisdom-related knowledge than people who are curious about other things. At the same time, they understand that life is uncertain and often unpredictable – that knowledge is not only limited, but also much of what one ideally would like to know is, at a given time, unknowable.

The affective dimension involves sympathy and compassion for others, including people who are unlike oneself and who may have value systems different from one's own. According to Ardelt, wise individuals refrain from behavior that shows negative emotions or indifference toward others, but instead accept and value them for who they are.

The reflective dimension requires a willingness to look at issues from different perspectives. People who are reflective realize that two people may claim, cognitively, to understand something, and yet have wholly different understandings of the same thing. They are also willing to question their own beliefs and behaviors and to see where their own judgment may be biased.

With respect to Max's problem, Ardelt might agree with the Berlin group that if Max is a wise teacher, he can draw on a lot of knowledge. As he has always been very interested in people and their relationships, he has learned a lot about life. Ardelt would suggest that Max should try to take everyone's perspective and put himself in their shoes. How does the young teacher feel when he confronts her? How can he help her to develop a better relationship with the students? How do the students feel, and how can he support them? Ardelt would also suggest that Max should question his own motives. Does he truly want to help the new teacher, or does some part of him enjoy the fact that he is a better teacher than she is and that the students like him better?

4.2.5 Webster's HERO(E) Model of Wisdom

The model proposed by Jeffrey Dean Webster (2003, 2007, 2014, 2019) views wisdom as the ability to apply insights gained from past experiences in order to solve problems and help other people. Webster has suggested five elements of wisdom in what he refers to as his **HERO(E) model** – humor, emotional regulation, reminiscence/reflectiveness, openness to experience, and critical life experiences. Webster's basic idea is that wisdom is acquired through thinking about, and learning from, critical life experiences. Wisdom is something one acquires from life experience. One cannot learn it from textbooks, from sitting in classrooms, or from merely having conversations with wise people. Wise individuals reminisce and reflect on their experiences, trying to make meaning and gain insights from them. Openness is a willingness to try out new experiences and perspectives. Emotional regulation is particularly relevant in difficult situations that cause strong negative feelings, such as anger or anxiety. Wisdom involves acknowledging and accepting those feelings, but also being able to regulate them as the situation requires. Humor is included in the model because it is a way in which one can achieve some distance from a phenomenon – by looking at it humorously or ironically. Humor especially applies in the context of not taking oneself and one's ideas too seriously – that is, having a sense of humor about oneself and one's ideas. Once one takes one's own ideas too seriously, it becomes hard to take others' ideas as seriously, and one loses one's ability to consider others' ideas with careful judgment and respect.

As for Max's problem, Webster might advise him to apply insights gained from earlier experiences. When Max was a young teacher himself, what would have helped him to become a better teacher? What advice from an older colleague would have been helpful? Max should also pay attention to his own emotions – if he grows angry with his young colleague, maybe he can control those feelings by recalling his own early teaching years. Humor might help him a lot in building a relationship with the young colleague.

4.2.6 Wisdom as Self-Transcendence

Drawing on concepts from Buddhism, Michael R. Levenson and Carolyn Aldwin have proposed a **self-transcendence model** of wisdom (Aldwin et al., 2019; Levenson et al., 2005). Self-transcendent individuals are not focused on themselves as much as most of us are. They are at peace with who they are, and this includes their weaknesses. They are well aware of their own weaknesses, but they have accepted them and learned to deal with them. They do not depend on external validation, such as fame, riches, or constant reassurance from other people. They care a lot about others, and because they do not need reinforcement from their friends and family members, they can accept and love them just as they are. Self-transcendent individuals feel closely connected to other people, to humanity at large, and to nature. Many of them commit themselves to a common good.

With regard to Max's problem, a self-transcendent Max would not feel angry or affronted by the math teacher's emotional reaction. He would feel compassion both for the teacher, for her obvious insecurity, and for the students. He would try to help both sides to find a compromise without caring about the costs or benefits of the situation to him.

4.2.7   *The Polyhedron Model of Karami and Colleagues*

Karami and colleagues (Karami et al., 2020; Karami & Parra-Martinez, 2021) have suggested a **polyhedron model of wisdom (PMW)** based on a systematic review of wisdom studies in three different disciplines (Karami et al., 2020). Wisdom is a situational construct that involves the adequate use of knowledge, intelligence and creativity, self-regulation, openness and tolerance, altruism and moral maturity, and sound judgment to solve critical problems. The polyhedron model offers an organic approach to inform people's behaviors during times of crisis. Crises test a person's ability to find novel solutions to impending problems, while dealing with personal interest and emotions, and various levels of impact on the world.

A wise person actively acquires and retains knowledge that is relevant to understanding and processing a given situation in context. Sound judgment involves thinking through problematic situations in terms of what to believe or how to act in facilitating the decision-making process. Wise people carefully revisit their life events, critically evaluate processes and outcomes, and determine strategies to change themselves, their actions, the environment, or others. In addition, because of the intricate reciprocal relationship between self-reflection and self-regulation, wise individuals are constantly self-actualizing and persevering in order to learn from their experiences and attain their goals.

According to the polyhedron model, wise people understand that the validity of information available to humans is essentially limited, and individuals have access only to select parts of reality in which the present and future cannot be fully known in advance. Wise people consider the limitations of their knowledge, the uncertainty of the future, and the uncertainty of life events. Hence wisdom encompasses facing, understanding, and synthesizing a great diversity of beliefs, values, goals, and experiences.

Wise people develop prosocial behaviors. They understand morality and ethics, and consequently become sensitive to the injustices of the world. They are empathetic toward other people's suffering and struggles. They strive for personal growth and help others to grow.

The polyhedron model also includes creative thinking. Creative thinkers detect gaps, produce novel and useful ideas (fluency, originality), produce alternative ideational categories (flexibility), and introduce details to ideas (elaboration).

Dynamic balance translated into action is perhaps the most important component of the polyhedron model. It refers to balancing interests and points of view, and, where possible, to synthesizing them in such a way that they can be understood in relation to each other. The model does not claim that every component is essential for a person to be wise. However, dynamic balance is the tacit recognition of what elements of wisdom are required to address a problem in each context, time, place, and set of circumstances. A wise person should be able to read into the complexities of reality and use their skills to face each problem and decision that life presents.

According to the polyhedron model, Max would engage in solving this problem even if he has to sacrifice his personal benefits (such as time and energy) to benefit everyone's well-being. He needs to build a body of relevant information from different sources (e.g., students, teacher, parents, and students' records) in order to understand all the components of the problem. He needs to consider the perspectives, goals, values, and interests of all sides if he is to come up with a useful and novel solution. Max would evaluate the potential consequences of a proposed solution or decision in the short and long term. The solution would probably involve several steps. He needs to monitor his emotional control, processing action plans, and learning from mistakes.

4.2.8 The Common Model of Wisdom of Grossmann and Colleagues

Igor Grossmann and his colleagues have suggested a **common model of wisdom** that seeks to combine elements of previous models. They define wisdom as "morally-grounded excellence in social-cognitive processing" (Grossmann et al., 2020, p. 133). "Morally-grounded" wisdom is that which balances one's own interests with those of others, pursues truth rather than dishonesty, and cares about the needs of all of humanity. "Excellence in social-cognitive processing" means that wise individuals (1) consider different contexts, (2) take different perspectives and consider the short- and long-term effects of their decisions, (3) think reflectively and dialectically, and (4) are aware of the limitations of their own knowledge and the subjectivity of their thinking. Indeed, it is often the case that the more people know, the more they realize they do not know.

According to the model of Grossmann and his colleagues, Max would need to analyze the problem carefully. He would have to consider the situations of everyone involved, and their different perspectives, needs, and goals. He would need to reflect critically on his own thinking to make sure that his personal biases – perhaps a bias favoring the students – do not play a role in how he handles the situation. Finally, he would have to look for a solution that benefits everyone, not just himself.

4.3 A 6P Theoretical Framework

We have looked at a number of wisdom theories. All of them have somewhat different components, but together they seem to produce a comprehensive picture of wisdom. How does one integrate the ideas in these various theories? An attempt has been made to achieve some kind of systematization through a so-called "6P theoretical framework" (Sternberg & Karami, 2021a). What exactly does this mean?

According to this framework, wisdom can be understood in terms of six Ps. This framework is an expansion of a 4P framework originally proposed for creativity (Rhodes, 1961). Phan et al. (2021) have tried to apply Rhodes' original 4P model to wisdom.

The six Ps of Sternberg and Karami (2021a) are (1) the Purpose of wisdom, (2) the environmental/situational Presses that lead to wisdom, (3) the kinds of Problems that require or, at least, are better solved through wisdom, (4) the cognitive, metacognitive, affective, and motivational characteristics of Persons who are wise in their thought and action, (5) the psychological Processes that contribute to wisdom, and (6) the Products of wisdom.

The six Ps are not independent of each other. Clearly, they all interact with each other in various ways. For example, one's purpose in solving a wisdom-based problem will influence the mental processes that one chooses to use to solve the problem. And the processes that one uses will affect the products of wise thinking. Table 4.1 summarizes the six Ps.

Not all theories address all six of the Ps. On the contrary, much of the apparent disagreement among psychological theories is that they actually deal with different aspects of wisdom as a psychological phenomenon. That is, the theories do not actually conflict, but rather they are like

Table 4.1 *6P Theoretical framework for understanding wisdom*

P element	Definition of the P	Example of the P
Purpose	What is accomplished by wisdom	Seeking a common good: seeking a solution that benefits Max's students, the math teacher, and possibly Max himself
Press	Environmental forces that contribute to wisdom	The students' upcoming final exams combined with the math teacher's defensiveness and limited experience
Problem	The challenge facing the person who is seeking to be wise	How to persuade the math teacher to find ways to improve her teaching
Person	The individual who is seeking to be wise	Max, with his background, knowledge, experience, and personality
Processes	The mental operations of wisdom	The questions that Max asks the students and the teacher, the conclusions he draws from their responses, and the steps he takes with the students and the teacher in finding a solution
Product	The outcome(s) of wisdom	For the teacher, improved teaching skills and greater self-confidence; for the students, success in the final exams

the proverbial blind men feeling parts of an elephant who conceive of different animals because they are only feeling small parts of the elephant.

4.3.1   *Purpose*

The first P in the theoretical framework is Purpose – what is accomplished by wisdom. Perhaps surprisingly, not many theories directly address this question.

Baltes and Staudinger (2000) emphasized that wisdom could help people to achieve the best of which they individually, and collectively in society, were capable not only with regard to their own development as individuals, but also with regard to the development of others. For those authors, wisdom seems to involve some combination of self-actualization and other-actualization (see also Kaufman, 2020; Maslow, 1943, 1954, 1962; Webster, 2003, 2007). As used here, the term "self-actualization" refers to reaching one's fullest potential as a person, and the term "other-actualization" refers to helping others to reach their fullest potential as individuals. But how would one know when one had achieved such actualization, of oneself or of others?

One way of knowing this might be through the attainment of some kind of common good that embraces both oneself and others. The theory that perhaps most directly addresses purpose, and in particular the common good, is the balance theory of Sternberg (1998, 2019b), according to which the purpose of wisdom is to achieve a common good. Related to this is the balancing of intrapersonal (one's own), interpersonal (others'), and extrapersonal (larger) interests over the long and short term in the balance theory. Although this purpose of achieving a common good through balancing is not explicit in other theories, it seems to be at least implicit in many of them, such as the Berlin paradigm.

Balance plays a part in other theories as well, such as the balance among cognitive, affective, and reflective elements of wisdom in Ardelt's theory (Ardelt, 2003), and the balance of viewpoints in the theory of Grossmann et al. (2020). Karami et al. (2020) speak of dynamic balance and synthesis. Thus one purpose of wisdom may be to achieve balance (the name of Sternberg's theory), whether among interests or among aspects of oneself. People who become out of balance, according to this viewpoint, find it difficult or impossible to be wise.

Why would balance and the achievement of some kind of good be so important to the purpose of wisdom across theories? One possible reason might be that it is precisely this balance that distinguishes wisdom from other human abilities. Typically, we think of both intelligence and creativity as unidimensional attributes – the more we have of them, the better. More wisdom may also be better, but wisdom, unlike intelligence and creativity as they are usually conceptualized, involves a kind of pulling back – a realization that often wisdom is to be found in moderation, in some kind of "golden mean," a concept introduced by one of the world's historical experts on wisdom, Aristotle.

4.3.2   Press

The second element in the 6P model of Sternberg and Karami (2021a), extending the work of Rhodes (1961), is environmental Press, or the aspects of the environment that push people toward wisdom. Press can be seen as the set of factors that motivate or enable people to think wisely (or unwisely), such as structures that force or motivate them to listen to (or ignore) others' perspectives.

Sternberg (1998, 2019b) and later Sternberg and Karami (2021a) identified three features of press that affect how one draws, in particular, upon wisdom in solving life problems.

First, environmental press derives from questions of *competing personal interests,* in particular one's own, others', and larger interests. All of the psychological theories recognize that wisdom is challenging. Sternberg (1998) specifically talks about balancing intrapersonal, interpersonal, and extrapersonal interests. Karami et al. (2020) recognize the importance of understanding multiple points of view. Grossmann et al. (2020) speak of context adaptability and multiple perspectives, as does Ardelt (2003). Intelligence and creativity, in contrast, do not always involve such competing interests, and may involve no competing interests at all.

Second, wisdom-based situations often pit *short-term interests* against *long-term interests.* Very often, what is positive in the short term turns out to be negative in the long term. The press of the short term is often quite different from the press of the long term. One has clients, or customers, or supervisors, or stockholders, or friends or family pressing for one thing, and yet one believes that, in the long run, what they are pressing for is the wrong thing. Of course, the press can go the opposite way. Sometimes people seek short-term gains at the expense of long-term ones, and others warn them that their short-term gains may result in long-term losses – the lures of smoking, ingestion of illegal drugs, and making a quick buck at others' expense come to mind immediately. Thus one purpose of wisdom is to accomplish short-term goals without compromising long-term ones.

The eternal challenge of wisdom is knowing what courses of action will compromise long-term goals. Few people predicted how social media would reward negative posts so much more than positive posts, in terms of reposting, so that the reward system would perversely favor people who have bad things to say. Because short-term consequences often have a more clear and immediate impact, short-term environmental press often ends up taking precedence over long-term press. The challenge for the wise individual is to balance them.

Third, different individuals and groups may interpret environmental press in different, and even in mutually incompatible or contradictory ways. As a simple example, when a country acts aggressively, some people may view an aggressive response to this as necessary in order to send a clear message that aggression will not be tolerated. Other people might view a response that defuses tension as far more appropriate, with the hope that a step-down type of response may ease tensions. Wisdom lies, in large part, in interpreting the complexities of the situation in a way that optimizes the goal of peace. Hitler was not to be appeased – Neville Chamberlain is infamous for proposing "peace in our time." At the same time, if John F. Kennedy had sought to destroy Russian missiles in Cuba rather than to establish a blockade, you might not be reading this chapter today!

People may respond wisely to some kinds of environmental press (e.g., professional ones) and unwisely to other kinds (e.g., personal ones). Any number of individuals known for their professional wisdom have been less wise in their personal lives (e.g., King David in the Old Testament of the Bible). This inconsistency in people's behavior has led some to argue that wisdom is largely domain-specific (e.g., Grossmann et al., 2016, 2019; Zachry et al., 2018; see also Chapter 5). Staudinger (2019) argued that wisdom about oneself needs to be distinguished from wisdom about life in general.

Grossmann's work (see Chapter 5) shows that situational press can be important in determining whether a person shows wisdom in solving a particular problem in a particular situation. Often there is pressure not to act wisely, such as when individuals or groups feel threatened by the consequences for them of a wise decision, or when a particular ideology actually leads them to act in an unwise way. What can be learned from this work is that one can have many elements of wisdom in place, but then environmental press can lead one to act unwisely, despite one's personal characteristics and skills in solving problems.

4.3.3   Problems

Problems that require wisdom for their solution are very different from problems that require the kinds of judgments often required in so-called tests of intelligence, aptitudes, and even many forms of achievement (Sternberg, 2019a, 2019b; Sternberg & Karami, 2021a, 2021b).

Although "problems" are not part of the original 4P framework offered for creativity, they need to be considered in order to identify the differences between wisdom-based problems and other kinds of problems. What are these differences?

First, real-life problems that require wisdom can never be presented in the multiple-choice format that is so popular for much of standardized testing. They typically require judgment of many diverse solutions, and those solutions are not just presented to the problem solver. The problem solver has to generate the solutions themselves.

Second, wisdom-based problems are ill-structured, in that they lack any kind of clear and unambiguous path to a solution. They are very unlike, say, the so-called "missionaries and cannibals" problem or "Tower of Hanoi" problem or many standardized test problems, which, despite their difficulty, have a path that leads clearly to a unique solution.

Third, one never knows for sure just how wise any given solution is. And solutions that at one time may appear to be wise may later appear to be supremely foolish. Many of us when solving problems have made decisions that seemed wise at the time, and later seemed foolish. Examples are poor relationship choices, choosing to live in a neighborhood or house that is a bad fit with us, or choosing a job that seemed like a good choice until one started it.

Fourth, wisdom-based problems are always deeply contextual. What constitutes a good solution may vary widely across cultures (Edmondson & Woerner, 2019) and even across temporal periods in history.

Fifth, problems that require wisdom are often high stakes, at least for the problem solver(s). Although a standardized test may be for high stakes, any single problem on it probably is not. In contrast, wisdom-based problems can influence or even determine the course of one's life. They are ecologically valid because they *are* real-world problems (Schwartz & Sharpe, 2011, 2019; Sternberg et al., 2019). There is a big difference, for example, between solving problems relating to distribution of COVID-19 vaccines, where lives are at stake, and solving problems on tests that require computation using mathematical formulas or comprehension of reading passages about nothing of note.

Sixth, wisdom-based problems typically do not lend themselves to quick solutions. They require engagement over long periods of time. In this way, they are the opposite of problems on standardized tests, which typically require very quick solutions.

Seventh, wisdom-based problems frequently need creative and often unexpected solutions. The paradigmatic case, of course, was King Solomon's decision to cut a baby in half and give half of the baby to each of the two women who claimed to be its mother. His plan, of course, was to see which woman would allow such a horrible solution to be put into effect.

Eighth, as discussed above, wisdom-based problems require the understanding and balancing of diverse interests, with wise decision makers often having to change their thinking as they go along.

Ninth, wisdom-based problems tend to be emotionally charged. People who may be good at solving theoretical problems may fall apart when their emotions become involved.

Tenth, wisdom-based problems tend to rely less on formal knowledge and more on tacit or informal knowledge (Sternberg & Horvath, 1999). As almost all the psychological theorists of wisdom have recognized, wisdom-based problems draw on life experience, and minimally if at all on what one learns in school.

Finally, wisdom-based problems typically have an ethical dimension (Sternberg, 1998). They require one to do the "right thing" (see Chapter 13). Wisdom is often challenging because, in the end, people do not want to do what they know is the right thing!

4.3.4 *Persons*

Most psychological theories of wisdom, historically, have emphasized characteristics of the person. Most of the models that we reviewed earlier focus mainly on wise individuals. Briefly, the Berlin Wisdom Model describes wise people as experts on the fundamental issues of human life (Baltes & Staudinger, 2000). Note, however, that according to Baltes and Kunzmann (2004) the Berlin model does not view wisdom exclusively as a characteristic of persons – wisdom can also be found, for example, in texts and documents, which would make it a characteristic of products. Ardelt (2004, 2019) explicitly states that wisdom is a personality characteristic of individuals; according to her, wisdom cannot be learned from books, but has to emerge as individuals deal with and reflect on personal experiences. Webster (2003, 2007) also conceptualized wisdom as the result of a person's reflecting on their experiences.

Only relatively recently have wisdom researchers started to consider wisdom as less of a stable characteristic that some people have in abundance and others (most of us) do not. In fact, most people have had some very wise moments in their life, and some very unwise moments as well (Grossmann, 2017; Grossmann et al., 2016; see Chapter 5). This perspective on wisdom emphasizes the role of environmental press (context) and concrete problems for wisdom more than the role of person characteristics.

4.3.5   *Processes*

The processes of wisdom proposed by a particular model derive, in large part, from what it takes to execute whatever the model views as the purpose of wisdom. These processes are not just about balancing, but also about how one actually balances interests in the face of many competing constraints. For example, in a conflict, such as that between Israelis and Palestinians, or between residents of Hong Kong who want freedom of the press and those who are satisfied with government suppression of the press, multiple groups may seek a common good. They just have very different ideas of what that common good will be.

Across models, wisdom seems to contain some combination of cognitive and metacognitive, affective, motivational, and existential or possibly spiritual processes. Some of the processes that have been proposed include abstract reasoning (Takahashi & Overton, 2005), dialectical reasoning (Grossmann et al., 2020), self-reflection (Glück & Bluck, 2013; Staudinger, 2019; Weststrate & Glück, 2017), and emotional regulation (Webster, 2003). As discussed earlier, Sternberg (2019b) has emphasized balance processes – working toward a common good by balancing intrapersonal, interpersonal, and extrapersonal interests, over the long term as well as the short term, by balancing adaptation to, shaping of, and selection of environments.

4.3.6   *Products*

Products of wisdom include decisions, judgments, problem solutions, and, in the final analysis, actions based on the concepts that emerge from deliberation. Kaufman and Beghetto (2009) have proposed a 4C model of creativity, which Sternberg and Karami (2021b) have generalized to wisdom. The products, according to this view, can be of four kinds.

Mini-w wisdom can occur when one is learning what constitutes proper or suitable wise behavior in a given domain. Sometimes what is wise is the same across domains – for example, sooner or later we learn that we are supposed to show in our behavior the golden rule of acting toward others as we would wish them to act toward us. However, in other instances what is wise differs across domains – for example, it may be wise to jump quickly into the water to try to save someone who is drowning in a lake, but unwise to quickly jump into the water to save the person if they are drowning in a rogue ("freak" or "killer") wave that is likely to take not only the already drowning person, but also the person who is trying to save them. In the latter case, more extensive aid will be needed than one individual jumping into the ocean to save the person in distress.

Little-w wisdom constitutes the products of wise decisions we make that may be of consequence for us personally or for those in our immediate surrounding, but that have no real broader implications. It is the wisdom, say, that we teach our children or our students – for example, that it is a bad idea to be a bully because it hurts others and also results in others seeing us as aggressive and inconsiderate of others.

Pro-w wisdom is professional wisdom, and is largely the result of the tacit knowledge that we gain during our socialization into our profession (see Sternberg & Horvath, 1999). It might be advice, for example, on balancing the interests of stockholders, customers, employees, and managers in a corporation.

Big-W wisdom is the wisdom that some people apply to major problems, such as how to distribute the COVID-19 vaccine to large numbers of people rapidly. It is the kind of wisdom that one hopes one's state and national leaders will show in their governance.

To summarize, products can be of four different magnitudes, ranging from mini-w to big-W. Often one cannot be sure what kind of product a judgment or decision is until some time has passed and one can look back on the situation and reflect on it and on the decision that one reached.

4.4 Conclusion

In this chapter we have reviewed some of the major psychological theories of wisdom. We began by reviewing some of the earliest work and then proceeded to discuss some of the more recent psychological theories. We then analyzed the composition of these theories in terms of the six Ps: purpose, press, problems, persons, processes, and products. A comprehensive theory of wisdom would encompass all six of the Ps, but the field of psychology is not yet close to having a theory that fully accounts for all of them. Nor is it yet clear exactly what such a theory would look like.

Wisdom is one of the most important characteristics that we need in our lives in order to thrive, and it is also perhaps what society today needs most of all. Understanding wisdom better through psychological theories is an important step toward seeing more infusion of wisdom into our lives throughout the world.

4.5 Comprehension and Discussion Questions

(1) Which definition(s) reviewed in the first part of this chapter do you find most convincing, and why?

(2) Try to come up with your own personal definition of wisdom. You can draw elements from all of the models reviewed in this chapter. You can also add elements if you think something is missing.

(3) One important question in wisdom psychology is how we can prove that a theory is valid – that is, that it really describes wisdom. How could you test whether your personal definition is really a good description of wisdom?

(4) Think about a difficult life problem that you or someone close to you has encountered. Can you identify the six Ps with respect to that problem, as in Table 4.1? What could a wise solution (i.e., the product of wisdom) have been?

(5) In the light of the theories of wisdom presented in this chapter, what can a person do to enhance their own wisdom?

4.6 Investigations

Robert J. Sternberg's research is focused on attempting to incorporate wisdom into people's notions of what it means to be "intelligent." Historically, wisdom has been seen as related to, but distinct from, intelligence. And certainly there are aspects of human intelligence that are distinct from wisdom. However, our "raw" intelligence is destroying the world as we know it. We humans are creating problems for ourselves that, in the long run, may become insurmountable, such as climate change, pollution, weapons of mass destruction, and pandemics resulting from ever greater proximity of humans to wildlife that used to have its own preserve. If we do not think of intelligence *adaptively,* as involving wisdom as well as sheer brainpower to solve complex but abstract problems removed from everyday life, future generations of humans that would have been may never come to be, as a result of our own short-sightedness in applying our intelligence to our individual needs rather than to our collective well-being.

Judith Glück's main topic of research is wisdom psychology. Having been trained in psychometrics, she has a strong interest in developing new ways to measure wisdom. She is also interested in the development of wisdom through an interplay of life experiences and internal and external resources, factors that influence wisdom in professional contexts, ways to foster wisdom through interventions and through changes in structures and systems, the relationship between wisdom and morality, and people's conceptions of wisdom in different cultures.

Sareh Karami's research involves the polyhedron model of wisdom and its applications. She has also done work on a 6P model of wisdom, and on applying that model to intelligence and creativity. In addition, she is interested in positive creativity – the use of creativity for positive purposes in order to make the world a better place. Sareh is especially interested in gifted children and how ideas such as those explored in this chapter can be applied to teaching such children to capitalize on their gifts.

4.7   Practical Applications

Theories of wisdom are important to everyday life because they can serve as a basis for our understanding of what wisdom is, of how best to measure it, and most importantly, of how to develop it in young and even older people. We need to teach people to be not just classically "smart," but also wise. Otherwise we put the world at risk because our intelligence destroys humanity and takes many other species with us.

Glossary

balance theory of wisdom the theory that wisdom is the utilization of one's abilities and knowledge toward the attainment of a common good, by balancing intrapersonal, interpersonal, and extrapersonal interests over the long term as well as the short term, through the infusion of positive ethical values, in order to adapt to, shape, and select environments.

Berlin Wisdom Model the theory that wisdom is an expert knowledge system comprising rich factual knowledge, rich procedural knowledge, lifespan contextualism, relativism of values, and awareness and management of uncertainty.

common model of wisdom the theory that wisdom comprises balance of viewpoints, epistemic humility, context adaptability, and multiple perspectives.

HERO(E) model the theory that wisdom comprises humor, emotional regulation, reminiscence/reflectiveness, openness to experience, and critical life experiences.

polyhedron model of wisdom (PMW) the theory that wisdom comprises knowledge, reflectivity, and self-regulation, pro-social behaviors and moral maturity, openness and tolerance, sound judgment and creativity, and dynamic balance and synthesis.

self-transcendence model the theory that wisdom comprises self-knowledge, self-acceptance, independence of external sources of reward, connectedness with all of humanity and nature, and an orientation toward a greater good.

three-dimensional model of wisdom the theory that wisdom comprises cognitive, affective, and reflective dimensions.

REFERENCES

Aldwin, C. M., Igarashi, H., and Levenson, M. R. (2019). Wisdom as self-transcendence. In R. J. Sternberg and J. Glück, eds., *The Cambridge Handbook of Wisdom*. Cambridge University Press, pp. 122–43.

Ardelt M. (2003). Empirical assessment of a Three-Dimensional Wisdom Scale. *Research on Aging*, 25(3), 275–324.

(2004). Wisdom as expert knowledge system: a critical review of a contemporary operationalization of an ancient concept. *Human Development*, 47(5), 257–85.

(2005). How wise people cope with crises and obstacles in life. *ReVision*, 28(1), 7–20.

(2019). Wisdom and well-being. In R. Sternberg and J. Glück, eds., *The Cambridge Handbook of Wisdom*. Cambridge University Press, pp. 602–25.

Baltes, P. B. and Kunzmann, U. (2003). Wisdom: the peak of human excellence in the orchestration of mind and virtue. *The Psychologist*, 16, 131–33.

(2004). The two faces of wisdom: wisdom as a general theory of knowledge and judgment about excellence in mind and virtue vs. wisdom as everyday realization in people and products. *Human Development*, 47(5), 290–99.

Baltes, P. B. and Smith, J. (1990). The psychology of wisdom and its ontogenesis. In R. J. Sternberg, ed., *Wisdom: Its Nature, Origins, and Development*. Cambridge University Press, pp. 87–120.

(2008). The fascination of wisdom: its nature, ontogeny, and function. *Perspectives on Psychological Science*, 3(1), 56–64.

Baltes, P. B. and Staudinger, U. M. (1993). The search for a psychology of wisdom. *Current Directions in Psychological Science*, 2(3), 75–80.

(2000). A metaheuristic (pragmatic) to orchestrate mind and virtue toward excellence. *American Psychologist*, 55(1), 122–36.

Clayton, V. (1976). *A multidimensional scaling analysis of the concept of wisdom*. Unpublished doctoral dissertation, University of Southern California, Los Angeles, CA.

(1982). Wisdom and intelligence: the nature and function of knowledge in the later years. *The International Journal of Aging and Human Development*, 15(4), 315–23.

Clayton, V. P. and Birren, J. E. (1980). The development of wisdom across the life span: a re-examination of an ancient topic. In P. B. Baltes and O. G. Brim, Jr., eds., *Life-Span Development and Behavior*, Vol. 3. Academic Press, pp. 103–35.

Curnow, T. (2015). *Wisdom: A History*. University of Chicago Press.

Edmondson, R. and Woerner, M. H. (2019). Sociocultural foundations of wisdom. In R. J. Sternberg and J. Glück, eds., *The Cambridge Handbook of Wisdom*. Cambridge University Press, pp. 40–68.

Glück, J. and Bluck, S. (2013). The MORE Life Experience Model: a theory of the development of personal wisdom. In M. Ferrari and N. M. Weststrate, eds., *The Scientific Study of Personal Wisdom*. Springer, pp. 75–98.

Glück, J., Bluck, S., and Weststrate, N. M. (2019). More on the MORE Life Experience Model: what we have learned (so far). *The Journal of Value Inquiry*, 53, 349–70.

Grossmann I., (2017). Wisdom in context. *Perspectives on Psychological Science*, 12(2), 233–57.

Grossmann, I., Gerlach, T. M., and Denissen, J. J. A. (2016). Wise reasoning in the face of everyday life challenges. *Social Psychological and Personality Science*, 7(7), 611–22.

Grossmann, I., Kung, F. Y. H., and Santos, H. C. (2019). Wisdom as state versus trait. In Sternberg R. J and J. Glück, eds., *The Cambridge Handbook of Wisdom*. Cambridge University Press, pp. 249–73.

Grossmann, I. Weststrate, N. M., Ardelt, M. et al. (2020). The science of wisdom in a polarized world: knowns and unknowns. *Psychological Inquiry*, 31(2), 103–33.

Karami, S. and Parra-Martinez, F. A. (2021) Foolishness of COVID-19: applying the polyhedron model of wisdom to understand behaviors in a time of crisis. *Roeper Review*, 43(1), 42–52.

Karami, S., Ghahremani, M., Parra-Martinez, F., and Gentry, M. (2020). A polyhedron model of wisdom: a systematic review of the wisdom studies in three different disciplines. *Roeper Review*, 42(4), 241–57.

Kaufman, J. C. and Beghetto, R. A. (2009). Beyond big and little: the four C model of creativity. *Review of General Psychology*, 13(1), 1–12.

Kaufman, S. B. (2020). *Transcend: The New Science of Self-Actualization*. Tarcher-Perigree.

Levenson M. R., Jennings P. A., Aldwin C. M., and Shiraishi R. W. (2005). Self-transcendence: conceptualization and measurement. *The International Journal of Aging and Human Development*, 60(2), 127–43.

Maslow, A. H. (1943). A theory of human motivation. *Psychological Review*, 50(4), 370–96.

(1954). *Motivation and Personality*. Harper and Row.

(1962). *Toward a Psychology of Being*. D. Van Nostrand Company.

Phan, L. V., Blackie, L. E. R., Horstmann, K., and Jayawickreme, E. (2021). An integrative framework to study wisdom. In Rauthmann, ed., *The Handbook of Personality Dynamics and Processes*. Elsevier, pp. 1159–82.

Rhodes, M. (1961). An analysis of creativity. *The Phi Delta Kappan*, 42(7), 305–10.

Schwartz, B. and Sharpe, K. E. (2011), *Practical Wisdom: The Right Way to Do the Right Thing*. Penguin.

(2019). Practical wisdom: what Aristotle might add to psychology. In R. J. Sternberg and J. Glück, eds., *The Cambridge Handbook of Wisdom*. Cambridge University Press, pp. 226–48.

Staudinger, U. (2019). The distinction between personal and general wisdom: how far have we come? In R. J. Sternberg and J. Glück, eds., *The Cambridge Handbook of Wisdom*. Cambridge University Press, pp. 182–201.

Sternberg, R. J. (1998) A balance theory of wisdom. *Review of General Psychology*, 2(4), 347–65.

(2003). *Wisdom, Intelligence, and Creativity*. Cambridge University Press.

(2019a). Race to Samarra: the critical importance of wisdom in the world today. In R. J. Sternberg and J. Glueck, eds., *The Cambridge Handbook of Wisdom*. Cambridge University Press, pp. 3–9.

(2019b). Why people often prefer wise guys to guys who are wise: an augmented balance theory of the production and reception of wisdom. In R. J. Sternberg and J. Glueck, eds., *The Cambridge Handbook of Wisdom*. Cambridge University Press, pp. 162–81.

Sternberg, R. J. and Glück, J. (2022). *Wisdom: The Psychology of Wise Thoughts, Words, and Deeds*. Cambridge University Press.

Sternberg, R. J. and Horvath, J. A., eds. (1999). *Tacit Knowledge in Professional Practice*. Lawrence Erlbaum Associates.

Sternberg, R. J. and Karami, S. (2021a). What is wisdom? A unified 6P framework. *Review of General Psychology*, 25(2), 134–51.

(2021b). A 4W model of wisdom and giftedness in wisdom. *Roeper Review*, 43(3), 153–60.

Sternberg, R. J., Nusbaum, H., and Glueck, J., eds. (2019). *Applying Wisdom to Contemporary World Problems*. Palgrave Macmillan.

Takahashi, M. and Overton, W. F. (2005). Cultural foundations of wisdom: an integrated developmental approach. In R. J. Sternberg and J. Jordan, eds., *A Handbook of Wisdom: Psychological Perspectives*. Cambridge University Press, pp. 32–60.

Webster, J. D. (2003). An exploratory analysis of a self-assessed wisdom scale. *Journal of Adult Development*, 10(1), 13–22.

(2007). Measuring the character strength of wisdom. *The International Journal of Aging and Human Development*, 65(2), 163–83.

(2019). Self-report wisdom measures: strengths, limitations, and future directions. In R. J. Sternberg and J. Glück, eds., *The Cambridge Handbook of Wisdom*. Cambridge University Press, pp. 297–320.

Weststrate, N. M. and Glück, J. (2017). Hard-earned wisdom: exploratory processing of difficult life experience is positively associated with wisdom. *Developmental Psychology*, 53(4), 800–14.

Zachry, C. E., Phan, L. V., Blackie, L. E. R., and Jayawickreme, E. (2018). Situation-based contingencies underlying wisdom-content manifestations: examining intellectual humility in daily life. *Journal of Gerontology B: Psychological Science & Social Science*, 73(8), 1404–15.

CHAPTER 5

Wisdom
Situational, Dispositional, or Both?

Igor Grossmann

5.1 Introduction

King Solomon in the Old Testament was known for his wisdom. People came from far and wide to his court, seeking his wise judgment on challenging, seemingly intractable life matters. However, despite allegedly being the wisest (and wealthiest) man in his era, his personal life was anything but exemplary. It was riddled with misjudgments. Known for dispassionate self-restraint when evaluating others' problems, his personal passions resulted in a vast harem. Solomon accumulated luxury at the expense of his nation via increasingly unpopular taxation. He showed off the opulence of his court and palaces to representatives of other kingdoms. Most importantly, he did not spend much time on the education of his son Rehoboam, whose actions after Solomon's death led to the kingdom's quick demise (Parker, 1992) (Figure 5.1).

Irrespective of the exact details (and veracity) of this Biblical narrative, the general structure of the narrative seems familiar – a person shows wisdom when reflecting on others' concerns, yet shows little critical acumen in their own life. You can probably think of a friend or two whose lives appear as paradoxical as King Solomon's. Yet there is a deeper lesson to be learned here, which has to do with the core nature of how we perceive wisdom in others and in ourselves, and how a whole range of biases and illusions prevent us from fully grasping how wisdom unfolds in our lives.

5.2 Essentialist and Constructivist Views on Wisdom

To appreciate Solomon's story, we need to take a small detour to characterize how scholars in philosophy, education, and psychology understand wisdom. In this textbook you will encounter a range of perspectives on the core psychological features of wisdom. Some of them are about how to make a wise decision in a challenging situation (e.g., Grossmann, 2017a), while others are about regulating one's emotions (Bangen et al., 2013) or contributing toward a common good (for a review, see Chapter 4 of this textbook). However, beyond specific ingredients, there is a fundamental distinction between a perspective of wisdom as a "fixed" characteristic or as a "malleable" process. For instance, the general public and some scholars often subscribe to the notion that wisdom is a discrete **trait** that is stable and invariable. We shall call this view an essentialist perspective of wisdom (Grossmann, 2017b). **Essentialism** in relation to a psychological characteristic is a belief that the characteristic is typically stable and invariable across time. According to this belief, a given characteristic is a **natural kind**, representing the structure of the natural world, uniform in structure and composition (Haslam et al., 2004). An essentialist belief about wisdom suggests that wisdom is largely stable from one situation to the next and over time.

Figure 5.1 *The Judgement of Solomon*, whose wisdom is exemplified in the Biblical story in which he gives his verdict; he commands a soldier to cut the living child in two, and the true mother objects to Solomon's verdict (1 Kings 3:25-27). Painting by Peter Paul Rubens, *c.* 1617. Delft, Stedelijk Museum Het Prinsenhof https://rkd.nl/explore/images/5235

This essentialist perspective is captured in our fascination with **exemplars of wisdom** (Weststrate et al., 2016). These are stories of remarkable and unique individuals, sages, political leaders, or social activists, in history, folklore, and the popular media. Think of Confucius, Merlin, Gandalf in *The Lord of the Rings*, Dumbledore in the Harry Potter series, or Yoda in *Star Wars*. Or think of Mother Teresa, Mahatma Gandhi, or Malala Yousafsai. Each of these exemplars signals that wisdom is personal and unique to remarkable, admirable individuals. Yet, as King Solomon's example demonstrates, this perspective runs into problems in accounting for possible variability in exemplars' wisdom across situations and over time. Is King Solomon a bad exemplar of wisdom, given his variability? Should we ignore his experiences? As we shall learn in this chapter, the answer to these questions requires some reconsidering of what wisdom is about.

There is another perspective on the nature of wisdom. This **constructivist perspective** assumes that the socio-cultural context in which people find themselves determines their experiences and their reflections on those experiences. This perspective assumes that wisdom, like many other psychological processes, is manifested through subjective interpretation of reality (Griffin & Ross, 1991). It assumes that wisdom is malleable and changeable, and that it is not a natural kind. In contrast to viewing wisdom as a stable and invariable natural kind, the constructivist perspective suggests that a person's wisdom is not very stable from one situation to the next. This perspective can even be found in the writing of some of the remarkable individuals whom others typically essentialize as paragons of wisdom.

Like King Solomon, many wisdom exemplars, such as Mahatma Gandhi, Martin Luther King, Jr., Mother Teresa, and Leo Tolstoy, showed large inconsistencies in their wisdom across different domains of their lives (Grossmann & Kross, 2014). According to the constructivist view, it is valuable to study specific experiences or *states* in which people find themselves. Attention to cultural, experiential, and situational contexts can help to shed light on factors that promote as well as inhibit wisdom in people's lives. Critically, the constructivist perspective does not assume that wisdom has a unitary stable core. Rather, this perspective acknowledges how cultural–historical and individual contexts aid the expression of wisdom-related characteristics. As we shall also see below, constructivist insights have implications for the measurement of wisdom, shifting the focus from abstract traits to concrete responses to specific situations.

5.3   Dispositional versus Situational Approaches in Psychology

Essentialist and constructivist perspectives map onto different approaches to understanding psychological characteristics at large. On the one hand, there is a long tradition in philosophy and psychology of viewing psychological characteristics through the lens of (stable) *dispositions* – that is, natural tendencies of character or habit to act in a specified way. Yet another prevalent tradition involves viewing the same characteristics through the lens of (variable) *situations* – that is, environmental and situational cues that influence how we experience, understand, and react to an issue at hand.

Consider the following example. You are sitting in a new restaurant, waiting for your food. Unfortunately, your order was mixed up and the waiter nervously asks you to wait another half hour for your food. When you finally get your meal, the waiter just quickly arranges it and leaves. As the food is lacklustre, and you have spent more than an hour longer at the restaurant than you had anticipated, you just want to leave. Unfortunately, the waiter is not easy to find, and when you finally locate them at another table and tell them you need a check, it takes another half an hour for them to bring it you. The waiter also appears somewhat confused. If somebody asked you about your waiter's competence, you would probably state that they are largely incompetent. You might further vow never to set foot in that restaurant again.

In this situation, you make a **dispositional** judgment, passing a global judgment on a person or a place (in this case, evaluating the waiter's competence and conscientiousness). However, imagine that you bump into this waiter a few days later in the street, and they tell you that the restaurant did not get their food supplies on time due to a range of unprecedented circumstances, and that the chef's young daughter ended up in hospital right when the chef was preparing your meal, so that he had to leave halfway through his preparations. Moreover, the restaurant was severely understaffed due to three other waiters calling in sick an hour before it opened that night. Finally, your waiter was not even supposed to be working that day. They were called on to help on their night off, and were not informed that all the other waiters were off sick. Your waiter ended up serving three times the usual number of meals. Would you still view the waiter as incompetent and unconscientious?

Bombarded by all this **situational** information, you may attempt to revise your earlier judgment. Now you may view the waiter as highly competent – there was no chef present and no other waiters, yet you were able to get a halfway decent meal! Under such circumstances, the waiter's willingness to come for help appears highly conscientious, and his ability to juggle the limitations at the restaurant seems to indicate a high level of competence.

Situations like the one depicted in this example apply not only to our evaluation of competence of waiters in restaurants, but also to our views of the wisdom of political leaders. Consider another example. At a family dinner, a conversation swerves dangerously into politics. Some of the relatives view a new politician as an ultra-liberal, naive fool, and consider the elder-stateswoman politician a conservative bastion of wisdom, much needed in uncertain times. Other relatives view the conservative politician as a dictatorial fool, who is insensitive to pressing social injustices, and deaf to calls for change. They regard the new politician as a hopeful candidate for a wise new age. How easy it is to assign wisdom and folly to politicians! Yet what does the family actually know about these individuals, beyond the caricatured and stylized portrayals in their social-media campaigns and in the press? How much do they know about the social pressures on politicians that force them to make certain decisions? Despite the lack of insight into the nuanced experiences of political leaders at a family dinner, such considerations are missing. Instead, the family makes dispositional judgments about the politicians' wisdom (or folly) based on abstract, limited fragments of information that have been fed to them via various media channels, as well as through general impressions they have gained from family and other friends.

This **folk psychology** approach to individual characteristics is not only common among the general public, but also prevalent among some experts in the psychological literature. Often psychologists ask people to judge others, or themselves, in an abstract fashion. For example, how conscientious are you? How open-minded are you? What about your perspective-taking abilities? If a given characteristic is a stable disposition, one should be easily able to provide an accurate assessment of such characteristics, both for oneself and for others. After all, one has had plenty of chances to observe oneself in the past. If the characteristic is uniform in structure and composition (both of which are defining features of essentialism), the meaning and the expression of these characteristics should not be subject to cross-situational **variability**.

The dispositional approach has long been dominant in many areas of psychological research, including clinical psychology, industrial and organizational psychology, and personality research. Similarly, numerous scholars employ measures that assume wisdom to be a stable disposition (e.g., Ardelt, 2003; Thomas et al., 2019; Webster, 2007). These measures rely on questionnaires in which people report how **empathetic**, thoughtful, or benevolent they consider themselves to be.

At the same time, several research groups have employed the situation-focused approach to measuring wisdom. For instance, Paul Baltes and his colleagues used this approach within the Berlin Wisdom Paradigm that you read about in Chapter 4 of this textbook. Aspects of this paradigm explicitly target awareness of situational forces on human behavior. As Aristotle pointed out long ago, wise judgment is by default variable across situations. There is no single rule that would be "wise" in all situations (Kristjánsson, 2013). According to this Aristotelian perspective on wisdom, it is very important to pay attention to the specific contextual factors for action in response to concrete situations. Consequently, scientists who aim to realize this insight empirically study wisdom in the context of specific situations that people encounter in their lives.

Overall, as is summarized in Table 5.1, the essentialist perspective on wisdom as a stable disposition is aligned with the use of self-reported abstract personality-style measures, aiming to capture wise dispositions – that is, one's general tendencies (Ardelt, 2003; Levenson et al., 2005; Webster, 2003). In contrast, the constructivist perspective on wisdom is aligned with measuring

Table 5.1 *Perspectives on the nature of wisdom and their implications for measurement*

	Essentialism	*Constructivism*
Perspective	• Wisdom as a natural kind • Stable • Similar structure in different situations	• Wisdom as construed and embedded in socio-cultural experiences • Highly variable • Variable structure in different situations
Approach	*Dispositional* • Individual differences/traits • Focus on general tendencies of character or habit	*Situational* • Judgment in concrete situations • Focus on factors that influence how we experience, understand, and react to an issue
Measures	*Context-free* • Self-report questionnaires on general characteristics	*Context-dependent* • Human-coded ratings of reflections on specific situations

expression of wisdom-related characteristics in specific situations (e.g., Baltes & Smith, 2008; Grossmann et al., 2012, 2013; Weststrate & Glück, 2017).

5.4   What Do the Data Tell Us?

Given the differences between the essentialist and constructivist perspectives on the nature of wisdom, it appears prudent to ask which of these perspectives has greater support from research. Is wisdom a highly stable characteristic, as essentialists assume? Or is it a pure construction without any core to it, as constructivists suggest? As the last two decades of empirical research have revealed, there is some evidence to support both perspectives.

5.4.1   Initial Observations about Dispositions and Situations

Judith Glück (2018) and her research team were among the first to explore the stability of wisdom. The researchers were interested in autobiographical reflections of wisdom nominees. They invited nominees and comparable control participants to come into the laboratory on two occasions. Each time, the researchers interviewed the participants about a challenging event from their lives, with unbiased coders scoring participants' responses for commonly measured attributes of wisdom. Next, the researchers compared how wisdom scores from reflection on one experience overlapped with wisdom scores from reflection on another experience. They also compared how much different wisdom categories overlapped in each situation – whether a person who showed greater recognition of their limits was also more likely to consider the broader role of contexts in their life. The results showed that scores on one category showed a high degree of overlap with scores on another wisdom category (**Pearson's correlation coefficient** $r = 0.70$). In other words, the responses were internally consistent. However, wisdom nominees showed only a small degree of convergence between scores for reflection on different situations, as exemplified by a weak correlation between wisdom scores in reflections on different situations ($r = 0.30$). In other words, there was a high level of cross-situational variability in responses among wisdom nominees.

Analyses from autobiographical experiences suggest that there is some variability in wisdom, but how common is such variability in real life? Together with scholars from Berlin, Germany, I asked a large group of local participants to take part in a 9-day diary study (Grossmann et al., 2016). Each day, the participants reported what was the most challenging issue of the day, reflected on their experience, and provided responses that captured wisdom-related characteristics such as **intellectual humility**, consideration of diverse perspectives, and consideration of events in flux and in the process of change. Using these responses, we could examine how stable and variable wisdom is in everyday life. It turned out that the overlap between wisdom in response to one situation was only modestly associated with wisdom in response to another situation on a different day. The percentage of within-person **variance** in wisdom (versus variance between persons) ranged from 94 percent for consideration of others' perspectives to 66 percent for self-transcendence (average of 81 percent). In comparison, Big Five personality traits typically vary between 78 percent and 49 percent within a person (Fleeson & Gallagher, 2009). In other words, a given person's wisdom when facing a challenging situation is not likely to tell us how they will react to another challenge. In addition, the findings were the same when we only looked at the top scorers on wisdom – **stability** in wisdom among the top 25 percent of participants was equally low.

However, despite substantial variability in wisdom across situations, both the diary study and subsequent research have suggested that wisdom characteristics show at least some stability. Moreover, estimates of stability in wisdom from diary studies may provide an overly conservative estimate. This is because one would ideally want to compare wisdom in response to similar situations. Yet we are unlikely to experience the same challenges day after day in a diary situation. And when comparing more similar situations, such as major adversities, the stability of wisdom appears to be higher (r = 0.35; Dorfman et al., 2021).

Overall, the current empirical results suggest that there is some evidence of within-person stability in wisdom from one situation to the next (supporting the dispositional approach). Yet there is also substantial between-person variability in wisdom (supporting the situational approach).

5.4.2 Variability in Wisdom Is Systematic

Variability in wisdom could be just random noise, and thus something to be ignored. However, new evidence shows that this variability is quite systematic, both in terms of its associations with other psychological processes, and when examining social and cognitive factors that may promote and inhibit wisdom in different challenges that people encounter in their lives. In the diary study mentioned above (Grossmann et al., 2016), even though we observed substantial variability in wisdom from one diary day to another, this variability followed a systematic pattern. When participants reflected on challenges involving other people, they reported greater wisdom compared with challenges they faced on their own (e.g., a work-related challenge not involving colleagues) (Grossmann et al., 2016). Researchers have since replicated this pattern when examining wisdom in response to major adversities that participants reported in a 1-year longitudinal study (Dorfman et al., 2021). When participants reported adversities with a focus on themselves (e.g., economic hardship, major health problems), they reported lower wisdom compared with events that involved other people (e.g., social conflict, health problem of a close family member).

One further insight about the systematic variability of wisdom concerns its association with prosocial behavior. This association is often assumed, and this is exemplified in the idea that wisdom is oriented toward the "common good" (for a review, see Grossmann et al., 2020). However, until recently this assumption has not been tested. Note that dispositional and situational approaches to wisdom would make different predictions about *how* wisdom would relate to prosocial behavior or other moral characteristics. A **dispositional** approach to wisdom would assume a rather straightforward hypothesis, namely that wiser people are more prosocial, charitable, giving, or benevolent. Moreover, this association should be stable across situations. Conversely, a **situational** approach to wisdom would emphasize how certain features of a situation (or its subjective construal) have an impact on the association of wisdom with prosocial behavior.

Together with Justin Brienza and Ramona Bobocel, I have recently decided to address this question empirically (Grossmann et al., 2017). We presented a large group of participants with a **public goods game**. In this game, one is asked how much of a bonus payment one would be willing to place into a common pool shared with several other anonymous members of a group to whom one is assigned. Whatever the person and the other members of their group put into the common pool will be doubled and split equally among all members of the group. Typically, from a perspective of economic self-interest, one would not put anything from the bonus into the common pool – let other suckers contribute instead. However, the maximum gain in the public goods game can be achieved if each member cooperates. Thus monetary contributions to the common pool are typically considered a marker of cooperation. This version of the public goods game included a twist. Before deciding, one group of participants took extra time to reflect on their decision, whereas another group was asked to act spontaneously. In addition to the game, we assessed participants' wisdom in reflection on an unresolved conflict that they had recently experienced.

Our empirical results showed that greater wisdom was indeed associated with more cooperative behavior in the public goods game. Yet these results came with a caveat. This positive association was present only when participants were given extra time to reflect on their decision, and not when they made a spontaneous decision about their contribution to the common pool. Overall, this study provides support for the constructivist perspective rather than the essentialist perspective on wisdom. The association of wisdom with pro-sociality exists, and yet it also systematically varies, depending on the features of the situation.

5.4.3   Solomon's Paradox

Perhaps the strongest evidence for systematic cross-situational differences in wisdom comes from experiments that involve random assignment of participants to conditions that emphasize the unique features of a situation in a controlled laboratory setting. One situational feature that is worth exploring concerns the role of personal relevance. Let us return to the example of the Biblical King Solomon, who apparently showed great wisdom in response to other people's challenges, but failed to exercise wisdom when facing personal issues. This Biblical story suggests an interesting hypothesis involving an asymmetry between expression of wisdom for the personal versus other people's issues (Staudinger, 2013), namely that wisdom may be greater during reflection on other people's dilemmas than during reflection on our own challenges.

One of the first experimental studies on wisdom indirectly captured this asymmetry. Staudinger and Baltes (1996) asked participants to come to the lab to reflect on a range of scenarios. As is usual with experiments, the researchers randomly assigned the participants to several different conditions. In the first condition, participants thought about an interpersonal dilemma on their own. In the second condition, participants considered what other people whose opinion they valued might say about the same dilemma. The results showed that reflections of participants in the second, other-focused condition were richer in themes consistent with core features of wisdom. They were more likely to recognize uncertainty and change, and to acknowledge intellectual humility (i.e., the limits of their knowledge) compared with participants in the first, think-alone condition. Yet those of you who are more critical of experimental designs may already see why this experiment may be problematic. When considering other people's opinions, participants spent more time deliberating on the scenario – a serious confounding factor in the researchers' experimental design (Staudinger & Baltes, 1996; table 4). Perhaps, if people in the first condition had had more time to reflect on the situation, they would have produced similarly wise responses even when continuing to think about the issue on their own.

Building on the Biblical analogy concerning Solomon's judgments about personal versus non-personal challenges directly, Ethan Kross and I decided to address these limitations and to examine a possible mechanism that could account for "Solomon's paradox" (Grossmann &

Kross, 2014). We designed a series of experiments in which we carefully controlled the length of time for which participants reflected on a problem with which they were presented. In one such study, we invited college students from the University of Michigan, all of whom were in a monogamous relationship, to visit our laboratory to reflect on a range of interpersonal scenarios. We randomly assigned the participants to two groups. In the self-centered condition, participants reflected on situations involving their partner, whereas in the non-self-centered condition, participants reflected on a comparable situation involving their friend's partner. Here is an example of the kind of situation that we instructed participants in the self-centered condition to reflect on:

> Your partner has admitted being unfaithful. You have been in a serious relationship, and now you suddenly learn that your partner had sex with your close friend.

And here is the corresponding non-self-centered scenario:

> Your friend's partner has admitted being unfaithful. Your friend has been in a serious relationship, and now your friend suddenly learns that their partner had sex with their close friend.

After the participants had reflected on the presented situation, we assessed their wisdom in responses to the situation, including measures of their intellectual humility, consideration of compromise, and consideration of diverse ways in which the situation might unfold after the incident. For each of the aspects of wisdom, the participants who had reflected on the non-self-centered scenario were overall more likely to report wisdom compared with the participants who had reflected on the self-centered scenario. Similar self–other asymmetries in wisdom appear for scenarios in which a friend betrays one's trust, and when examining non-college student populations of younger and older age (Grossmann & Kross, 2014; study 3).

Several interesting insights can be gained from this experimental research. First, the variability across situations appears to be systematic, and varies depending on the degree of self-involvement. No matter how wise you are in relation to others' dilemmas, you can still be a fool in your own life. Second, the capacity for wisdom may be higher than expected when judging based solely on decisions that people make about their personal lives.

5.5 Integrating Dispositional and Situational Approaches to Wisdom

It appears that there is both substantial, systematic variability in wisdom, consistent with the situational approach, and also some evidence of cross-situational and cross-temporal stability in key wisdom characteristics (e.g., intellectual humility, consideration of change, or perspective taking), consistent with the dispositional approach. Fortunately, new insights in personality psychology allow us to integrate these approaches. One way to integrate these insights is to consider wisdom as a broad system, including one's culture and ecology (e.g., how culture and ecology influence thoughts, feelings, and behaviors) (Grossmann, 2017b), as well as experiences and situations that one encounters over the course of one's life. Viewing wisdom as a system allows us to consider its dispositional features. Just as modern theory of personality and corresponding empirical work have shown (Fleeson, 2001), dispositional and situational features of wisdom can work together, integrated in a mutually reinforcing multi-level framework.

Let us consider Figure 5.2, which shows how wisdom responses may be distributed across individuals in a society. On the right side of the figure is a set of bell-shaped distributions. The

Wisdom as a multi-level system

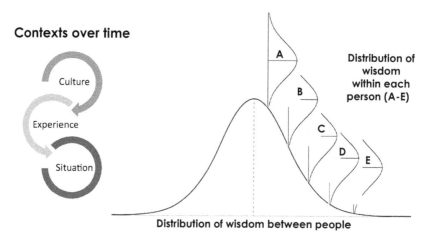

Contexts over time

Culture

Experience

Situation

A

B

C

D

E

Distribution of wisdom within each person (A–E)

Distribution of wisdom between people

Figure 5.2   Wisdom as a multi-level system. The diagram on the right depicts the distribution of wisdom between and within people. The diagram on the left depicts wisdom embedded in a range of socio-cultural and situational contexts, which in turn can vary over time.

horizontal distribution corresponding to *between*-person differences is average wisdom. As with many individual characteristics, when sampled at random, average wisdom may follow a bell-curve-shaped distribution. Thus Persons A–E depicted on this graph have their average placement somewhere on this bell-shaped curve. For instance, Aram may be on average more likely to show wisdom than Elizabeth. But note that Aram, Elizabeth, and each other person also has their own **intra-individual** distribution. These distributions are depicted with a vertical bell-shaped curve (although, arguably, the shape of the curves may vary between individuals as well). Here we see that, under some circumstances, Elizabeth's wisdom may be quite similar to if not greater than Aram's. What could such circumstances be? First, as we have already learned, Elizabeth may be in a situation involving family and friends, whereas Aram may be on his own. Or, as we shall learn below, the perception of the situation may have prompted Elizabeth to express greater wisdom than Aram. This view of wisdom as consisting of a distribution of characteristics is not unique to wisdom. As William Fleeson and Eranda Jayawickreme have shown (Fleeson & Jayawickreme, 2015), it is prevalent for most individual characteristics in psychology. As Figure 5.2 shows, situation-specific responses reflect individual behavior in a particular moment. A person's distribution of such behaviors, across situations and over time, shows the typical frequency with which that individual is at each level of their own continuum. At the same time, one can also average a single person's responses to understand their average tendency. The distribution of these average tendencies would indicate the variability in dispositions between individuals.

From this perspective, a person has an overall tendency to think and act wisely (i.e., their disposition). Yet this same person can vary in their wisdom from one situation to the next, thereby accounting for the findings of both consistency and variability in wisdom that we have seen so far. This perspective makes some interesting predictions about the nature of wisdom and its measurement. For instance, we can view dispositional wisdom as a series of probabilistic and event-contingent responses captured across multiple points in a person's timeline. In other words, researchers who are interested in people's general disposition for wisdom are well advised to assess relevant characteristics across multiple domains and time points.

On the left side of Figure 5.2, you can also see how different contexts shape people's wisdom over time. Our culture affects our cognitions and social behavior, including how we approach other people (Varnum et al., 2010). Indeed, some preliminary work suggests that cultures which endorse an interdependent view of the world and relationships are more likely to express wisdom in reasoning about social conflicts compared with cultures that endorse an independent view of the world and relationships (Grossmann et al., 2012). Furthermore, our experiences in the ecological context, including safety and resources available, may be associated with different propensities to show wisdom during reflection on interpersonal challenges (Brienza & Grossmann, 2017). When resources are scarce, as is the case for many less educated, lower-income individuals, wisdom-related strategies conducive to cooperation and planning for navigating an uncertain environment may be adaptive. Consistent with this idea, some research shows that blue-collar, less educated individuals are more likely to show wisdom in reflection on interpersonal conflicts compared with white-collar, college-educated individuals in the USA (Brienza & Grossmann, 2017). In short, wisdom appears to be greatly shaped by our culture, our experiences, and the ways in which we understand the situations that are unfolding in front of our eyes.

5.6   Mismeasurement of Wisdom and the Objectivity Illusion

Insights from the debate about the dispositional stability versus contextual variability of wisdom have substantial implications for **reliability** of measurement. Reliability is a psychometric concept that refers to the overall consistency of the measure, such that high reliability would lead to comparable results under consistent conditions. If wisdom were stable, this could make it unnecessary to measure wisdom repeatedly. Understanding the features of a context in which wisdom is measured would not matter much either. Instead, context would be just noise in the data – something to be avoided. From an essentialist perspective, it seemed methodologically prudent and cost-effective to rely on abstract and decontextualized evaluations of wisdom. Indeed, many scholars pursued this approach. Unfortunately, as the empirical evidence reviewed above shows, a purely essentialist perspective is not supported by the data. Moreover, according to the systematic perspective depicted in Figure 5.2, wisdom cannot be truly separated from contextual considerations.

Measuring wisdom in a decontextualized fashion is problematic for a set of other reasons. Consider a tweet from a former US president, Donald Trump, from December 25, 2013: "The new Pope is a humble man, very much like me, which probably explains why I like him so much!" Is Donald Trump justified in his self-assessment when he claims to be as humble as the Pope? Arguably, past evidence of his behavior paints an opposite picture. The tweet from the former US president seems ironic. Unfortunately, there is nothing ironic about abstract self-report measures devised from the dispositional approach to wisdom, many of which suffer from similar problems to Donald Trump's claim about his humility. Many wisdom measures start by asking participants about their humility, appreciation of humor, empathy, or open-mindedness. As Trump's response shows, such an approach can be misleading. Are people who claim to be especially humble or empathetic paragons of wisdom? Or are they just trying to present themselves in the most favorable light to impress others? Or are they mostly deceiving themselves? It is impossible to know for sure, though there is accumulating evidence which suggests that the latter two possibilities are quite likely (Glück, 2018; also see Chapter 6 in this textbook).

In fact, empirical research shows that people who report higher scores on global self-report measures of wisdom are prone to self-deception and **impression management** (Brienza et al., 2018; Taylor et al., 2011). Such abstract self-evaluations take a heavy toll on participants. Even if one were not interested in impressing others, one might still not be able to help deceiving oneself or being prone to **memory biases** in self-evaluations. Imagine that a researcher asks you about your humility. To provide an accurate answer to their question, you would have to dive deep into your personal history and how you view yourself. This is not an easy task. To have a reliable assessment of our humility, we would have to spend a great deal of time pondering this question – something that we don't do very often. After reading the insights from this chapter, you may be tempted to think of a past concrete instance in which you did or did not show much humility, to anchor your self-assessment. Yet this approach is problematic, too. When searching through your memory for instances of exemplary behavior (or its absence), you are more likely to consider the most vivid experiences – those that stayed in your mind. Unfortunately, such experiences are rarely typical of our everyday life. Our memory is biased in such a way that we are more likely to recall the most vivid experiences, ones that are usually atypical of our everyday life (and hence remain vivid in our memory), whereas mundane experiences are often forgotten. Unfortunately, it is the mundane experiences that make up most of our life. Therefore, even when you use concrete past events as a basis for your self-assessment, you may end up providing a distorted view of yourself.

What is worse, you may end up believing this distorted self-view! And you would not be alone. We are all tempted by **naive realism** – that is, an illusory idea that the world is what we perceive it to be. Naive physics often does not correspond to the actual physical forces. For instance, do you think the perception of a solid surface from the chair or sofa you are sitting on right now really reflects the pressure of the chair's atoms against your atoms? It is not really the case. In fact, unless your body defies the laws of physics, you are levitating one hundred millionth of a centimeter above the chair, with negatively charged fields of the electrons from the chair and your body repelling each other (Ross, 2018). In other words, our subjective perspection of the world takes numerous detours on the way to our consciousness. Most of the time, we don't realize this, instead relying on the assumption that our perception of the world is objective – often a useful and efficient heuristic when processing a huge load of consciously, and unconsciously, appearing information. Nevertheless, this **objectivity illusion** (Griffin & Ross, 1991; Ross, 2018) plays a fundamental role in our view of ourselves and the way in which we perceive others. Assuming that our memory is an unbiased representation of who we are, we may be tempted to view ourselves as humble if we are recalling an extraordinary event in which we exercised some humility. Perhaps, when Donald Trump tweeted about comparing himself to Pope Francis, he might have had some examples of humility in his mind. Although some of you may be tempted to discount Trump's humility and wisdom due to a range of scenarios in which he apparently showed little of either, don't forget that, for each of us, wisdom is not equally present across all of the situations we experience – rather, it follows a distribution, as depicted in Figure 5.2. Moreover, who is to say that our memory is not distorted when we bring examples of Trump's folly to mind?

5.7   Toward Better Measurement

Systematic variability in wisdom within each person across situations and over time yields a practical insight – measuring wisdom-related characteristics only once produces a poor estimate of one's wisdom. Indeed, modern standards in personality research (e.g., Fleeson & Jayawickreme, 2015) point to the benefits of measuring individual differences in a range of different contexts to evaluate one's general tendencies (or traits). According to this research, there are also some recommendations for the number of measurement points needed to reliably assess general tendencies. For instance, based on the degree of cross-situational stability in wisdom that we discussed above, one would need at least *three* measurement points to obtain a reliable estimate of one's average tendency.

The situational approach to measuring wisdom is not without limitations. Typically, it relies on human coders, who score wisdom in reflections that participants provide in response to hypothetical situations (e.g., Baltes & Smith, 2008; Grossmann et al., 2013) or specific autobiographical experiences (Glück et al., 2005; Weststrate & Glück, 2016). Such human-coded scores are often impractical, introducing a substantial burden for researchers, as usually one needs at least two observers to rate the same reflections, and one must also ensure that they are reliable and unbiased in their scoring. Consequently, this method is not easy to scale up to large-scale investigations across many domains. Moreover, human-coded measures of wisdom usually rely on participants providing stream-of-thought reflections on challenging issues. Although this approach works well when reflecting on hypothetical scenarios in the laboratory, it may not be feasible or ethical when examining acute challenges that people may be facing in their lives. Thus, although the situational approach avoids some of the major issues common to abstract self-report measures, it is not a panacea. It has limited reach when one aims to obtain an **ecologically valid** estimate of a person's wisdom across many situations in everyday life.

To bridge these limitations, Justin Brienza and I recently proposed a compromise solution – the Situated Wise Reasoning Scale (SWIS; Brienza et al., 2018). To avoid the biases associated with decontextualized self-reports, we used recent advances in survey methods concerning event reconstruction (Schwarz et al., 2009). Participants first recalled a recent challenge that they had experienced, bringing to mind when, where, at what time, and with whom this event occurred. They then recalled thoughts and feelings that came into their mind during the experience. Finally, they answered a set of questions designed to assess wisdom-related characteristics (for further details, see Chapter 6). This method allows the investigators to measure multiple situations at the same time, and it is also unrelated or inversely related to a wide range of social and **cognitive biases**, unlike abstract self-report measures for assessing wisdom (Brienza et al., 2018). However, like any self-report measure, it may still be subject to some of the biases and illusions, albeit to a smaller degree than the abstract measures discussed above.

5.8   Boosting and Training Wisdom

One of the most exciting implications of cross-situational variability in wisdom is that we can possibly shape situations to our benefit. Here the insight about relative lower wisdom when dealing with personal rather than other people's issues appears troublesome. In many domains of our lives, we cannot always defer decisions to someone else, so what should we do? As we discussed earlier when introducing the idea of naive realism in perception of reality, people tend to subjectively represent and construct the events that they encounter (Griffin & Ross, 1991). The notion of **subjective construal** can possibly help to shed light on the difference in wisdom when one is reflecting on person- and non-person-centric situations. Ethan Kross and I reasoned that wisdom appeared to be heightened during reflection on non-personal challenges because of a particular vantage point that one adopts when construing other people's dilemmas compared with one's personal problems. When thinking about others, we often take the perspective of an impartial third-person observer of events from afar. In contrast, when we reflect on personal issues we typically do so from an immersed, first-person perspective. If this difference in vantage point is elemental for the self–other asymmetry in manifest wisdom, it may be possible to boost wisdom in reflection on personal issues by construing personal situations as a hypothetical "impartial observer."

We first sought to test this idea in the context of job prospects at the peak of the "great recession" in the USA, asking college seniors, none of whom had a secured job at this point, to consider their future career prospects (Kross & Grossmann, 2012). Participants were randomly assigned to two conditions. In one condition, we instructed participants to reflect on their job prospects from the perspective of a "distant observer," envisioning the situation unfolding from afar. In the control condition, seniors envisioned the situation unfolding before their own eyes. We found that, compared with the control group, the "distant-observer" instructions prompted greater wisdom – that is, greater recognition of the limits of their knowledge, and consideration of how things might unfold and change. In a follow-up set of experiments, we obtained equivalent results when instructing participants to reflect on a polarized political issue at the peak of the 2008 US presidential election (Kross & Grossmann, 2012), trust and infidelity conflicts (Grossmann & Kross, 2014), and personal *autobiographical experiences* – that is, recent unresolved conflicts that people had experienced in their own lives (Grossmann et al., 2019; Huynh et al., 2016). In each case, linguistic and temporal prompts that promoted a distant-observer vantage point (e.g., by using third-person language, "he"/"she," or the perspective of "one year from now") fostered wisdom (recognition of the limits of one's knowledge and recognition of change) in reflections on hypothetical and autobiographical issues compared with prompts that promoted an immersed vantage point (e.g., by using first-person language, "me"/"mine," or the perspective of "here and now"). Moreover, using this manipulation, we were able to attenuate the self–other asymmetry discussed above. That is, the observer vantage point led to greater wisdom both about personal problems and about a friend's problems, thereby reducing self–other asymmetry (Grossmann & Kross, 2014; studies 2–3). It appears that experimental instructions altered the perception of the situation from being exclusively self-focused to considering the viewpoints of the other individuals involved, in turn recreating wisdom-enhancing contexts in one's mind. Overall, it appears that a wide range of construal-altering instructions (see Figure 5.3) increase participants' ability to apply central features of wisdom in hypothetical and real-world situations, in the context of both interpersonal and intergroup conflicts.

Can the distanced-observer construal be *trained* to promote changes in wisdom over time? Building on the insights from the contextual view of wisdom, my colleagues and I decided to address this question (Grossmann et al., 2021). Given that people experience a range of issues in their lives, we reasoned that an effective shift in subjective construal toward the vantage point of an impartial observer requires repeated practice of wisdom-enhancing strategies over time. In turn, practice-driven shifts in subjective construal should promote greater wisdom after the

Figure 5.3   Factors that promote wisdom (adapted from Santos et al., 2017), based on experimental insights showing effective boosts in wisdom in the laboratory and in people's daily lives.

Figure 5.4   Training effects on shifts in wisdom, when examining reflections before and after the intervention. For several single features of wisdom (intellectual humility, consideration of diverse perspectives, search for compromise, and conflict resolution), and for the average wisdom score (left), participants in the third-person training (but not the control) condition showed growth in wisdom over a period of 1 month. Estimates show means and 95 percent confidence intervals.

practice. We tested this idea in a set of **randomized control trial (RCT)** intervention studies. In each study, participants reflected on their interpersonal conflicts twice – before and after the intervention – and we then analyzed their reflections for the presence of wisdom-related themes. In between these measurement points, participants were randomly assigned to the third-person intervention condition or the first-person control condition (in the second study we also added a no-instruction control condition). In each condition, participants were instructed to keep a diary, each day writing a short reflection on the most significant (positive or negative) issue of the day. Based on the earlier experimental work, in the intervention condition, participants had to write the diary using third-person language, reflecting on the event from an observer's perspective. In the control condition(s), participants wrote their diary in first-person language, as one would typically do when keeping a diary. Figure 5.4 shows the results we obtained in the first study, which demonstrate that this 1-month intervention had an impact on a range of features of wisdom, resulting in post-intervention growth in wisdom in the third-person condition compared with the control condition. These results were statistically accounted for by a shift toward more inclusive subjective construal of the interpersonal conflicts that participants reflected on in the experimental conditions. These training results are preliminary, and require further replication and extension to other cultures. Nonetheless, they are encouraging, for the first time providing empirical support from RCTs for training-based shifts in wisdom over time.

Is wisdom dispositional or situational? As we have learned in this chapter, it is a bit of both. By paying attention to the contextual factors and being mindful of the cultural, situational, and subjective experiential forces that exert an influence on people's behavior, we can both improve measurement and start to develop evidence-based wisdom interventions. By measuring these contextual factors as part of a person's behavioral profile of wisdom across different situations, we can also obtain a richer picture of that person's wise dispositions.

5.9   Comprehension and Discussion Questions

(1)   What are the key differences between essentialist and constructivist views? How are they supported by current research?
(2)   What are some of the issues with modern wisdom measurements, in terms of dispositional versus situational approaches to wisdom?
(3)   What are the potential implications of wisdom research for everyday life? Is wisdom trainable?
(4)   Can you think of an instance where someone acted with uncharacteristic wisdom? What did they do, and why was it particularly wise of them to do this in that particular situation?
(5)   How do you think your wisdom has been fluctuating over time? Do you notice any changes when you compare your wisdom today with how you were a few years ago?
(6)   Discuss examples of naive realism in real life. How does it affect your perception of other people and of yourself?

5.10   Investigations

Igor Grossmann studies people and cultures, sometimes together, and often across time. His interests span multiple disciplines and methods, including big data, intensive longitudinal surveys, and behavioral experiments to target complex societal issues. His chief work aims to uncover cultural and psychological processes that enable people to think and act wisely. Beyond introducing experimental, intensive longitudinal, and psychological network methods to the study of wisdom-related characteristics, he has led several community initiatives in the field aiming to uncover the "jingle-jangle" fallacies in wisdom science, guiding the academic community toward a shared, clearly specified language with which to characterize wisdom's central features as a foundation for the growing field. Most recently, his program of research has also included exploration of the core features of sound judgment, including how the concept of wisdom differs from related concepts in other disciplines, such as the notion of rational judgment, as well as the relationship between wisdom and foresight in the geopolitical and societal realm to better understand the world after the COVID-19 pandemic.

5.11   Practical Applications

The insights featured in this chaper directly emphasize the role of studying wisdom in the context of real-world events that people experience in their lives, including trust and infidelity transgressions in interpersonal relationships, political polarization and intergroup conflicts. Insights from the experimental work on variability in wisdom across social contexts has implications for designing and choosing environments in a way that can promote greater wisdom. Insights from the initial training work suggest an evidence-based path toward cultivation of wisdom in everyday life. And at the broadest level, insights about subjective construal of the situations and our self views can help us to be more critical of our beliefs versus the beliefs of other people with whom we disagree.

Glossary

cognitive bias in thinking, systematic as opposed to random error when processing and interpreting information in one's world that affects the decisions and judgments one makes.

constructivist perspective the assumption that wisdom, like many other psychological processes, is filtered through subjective experience and interpretation of reality.

dispositional referring to a natural tendency of character or habit to act in a specified way.

ecologically valid the extent to which a measure or observation can be generalized to real-life situations.

empathetic understanding, being aware of and sensitive to, and vicariously experiencing the feelings, thoughts, and experiences of another person or group of people.

essentialism a philosophical belief about the nature of the world that views personal characteristics such as wisdom as natural kinds, easily distinguishable and heritable, and uniform in structure and composition.

exemplar of wisdom any remarkable and unique individual, sage, political leader, or social activist, in folklore or in the popular media, who is viewed as an ideal model of widsom.

folk psychology intuitive understanding of psychology, especially the attribution of mental states, by everyday people without formal training in relevant academic fields of science.

impression management a process in which people aim to influence the perceptions of other people about themselves by regulating and controlling information during social interactions.

intellectual humility recognition of the limits of one's knowledge and one's fallibility.

inter-individual referring to the comparison of (psychological) processes or characteristics between people.

intra-individual referring to the comparison of (psychological) processes or characteristics within the same person, across different situations or over time.

memory bias a cognitive bias that either impairs or enhances memory recall, or that alters the content of a reported memory.

naive realism the illusory idea that the world is what we perceive it to be through our senses.

natural kind a philosophical position, according to which linguistic terms used to communicate ideas about the world reflect the structure of the natural world (e.g., a position that common terms used in the English language to describe emotions reflect the fundamental emotional facets that humans in all cultures as well as non-human animals share).

objectivity Illusion an illusion of personal objectivity, which follows from naive realism. It is the view that one's perceptions are realistic and "objective," and that other people should share them. It applies to perception of objects, events, beliefs, preferences, and feelings.

Pearson's correlation coefficient a statistical measure of the strength of a relationship between two variables (or of one variable over time).

public goods game in experimental economics, a standard game in which participants secretly choose how many of their private tokens to put into the public pot. Each person keeps the tokens they do not contribute plus an even split of the tokens in the pot (researchers running the game multiply the number of tokens in the pot before it is distributed, to encourage contribution).

randomized control trial (RCT) a type of scientific experiment that aims to reduce certain sources of bias when testing the effectiveness of treatments by randomly allocating subjects to two or more groups, treating them differently, and then comparing them with respect to a measured response.

reliability a psychometric concept, referring to overall consistency of the measure, such that high reliability would lead to similar results under consistent conditions.

situational referring to an approach to studying wisdom in which attention is paid to the expression of wisdom in specific situations.

stability the extent to which a given psychological characteristic remains the same across different situations or over time. It can be assessed by examining interindividual differences in a trait (rank-order stability), or the stability of one's profile.

subjective construal the idea that people are governed by their own subjective representations and constructions of the events that unfold around them.

trait any characteristic that is studied within the dispositional approach to the study of individual differences in psychology, reflecting habitual patterns of behavior, thoughts, and feelings.

variability the extent to which a distribution is stretched or squeezed, showing the distribution of a certain characteristic relative to the central tendency.

variance a statistical term that refers to a way of measuring the typical squared distance of responses from the sample mean.

REFERENCES

Ardelt, M. (2003). Empirical assessment of a three-dimensional wisdom scale. *Research on Aging*, 25(3), 275–324.

Baltes, P. B. and Smith, J. (2008). The fascination of wisdom: its nature, ontogeny, and function. *Perspectives on Psychological Science*, 3(1), 56–64.

Bangen, K. J., Meeks, T. W., and Jeste, D. V. (2013). Defining and assessing wisdom: a review of the literature. *The American Journal of Geriatric Psychiatry*, 21(12), 1254–66.

Brienza, J. P. and Grossmann, I. (2017). Social class and wise reasoning about interpersonal conflicts across regions, persons and situations. *Proceedings of the Royal Society B: Biological Sciences*, 284(1869), 20171870.

Brienza, J. P., Kung, F. Y. H., Santos, H. C., Bobocel, D. R. R., and Grossmann, I. (2018). Wisdom, bias, and balance: toward a process-sensitive measurement of wisdom-related cognition. *Journal of Personality and Social Psychology*, 115(6), 1093–126.

Dorfman, A., Moscovitch, D. A., Chopik, W. J., and Grossmann, I. (2021). None the wiser: year-long longitudinal study on effects of adversity on wisdom. *European Journal of Personality*. DOI:10.1177/08902070211014057

Fleeson, W. (2001). Towards a structure and process integrated view of personality: traits as density distributions of state. *Journal of Personality and Social Psychology*, 80(6), 1011–27.

Fleeson, W. and Gallagher, P. (2009). The implications of Big Five standing for the distribution of trait manifestation in behavior: fifteen experience-sampling studies and a meta-analysis. *Journal of Personality and Social Psychology*, 97(6), 1097–114.

Fleeson, W. and Jayawickreme, E. (2015). Whole trait theory. *Journal of Research in Personality*, 56, 82–92.

Glück, J. (2018). Measuring wisdom: existing approaches, continuing challenges, and new developments. *The Journals of Gerontology, Series B: Psychological Sciences*, 73(8), 1393–403.

Glück, J., Bluck, S., Baron, J., and McAdams, D. P. (2005). The wisdom of experience: autobiographical narratives across adulthood. *International Journal of Behavioral Development*, 29(3), 197–208.

Griffin, D. W. and Ross, L. (1991). Subjective construal, social inference, and human misunderstanding. In *Advances in Experimental Social Psychology*, 24, 319–59.

Grossmann, I. (2017a). Wisdom in context. *Perspectives on Psychological Science*, 12(2), 233–57.

(2017b). Wisdom and how to cultivate it. *European Psychologist*, 22(4), 233–46.

Grossmann, I. and Kross, E. (2014). Exploring Solomon's paradox: self-distancing eliminates the self-other asymmetry in wise reasoning about close relationships in younger and older adults. *Psychological Science*, 25(8), 1571–80.

Grossmann, I., Karasawa, M., Izumi, S. et al. (2012). Aging and wisdom: culture matters. *Psychological Science*, 23(10), 1059–66.

Grossmann, I., Na, J., Varnum, M. E. W., Kitayama, S., and Nisbett, R. E. (2013). A route to well-being: intelligence versus wise reasoning. *Journal of Experimental Psychology: General*, 142(3), 944–53.

Grossmann, I., Gerlach, T. M., and Denissen, J. J. A. (2016). Wise reasoning in the face of everyday life challenges. *Social Psychological and Personality Science*, 7(7), 611–22.

Grossmann, I., Brienza, J. P., and Bobocel, D. R. (2017). Wise deliberation sustains cooperation. *Nature Human Behaviour*, 1(3), 0061.

Grossmann, I., Oakes, H., and Santos, H. C. (2019). Wise reasoning benefits from emodiversity, irrespective of emotional intensity. *Journal of Experimental Psychology: General*, 148(5), 805–23.

Grossmann, I., Weststrate, N. M., Ardelt, M. et al. (2020). The science of wisdom in a polarized world: knowns and unknowns. *Psychological Inquiry*, 31(2), 103–33.

Grossmann, I., Dorfman, A., Oakes, H. et al. (2021). Training for wisdom: the distanced-self-reflection diary method. *Psychological Science*, 32(3), 381–94.

Haslam, N., Bastian, B., and Bissett, M. (2004). Essentialist beliefs about personality and their implications. *Personality and Social Psychology Bulletin*, 30(12), 1661–73.

Huynh, A. C., Yang, D. Y.-J., and Grossmann, I. (2016). The value of prospective reasoning for close relationships. *Social Psychological and Personality Science*, 7(8), 893–902.

Kristjánsson, K. (2013). *Virtues and Vices in Positive Psychology: A Philosophical Critique*. Cambridge University Press.

Kross, E. and Grossmann, I. (2012). Boosting wisdom: distance from the self enhances wise reasoning, attitudes, and behavior. *Journal of Experimental Psychology: General*, 141(1), 43–48.

Levenson, M. R., Jennings, P. A., Aldwin, C. M., and Shiraishi, R. W. (2005). Self-transcendence: conceptualization and measurement. *The International Journal of Aging and Human Development*, 60(2), 127–43.

Parker, K. I. (1992). Solomon as philosopher king? The nexus of law and wisdom in 1 Kings 1-11. *Journal for the Study of the Old Testament*, 17(53), 75–91.

Ross, L. (2018). From the fundamental attribution error to the truly fundamental attribution error and beyond: my research journey. *Perspectives on Psychological Science*, 13(6), 750–69.

Santos, H. C., Huynh, A. C., and Grossmann, I. (2017). Wisdom in a complex world: a situated account of wise reasoning and its development. *Social and Personality Psychology Compass*, 11(10), Article e12341.

Schwarz, N., Kahneman, D., and Xu, J. (2009). Global and episodic reports of hedonic experience. In R. Bell, F. Stafford and D. Alwin, eds., *Calendar and Time Diary: Methods in Life Course Research*. Sage Publishing, pp. 157–74.

Staudinger, U. M. (2013). The need to distinguish personal from general wisdom: a short history and empirical evidence. In *The Scientific Study of Personal Wisdom*. Springer, pp. 3–19.

Staudinger, U. M. and Baltes, P. B. (1996). Interactive minds: a facilitative setting for wisdom-related performance? *Journal of Personality and Social Psychology*, 71(4), 746–62.

Taylor, M., Bates, G., and Webster, J. D. (2011). Comparing the psychometric properties of two measures of wisdom: predicting forgiveness and psychological well-being with the Self-Assessed Wisdom Scale (SAWS) and the Three-Dimensional Wisdom Scale (3D-WS). *Experimental Aging Research*, 37(2), 129–41.

Thomas, M. L., Bangen, K. J., Palmer, B. W. et al. (2019). A new scale for assessing wisdom based on common domains and a neurobiological model: the San Diego Wisdom Scale (SD-WISE). *Journal of Psychiatric Research*, 108, 40–47.

Varnum, M. E. W., Grossmann, I., Kitayama, S., and Nisbett, R. E. (2010). The origin of cultural differences in cognition: evidence for the social orientation hypothesis. *Current Directions in Psychological Science*, 19(1), 9–13.

Webster, J. D. (2003). An exploratory analysis of a self-assessed wisdom scale. *Journal of Adult Development*, 10(1), 13–22.

(2007). Measuring the character strength of wisdom. *The International Journal of Aging and Human Development*, 65(2), 163–83.

Weststrate, N. M. and Glück, J. (2016). Wiser but not sadder, blissful but not ignorant: exploring the co-development of wisdom and well-being over time. In M. Robinson and M. Eid, eds., *The Happy Mind: Cognitive Contributions to Well-Being*. Springer International Publishing/Springer Nature, pp. 459–80.

(2017). Hard-earned wisdom: exploratory processing of difficult life experience is positively associated with wisdom. *Developmental Psychology*, 53(4), 800–14.

Weststrate, N. M., Ferrari, M., and Ardelt, M. (2016). The many faces of wisdom: an investigation of cultural-historical wisdom exemplars reveals practical, philosophical, and benevolent prototypes. *Personality and Social Psychology Bulletin*, 42(5), 662–76.

CHAPTER 6

Measurement of Wisdom

Judith Glück[1]

6.1 Introduction

As psychologists, we consider it important to test our hypotheses about concepts such as wisdom empirically – that is, we run studies that assess people's wisdom and analyze how it relates to other variables, such as age or intelligence. To study wisdom empirically, we need to devise good ways to **measure** it. Take a few minutes to think about how you would measure wisdom. If someone gave you money to develop a wisdom test, what might it look like?

Ever since psychologists began to study wisdom empirically, the question of how best to measure it has been under debate. We still do not have the perfect measure, but there are some promising approaches. This chapter will take you on a hands-on sightseeing tour of the current ways in which we can measure wisdom. You will get to try out the various approaches and form your own opinion about which approach works best.

Most wisdom measures fall into one of two groups: **self-report scales** and **performance measures**. Self-report tests build on how we typically measure personality – participants indicate how much they agree or disagree with statements (so-called "items") about themselves. Performance measures build on how we usually measure abilities – participants are asked to come up with solutions to life problems. We shall look at examples of both groups in turn.

6.2 Self-Report Wisdom Scales

As a first step, you may want to take a short self-report test. Please indicate your response to each of the items in Box 6.1, using a scale from 1 (= "disagree completely") to 5 (= "agree completely").

This scale is called the Brief Wisdom Screening Scale (BWSS; Glück et al., 2013). It consists of those items from three popular wisdom scales that were most strongly related to a "common factor" across the scales. Table 6.1 describes the three wisdom scales on which the BWSS is based (see also Webster, 2019). Each scale is based on one of the definitions of wisdom that were discussed in Chapter 4.

As you probably noticed, for most of the statements in Box 6.1, agreeing more strongly corresponds to greater wisdom. For statements 10, 15, and 20, the reverse is true, and agreeing more strongly corresponds to less wisdom. Therefore, to compute your "wisdom score," you first need to reverse your responses to these three statements ($1 \rightarrow 5$, $2 \rightarrow 4$, $3 = 3$, $4 \rightarrow 2$, $5 \rightarrow 1$). Next, compute the sum across all your responses, which should be a number between 21 and 105.

---

[1] Portions of this chapter draw on ideas expressed in Sternberg, R. J. and Glück, J. (2022). *Wisdom: The Psychology of Wise Thoughts, Words, and Deeds*. Cambridge University Press.

Table 6.1 *The three most popular self-report measures of wisdom*

Measure/authors	Wisdom definition	Subscales	Sample items	Correlates
Adult Self-Transcendence Inventory (ASTI) (Levenson, Jennings, Aldwin, & Shiraishi, 2005; Koller, Levenson, & Glück, 2017)	Self-transcendence: independence from external self-definitions and dissolution of rigid boundaries between the self and others	Total sum score across five subscales (Koller et al., 2017): (1) Self-knowledge and self-integration (2) Non-attachment (3) Presence in the here and now and growth (4) Self-transcendence (5) Peace of mind	35 items, e.g., "I can learn a lot from others." "My peace of mind is not easily upset." "I feel that my individual life is part of a greater whole."	Openness to experience, personal growth, self-acceptance, emotional competence, extraversion, empathy, meditation practice, egalitarianism (Glück et al., 2013; Le & Levenson, 2005; Levenson et al., 2005)
Self-Assessed Wisdom Scale (SAWS) (Webster, 2007)	"the competence in, intention to, and application of, critical life experiences to facilitate the optimal development of self and others" (Webster, 2007, p. 164)	(1) Critical life experience (2) Openness (3) Emotional regulation (4) Reminiscence and reflectiveness (5) Humor	40 items, e.g.: "I have had to make many important life decisions." "I can regulate my emotions when the situation calls for it." "I can chuckle at personal embarrassments."	Openness to experience, personal growth, emotional competence, self-efficacy, ego integrity, forgiveness, personal wellbeing, empathy, generativity, and positive psychosocial values (Glück et al., 2013; Taylor et al., 2011; Webster, 2003, 2007, 2010)
Three-Dimensional Wisdom Scale (3D-WS) (Ardelt, 2003)	Wisdom as a combination of personality traits that enable individuals to take others' perspectives and overcome biases and blind spots, learn from life, and care for others	(1) Cognitive dimension (2) Reflective dimension (3) Compassionate dimension	39 items, e.g.: "Things often go wrong for me by no fault of my own" (reverse-coded "Sometimes I feel a real compassion for everyone" "Ignorance is bliss" (reverse-coded)	Openness to experience, personal growth, emotional competence, empathy, mastery, purpose in life, forgiveness, wellbeing (Ardelt, 2003, 2011; Glück et al., 2013)

Source: Adapted from Glück & Weststrate, unpublished review article.

Box 6.1 A self-report wisdom scale.

(1) My peace of mind is not easily upset. *Response:* ....
(2) I have a good sense of humor about myself. *Response:* ....
(3) I have dealt with a great many different kinds of people during my lifetime. *Response:* ....
(4) I have learned valuable life lessons from others. *Response:* ....
(5) At this point in my life, I find it easy to laugh at my mistakes. *Response:* ....
(6) My happiness is not dependent on other people and things. *Response:* ....
(7) I can accept the impermanence of things. *Response:* ....
(8) I like to read books which challenge me to think differently about issues. *Response:* ....
(9) I am "tuned in" to my own emotions. *Response:* ....
(10) I either get very angry or depressed if things go wrong. *Response:* ....
(11) I am able to integrate the different aspects of my life. *Response:* ....
(12) I often have a sense of oneness with nature. *Response:* ....
(13) It seems I have a talent for reading other people's emotions. *Response:* ....
(14) I feel that my individual life is a part of a greater whole. *Response:* ....
(15) There are some people I know I would never like. *Response:* ....
(16) I have grown as a result of losses I have suffered. *Response:* ....
(17) I can freely express my emotions without feeling like I might lose control. *Response:* ....
(18) I am very curious about other religious and/or philosophical belief systems. *Response:* ....
(19) I don't worry about other people's opinions of me. *Response:* ....
(20) Sometimes I get so charged up emotionally that I am unable to consider all ways of dealing with my problems. *Response:* ....
(21) I always try to look at all sides of a problem. *Response:* ....

Divide the sum by 21, and you have your average. The maximum possible average would obviously be 5, which would indicate extremely high wisdom. Or would it? What do you think? Is a person who scores a 5 on this test guaranteed to be extremely wise?

It seems a bit too easy, doesn't it? If this test were to be used to select job applicants, most candidates would probably figure out how to present themselves as very wise. Few would admit, even if it were true, that they have difficulty laughing about themselves, that their happiness is strongly dependent on other people, or that they sometimes do not look at all sides of a problem. Here are four reasons why self-report scales may not be the best possible approach to measuring wisdom.

6.2.1 Fakeability

Look over the items of the BWSS again, but this time imagine that you are applying for a position as a community's resident sage and trying to make yourself look as wise as possible. You'd probably come out well at the top, right? The measure becomes less one of wisdom than one of the ability to guess what counts as a wise response. In other words, people can intentionally distort their scores in self-report scales to present themselves in the most positive way.

6.2.2 The Self-Reflection Paradox

Perhaps then we should not use the BWSS to select resident sages, but we might still use it, for example, in a study. Study participants would have no incentive to fake wisdom, so they would respond accurately, right? If you want to, go over the BWSS one more time, this time trying to channel the wisest person you know. How would that person respond to the items? Would they really give themselves a 5 on every single statement? Probably they would not. Wise people tend to be more critical of themselves than other people are. Very wise people might know that they have quite a good sense of humor about themselves, but they know people who are even funnier. A wise person might feel that they can accept the impermanence of things most of the time, but sometimes they just want to hold on to a good moment. A wise person might actually have a talent for reading people's emotions, but they also know how easily one can misinterpret facial expressions. In short, wise people might be more likely to give themselves a 4 than a 5 on some items. People who give themselves all 5s may just be a bit too self-confident to be truly wise. This creates an interesting paradox. If critical self-reflection is part of wisdom, then those who describe themselves as wisest cannot be the wisest (Aldwin, 2009; Glück, 2018).

6.2.3 Typical Situations vs. Challenging Situations

Scales like the BWSS also ask you to describe your typical state of mind. If you agree that your peace of mind is not easy to disturb or that you always try to look at all sides of a problem, your response is probably based on a kind of mental averaging across many situations in your everyday life. However, the problem with wisdom is that the situations where we need it most may be the situations where it is least accessible to us. You can try this out for yourself. Think of the last really unpleasant conflict that you had with someone who is at least moderately important to you. This could be an argument with a partner or family member, or a conflict at work or school. Think back about the experience for a few minutes, and then fill out the scale in Box 6.2. Use a response scale from 1 (= "disagree completely") to 5 (= "agree completely").

This is an abbreviated version of the Situated Wise Reasoning Scale (SWIS; Brienza et al., 2018). It was developed to account for the fact that, as was outlined in Chapter 5 of this book, wisdom varies between situations. Your score is the average across your responses. It may well be a bit lower than your score on the BWSS. This does not mean that you were lying when you filled out the BWSS. In the BWSS, you described yourself in general, whereas in the SWIS, you described yourself in one particular difficult situation. In fact, in those situations where we most need wisdom, we may be least likely to show wisdom – because we are angry, upset, stressed out and unable to access all of our wisdom-related knowledge. Measures such as the SWIS assess people's recollections of actual difficult situations. However, self-report scales can only ask people how they think or feel about problems. They cannot assess how well people actually solve problems.

Box 6.2 A self-test of situational wisdom.

While this situation was unfolding, I did the following:

(1) Made an effort to take the other person's perspective: . . . .
(2) Considered alternative solutions as the situation evolved: . . . .
(3) Thought the situation could unfold in many different ways: . . . .
(4) Double-checked whether my opinion on the situation might be incorrect: . . . .
(5) Looked for any extraordinary circumstances before forming my opinion: . . . .
(6) Tried my best to find a way to accommodate both of us: . . . .
(7) Tried to see the conflict from the point of view of an uninvolved person: . . . .

6.2.4   *Judging Our Own Abilities*

People are notoriously bad at judging their own abilities and competencies. Imagine an intelligence test that just asked people how intelligent they are – some people would grossly overestimate their intelligence, whereas others would underestimate it. After all, how could we judge how intelligent we are? We cannot compare our own inner-thinking experience with that of other people, so we cannot know whether our thinking is faster, more logical, or more complex than that of others. For this reason, self-report tests are typically used to measure personality components, attitudes, emotions, and the like – qualities of how we feel, not how we think. To test intelligence or more specific abilities and competencies, we ask participants to solve problems that require these abilities and competencies. To measure wisdom-related competencies, researchers have developed so-called performance measures of wisdom (Kunzmann, 2019). These approaches will be reviewed next.

6.3   Performance Measures of Wisdom

Box 6.3 shows another self-test. This time, it is a **closed-response problem**. Read the description of the problem and then decide which of the five responses below is the wisest.

As you have already read five chapters of this book, it is probably obvious to you that (4) is the wisest answer. (It also happens to be three times as long as the others, which is no coincidence – as wise responses consider many different aspects and perspectives, they tend to be longer than simple and bold but unwise responses.) The problem is that you possibly would have guessed correctly even if you had not read Chapters 1–5. Even a very unwise person might guess that (4) is the wisest answer. But would a very unwise person, or even you, be able to actually *act* wisely in Tessa's situation? Maybe not. Many people might recognize (4) as the wisest response, but if they were faced with a terribly jealous partner, their reaction would be (1), (2), (3), or (5). In other

---

Box 6.3 A closed-response wisdom problem.

Tessa has been dating Max for almost 2 years. She is happy with the relationship, but there is one problem – Max is terribly jealous, and his jealousy seems to be increasing. Tessa feels that she is not giving him any reason to be jealous. Recently, they had a big fight because Max did not want Tessa to go out on a "girls' night" with her friends. What could Tessa consider and do?

(1)   Tessa should just leave Max, as fast as possible. This relationship has no future.

(2)   Tessa should not go on her girls' night if it is such a problem for Max. If she really loves him, she should do that for him. She should prove to him that he can trust her.

(3)   Tessa should tell Max that if his behavior does not change, she is going to leave him. She should not tolerate his jealousy.

(4)   Tessa should not just let Max's jealousy control her life, but she should consider that it may have reasons that are not his fault. Perhaps he had a very bad experience in an earlier relationship. She should talk to him and try to understand his perspective, but she should also make sure that he understands hers. Maybe they can work out a compromise that helps Max to gain trust in her over time.

(5)   Tessa and Max are obviously very different. Either they can each develop a lot of tolerance for the other's need, or their relationship is going to be a constant battle of wills.

words, many people are able to *recognize* wisdom when they see it, but not to *produce* as much wisdom on their own.

Therefore we cannot adequately measure wisdom in the same way as we measure intelligence, assessing whether people are able to select the correct solution to a problem from a set of alternatives. Also, wisdom problems typically do not have only one correct solution. There may actually be many ways in which Tessa can approach her problem, but none of them will be perfect. The best way to measure wisdom is to use **open-ended problems**. These involve presenting people with a problem, letting them talk or write about possible solutions, and then evaluating the wisdom of their responses.

This approach was already being used in the Berlin Wisdom Paradigm, the first psychological measure of wisdom (Baltes & Smith, 1990; Baltes & Staudinger, 2000). To try it out, take a look at Box 6.4. Typically, the Berlin Wisdom Paradigm is administered as an interview. You would first get to practice speaking all your thoughts out loud, and then you would be presented with a problem and asked to speak aloud everything that comes to your mind about it. Your response would be recorded and transcribed. If you want to try it out, just write down your thoughts about the problem in Box 6.4.

Box 6.5 gives examples of a relatively wise and a relatively unwise response (Sternberg & Glück, 2022). The wise response clearly sounds wiser – and again is a lot longer – than the unwise response. But what is it exactly that makes the wise response wise? If you want, try to identify the specific statements that demonstrate wisdom.

The Berlin researchers use five criteria to evaluate the amount of wisdom in participants' responses to this type of problem:

Box 6.4 An open-ended wisdom problem.

A 15-year-old girl wants to move out of her family home immediately. What could one consider and do in such a situation?

---

(1) *Factual knowledge* indicates how much participants know about an issue – how much they seem to know about 15-year-old girls, their interests and priorities, potential reasons why they want to move out, possible alternatives, and so on. Wise individuals have a lot of factual knowledge about life.

(2) *Procedural knowledge* indicates how much participants seem to know about how to deal with such problems – what questions to ask the 15-year-old girl and her parents, how to help the family find a compromise, and so on. Wise individuals have a lot of procedural knowledge.

(3) *Value relativism* indicates whether participants take into account the fact that different people have different values, priorities, and goals. Wise individuals know and accept that other people's values and goals might be very different from their own. A wise person would never say that the girl is just wrong. They would always try to understand her perspective.

(4) *Lifespan contextualism* indicates whether participants consider how contexts – a person's life phase, life situation, and environment – influence behavior. Wise individuals would consider contextual factors that may influence the girl – maybe she has a stepfather whom she doesn't like, or her family's religious or cultural norms are at odds with those of her friends.

(5) Finally, *recognition and management of uncertainty* indicates whether participants know how uncertain and unpredictable life is. Wise individuals know how much they don't know. They would ask a lot of questions first, and even when they feel they have a pretty good understanding of the situation, they would still consider various options and possible developments. They would not just tell the parents what to do.

The wise response fulfills all of these criteria. The participant seems to know quite a lot about adolescents and ways to deal with this type of problem, acknowledges that the girl's priorities are different from those of her parents and that her current life phase is influencing how she sees the world, and considers several different options. The unwise response simply dismisses teenagers' ideas as ridiculous. The participant seems to be absolutely certain about what is right and wrong.

When you compare this approach to measuring wisdom with the self-report scales discussed earlier, what do you conclude? A very unwise person would certainly have a hard time faking a wise response to such a problem. So fakeability is not an issue here, nor is critical self-reflection – a self-reflective person would probably show more value relativism and awareness of uncertainty than a highly self-confident person. Still, using life problems to measure wisdom has two disadvantages. The first is practical, in that collecting, transcribing, and evaluating open-ended responses requires much more effort and time than just administering a self-report scale. The second problem is, again, whether a person who seems to be wise according to this measure would also be wise in real life. Suppose that a participant talks extremely wisely about the 15-year-old girl's problem. Can we be sure that they will act equally wisely if their own 15-year-old daughter wants to move out? As Ursula Staudinger and her colleagues have argued (Staudinger, 2019; see also Chapter 4), there is a big difference between how wise we are with respect to theoretical problems of fictitious characters, and how wise we are with respect to real problems of our own. The Berlin Wisdom Paradigm and similar measures assess people's ability to *think* wisely, but not necessarily their ability to *act* wisely in challenging real-life situations.

Earlier in this chapter, you filled out the Situated Wise Reasoning Scale (SWIS) with respect to a difficult situation that you have experienced. In my lab, we use a similar but open-ended

---

Box 6.5 Wise and unwise responses in the Berlin Wisdom Paradigm.

(1) WISE RESPONSE

The first question is obviously why the girl wants to move out. There could be some kind of abuse occurring in the family – there definitely are situations where she should get support in moving out of her home right away. But given that she's 15, it might also be more of an emotional problem. At this age, sometimes things may be extremely important to her that adults don't really find so important. If that seemed to be the case, I would first try to talk both to her and to her parents. It's important to understand the parents' view. Maybe it's possible to find a good compromise. Or maybe she can move out for a limited time. Often things get better, especially at that age she may see things differently soon. So it may be important to choose options that can be reversed if the circumstances or her feelings change.

(2) UNWISE RESPONSE

No way. A girl so young just can't move out. What is she even thinking? There are all kinds of dangers out there. That's just one of those ridiculous ideas that teenagers have.

approach. We assume that people's wisdom manifests itself in how they think about past experiences. As will be discussed in Chapter 11, we assume that wisdom develops because some individuals think deeply about difficult experiences, trying to understand what happened and what they can learn from it (Glück & Bluck, 2013; Glück et al., 2019; Weststrate & Glück, 2017). Therefore we interview participants about difficult events from their life and then look for indicators of wisdom in their responses. Box 6.6 shows a written version of our Life Challenge Wisdom Interview.

If you were a participant in our research, your interview would be transcribed and rated for specific wisdom criteria and developmental wisdom resources (see Chapter 11). One important difference from the SWIS is that we would not focus on what you did, thought, and felt at the time when the conflict happened – after all, you may have learned and grown since then. We would look at how you reflect on the event now. For example, maybe you did not understand your opponent's perspective when the conflict happened, but now you can see why they felt the way they did. So we look at how wisely you now reflect back on the conflict.

Box 6.7 gives an example from one of our studies (Glück, 2016; Sternberg & Glück, 2022). Again, as you read this passage, try to identify aspects of wisdom.

Box 6.6 A written version of the Life Challenge Wisdom Interview.

Take a sheet of paper and make a list of difficult conflicts you have had in your life. Then choose the most difficult conflict that fulfills the following criteria: (1) the conflict is no longer ongoing, (2) you were at least 18 years old when the conflict happened, and (3) you are willing to think back about the conflict (in our studies, you would have to be willing to be interviewed about it).

Now think back about the conflict you selected and imagine (or write down) how you would tell the story to a stranger. What was the conflict about? How did you try to resolve it at the time? How did it unfold? How did it end?

Once you have told the story, answer the following questions.

(1) What were your dominant thoughts at the time of the conflict? How did you feel?
(2) What do you think the other person was thinking, and how do you think they felt at the time?
(3) How do you feel about the conflict now as you remember it?
(4) Do you think you took away a lesson or insight from that experience? If yes, what is it?

Box 6.7 A sample response from a conflict interview.

This participant got a new job as a manager and found that she was supposed to work with an assistant who essentially refused to work. Her first reaction was to have the woman transferred to another department. However, as she tried to do that, she *"met someone else who had worked with that woman earlier. And that person told me the story in a very different way. She said, imagine being in the situation that you are just not good at your work. That was a completely new thought for me; I was totally a rising star at the time! Imagine, she said, what it would feel like to be unable to do things on the computer that everyone else knows how to do; everyone else constantly lets you feel how annoying it is when you ask them for help. And that got me thinking. Maybe it was not, or not only, that woman who was acting weird. Maybe she was in a weird situation, too. I was coming in as the new superstar boss, and she was scared of me and just didn't know what to do."*

In our view, this passage shows several indicators of wisdom.

(1) First, the participant clearly shows *contextualism:* she understands how the co-worker's behavior was not a result of "bad" personality characteristics such as laziness or disloyalty, but that it was a result of her situation – of being faced with tasks that she just knew she was not good at.

(2) In fact, this was an actual *insight* that the participant gained from the situation. Later in the interview, she explained that beyond the fact that she was able to resolve the situation by assigning the co-worker different tasks, she learned the more general lesson that people's behavior is often shaped by their situation. That insight later helped her in other challenging situations as well.

(3) The participant also clearly shows *empathy and perspective taking*, as she is able to imagine how the co-worker felt. She understands that the co-worker was feeling helpless and scared of her new boss.

(4) Finally, she demonstrates *self-reflection*. She talks about how the idea that someone might not be good at their work was totally alien to her at the time, and she imagines how she must have looked to the co-worker.

We believe that interviews about challenging experiences from participants' past can tell us a lot about their wisdom. When they talk about past conflicts, some people can clearly see the other side's perspective, understand their feelings, and reflect on their own behavior. Other people are much less wise. They might tell the story of how they quickly got rid of a co-worker who did not perform well. They might have been smarter than the participant cited above as they tricked some other department into taking on the "problem person", and they might even be more professionally successful, but we would not consider them to be wise.

Our autobiographical interviews provide us with very interesting data about wisdom in real life. However, as measures of wisdom, they pose two important problems. First, when we present people with the problem about the 15-year-old girl, all of them talk about 15-year-old girls. In our interviews, participants talk about very different problems. We have had participants whose most significant conflict was with their neighbor about felling a tree next to the boundary fence, and others for whom their acrimonious divorce was their most significant conflict. Although almost all conflicts require wisdom, the components of wisdom that they most require can be quite different. For example, the conflict with the neighbor might require some empathy, perspective taking, and tolerance, whereas the acrimonious divorce may require a lot of emotion regulation and self-reflection. We cannot compare people's levels of these wisdom components across different conflicts. To obtain some level of comparability, we would have to ask participants for more than one story, perhaps setting a topic for each (a family conflict, a work- or school-related conflict, a conflict with a friend, and so on). That would make our measure extremely time-consuming.

And there is another problem. In our first interview study, just to see which approach would work better as a measure of wisdom, we asked each participant for two stories: (1) a difficult conflict, and (2) a difficult event from whatever domain they chose. As you can imagine, the second approach brought up an even wider range of stories than the first. Still, we felt that most of the stories were quite indicative of their narrators' wisdom. As we had two stories from each participant, we also had two estimates of each participant's wisdom. We were expecting a strong correlation between these two estimates – a person who talked very wisely about the conflict from their life would probably also talk very wisely about the other difficult event. However, that was not what we found. The **correlation coefficient** between the two wisdom scores was about 0.30 (Glück, 2018), which is quite low for two measures of the same thing. Some of our participants talked quite wisely about one event in their life and quite unwisely about another.

From a scientific perspective, this is quite interesting. Perhaps we are all wiser about some events from our life than about others. We talk to other people about some experiences, which may help us to gain insights from them. Other experiences may be so challenging or embarrassing that we prefer never to think about them again, until they come back to us in a wisdom interview 30 years later. If we wanted to get a representative picture of a person's wisdom, we would have to ask them to recount several different events, probably at least five, which would require hours of interviewing and days of analyzing the data. The same problem arises with the SWIS that you tried out earlier – we would have to ask each participant to recall far more than one conflict in order to get a clear picture of their wisdom (Brienza et al., 2018).

In summary, both self-report measures and performance measures of wisdom have their problems.

6.4   The Main Problems with Performance Measures

6.4.1   Time, Effort, and Costs

When you use a measure such as the Berlin Wisdom Paradigm or our autobiographical wisdom interview, you have to (1) interview the participants, sometimes at length, (2) transcribe their responses (or pay to have them transcribed), and (3) have trained raters evaluate the transcripts using wisdom criteria (ideally, there should be different raters for each criterion). You can probably imagine how much time and money this effort would require compared with administering a self-report scale. Some researchers have been experimenting with written responses and with having raters rate directly for wisdom (e.g., Zacher et al., 2015), but it is not yet clear how well this approach works.

6.4.2   Lack of Emotional Engagement (If Problems Are Pre-Defined)

When you use pre-defined wisdom problems, as in the Berlin Wisdom Paradigm, you are essentially asking participants to think about a theoretical problem faced by a fictitious person. Some people may sound very wise as they talk about those theoretical problems, but much less wise if faced with wisdom-requiring problems in their own life (Staudinger, 2019). Other participants may actually have experienced similar situations in their own life, so the problem may be much more emotional for them.

6.4.3   Lack of Comparability (If Problems Are Autobiographical)

The alternative approach is to interview people about problems from their own life. The main disadvantage of this approach is that, as mentioned earlier, participants may have had very different experiences, which may elicit quite different components of wisdom.

Some recent approaches to measuring wisdom have tried to find other ways to use the same problem for all participants, but still engage them emotionally.

6.5   Interesting New Approaches

One classical way to get people emotionally involved is to show them a video – we get much more immersed in a situation if we see and hear actual people than if we just read a brief text. Stefanie Thomas and Ute Kunzmann used videos of young real-life couples talking about real-life problems in their real-life relationships (Thomas & Kunzmann, 2014). They found that their participants, especially the young ones, became more emotionally involved by watching the videos than by reading two lines about a fictitious 15-year-old. To evaluate the participants' responses, they used the criteria of the Berlin Wisdom Model. The results revealed that young participants actually showed more wisdom than older participants, probably because the relationship problems discussed in the videos were more relevant to them.

Chao Hu and his colleagues used a different method to engage participants emotionally (Hu et al., 2017). They presented them with a wisdom problem and asked them to imagine that someone they knew was faced with that problem and they were giving advice to that person. The participants were told to talk into a camera, imagining that the camera was the advice seeker. This approach still has room for improvement (it would probably feel more natural to talk to a person instead of a camera), but you can probably imagine the difference between talking about an imaginary person's life crisis and talking to a friend going through a life crisis. Another interesting feature of this study is that the videos of the participants giving advice were coded using software that identifies emotional expressions. Such data, in combination with ratings of the actual content of the participants' responses, may offer exciting additional information in future measures (Glück, 2018).

A third way to bring the measurement of wisdom closer to real life might be to collect **informant ratings** – to ask other people about a person's wisdom. Maybe people who know you well are the best sources of information about your wisdom. We once tried this out. Using a complicated anonymization procedure involving sealed urns, Uwe Redzanowski and I asked people from several university departments to (1) rate themselves for wisdom, (2) rate their colleagues for wisdom, and (3) fill out the Three-Dimensional Wisdom Scale. We found that a small number of people were quite unanimously rated as wise by their colleagues (Redzanowski & Glück, 2013). Interestingly, none of them rated themselves as particularly wise or scored particularly high on the Three-Dimensional Wisdom Scale. In fact, people's views of their own wisdom were completely unrelated to their colleagues' views of their wisdom. Some participants felt that they were very wise, but their colleagues disagreed with this view. Others rated themselves low, but their colleagues rated them high. We found every possible combination! At least according to this one study, either people's colleagues cannot tell how wise they are, or people aren't very good at judging their own wisdom.

If you think about the different components of wisdom, it makes sense that some components would be hard to judge from the inside, whereas others may be hard to judge from the outside. If we want to find out whether a person is a wise listener or good at giving advice, we should ask other people. If we want to know whether a person is able to regulate their feelings well, no other person can really judge this. If we want to know whether a person is able to consider and balance many different viewpoints, we should just look at how the person deals with a complex problem. Some aspects of wisdom are invisible from the outside, but others, especially the abilities and competencies that wisdom involves, are difficult to judge from the inside. An optimal measure of wisdom might actually include a combination of different assessment methods.

6.6   Different Results for Different Measures

Because wisdom measures are so different, study results are somewhat dependent on the measures used. Take the relationship between wisdom and age as an example. Performance in the Berlin Wisdom Paradigm increases in adolescence and young adulthood (Pasupathi et al., 2001), but after that it seems to be largely independent of age (Staudinger, 1999), as are scores on the Adult Self-Transcendence Inventory (Glück et al., 2013). Scores on the Three-Dimensional Wisdom Scale and the Self-Assessed Wisdom Scale are highest in middle age (Ardelt et al., 2018; Webster et al., 2014). However, scores on the Situated Wise Reasoning Scale seem to be *lowest* in middle age (Brienza et al., 2018). Finally, Grossmann et al. (2010) found that scores on an open-ended wise reasoning measure actually increased with age well into participants' nineties. So the way in which wisdom is related to age depends on how we measure wisdom (you will read more about the relationship between wisdom and age in Chapter 11). Some recent studies have therefore used more than one measure of wisdom and then analyzed how consistent the results were across measures (e.g., Glück et al., 2019; Webster et al., 2018; Weststrate & Glück, 2017). These studies show that correlations with other variables tend to be higher when all variables are measured using similar methods. Self-report wisdom measures will be more highly correlated with other self-report measures, such as personality, and performance measures will be more highly correlated with other performance measures, such as intelligence. When you select a measure of wisdom for a study, it is important to consider the model of wisdom underlying each measure, so that your measure fits with your research questions. For example, if you are interested in interpersonal aspects of wisdom, you would want to use the Three-Dimensional Wisdom Scale, whereas if you are more interested in wisdom as learning from one's experiences, you would use the Self-Assessed Wisdom Scale.

There is much room for creative new measures of wisdom. Perhaps you will come up with the next step toward the perfect measure!

6.7   Comprehension and Discussion Questions

(1) Imagine that someone paid you a lot of money to develop an ultra-brief wisdom measure. It is supposed to consist of no more than three questions or items. Which questions or items would you choose to capture the essence of wisdom? If you find it hard to come up with items of your own, look at the items of the Brief Wisdom Screening Scale in Box 6.1. Which ones would you select for your ultra-brief measure?

(2) Pick three of the wisdom measures that were introduced in this chapter. For each of them, try to come up with one research question for which you would want to use this particular measure. Why is this measure particularly suited to answering this question?

(3) Explain the main problems with self-report wisdom scales using examples of your own.

(4) Explain the main problems with performance measures of wisdom using concrete examples.

(5) "Ecological validity" is the extent to which a measure of a psychological construct predicts people's behavior in real life. A good measure of wisdom should be able to predict a person's real-life wisdom. Think of a typical situation in which people need a lot of wisdom. Can you think of a way to "emulate" this situation in a psychological test or questionnaire? What could such a measure look like?

(6) Imagine that you are starting a long-term study of how wisdom develops, in which people's wisdom gets measured every year over a period of 20 years. Which measure(s) of wisdom would you use in this study? Why?

6.8   Investigations

Judith Glück's main topic of research is wisdom psychology. Having been trained in psychometrics, she has a strong interest in developing new ways to measure wisdom. She is also interested in the development of wisdom through an interplay of life experiences and internal and external resources, factors that influence wisdom in professional contexts, ways to foster wisdom through interventions and through changes in structures and systems, the relationship between wisdom and morality, and people's conceptions of wisdom in different cultures.

6.9   Practical Applications

Judith Glück's work is relevant to many areas of everyday life. Ways to foster the development and manifestation of wisdom seem very important for today's world. Although research on measuring wisdom may seem less directly relevant than applied research, we need to provide the best tools for measuring wisdom if we want to study the factors that influence whether people grow toward wisdom and display wisdom in their everyday lives.

Glossary

closed-response problem a type of problem used in tests or questionnaires where participants select one response from a given set of responses. For example, in a test of mathematical ability, participants might be presented with a math problem and five possible solutions, only one of which is correct.

correlation coefficient a number between −1 and +1 that describes how closely related two variables are in a sample of participants. A correlation coefficient of +1 means that there is a perfect positive linear relationship between the two variables – the higher people score in one variable, the higher they score in the other. A correlation coefficient of −1 means that there is a perfect negative linear relationship – the higher people score in one variable, the lower they score in the other. A correlation coefficient of zero means that there is no relationship at all – for example, if we know a person's wisdom, we cannot predict their shoe size from it. If we have two different measures of the same variable, we would expect a correlation of about 0.70 between them. A correlation of 0.30 might be found between variables that are somewhat but not closely related, such as well-being and personality.

informant ratings ratings of characteristics of people that are not collected from the people themselves but from others who are assumed to be sufficiently familiar with them.

measure in psychology, to assign numbers to people based on specific rules. IQ, for example, is a number that is supposed to describe a person's intelligence based on how many problems the person solved in an intelligence test. Psychometrics is the subdiscipline of psychology that looks at how we can develop good measures of psychological characteristics.

open-ended problem a type of problem used in tests or questionnaires where participants are not presented with a pre-defined set of solutions. Participants generate their own solutions by writing or speaking. For example, in a creativity test, participants might be asked to name as many possible uses for a small box as they can.

performance measure a measure that is typically used to evaluate abilities or competencies. Performance measures typically consist of problems that require the specific ability or competency. The levels of the ability or competency possessed by participants are estimated based on how many problems they are able to solve correctly.

self-report scale a scale that is typically used to measure personality characteristics, emotions, or attitudes. Self-report scales typically consist of words or statements that describe certain characteristics. Participants use response scales (often five-point scales) to indicate to what extent each statement is true for them. Typical response scales range from "disagree completely" to "agree completely," or from "never" to "always."

REFERENCES

Aldwin, C. M. (2009). Gender and wisdom: a brief overview. *Research in Human Development*, 6(1), 1–8.

Ardelt, M. (2003). Empirical assessment of a three-dimensional wisdom scale. *Research on Aging*, 25(3), 275–324.

(2011). The measurement of wisdom: a commentary on Taylor, Bates, and Webster's comparison of the SAWS and 3D-WS. *Experimental Aging Research*, 37(2), 241–55.

Ardelt, M., Pridgen, S., and Nutter-Pridgen, K. L. (2018). The relation between age and three-dimensional wisdom: variations by wisdom dimensions and education. *The Journals of Gerontology, Series B: Psychological Sciences and Social Sciences*, 73(8), 1339–49.

Baltes, P. B. and Smith, J. (1990). Toward a psychology of wisdom and its ontogenesis. In R. J. Sternberg, ed., *Wisdom: Its Nature, Origins, and Development*. Cambridge University Press, pp. 87–120.

Baltes, P. B. and Staudinger, U. M. (2000). Wisdom: a metaheuristic (pragmatic) to orchestrate mind and virtue toward excellence. *American Psychologist*, 55(1), 122–36.

Brienza, J. P., Kung, F. Y. H., Santos, H. C., Bobocel, D. R., and Grossmann, I. (2018). Wisdom, bias, and balance: toward a process-sensitive measurement of wisdom-related cognition. *Journal of Personality and Social Psychology*, 115(6), 1093–126.

Glück, J. (2016). *Weisheit – Die 5 Prinzipien des gelingenden Lebens. [Wisdom – The Five Principles of the Good Life.]* Kösel.

(2018). Measuring wisdom: existing approaches, continuing challenges, and new developments. *The Journals of Gerontology, Series B: Psychological Sciences*, 73(8), 1393–403.

Glück, J. and Bluck, S. (2013). The MORE Life Experience Model: a theory of the development of personal wisdom. In M. Ferrari and N. M. Weststrate, eds., *The Scientific Study of Personal Wisdom*. Springer, pp. 75–97.

Glück, J., König, S., Naschenweng, K. et al. (2013). How to measure wisdom: content, reliability, and validity of five measures. *Frontiers in Psychology*, 4, 405.

Glück, J., Bluck, S., and Weststrate, N. M. (2019). More on the MORE Life Experience Model: what we have learned (so far). *The Journal of Value Inquiry*, 53(3), 349–70.

Grossmann, I., Na, J., Varnum, M. E. W. et al. (2010). Reasoning about social conflicts improves into old age. *Proceedings of the National Academy of Sciences of the United States of America*, 107(16), 7246–50.

Hu, C. S., Ferrari, M., Wang, Q., and Woodruff, E. (2017). Thin-slice measurement of wisdom. *Frontiers in Psychology*, 8, 1378.

Koller, I., Levenson, M. R., and Glück, J. (2017). What do you think you are measuring? A mixed-methods procedure for assessing the content validity of test items and theory-based scaling. *Frontiers in Psychology*, 8, 126.

Kunzmann, U. (2019). Performance-based measures of wisdom: state of the art and future directions. In R. J. Sternberg and J. Glück, eds., *The Cambridge Handbook of Wisdom*. Cambridge University Press, pp. 277–96.

Le, T. N. and Levenson, M. R. (2005). Wisdom as self-transcendence: what's love (and individualism) got to do with it? *Journal of Research in Personality*, 39(4), 443–57.

Levenson, M. R., Jennings, P. A., Aldwin, C. M., and Shiraishi, R. W. (2005). Self-transcendence: conceptualization and measurement. *The International Journal of Aging and Human Development*, 60(2), 127–43.

Pasupathi, M., Staudinger, U. M., and Baltes, M. M. (2001). Seeds of wisdom: adolescents' knowledge and judgement about difficult life problems. *Developmental Psychology*, 37(3), 351–61.

Redzanowski, U. and Glück, J. (2013). Who knows who is wise? Self and peer ratings of wisdom. *The Journals of Gerontology: Series B, Psychological Sciences and Social Sciences*, 68(3), 391–94.

Staudinger, U. M. (1999). Older and wiser? Integrating results on the relationship between age and wisdom-related performance. *International Journal of Behavioral Development*, 23(3), 641–64.

(2019). The distinction between personal and general wisdom: how far have we come? In R. J. Sternberg and J. Glück, eds., *The Cambridge Handbook of Wisdom*. Cambridge University Press, pp. 182–201.

Sternberg, R. J. and Glück, J. (2022). *Wisdom: The Psychology of Wise Thoughts, Words, and Deeds*. Cambridge University Press.

Taylor, M., Bates, G., and Webster, J. D. (2011). Comparing the psychometric properties of two measures of wisdom: predicting forgiveness and psychological well-being with the Self-Assessed Wisdom Scale (SAWS) and the Three-Dimensional Wisdom Scale (3D-WS). *Experimental Aging Research*, 37(2), 129–41.

Thomas, S. and Kunzmann, U. (2014). Age differences in wisdom-related knowledge: does the age relevance of the task matter? *The Journals of Gerontology: Series B, Psychological Sciences and Social Sciences*, 69(6), 897–905.

Webster, J. D. (2003). An exploratory analysis of a self-assessed wisdom scale. *Journal of Adult Development*, 10(1), 13–22.

(2007). Measuring the character strength of wisdom. *The International Journal of Aging and Human Development*, 65(2), 163–83.

(2010). Wisdom and positive psychosocial values in young adulthood. *Journal of Adult Development*, 17(2), 70–80.

(2019). Self-report wisdom measures: strengths, limitations, and future directions. In R. J. Sternberg and J. Glück, eds., *The Cambridge Handbook of Wisdom*. Cambridge University Press, pp. 297–320,

Webster, J. D., Westerhof, G. J., and Bohlmeijer, E. T. (2014). Wisdom and mental health across the lifespan. *The Journals of Gerontology: Series B, Psychological Sciences and Social Sciences*, 69(2), 209–18.

Webster, J. D., Weststrate, N. M., Ferrari, M., Munroe, M., and Pierce, T. W. (2018). Wisdom and meaning in emerging adulthood. *Emerging Adulthood*, 6(2), 118–36.

Weststrate, N. M. and Glück, J. (2017). Hard-earned wisdom: exploratory processing of difficult life experience is positively associated with wisdom. *Developmental Psychology*, 53(4), 800–14.

Zacher, H., McKenna, B., Rooney, D., and Gold, S. (2015). Wisdom in the military context. *Military Psychology*, 27(3), 142–54.

PART II

Foundations of Wisdom in the Individual and in the World

CHAPTER 7

Wisdom, Creativity, and Intelligence

Dowon Choi, Sarah F. Lynch, and James C. Kaufman

Your scientists were so preoccupied with whether or not they could, they didn't stop to think if they should.

Dr. Ian Malcolm, *Jurassic Park* (Kennedy et al., 1993)

Are you a good witch or a bad witch?

Glinda, *The Wizard of Oz* (Leroy & Fleming, 1939)

7.1 Introduction

Intelligence and **creativity** are often considered to be inherently positive traits. Creativity, in particular, is often associated with benevolence to the point that some scholars include societal benefit as part of its definition (Kampylis & Valtanen, 2010). Yet many studies have found creativity to be associated with less positive traits, such as low integrity (Beaussart et al., 2013), deception (De Dreu & Nijstad, 2008), or dishonesty (Gino & Ariely, 2012). Indeed, in one study, it was often the more complex or morally ambiguous solution, as opposed to the most benevolent one, that was rated as most creative (Cropley et al., 2014).

Intelligence, similarly, has shown no relationship to positive personality **constructs** such as agreeableness or emotional stability (Bipp et al., 2008), although it is positively correlated with openness (Ackerman & Heggestad, 1997). Intelligence and creativity can be used for amazing and beneficial advances – consider the invention of the polio vaccine and other medical advances, continued global efforts for human rights, or the continual inventions and innovations that make life easier for those in need. Yet there are many examples of a dark side of creativity and intelligence. A successful act of terrorism requires intelligence and creativity (Gill et al., 2013). Computer hacking, industrial espionage, or smuggling all require high levels of intelligence and creativity, and we can probably easily come up with many more examples. Hollywood also jumps on this train of thought, often writing the mastermind of a heist or criminal organization as a brilliant and creative problem solver (e.g., in *Ocean's 11*, *Baby Driver*, or *Catch Me If You Can*).

What determines if someone uses their intellectual and creative abilities for good or evil? We argue in this chapter, as proposed in the landmark theoretical work by Sternberg (1998, 2007, 2019b), that wisdom is the lever that determines the direction in which people choose to use their intelligence and creativity. Just as interests, exposure, and personality can lead some people to use their gifts in art and others in science (Kaufman & Baer, 2005; Kaufman et al., 2013), wisdom can help to guide people toward one side or another on the spectrum of good versus evil.

Before we dive into the theory and research on how these constructs intersect, we shall briefly present an overview of the three constructs.

7.1.1   *Creativity*

Although there are many different theories and conceptions of creativity, there is strong agreement on the basic components of how creativity should be defined. Most scholars agree that to be creative something must be both (1) new/original and (2) useful/appropriate/valuable (Guilford, 1950; Hennessey & Amabile, 2010; Kaufman, 2016; Simonton, 2012).

There are many approaches to studying creativity. One common framework consists of the Four Ps – the person, the process, the product, and the press (meaning the environment) (Rhodes, 1961). More recently, there has been a push to include sociocultural components, and a modification called the Five As (Glăveanu, 2013) has been proposed. The first three As – the actor, the action, and the artifact – mirror the first three Ps. The environment concept is then split into two components, namely the audience (both the initial people one might share work with and the ultimate intended consumers) and affordances (the physical, psychological, and intellectual resources needed for creation). When studying the creative person (or actor), one recurring finding is that the personality trait of openness to experience is related to higher levels of creativity (e.g., Feist et al., 2017).

There are many other theoretical or empirical works on creativity that are relevant to its intersection with intelligence and wisdom. The Geneplore model takes a cognitive perspective by viewing creativity as a series going back and forth between generating ideas and exploring solutions (Finke et al., 1992). Modern creative problem-solving models often include multiple stages, commonly beginning with problem recognition – finding the problem that needs to be solved (Reiter-Palmon & Robinson, 2009). The next two stages are similar to the Geneplore model – idea exploration and idea evaluation. The final stage is usually implementation or validation – actually testing the creative idea (Mumford et al., 1991).

7.1.2   *Intelligence*

For many years, intelligence was conceptualized as a single entity, *g* (Spearman, 1904). This approach considered intelligence to be a generalized construct – all cognitive abilities would be tied into *g*. One of the early theories to move beyond *g* was Horn and Cattell's idea of fluid intelligence (solving new problems and considering new stimuli) and crystallized intelligence (acquired knowledge) (Horn & Cattell, 1966). More recently, Horn and Cattell's theories, Horn's further scholarship, and the **psychometric** studies of Carroll (1993) have been integrated into the Cattell–Horn–Carroll (CHC) theory (Schneider & McGrew, 2012). The CHC theory expanded on fluid and crystallized intelligence to include **visual-spatial processing, short-term memory, long-term storage and retrieval**, and several other additions.

As intelligence theories have developed, scholars have looked beyond traditional analytic-based concepts. Gardner's theory of multiple intelligences (Gardner, 1999) includes some intelligences that are more traditional, such as linguistic, logical-mathematical, and spatial intelligences, and others that expand the boundaries of intelligence, such as bodily-kinesthetic, musical, interpersonal, intrapersonal, and naturalist intelligences. Robert Sternberg's triarchic theory (Sternberg, 1985a), later revised to become the theory of successful intelligence (Sternberg, 1996), includes analytic intelligence but also two often overlooked ideas. One of these is creative intelligence (comparable to some of the ideas discussed in creativity). The other, namely practical intelligence, taps the essential skills that one needs to survive day-to-day, which is similar to "street smarts"

(Sternberg & Hedlund, 2002). For example, can someone find the best fit between their strengths and the demands of the surrounding environment (Sternberg, 2000)? If so, they are exhibiting practical intelligence to be successful. The most recent evolution of this theory, namely the augmented theory of successful intelligence, explicitly includes wisdom as a desired outcome (Sternberg, 2020) and core component (Sternberg, 2019a).

7.1.3 Wisdom

Given that wisdom is the topic of this textbook, we shall focus on some specific concepts that particularly connect to intelligence and creativity. **Implicit theories** of wisdom are common-sense conceptions of wisdom expressed in everyday language (Bangen et al., 2013; see also Chapter 3 in this volume). In this everyday context, wisdom is seen as clearly distinct from social intelligence and creativity, and is viewed more as an exceptional level of human functioning. It encompasses the balanced intersection of motivational and intellectual aptitude in conjunction with interpersonal competence, including the ability to listen, evaluate, and give advice (Baltes & Staudinger, 2000). The overarching, commonplace, implicit belief about wisdom is the push toward good. It assumes that actions are done in pursuit of a good life.

Partly based on the implicit theories, explicitly written theories provide a multifaceted, multidimensional concept of wisdom. It is a dynamic process that is self-reinforcing in nature (Ardelt, 2003). Given its complex nature, it is hard to narrow down wisdom to a simple definition. There is a significant degree of overlap within the various definitions of wisdom. Five concepts regularly occur across definitions – social decision making and life knowledge, prosocial attitudes and behaviors, reflection and self-understanding, acknowledgement and coping with uncertainty, and emotional homeostasis (Bangen et al., 2013).

7.2 Wisdom, Intelligence, and Creativity: Intersections

7.2.1 Implicit Theories of Wisdom, Intelligence, and Creativity

Implicit and explicit theories, as we have briefly discussed, are both important. Implicit theories reflect what people who are not experts believe about different constructs or people (Sternberg et al., 1981). Such beliefs may even be unconscious, with laypeople potentially being unaware that they hold these opinions (Greenwald & Banaji, 1995). Implicit theories often inform the framework for explicit theories or research programs (Bluck & Glück, 2005).

There have been several studies on implicit beliefs about intelligence (Lim et al., 2002; Sternberg et al., 1981) and creativity (Kaufman & Beghetto, 2013; Lim & Plucker, 2001), but for the purposes of this chapter we shall emphasize a key study that distinguished between implicit beliefs about intelligence, creativity, and wisdom (Sternberg, 1985b). In a series of experiments, Sternberg asked different groups (professors, students, and laypeople) to list and then rate behavioral characteristics associated with the three constructs. He found several interesting results.

People believed that intelligence included the ability to solve problems, integrate different types of information, and learn from the environment. Their implicit beliefs about creativity included being a free spirit, having aesthetic tastes, and showing defiance and curiosity. And finally, people believed that wisdom encompassed reasoning, learning from the past, and being able to use information. Beliefs about creativity, intelligence, and wisdom were all positively linked, but the relationship between intelligence and wisdom was viewed as much stronger. The weaker (although still significant) relationship between wisdom and creativity may reflect the fact that laypeople saw wise people as growing from lived experience, whereas they saw creative people as rebelling against the system and in doing so perhaps not learning as much from life lessons (Sternberg, 2005b).

Experts in different fields had slightly different interpretations of the three constructs (for example, business experts attached more value to logic's role in intelligence than did art experts). Such differences are consistent with domain-specific approaches to creativity (Kaufman et al., 2017).

Glück and Bluck (2011) explored laypersons' conceptions of wisdom by having participants answer questionnaires on what wisdom is and how someone can become wise. Two primary clusters emerged, as hypothesized: (1) a cognitive cluster, which placed a greater emphasis on knowledge, and (2) an integrative cluster, which also valued more affective components. Interestingly, the clusters were quite similar in how they rated the importance of intelligence in wisdom – neither of them saw intelligence as being notably important in determining wisdom. In general, creativity was seen as even less relevant to wisdom than intelligence.

If someone possesses knowledge, good decision-making skills, and an ability to generate solutions, and yet lacks prosocial values, then this individual may be smart and creative, but not wise (Bangen et al., 2013). Although creativity may allow for an individual to develop complex solutions to difficult ethical problems (Bierly et al., 2009), creative people also tend to be more likely to use context and individual situations to determine whether their behaviors are ethically appropriate to a situation, rather than blindly subscribing to a universally accepted concept of morality (Mumford et al., 2010). Forsyth (1980) found that there are two dimensions of ethical ideologies – idealism and relativism. Creative people showed a complex pattern including high idealism and relativism, meaning that they tend to hold high ethical values but are relatively flexible in each situation (Bierly et al., 2009).

Even if people are creative in the service of unethical or evil pursuits (e.g., Cropley et al., 2008, 2010), a lack of wisdom may not be the reason for this. Acting in an unwise manner does not necessarily mean being evil. Many of the leaders who have committed atrocities that have killed millions of people have, at least initially, believed that their actions were wise. Furthermore, people may act poorly and be aware that their actions are bad; they may simply give in to greed, power, or another desire. Our human history is littered with stories of many passionate and educated political, economic, or religious ideologists who fell into these complicated categories. The Cambodian dictator Pol Pot, who was ultimately responsible for the mass killings of his own people, initially had a vision (or so he claimed) of making a self-sufficient country independent from foreign powers (Locard, 2005).

7.2.2   *Empirical Studies of Creativity, Intelligence, and Wisdom*

Unfortunately, there are few studies that have explicitly researched all three constructs together. One notable exception is that by Staudinger et al. (1997), who measured wisdom using a think-aloud protocol in which participants answered questions about possible real-life problems that would require wisdom to solve. Standardized tests were used for creativity (divergent thinking) and intelligence (crystallized and fluid assessments). The authors also measured personality and cognitive styles. Wisdom was significantly correlated with intelligence and creativity; it was also correlated with openness to experience, which is associated with both creativity and intelligence. These researchers' findings showed that both cognitive styles and creativity better predicted wisdom than did either measure of intelligence.

Mickler and Staudinger (2008) used a similar think-aloud protocol to that adopted by Staudinger et al. (1997) to assess general wisdom, but added separate questions about the participants' own experiences to create a new measure of personal wisdom. They then tested the relationship of the two measures to a number of variables, including intelligence and other creativity-related variables. For example, tolerance of ambiguity is a trait that has been both theoretically (Amabile, 1983) and empirically (Zenasni et al., 2008) associated with creativity (although, of course, other abilities and traits are also needed for creativity). Tolerance of ambiguity was highly correlated with personal wisdom ($r = 0.71$). In addition, openness to experience was significantly correlated with both personal and general wisdom. Furthermore, both personal and general wisdom were significantly correlated with both crystallized and fluid intelligence.

Grossmann et al. (2013) primarily focused on wisdom and wellbeing, but also included intelligence and personality. They focused on wise reasoning in thinking, which was measured via participants' responses to scenarios in a similar manner to the way in which Staudinger et al. (1997) tested for general wisdom. Grossmann et al. (2013) found that wise reasoning was significantly related to scores on acquired knowledge measured by a vocabulary test, but there were no significant relationships to additional intelligence test scores of verbal comprehension or certain memory skills. Openness to experience also showed no relationship with wise reasoning. Given that the paper's emphasis was on wisdom and well-being, the authors did not explore why openness to experience and two of the three intelligence measures did not relate to wisdom, in contrast to findings in previous studies. Weststrate and Glück (2017), in their investigation of life experiences and wisdom, included crystallized and fluid intelligence tests; neither was significantly correlated with multiple measures of wisdom.

In summary, intelligence and creativity (or creativity-related attributes) are inconsistently correlated with wisdom. However, when these relationships do exist, they tend to be weak and are not the best predictors of wisdom.

7.2.3   *Theoretical Relationships between Creativity, Intelligence, and Wisdom*

Much (if not all) of the theoretical groundwork for exploring the commonality of these three constructs has been developed by Robert Sternberg across two primary theories. The first is his balance theory of wisdom (Sternberg, 1998, 2001), which also encompasses creativity and intelligence. The balance theory defines the core tenets of wisdom as balancing goal-setting ability, responses to the environment, interests, and short- and long-term goals, all in conjunction with values and morals. It states that wise decisions are based not purely on intelligence or factual knowledge, but also on tacit knowledge (part of the practical intelligence described earlier in this chapter).

In this model, overall, wisdom can be viewed as the balanced outcome between these different tenets with both immediate and lasting effects. It comes with the recognition of intrapersonal, interpersonal, and extrapersonal interests (that is, the needs of oneself, others, and the community, respectively). In an individual, these combined characteristics define a person who most likely possesses critical aspects of both intelligence and creativity. These are the differentiation factors that separate those who are intelligent, creative, and wise from those who are intelligent, creative, and foolish.

Next, Sternberg addressed all three constructs together in his **WICS model** (Wisdom, Intelligence, and Creativity Synthesized), which was presented as a model of thinking processing (Sternberg, 2003b). Cognitive dimensions of processing are an individual's ability to understand life, comprehend significance, and appreciate deeper meaning, particularly regarding individual and social matters (Ardelt, 2003).

This model considers cognitive ability beyond traditional standardized tests. In a similar way to Sternberg's earlier triarchic and successful intelligence theories (Sternberg, 1985a, 1996), WICS is grounded in the idea that intelligence must include creative abilities. A smart person needs to be able to go beyond information presented in explicit terms, and imagine a new angle for the old problem. The WICS model takes wisdom into account not as a bonus or supplemental construct, but rather as an essential part of the ability to act pragmatically. It is applicable across a whole range of contexts, such as gifted identification (Sternberg, 2003a), gifted education practices (Dai, 2003), leadership (Sternberg, 2005), classroom settings (Sternberg, 2010), university admissions (Sternberg et al., 2012), and awarding scholarships (Sternberg & Grigorenko, 2004), among many others.

The WICS model systematically combines the above-mentioned areas, resting on the assumption that someone who possesses and combines these attributes can use each area in a comprehensive fashion (Sternberg, 2003b). Creativity can be used to generate depictions of and solutions to problems. Intelligence (both analytic and practical) can help one to implement decisions and persuade others of the intrinsic value of these choices. Wisdom is used to ensure that when one uses intelligence and creativity to advance in life, the pathway chosen will be beneficial to the global community.

Other theories of wisdom do not explicitly address intelligence and creativity, but include related concepts. For example, the Berlin Wisdom Paradigm (Baltes & Smith, 2008) encompasses factual and strategic knowledge about the fundamental pragmatics of life, which would likely overlap with intelligence. Furthermore, the paradigm also includes the ability to manage the uncertainties of life, which would require tolerance of ambiguity (which, as discussed earlier, is related to creativity).

7.3   Conclusion

Within both creativity and intelligence research and theory there are many models of different domains, disciplines, and abilities. Within creativity, for example, there might be divisions between art, writing, science, and business (e.g., Kaufman et al., 2010) or different stages of creative problem solving (Mumford et al., 1991) or different levels of ability (Kaufman & Beghetto, 2009). Both traditional (e.g., Schneider & McGrew, 2012) and more contemporary models of intelligence (e.g., Sternberg, 1996) identify different abilities and processes that comprise the larger construct.

Wisdom is a new way of potentially understanding the value of both creativity and intelligence. The primary moderating variable that determines the manner in which someone uses their gifts is wisdom (Craft, 2006). Isolated from context, creativity and intelligence are simply tools. Is a hammer good or bad? It depends on whether the hand wielding it is building a house or attacking someone. Wisdom can be that hand. Wise people would be able to use their creativity and intelligence to do meaningful things that contribute to society in some way. A very wise person with less prominent levels of intellect or creativity can do more good than a creative and intellectual genius with low wisdom.

7.4 Comprehension and Discussion Questions

(1) Consider a situation involving an ethical dilemma. For example, imagine a situation in which a person must break a common law so as to benefit another person or group (e.g., stealing to feed a hungry person), or perhaps a situation in which helping one disenfranchised group involves harming another group. Do you think that, in these cases, creative or intelligent people might use their strengths to resolve such a conflict compared with a situation in which no such ethical dilemma is involved?

(2) People can have different conceptions of wisdom. How do you imagine a wise person? Imagine a highly wise person, a highly intelligent person, and a highly creative person. What do these three individuals have in common? In what respects do they differ? Does your image match with the perspectives of wisdom discussed in this chapter?

(3) As mentioned above, some scholars define creativity as being a construct that is only morally good. Other scholars include the idea of malevolent creativity. Which idea makes more sense to you? Can you think of a highly creative person from history or fiction who intentionally harmed other people?

(4) In this chapter, the dimension of time and perspective were not necessarily considered in relation to how we judge whether a certain behavior is more good or more evil. Can creative or intelligent behavior that was once considered morally good come to be seen as malevolent after a period of time? Similarly, can behavior that was seen as morally good by one group of people be seen as evil by another group of people? Can you think of any examples?

(5) We have discussed studies that linked higher creativity with lower integrity and a more flexible morality. Historically, Korean Buddhist monks fought on the battlefield to defend their community, allowing themselves to violate their canonical rule, "Do not kill living things." How can you interpret such a violation of their own principles? Would you consider the monks' fighting behavior as an example of low integrity or creative justification? Overall, would you consider their behavior to be a wise judgment? Do you think there are circumstances in which it may be wise to kill someone?

(6) Do you think intelligence, creativity, and wisdom can be taught over time as in the WICS model? If not, why do you think this? If you think they can be taught over time, how do you think we can teach them?

7.5 Investigations

James Kaufman, in collaboration with Hansika Kapoor, has proposed a model of dark creativity that explores how people use their creativity to enable actions or produce artifacts that may be considered malevolent or harmful. The relationship with intelligence and wisdom can be seen in a set of individual mechanisms, which include both intellectual ability and values. Although higher intelligence will often lead to malevolent creative acts that are more likely to have a negative impact upon society (i.e., they are more likely to be successful and carried out on a grander scale), wisdom (as represented by a component called "personal values") is more likely to temper dark creativity. Two examples of wise values that may dissuade individuals from pursuing malevolently creative acts are general benevolence and universalism (consideration for all people).

Dowon Choi, with James Kaufman, has focused on developmental and multicultural theoretical perspectives to foster the creativity of all students (not only those who are academic high achievers) in their own contexts, which may lead to an increased community level of wisdom. Choi and Kaufman have also highlighted the interdependence between top-down leadership and an individual's bottom-up leadership to govern their communities and live wisely for the benefit of the world community. Recently, Choi collaborated with Alan Kaufman in a study of the historical and contemporary vestige of the malleable nature of human intelligence in IQ tests.

7.6   Practical Applications

Creativity is most commonly associated with the arts and science, but it can be found and experienced everywhere. As discussed in this chapter, creativity broadly consists of two components – novelty and usefulness. We can probably easily come up with a surprising situation that requires our creative adaptation and modification of the environment (e.g., an unexpected detour). In the future we can expect to have to deal with massive levels of changes (e.g., climate change, pandemics, and shifts in global power) in a convoluted context. Intelligence, creativity, and wise decision making will be critical if individuals and leaders are to navigate information saturation, fast communication, and the emergence of brand-new problems. At an individual level, wisdom may help to reduce the anxiety caused by this ambiguity and uncertainty, and increase emotional equilibrium and well-being. At a community level, if individuals develop intelligence to think critically, creativity to solve problems, and wisdom to incorporate intelligence and creativity together, flexibly and prosocially, they may be able to make better collaborative decisions that help all of us to coexist far into the future.

Glossary

constructs in psychology, tools for understanding psychological concepts and phenomena that may not exist in a directly observable or measurable form. Examples of constructs include intelligence, wisdom, self-esteem, creativity, and anxiety.

creativity the capacity of a person or thing to produce something that is both new and useful. Since newness and usefulness can be judged differently in different situations, creativity is often understood in context.

implicit theories ideas and opinions that people may hold without fully understanding why they think that way; often people may not even know that they hold some beliefs.

intelligence this is conceptualized in many different ways, from a globalized cognitive ability to perceive, process, and produce information, to the interactions of many different components.

long-term storage and retrieval the ability to remember previously stored information (e.g., a friend's name, an order of objects, or a short story) and then to produce this information when it is needed.

psychometric relating to a field of study that focuses on measuring psychological constructs in a relatively objective way, such as the measurement of intelligence, personality, knowledge/skills, or clinically meaningful symptoms in tests or questionnaires.

short-term memory the ability to maintain, momentarily manipulate, and immediately reproduce or focus on information within primary memory.

visual-spatial processing the ability to accurately and quickly identify, remember, manipulate, and produce two-dimensional or three-dimensional visual information, including imagery.

WICS model a model (Wisdom, Intelligence, and Creativity Synthesized) that includes the ethical components necessary to be successful in life.

REFERENCES

Ackerman, P. L. and Heggestad, E. D. (1997). Intelligence, personality, and interests: evidence for overlapping traits. *Psychological Bulletin,* 121(2), 219–45.

Amabile, T. M. (1983). The social psychology of creativity: a componential conceptualization. *Journal of Personality and Social Psychology,* 45(2), 357–76.

Ardelt, M. (2003) Empirical assessment of a three-dimensional wisdom scale. *Research on Aging.* 25(3), 275–324.

Baltes, P. B. and Smith, J. (2008). The fascination of wisdom: its nature, ontogeny, and function. *Perspectives on Psychological Science,* 3(1), 56–64.

Baltes, P. and Staudinger, U. (2000). Wisdom: a metaheuristic (pragmatic) to orchestrate mind and virtue toward excellence. *American Psychologist,* 55(1), 122–36.

Bangen, K. J., Meeks, T. W., and Jesete, D.V. (2013) Defining and assessing wisdom: a review of the literature. *American Journal of Geriatric Psychiatry,* 21(12). 1254–66.

Beaussart, M. L., Andrews, C. J., and Kaufman, J. C. (2013). Creative liars: the relationship between creativity and integrity. *Thinking Skills and Creativity,* 9, 129–34.

Bierly, P. E., Kolodinsky, R.W., and Charette, B. J. (2009) Understanding the complex relationship between creativity and ethical ideologies. *Journal of Business Ethics,* 86(1), 101–12.

Bipp, T., Steinmayr, R., and Spinath, B. (2008). Personality and achievement motivation: relationship among Big Five domain and facet scales, achievement goals, and intelligence. *Personality and Individual Differences,* 44(7), 1454–64.

Bluck, S. and Glück, J. (2005). From the inside out: people's implicit theories of wisdom. In R. J. Sternberg and J. Jordan, eds., *A Handbook of Wisdom: Psychological Perspectives.* Cambridge University Press, pp. 84–109.

Carroll, J. B. (1993). *Human Cognitive Abilities: A Survey of Factor-Analytic Studies.* Cambridge University Press.

Craft, A. (2006). Fostering creativity with wisdom. *Cambridge Journal of Education,* 36(3), 337–50.

Cropley, D. H., Kaufman, J. C., and Cropley, A. J. (2008). Malevolent creativity: a functional model of creativity in terrorism and crime. *Creativity Research Journal,* 20(2), 105–15.

Cropley, D. H., Cropley, A. J., Kaufman, J. C., and Runco, M. A., eds., (2010). *The Dark Side of Creativity.* Cambridge University Press.

Cropley, D. H., Kaufman, J. C., White, A. E., and Chiera, B. A. (2014). Layperson perceptions of malevolent creativity: the good, the bad, and the ambiguous. *Psychology of Aesthetics, Creativity, and the Arts,* 8(4), 400–12.

Dai, D. Y. (2003). The making of the gifted: implications of Sternberg's WICS model of giftedness. *High Ability Studies,* 14(2), 141–42.

De Dreu, C. K. W. and Nijstad, B. A. (2008). Mental set and creative thought in social conflict: threat rigidity versus motivated focus. *Journal of Personality and Social Psychology,* 95(3), 648–61.

Feist, G. J., Reiter-Palmon, R., and Kaufman, J. C., eds., (2017). *The Cambridge Handbook of Creativity and Personality Research.* Cambridge University Press.

Finke, R. A., Ward, T. B., and Smith, S. M. (1992). *Creative Cognition: Theory, Research, and Applications.* MIT Press.

Forsyth, D. R. (1980). A taxonomy of ethical ideologies. *Journal of Personality and Social Psychology,* 39(1), 175–84.

Gardner, H. (1999). *Intelligence Reframed: Multiple Intelligences for the 21st Century.* Basic Books.

Gill, P., Horgan, J., Hunter, S. T., and Cushenbery, L. D. (2013). Malevolent creativity in terrorist organizations. *The Journal of Creative Behavior,* 47(2), 125–51.

Gino, F. and Ariely, D. (2012). The dark side of creativity: original thinkers can be more dishonest. *Journal of Personality and Social Psychology,* 102(3), 445–59.

Glăveanu, V. P. (2013). Rewriting the language of creativity: the Five A's framework. *Review of General Psychology,* 17(1), 69–81.

Glück, J. and Bluck, S. (2011). Laypeople's conceptions of wisdom and its development: cognitive and integrative views. *The Journals of Gerontology: Series B: Psychological Sciences and Social Sciences,* 66B, 321–24.

Greenwald, A. G. and Banaji, M. R. (1995). Implicit social cognition: attitudes, self-esteem, and stereotypes. *Psychological Review,* 102(1), 4–27.

Grossmann, I., Na, J., Varnum, M. W., Kitayama, S., and Nisbett, R. E. (2013). A route to well-being: intelligence versus wise reasoning. *Journal Of Experimental Psychology: General,* 142(3), 944–53.

Guilford, J. P. (1950). Creativity. *American Psychologist,* 5(9), 444–54.

Hennessey, B. A. and Amabile, T. M. (2010). Creativity. *Annual Review of Psychology,* 61, 569–98.

Horn, J. L. and Cattell, R. B. (1966). Refinement and test of the theory of fluid and crystallized general intelligences. *Journal of Educational Psychology,* 57(5), 253–70.

Kampylis, P. G. and Valtanen, J. (2010). Redefining creativity—analyzing definitions, collocations, and consequences. *The Journal of Creative Behavior,* 44(3), 191–214.

Kaufman, J. C. (2016). *Creativity 101,* 2nd ed. Springer.

Kaufman, J. C. and Baer, J. (2005). The Amusement Park Theoretical (APT) Model of creativity. *Korean Journal of Thinking and Problem Solving,* 14, 15–25.

Kaufman, J. C. and Beghetto, R. A. (2009). Beyond big and little: the Four C Model of creativity. *Review of General Psychology,* 13(1), 1–12.

  (2013). Do people recognize the Four Cs? Examining layperson conceptions of creativity. *Psychology of Aesthetics, Creativity, and the Arts,* 7(3), 229–36.

Kaufman, J. C., Beghetto, R. A., Baer, J., and Ivcevic, Z. (2010). Creativity polymathy: what Benjamin Franklin can teach your kindergartener. *Learning and Individual Differences,* 20(4), 380–87.

Kaufman, J. C., Pumaccahua, T. T., and Holt, R. E. (2013). Personality and creativity in realistic, investigative, artistic, social, and enterprising college majors. *Personality and Individual Differences,* 54(8), 913–17.

Kaufman, J. C., Glăveanu, V., and Baer, J., eds. (2017). *The Cambridge Handbook of Creativity Across Domains.* Cambridge University Press.

Kennedy, K., Molen, G.R., and Spielberg, S. (1993). *Jurassic Park* [Motion picture]. Amblin Entertainment.

LeRoy, M. and Fleming, V. (1939). *The Wizard of Oz* [Motion picture]. Metro-Goldwyn-Mayer.

Lim, W. and Plucker, J. (2001). Creativity through a lens of social responsibility: implicit theories of creativity with Korean samples. *Journal of Creative Behavior,* 35(2), 115–30.

Lim, W., Plucker, J. A., and Im, K. (2002). We are more alike than we think we are: implicit theories of intelligence with a Korean sample. *Intelligence,* 30(2), 185–208.

Locard, H. (2005). State violence in democratic Kampuchea (1975–1979) and retribution (1979–2004). *European Review of History: Revue Européenne d'Histoire,* 12(1), 121–43.

Mickler, C. and Staudinger, U. M. (2008). Personal wisdom: validation and age-related differences of a performance measure. *Psychology and Aging,* 23(4), 787–99.

Mumford, M. D., Mobley, M. I., Uhlman, C. E., Reiter-Palmon, R., and Doares, L. M. (1991). Process analytic models of creative capacities. *Creativity Research Journal,* 4(2), 91–122.

Mumford, M. D., Waples, E. P., Antes, A. L. et al. (2010). Creativity and ethics: the relationship of creative and ethical problem-solving. *Creativity Research Journal,* 22(1), 74–89.

Reiter-Palmon, R. and Robinson, E. J. (2009). Problem identification and construction: what do we know, what is the future? *Psychology of Aesthetics, Creativity, and the Arts,* 3(1), 43–47.

Rhodes, M. (1961). An analysis of creativity. *Phi Delta Kappan,* 42(7), 305–11.

Schneider, W. J. and McGrew, K. (2012). The Cattell–Horn–Carroll model of intelligence. In D. Flanagan and P. Harrison, eds., *Contemporary Intellectual Assessment: Theories, Tests, and Issues*, 3rd ed. Guilford, pp. 99–144.

Simonton, D. K. (2012). Taking the U.S. Patent Office criteria seriously: a quantitative three-criterion definition and its implications. *Creativity Research Journal*, 24(2–3), 97–106.

Spearman, C. (1904). "General intelligence," objectively determined and measured. *The American Journal of Psychology*, 15(2), 201–92.

Staudinger, U. M., Lopez, D. F., and Baltes, P. B. (1997). The psychometric location of wisdom-related performance: intelligence, personality, and more? *Personality and Social Psychology Bulletin*, 23(11), 1200–14.

Sternberg, R. J. (1985a). *Beyond IQ: A Triarchic Theory of Human Intelligence*. Cambridge University Press.

(1985b). Implicit theories of intelligence, creativity, and wisdom. *Journal of Personality and Social Psychology*, 49(3), 607–27.

(1996). *Successful Intelligence*. Simon & Schuster.

(1998) A balance theory of wisdom. *Review of General Psychology*, 2(4), 347–65.

(2000). *Practical Intelligence in Everyday Life*. Cambridge University Press.

(2001). Why schools should teach for wisdom: the balance theory of wisdom in educational settings. *Educational Psychologist*, 36(4), 227–45.

(2003a). WICS as a model of giftedness. *High Ability Studies*, 14(2), 109–37.

(2003b). *Wisdom, Intelligence, and Creativity Synthesized*. Cambridge University Press.

(2007). A systems model of leadership: WICS. *American Psychologist*, 62(1), 34–42.

(2010). WICS: a new model for school psychology. *School Psychology International*, 31(6), 599–616.

(2019a). A theory of adaptive intelligence and its relation to general intelligence. *Journal of Intelligence*, 7(4), 23.

(2019b). Why people often prefer wise guys to guys who are wise: an augmented balance theory of the production and reception of wisdom. In R. J. Sternberg and J. Glück, eds., *The Cambridge Handbook of Wisdom*. Cambridge University Press, pp. 162–81.

(2020). The augmented theory of successful intelligence. In R. J. Sternberg, ed., *The Cambridge Handbook of Intelligence*, 2nd ed. Vol. 2. Cambridge University Press, pp. 679–708.

Sternberg, R. J. and Grigorenko, E. L. (2004). WICS: a model for selecting students for nationally competitive scholarships. In A. S. Ilchman, W. F. Ilchman, and M. H. Tolar, eds., *The Lucky Few and the Worthy Many: Scholarship Competitions and the World's Future Leaders*. Indiana University Press, pp. 32–61.

Sternberg, R. J. and Hedlund, J. (2002). Practical intelligence, g, and work psychology. *Human Performance*, 15(1–2), 143–60.

Sternberg, R. J., Conway, B. E., Ketron, J. L., and Bernstein, M. (1981). People's conceptions of intelligence. *Journal of Personality and Social Psychology*, 41(1), 37–55.

Sternberg, R. J., Bonney, C. R., Gabora, L., and Merrifield, M. (2012). WICS: a model for college and university admissions. *Educational Psychologist*, 47(1), 30–41.

Weststrate, N. M. and Glück, J. (2017). Hard-earned wisdom: exploratory processing of difficult life experience is positively associated with wisdom. *Developmental Psychology*, 53(4), 800–14.

Zenasni, F., Besançon, M., and Lubart, T. (2008). Creativity and tolerance of ambiguity: an empirical study. *Journal of Creative Behavior*, 42(1), 61–73.

CHAPTER 8

Wisdom, Morality, and Ethics[1]

Judith Glück and Robert J. Sternberg

8.1   Introduction

Box 8.1 presents a classical moral dilemma. What do you think about it?

Box 8.1 A moral dilemma (adapted from Colby et al., 1987).

Heinz's wife is suffering from a rare and deadly cancer. As it happens, a druggist in the same town recently discovered a drug that her doctors think might save her life. The drug is expensive to make, but the druggist is charging ten times his cost. This is far more than Heinz can afford to pay, even after asking all his friends for help. He desperately begs the druggist to sell him the drug at a lower price or to let him pay the balance later, but the druggist refuses. Desperately, Heinz considers breaking into the drugstore to steal the drug for his wife.

Why is this a "moral" dilemma, and what does morality have to do with wisdom? Simply put, **morality** is about what is right and what is wrong, and about how we can decide what is right and what is wrong. According to Greene (2013), morality is the reason why humans do unselfish things, even at a cost to themselves, for the benefit of a greater good. This chapter, and much of the literature, uses the terms "moral" and "ethical" largely interchangeably, but one possible distinction is that morality refers to the principles on which one's judgments of right and wrong are based, whereas ethics are principles of "right conduct."

Moral dilemmas, such as the one outlined above, typically describe situations in which moral rules clash. For example, it is wrong to steal, and it is wrong to let a person die. Is it right to steal so that a person doesn't die? Why exactly is one person's life more valuable than another person's profit? What if it were not Heinz's wife dying, but a stranger? What if it were Heinz's dog? Why does this make a difference? There is no objectively right answer to these questions, because they all come down to values (see also Chapter 2).

In our everyday lives, we often encounter moral dilemmas that are even less clear-cut. If your friend tells you that she cheated on an important exam and you consider cheating to be deeply wrong, what should you do? There are many different values involved here, some of which are moral (you think it's wrong to cheat, but you also think it's wrong to betray a friend's confidence),

---

[1] Portions of this chapter draw on ideas earlier expressed in:
  Sternberg, R. J. and Glück, J. (2019). Wisdom, morality, and ethics. In R. J. Sternberg and J. Glück, eds., *The Cambridge Handbook of Wisdom*. Cambridge University Press, pp. 551–74.
  Sternberg, R. J. and Glück, J. (2022). *Wisdom: The Psychology of Wise Thoughts, Words, and Deeds.* Cambridge University Press.

while others are not moral but are still important to you (you don't want to lose her as a friend; you don't want people to consider you a grind). How do you balance these different values so as to make the best possible decision?

As we explained in Chapter 4, wisdom involves the ability to balance different intrapersonal, interpersonal, and extrapersonal interests, considering both short- and long-term outcomes, so as to optimize the outcome with respect to a common good (Sternberg, 1998). Clearly, then, wisdom can help us to deal with moral dilemmas. However, surprisingly few studies have examined the links between wisdom and morality. In this chapter, we shall discuss three aspects of the relationship between wisdom and morality – how wisdom is related to moral reasoning and moral intuitions, what moral values wise individuals hold, and how wise individuals may manage to act ethically even in difficult situations.

8.2 Moral Reasoning and Wisdom: Kohlberg's Theory of Moral Development

Lawrence Kohlberg was one of the first psychologists to study the development of moral reasoning (Kohlberg, 1958). Participants were presented with dilemmas such as the story about Heinz and asked questions about them. Should Heinz steal the drug? Why, or why not? Should he also steal it for a stranger? Why, or why not? And so on. In a class on moral development that one of us is teaching, students vote online in response to these questions. Typically, a large majority (but by no means all) of the students think Heinz should steal the drug. The majority is much smaller when students are asked if Heinz should steal the drug for a stranger. Only a minority of students think Heinz should steal the drug for a dog. What do you think, and why? In Box 8.2 is a list of possible arguments why Heinz should or should not steal the drug for his wife. To what extent does each of these reasons sound convincing to you? Indicate how much you agree with each statement on a scale from 1 (= not at all) to 5 (= very much).

You probably noticed that the arguments in Box 8.2 represent quite different ways of thinking. Kohlberg distinguished three basic levels of **moral reasoning**, each consisting of two stages. We shall describe them very briefly here.

The first level, usually seen in children, is *preconventional morality*. Preconventional morality is essentially selfish, and assumes that people should only follow rules when it is to their benefit. Responses (1) and (5) in Box 8.2 would be preconventional. They only look at the outcome for Heinz; no one else's interests or more general moral values are considered.

The second level is *conventional morality*. People at this stage consider morality as a matter of conformity, norms, and mutual expectations. Responses (2) and (4) in Box 8.2 are examples of conventional morality. Participants at this stage consider it essential that people follow the rules. Response (2) is not about Heinz's wife's right to live – it is just about Heinz's obligations toward her. Response (4) is typical of the so-called the "law and order" stage of conventional morality. People at this stage consider laws and rules as absolute, with no exceptions.

The third level is *post-conventional morality*. At this stage, people see the importance of social contracts, but they also know that rules are not absolute. They understand that some values, such as individual rights to life or liberty, should be protected independent of the circumstances. They know that there are situations where rules clash, they know that people differ in their needs and value orientations, and they know that weighing different ethical aspects against each other can be difficult. A postconventional person might say that the right of Heinz's wife to live is more

---

Box 8.2 Some arguments concerning the Heinz dilemma.

(1) Heinz should not steal the drug because he might get caught – it's not worth it if his wife gets well again, but he is in prison!

(2) Heinz should steal the drug because when he got married he promised to take care of his wife. He is bound by that promise.

(3) Heinz should steal the drug both for his wife and for a stranger, because a person's right to life is worth more than the druggist's right to profit.

(4) Heinz should not steal the drug. What would happen to our society if everybody just stole what they need?

(5) Heinz should steal the drug because if he doesn't, his wife might die and that would be very sad for him.

(6) Heinz should steal the drug and then confess and accept his verdict. That way, he will have followed his conscience, even if it is against the law.

---

important than any law about stealing, but that once she is saved, Heinz should have to compensate the druggist even if it takes many years to do so. If a law violates universal ethical principles, postconventional individuals will not follow that law.

8.2.1   Wisdom and Kohlberg's Levels of Moral Reasoning

What stage of moral reasoning would you expect a wise person to be at? As you have read in earlier chapters, wise individuals think deeply about complex issues, care about the wellbeing of others, and are motivated to achieve the best possible outcome for the community, so most people would probably expect wise people to be at the postconventional level. Only one study to date has investigated the relationship between wisdom and Kohlberg's levels of moral reasoning. Pasupathi and Staudinger (2001) found that about 70 percent of their postconventional participants were also among the top 20 percent of scorers in the Berlin Wisdom Paradigm (Baltes & Staudinger, 2000; see Chapter 6). In other words, postconventional moral thinkers were indeed likely also to be wise.

8.3   Beyond Moral Reasoning: Moral Intuitions

There is one problem with Kohlberg's approach – it is somewhat theoretical. When you were reading the Heinz dilemma at the beginning of this chapter, how did you decide whether or not Heinz should steal the drug? Did you make a long list of pros and cons in your head, weigh them carefully, and then decide? If you are like most people, you didn't. You probably had an immediate "gut feeling" about what Heinz should do. Only if someone had asked you why exactly Heinz should do what you thought he should do would you have searched for rational arguments supporting your position.

The moral psychologist Jonathan Haidt and others have shown that our moral judgments rarely arise from conscious moral reasoning (Haidt, 2001). People often have immediate **intuitions** about what is right or wrong, and then construct rational arguments to support their gut reaction: "When faced with a social demand for a verbal justification, one becomes a lawyer trying to build a case rather than a judge searching for the truth" (Haidt, 2001, p. 814).

Consider, for example, the story in Box 8.3.

Box 8.3 The Story of Julie and Mark (Haidt, 2001, p. 814).

Julie and Mark are siblings. They are traveling together in France on summer vacation from college. One night they are staying alone in a cabin near the beach. They decide that it would be interesting and fun if they tried making love. At the very least it would be a new experience for each of them. Julie is already taking birth control pills, but Mark uses a condom, too, just to be safe. They both enjoy making love, but they decide not to do it again. They keep that night as a special secret, which makes them feel even closer to each other. What do you think about this? Was it OK for them to make love?

Most people feel strongly that it was wrong for Mark and Julie to make love. A typical dialogue between an interviewer and an interviewee might go like this:

INTERVIEWER: Why was it wrong?
PARTICIPANT: Well, Julie might get pregnant, and the baby might be sick, or handicapped.
I: The story says she couldn't possibly get pregnant.
P: Okay, but it might destroy their relationship as brother and sister.
I: The story says it didn't.
P: But ... it's still wrong. I can't explain why, but it's wrong. It's just disgusting for a brother and sister to have sex.

If you have siblings of your own, you may also have a strong gut feeling that sex with a sibling would be disgusting. These gut feelings are clearly quite different from a rational consideration of different pro and con arguments.

So, are we helpless victims of our moral intuitions, using seemingly rational arguments only to support our gut feelings? Why, then, is it sometimes possible to convince someone to change their mind about a moral issue? Haidt (2001) argued that conscious reflection, especially when it involves taking the perspective of others, can sometimes overrule or change moral intuitions, but he considered this to be a relatively rare case. However, other researchers believe that people quite regularly rely on both intuitions and reasoning in their moral judgments.

8.4   Greene's Dual-Process Model

According to the philosopher and psychologist Joshua Greene, people can make moral judgments in two different ways (Greene, 2013). There is the fast, intuitive, effortless way to form judgments that you may have experienced when you were reading the story about Julie and Mark, but there is also a slower, conscious, effort-requiring process of reflection. If you are faced with a dilemma for which you do not have a strong gut feeling or for which you do not trust your gut feeling, you may actually try to collect information and weigh arguments rationally. The same distinction between "fast," intuitive and "slow," reflective thinking has been made for judgment and decision making in general (for an overview, see Kahneman, 2011).

In an interesting experiment, Paxton et al. (2012) told participants Haidt's story about Julie and Mark, followed by either a weak argument or a strong argument that went against their immediate disgust reaction. The weak argument was that making love is always a good thing. The strong argument explained that the disgust reaction stemmed from ancient times, when incest might indeed have had negative consequences, but that it was no longer relevant because the siblings used multiple means of contraception. After reading the strong argument and thinking about it for two minutes, participants judged the siblings' behavior as more acceptable than did participants who read the weak argument or were not given time to think.

How are the two processes related to wisdom? No research has investigated this question directly, but reflectivity – the willingness and ability to question one's own beliefs and take different perspectives – is an important cornerstone of wisdom (e.g., Ardelt, 2003; Baltes & Staudinger, 2000; Glück & Bluck, 2013; Sternberg, 1998; see Chapter 4). Wise people are unlikely to base their moral judgments solely on intuitions, because they aim to consider others' perspectives and needs, long-term as well as short-term outcomes, and the role of context in human behavior (Baltes & Staudinger, 2000; Grossmann, 2017; Sternberg, 1998).

In addition, wise people may have different moral intuitions from most of us. Experts in any field typically make quick and intuitive judgments in the domain of their **expertise** – for example, a chess master may grasp the whole layout on a chessboard with a single look, and immediately know the best move. This intuitive reaction is not innate, of course, but based on thousands of hours of practice. If wisdom is expert knowledge in matters of life (Baltes & Staudinger, 2000), it would be plausible that wise people do not just reflect more wisely on their intuitions – they may also have wiser intuitions than most people.

8.5   Moral Foundations Theory

Why do people have such different moral intuitions? Why do we have strong feelings about moral issues at all, especially if they do not concern us personally? Many people are willing to take to the streets and stand up for the rights of others. Why do we care so much about morality? Haidt (2001) argued that our moral feelings stem from the **evolution** of humanity – people are biologically predisposed to find certain things disgusting and deeply morally wrong. Prehistoric humans who did not have a predisposition against incest, for example, would simply have become extinct because their offspring would have been genetically compromised. And the incest taboo is not the only case of an evolved moral intuition. In other words, the foundations of our moral intuitions are much older than our modern brain's ability to think rationally about moral questions.

Haidt's **Moral Foundations Theory** (Haidt, 2013) proposes that six evolved mechanisms underlie most of our moral intuitions. However, due to differences in cultural background and upbringing, people differ greatly in how important each of the foundations actually is to them. Before we describe each of the six foundations, fill out the brief scale in Box 8.4 to find out how much each of the considerations matters to you.

(1)   Care

Items 1 and 7 in Box 8.4 refer to people's innate desire to care for and protect others in need, especially helpless creatures such as children or young animals. Humans everywhere in the world feel compassion for innocent victims of disaster, often combined with anger at those who caused them harm. The human capacity for empathy and compassion is larger than that of most animals, and is probably an important factor that kept early human communities functioning, although animals have shown impressive acts of compassion (de Waal, 2008).

Box 8.4 Sample items from the Moral Foundations Questionnaire (Graham et al., 2008).

When you decide whether something is right or wrong, to what extent are the following considerations relevant to your thinking? Please rate each statement using a scale from 0 = "not at all relevant (this consideration has nothing to do with my judgments of right and wrong)" to 5 = "extremely relevant (this is one of the most important factors when I judge right and wrong)."

_____(1) Whether or not someone suffered emotionally.
_____(2) Whether or not some people were treated differently than others.
_____(3) Whether or not someone's action showed love for his or her country.
_____(4) Whether or not someone showed a lack of respect for authority.
_____(5) Whether or not someone violated standards of purity and decency.
_____(6) Whether or not someone violated another person's personal freedom.
_____(7) Whether or not someone cared for someone weak or vulnerable.
_____(8) Whether or not someone acted unfairly.
_____(9) Whether or not someone did something to betray his or her group.
_____(10) Whether or not someone conformed to the traditions of society.
_____(11) Whether or not someone did something disgusting.
_____(12) Whether or not someone oppressed someone else.
Source for items 1–5 and 7–11: https://moralfoundations.org/questionnaires/.
Items 6 and 12 were designed by the authors of this chapter.

---

(2) Fairness

Items 2 and 8 in Box 8.4 refer to the universal human desire for fairness and justice. Many people engage themselves in righting injustices done to people they don't even know personally. We also become genuinely angry with people who cheat or exploit others. Research using economic games shows that many people are actually willing to pay a share of their own profit to get "freeriders" punished (Fehr & Gächter, 2000). If every person were only interested in their own profit, that behavior would be completely illogical. However, according to Haidt, humans have an innate desire for fairness – we want the rules to be the same for everyone.

(3) Loyalty

Items 3 and 9 in Box 8.4 refer to loyalty – standing up with and for the groups to which you feel you belong, which may include your family, your community, your political party, or your nation. Humans (and chimpanzees; see de Waal, 2008) have a strong need to belong to a group, which is why many of us identify as fans of sports teams, fashion brands, or influencers. Once people feel that they are part of a group, they tend to like other group members more than people outside the group – even if they have never met any of those people (Brewer, 1979). This is obviously a dubious side of our nature, and individuals and communities differ greatly in how much they value loyalty. The human desire to be part of a group has often been exploited by leaders fomenting nationalism or racism. From an evolutionary perspective, it makes sense that early humans who protected their group members against outsiders had a survival advantage.

(4) Authority

Items 4 and 10 in Box 8.4 refer to people's innate willingness to respect and obey authorities, hierarchies, and traditions. As with loyalty, views on authority vary widely across modern cultures and subcultures. When you ask people which values they want to convey to their children, their responses may cover the whole range from "obedience and discipline" to "the courage to stand up to authorities." It is not entirely clear how hierarchical human societies are by nature. Chimpanzees are closely related to us and live in more hierarchical structures than we do. Bonobos are equally closely related to us and much more egalitarian (de Waal, 2008). Interestingly, human hunter-gatherer societies seem to be quite egalitarian. Some archeologists argue that human societies became more authoritarian when humanity took up agriculture (Boehm, 1999).

(5) Sanctity/Purity

Items 5 and 11 in Box 8.4 refer to purity. Purity is closely related to disgust at things or practices that people view as unclean. In fact, the emotion of disgust evolved because it prevents people from getting sick or poisoned (which is why we find the smell of feces or rotten food disgusting). Interestingly, it seems to be relatively easy to teach humans to find things disgusting that are not really harmful, such as foods that a culture considers to be unclean. As a modern example, many vegans experience strong disgust when they imagine eating meat. Cultures differ in the extent to which they value virtues such as chastity and temperance and practices intended to keep one's body and mind clean.

(6) Liberty

Items 6 and 12 in Box 8.4 refer to the sixth moral foundation, liberty, which was added by Haidt in 2013. Across cultures, people have a strong desire for physical as well as psychological freedom. Humans may obey bullies who oppress the freedom of others, but they usually do not do so happily. Dictatorships that use draconian measures to oppress people's freedom often end because some citizens are willing to risk their lives to free their country.

As mentioned earlier, the moral foundations are considered to be evolution-based predispositions of human beings. At the same time, people differ considerably in the extent to which they endorse each moral foundation. The environmental and cultural influences of our upbringing influence how important the foundations become to us. If you want to test this out, present the scale in Box 8.4 to people with different ideological orientations. You may be able to replicate the findings of Graham et al. (2009). They reported that liberals tend to strongly endorse care and fairness, but not the other three foundations (liberty had not yet been added to the list in 2009), whereas conservatives also endorse care and fairness, but consider loyalty, authority, and purity as almost equally important. This finding explains why liberals and conservatives tend to view each other as immoral. Conservatives may think it is very important to teach children to respect and obey authorities, whereas liberals may think that children should be taught to speak up against authorities in order to protect weaker members of society.

8.6 Wisdom and Moral Values

Why are we talking about the moral foundations in a book about wisdom? Moral Foundations Theory is essentially a theory of people's moral **values**, suggesting that people differ in how much they endorse each of them. So which values do wise individuals care about? Box 8.5 shows a list of values. First, use a scale from 1 (= "not at all important") to 7 (= "extremely important") to indicate how important each value is to you. Then use the same scale to rate how important you think each value is to a very wise person.

The values in Box 8.5 are based on Shalom Schwartz's theory of basic human values (Schwartz, 2012). Schwartz's research has shown that these values matter to people all over the world, but both cultures and the people within each culture differ in how much they care about specific values. Some of the values are moral values, as they go beyond the individual's own interests, especially benevolence, universalism, and tradition. Other values, such as power and achievement, may actually come at a cost to other people.

What values do wise individuals endorse? From a theoretical perspective, we would expect them to care particularly for the moral values. Most wisdom theories include concern for the wellbeing of others or a larger common good (e.g., Ardelt, 2003; Sternberg, 1998). In addition, wise people are assumed to be tolerant of worldviews different from their own (e.g., Baltes & Staudinger, 2000; Grossmann et al., 2010), so they might also care about self-direction. In an expert survey, wisdom researchers considered both concern for a common good and value relativism and tolerance to be closely associated with wisdom (Jeste et al., 2010).

Box 8.5 Basic human values according to Schwartz (2012); adapted from Sternberg and Glück (2022).

Value	Personal importance	Importance for a wise person
Self-direction: making my own choices and thinking independently.	—	—
Stimulation: having excitement, novelty, and challenges in my life.	—	—
Hedonism: experiencing pleasure or positive sensations.	—	—
Achievement: being successful because of my competence and performance.	—	—
Power: having prestige and status, having dominance over people and resources.	—	—
Security: being safe and secure, living a stable, harmonic life.	—	—
Conformity: following social expectations and norms, not doing things that might upset or harm others.	—	—
Tradition: being respectful, committed to, or at least accepting of the customs and ideas of my culture or religion.	—	—
Benevolence: engaging myself for the welfare of the people I know or the people of my group.	—	—
Universalism: caring about the welfare of all people, nature, and the world at large.	—	—

But maybe that is just because the wisdom researchers who came up with those theories of wisdom care about those same values. Would an individual who cares a lot about power believe that wise people also care a lot about power? In a recent study, we asked participants to fill out value questionnaires for themselves and for a wise person, as you did in Box 8.5, and to report their political orientations (Glück et al., 2020). With respect to people's own values, conservatives cared more about security, conformity, and power than did liberals, and liberals cared more about universalism than did conservatives. (Both liberals and conservatives cared a lot about benevolence.) However, the main question was whether conservatives and liberals would also differ in their ideas about wise people's values. In other words, do people generally believe that wise people have the same values as themselves? Or do even people who care very little about, say, universalism, believe that wise people care about universalism?

The results were somewhere in between. Conservatives thought that wise people care more about security, conformity, and power than liberals thought they do. Liberals thought that wise people care more about universalism than conservatives thought they do. At the same time, virtually everyone thought that wise people cared less about security and power and more about universalism than they themselves did. Across several studies, participants felt that the three values most important to wise people are benevolence, universalism, and self-direction. In two of the studies, we also measured wisdom and analyzed whether wiser participants actually endorsed specific values. Just as people had thought, wisdom was positively related to benevolence, universalism, and self-direction, and negatively related to power and security.

Other studies have found similar results. Kunzmann and Baltes (2003) and Webster (2010) reported that wisdom was positively correlated with other-oriented values (wellbeing of friends, societal engagement, and ecological protection) and with striving for self-understanding and personal growth, and that it was negatively correlated with striving for a pleasurable life. In summary, wise people do seem to care more about ethical values – concern for members of one's own "tribe" as well as for all of humanity and nature – than other people do. They also care a lot about self-direction – thinking for themselves, making their own choices, and living the life that is right for them. Note that these results were obtained from studies in "Western" countries. In more traditional, hierarchical cultures, the results may be different (see, for example, Asadi et al., 2019). However, regardless of culture, it seems unlikely that a wise person would mindlessly submit to an authority that harms others. When you look at the popular wisdom exemplars that studies have identified (see Chapter 3), quite a number of them are associated with standing up for justice and against suppression (e.g., Mahatma Gandhi, Nelson Mandela, or Martin Luther King; see, for example, Paulhus et al., 2002; Weststrate et al., 2016). Importantly, these wisdom exemplars did not just stand by their cause, but they did so by peaceful means, and they succeeded. Typically, the hardest part of living a moral life is not the theoretical endorsement of moral values, but actually acting according to those values when things get difficult.

8.7   Wisdom and Ethical Behavior

Have you ever faced a difficult moral dilemma yourself? If so, do you feel that you acted in accordance with your own values? Research on **moral behavior** shows that people often do not act according to their own values. In 1970, Bibb Latané and John Darley opened up a new field of research by investigating what people actually did when faced with a person needing help, rather than what they said they would do (Latané & Darley, 1970). These researchers had found that when someone was in trouble, such as a person having an epileptic seizure (Darley & Latané, 1968) or falling and crying out in pain (Latané & Rodin, 1969), bystanders often did not intervene. Many did not intervene because they thought someone else might do so, or because they did not feel competent to help. Darley and Batson (1973) even showed that divinity students on their way to give a lecture on the parable of *The Good Samaritan* often did not stop to help a person lying on the ground in clear need of precisely that – a good Samaritan!

8.7.1 An Eight-Step Model for Ethical Behavior

Why do people who consider themselves to be good often do something bad? Obviously, it is much harder to actually act ethically than one would expect given the rules that we are taught by our parents, school, and religious training. Sternberg (2015) has proposed a model of ethical behavior that can be applied to a variety of ethical problems. According to Sternberg, people must go through a series of eight steps if they are to actually act ethically, and each step is a challenge in itself. In the following account we shall describe the eight steps in detail, using an example from university life as an illustration.

Importantly, no research has yet shown that wise individuals actually use these steps more often than other people do. Nevertheless, we have included them here because we believe that it is important for psychologists to look more at what people actually do than at what they think they might do (Baumeister et al., 2007). Living up to one's values is an important part of wisdom that should be investigated more in the future.

(1) Recognize that there is an event to which to react.

Laura is an associate professor at a university. She loves to teach and has a good relationship with her students. At some point, students tell her that an older professor in her department is treating some students badly. They say that this professor uses language suggestive of prejudice and gets very angry in class when students have difficulty understanding her ideas. Some students are deeply scared of that professor and afraid to speak up in class, as it seems that the professor laughs openly at students who make mistakes.

Should Laura do anything about this situation? Often we do not even notice (or we choose not to notice) other people's unethical behavior. Humans tend to mind their own business and let others mind theirs, which is usually a good rule, but it can become a bad rule when someone is doing something unethical. People may be particularly willing to accept unethical behavior from leaders if they have been taught not to question authority. Sometimes it can actually be quite appealing to hand over responsibility to political, educational, or religious leaders. Wise individuals take responsibility for their own life. They would want to stand up to leaders who abuse their power.

Laura is shocked by what the students tell her. It fits into a more general pattern. The same professor has been aggressively criticizing other people in department meetings, and two members of her team have recently quit their jobs. So there indeed seems to be a problem. But is it an ethical problem, and does Laura have a responsibility to act?

(2) Define the event as having an ethical dimension.

People differ in the extent to which they see an ethical dimension in everyday life. Some people consider the decisions to eat meat, to cheat in an exam, or to challenge one's boss about one's salary as moral questions, because these decisions involve the needs and rights of other beings. Other people do not think about ethics with respect to the same issues – they do what they consider as good for themselves without thinking much about it. Wise individuals are attentive to the potential moral impact of their own or others' behavior.

Ethical standards are very important to Laura. In fact, the conversation with the students took place after her class on moral psychology, in which she had talked about the importance of standing up against injustice! She feels that the students are hoping for her to do something about the situation.

(3)   Decide that the ethical dimension is significant.

Even if people see an ethical problem with someone else's behavior, they may still decide to do nothing about it because they consider the situation to be relatively harmless, or they feel that other benefits outweigh the ethical aspects. Sometimes, economic or strategic advantages can be gained from acting unethically. In other situations, people calm their conscience by telling themselves that "everyone else does the same thing."

The more she thinks about it, the more Laura feels that the problem with her older colleague is significant. Clearly, this is not just about different personal styles – two people have given up their academic career because of the professor's behavior, and students have been hurt emotionally. But is it really Laura's job to do something about it? The whole department has witnessed the professor's behavior in meetings, and nobody ever said anything. In a way, the professor is actually profiting from her aggressiveness, as few people are willing to stand up to her.

(4)   Take responsibility for generating an ethical solution to the problem.

As mentioned earlier, decades of social psychological research have shown how adept people are at looking away and waiting for someone else to take responsibility when something bad is happening. This is particularly the case if people regard the person who is acting unethically as a good friend, or if that person is superior to them in an institutional hierarchy.

Laura is not directly working with the professor who may have been acting unethically. However, she worries that if she takes action, other senior members of the department may consider her to be a troublemaker. She talks to a colleague who is, like her, in a junior position. That colleague cautions Laura against doing anything. She feels that the senior professors in the department are all good friends and will not tolerate someone "attacking" one of them. The colleague also tells Laura that the professor in question is having some serious problems in her personal life. She has recently been going through an unpleasant divorce.

(5)   Figure out what abstract ethical rule(s) might apply to the problem.

One difficult problem with ethical rules is that often more than one of them applies, and they tend to be in conflict with each other. For example, most of us have been taught as children to be honest. However, many of us also have childhood memories of adults either bursting into laughter or being horrified because we said something perfectly honest to the wrong person in the wrong situation. Clearly, in some cases, the rule about not hurting someone else's feelings takes precedence over the rule about not lying. In difficult situations, we need to make explicit for ourselves which ethical rules are actually relevant to a problem.

Laura is trying to figure out which ethical rules matter for her problem and how she should weigh them. The professor is struggling with personal troubles, and one should not hurt someone who is already hurting. But then, students and co-workers have been hurt by the professor's behavior. Laura wonders if she is maybe overestimating her own importance. After all, there are other places the students can turn to. Maybe she should just tell them to seek help from the university's student council or human resources department. But then, the consequences for the professor may be even harsher than if the issue stays within the department. Laura also wonders whether she should completely believe the students' accusations. Maybe they are exaggerating. Is it right to give the students so much power?

(6) Decide how these abstract ethical rules actually apply to the problem to suggest a concrete solution.

It is often difficult to weigh and balance different ethical rules with respect to a specific situation. Even people who are highly trained and skilled in working with ethical and judicial rules, such as judges and pastors, find this difficult, especially in situations where they themselves or their personal relationships are involved. As discussed in Chapter 4, wisdom researchers have been discussing why it is sometimes so much harder to show personal wisdom (wisdom realized in one's own life) than to show general wisdom (wisdom applied to other people's lives) (see Staudinger, 2019). Sometimes it helps to imagine looking at the situation from an outside perspective (Kross & Grossmann, 2012).

Laura has decided that she needs to do something. Students have told her that last week a student left class in tears after the professor yelled at him and told him he was too stupid for this university. In combination with the other things Laura has heard, she feels that the professor's transgressions are too severe and consistent to be justified by her personal troubles. Laura wonders if she should talk to another senior professor within the department whom she considers to be trustworthy and caring.

(7) Prepare for potential adverse consequences of acting.

As discussed earlier, one characteristic of ethical acts is that the person doing them does not stand to gain anything from them. In fact, acting ethically can have negative consequences. Sometimes doing the right thing may mean standing up against someone in public, which means that everybody will know who was responsible. This action may earn some people medals of honor, but more often it will earn them a lot of trouble. People who point out the unethical behavior of others may lose friends, be viewed as traitors themselves, or become the target of revenge by the people whose unethical behavior they uncovered. Whistleblowers often lose their jobs eventually.

Laura is quite worried that she may be wrong about the professor to whom she wants to talk. Perhaps his loyalty to the other professor goes further than Laura thinks. In any case, if the professor faces serious consequences for her behavior, she or other people in the department may find out that it was Laura who started the process. Laura is very worried about what this may mean for her position in the department and her relationships with her colleagues.

(8) Act.

Even after they have determined that they indeed need to do something, people sometimes end up not doing anything. They may just convince themselves that other things are more important.

They may never master the courage to actually do what they think is right, especially when negative consequences are likely. They may simply wait too long for the perfect moment, which somehow never comes.

Laura makes an appointment with the older professor. She asks him to treat the conversation as confidential and makes it clear that she is not sure whether she is doing the right thing, but then she tells him the whole story. The professor listens carefully. He says that Laura did the right thing. Similar things have happened before and he knows how to deal with them. He is going to work with the department head and the human resources department. They will talk to the professor about the allegations without giving away either Laura's name or any students' names. The professor will get a serious admonition and will be warned of consequences if she does not change her behavior. However, she will also be offered counseling to deal with her personal problems and develop her teaching strategies. A few weeks later, her students tell Laura that the professor's behavior has noticeably changed.

8.8   Conclusion

This chapter has summarized the theoretical and empirical relationships between wisdom and morality. Wise individuals are able to think carefully and rationally about moral dilemmas, recognizing their own intuitive impulses but not necessarily following them in making decisions. As they think about complex moral dilemmas, they aim to balance the different perspectives, interests, and needs optimally. Their value orientations are focused on a greater good that does not just include members of their own family or group, but humanity and the world at large. Because they are good at thinking about moral issues and dealing with the emotional and social aspects of complex situations, they are likely to also act ethically in difficult situations. Many of the great wisdom exemplars in history stood up for a just cause and accomplished major societal changes by peaceful means. We believe that the ethical aspect of wisdom is particularly important at a time when the world needs good decisions that do not focus on the needs of any particular nation or group. If we want to overcome serious world problems, such as climate change, global pandemics, and rising inequality, we need ethical and wise leaders.

8.9   Comprehension and Discussion Questions

(1)   Try to think of a difficult moral dilemma that a person might be facing nowadays – a problem that involves conflicting moral rules and that requires people to balance their own needs with those of others. How would people at the three levels of Kohlberg's model of moral reasoning think about that dilemma?

(2)   Are there domains in which you have strong moral intuitions – things that people may do that just feel deeply wrong to you, where even the thought of people doing them makes you deeply angry or disgusted? Try to think of an example. Where do you think these moral intuitions come from? Are they related to your upbringing, your cultural background, or specific experiences of your own, or could they be evolution-based?

(3)   Can you remember a situation in which you had a strong moral intuition but then changed your mind – perhaps because you found out more about the issue or someone convinced you of a different view? To what extent do you typically question your immediate intuitions?

(4)   Which values from Schwartz's model do you consider as most important for yourself? Are they moral values? Do you consider being an ethical person as a central part of your identity?

Why do you think you have these values, and why is being an ethical person so central or not central to your identity?

(5) Can you recall a moral dilemma that you have faced in your own life? Did you end up doing what you thought was right? Go through Sternberg's eight-step model and try to reconstruct whether and how you took each step. If you ended up not doing what was right, on which step did you stumble? If you did what was right, who or what helped you to do so?

8.10 Investigations

Judith Glück's main topic of research is wisdom psychology. Having been trained in psychometrics, she has a strong interest in developing new ways to measure wisdom. She is also interested in the development of wisdom through an interplay of life experiences and internal and external resources, factors that influence wisdom in professional contexts, ways to foster wisdom through interventions and through changes in structures and systems, the relationship between wisdom and morality, and people's conceptions of wisdom in different cultures.

Robert J. Sternberg studies wisdom, as well as intelligence and creativity. His major current concern in his research is with these processes as they apply in the everyday world. Too often tests are rather artificial, and give an impression of how people think they should answer the test questions, rather than how they would actually handle the situations in everyday life. Thus his current research presents real-world problems, asks participants how they would address those problems, and rates the responses for their wisdom in terms of the balance theory of wisdom.

8.11 Practical Applications

Judith Glück's work is relevant to many areas of everyday life. Ways to foster the development and manifestation of wisdom seem very important for today's world. Although research on measuring wisdom may seem less directly relevant than applied research, we need to provide the best tools for measuring wisdom if we want to study the factors that influence whether people grow toward wisdom and display wisdom in their everyday lives.

Robert J. Sternberg's research is oriented toward practical wisdom in the sense of understanding and assessing how people solve real problems. His research is maximum performance based – it looks at people's actual solutions to everyday problems and how effective those solutions are.

Glossary

evolution the process of change that all forms of life undergo over generations. Biological populations evolve through genetic changes that correspond to changes in the organisms' observable traits. Genetic changes include mutations, which are caused by damage or replication errors in organisms' DNA. As random genetic variations occur in a population over generations, natural selection gradually leads traits to become more or less common, depending on the relative reproductive success of organisms with those traits.

expertise the broad and deep competence in terms of knowledge, skill, and experience that distinguishes the best performers in a domain. Experts have acquired their skill and knowledge through long-term experience and practice.

intuitions the feelings or thoughts that people have about something without knowing why they feel or think that way – so-called "gut feelings" or "hunches." Intuitions are a function of the unconscious mind – those parts of one's brain/ mind (the majority of it, in fact) that one cannot consciously control or perceive.

moral behavior people's actions based on moral values and standards. Moral behavior is often equated with prosocial behavior. Typical examples of moral behavior include sharing, helping, cooperating, expressing sympathy, and standing up for the rights and needs of others.

moral dilemma any situation in which two moral values are in conflict and it is not clear that one of them should override the other. Any choice made by someone facing a moral dilemma will violate one moral value. Therefore they need to decide which value is more important in that situation, and which harm will have to be accepted as a consequence.

Moral Foundations Theory a social psychological theory that aims to explain the origins of and variation in human moral reasoning on the basis of innate, modular foundations. It was proposed by the psychologist Jonathan Haidt and his colleagues. Haidt's social intuitionist approach to morality assumes that moral judgment is caused by quick moral intuitions that are grounded in human evolution. The current version of the theory proposes six foundations: Care/Harm, Fairness/Cheating, Loyalty/Betrayal, Authority/Subversion, Sanctity/ Degradation, and Liberty/Oppression.

morality those intentions, decisions, and actions that people view as right and those which they view as wrong. Morality can refer to principles prescribed by a culture, religion, or philosophy, or it can be the set of principles that an individual person decides to follow.

moral reasoning the conscious thinking process by which people try to use logic to determine what is right and what is wrong with respect to a given problem.

values individuals' broad preferences concerning appropriate or desirable outcomes or courses of action. Values influence people's attitudes and behavior by guiding their choices according to their basic principles of right and wrong and their personal priorities.

REFERENCES

Ardelt, M. (2003). Empirical assessment of a three-dimensional wisdom scale. *Research on Aging*, 25(3), 275–324.

Asadi, S., Khorshidi, R., and Glück, J. (2019). Iranian children's knowledge about wisdom. *Cognitive Development*, 52, Article 100814.

Baltes, P. B. and Staudinger, U. M. (2000). A metaheuristic (pragmatic) to orchestrate mind and virtue toward excellence. *American Psychologist*, 55(1), 122–36.

Baumeister, R. F., Vohs, K. D., and Funder, D. C. (2007). Psychology as the science of self-reports and finger movements: whatever happened to actual behavior? *Perspectives on Psychological Science*, 2(4), 396–403.

Boehm, C. (1999). *Hierarchy in the Forest: The Evolution of Egalitarian Behavior*. Harvard University Press.

Brewer, M. B. (1979). In-group bias in the minimal intergroup situation: a cognitive-motivational analysis. *Psychological Bulletin*, 86(2), 307–24.

Colby, A., Kohlberg, L., Speicher, B. et al. (1987). *The Measurement of Moral Judgement: Volume 2, Standard Issue Scoring Manual*. Cambridge University Press.

Darley, J. M. and Batson, C. D. (1973). "From Jerusalem to Jericho": a study of situational and dispositional variables in helping behavior. *Journal of Personality and Social Psychology*, 27(1), 100–8.

Darley, J. M. and Latané, B. (1968). Bystander intervention in emergencies: diffusion of responsibility. *Journal of Personality and Social Psychology*, 8(4), 377–83.

De Waal, F. B. (2008). Putting the altruism back into altruism: the evolution of empathy. *Annual Review of Psychology*, 59, 279–300.

Fehr, E. and Gächter, S. (2000). Cooperation and punishment in public goods experiments. *The American Economic Review*, 90(4), 980–94.

Glück, J. and Bluck, S. (2013). The MORE life experience model: a theory of the development of personal wisdom. In M. Ferrari and N. M. Weststrate, eds., *The Scientific Study of Personal Wisdom: From Contemplative Traditions to Neuroscience.* Springer, pp. 75–97.

Glück, J., Gussnig, B., and Schrottenbacher, S. M. (2020). Wisdom and value orientations: just a projection of our own beliefs? *Journal of Personality*, 88(4), 833–55.

Graham, J., Haidt, J., and Nosek, B. A. (2008). *The Moral Foundations Questionnaire.* Downloaded from https://moralfoundations.org/questionnaires/.

Graham, J., Haidt, J., and Nosek, B. A. (2009). Liberals and conservatives rely on different sets of moral foundations. *Journal of Personality and Social Psychology*, 96(5), 1029–46.

Greene, J. (2013). *Moral Tribes: Emotion, Reason, and the Gap Between Us and Them.* Penguin.

Grossmann, I. (2017). Wisdom in context. *Perspectives on Psychological Science*, 12(2), 233–57.

Grossmann, I., Na, J., Varnum, M. E. W. et al. (2010). Reasoning about social conflicts improves into old age. *Proceedings of the National Academy of Sciences of the United States of America*, 107(16), 7246–50.

Haidt, J. (2001). The emotional dog and its rational tail: a social intuitionist approach to moral judgment. *Psychological Review*, 108(4), 814–34.

(2013). *The Righteous Mind: Why Good People are Divided by Politics and Religion.* Vintage.

Jeste, D. V., Ardelt, M., Blazer, D. et al. (2010). Expert consensus on characteristics of wisdom: a Delphi method study. *The Gerontologist*, 50(5), 668–80.

Kahneman, D. (2011). *Thinking, Fast and Slow.* Macmillan.

Kohlberg, L. (1958). *The Development of Modes of Thinking and Choices in Years 10 to 16.* PhD dissertation, University of Chicago.

Kross, E. and Grossmann, I. (2012). Boosting wisdom: distance from the self enhances wise reasoning, attitudes, and behavior. *Journal of Experimental Psychology: General*, 141(1), 43–48.

Kunzmann, U. and Baltes, P. (2003). Wisdom-related knowledge: affective, motivational, and interpersonal correlates. *Personality and Social Psychology Bulletin*, 29(9), 1104–19.

Latané, B. and Darley, J. M. (1970). *Unresponsive Bystander: Why Doesn't He Help?* Prentice-Hall.

Latané, B. and Rodin, J. (1969). A lady in distress: inhibiting effects of friends and strangers on bystander intervention. *Journal of Experimental Social Psychology*, 5(2), 189–202.

Pasupathi, M. and Staudinger, U. M. (2001). Do advanced moral reasoners also show wisdom? Linking moral reasoning and wisdom-related knowledge and judgement. *International Journal of Behavioral Development*, 25(5), 401–15.

Paulhus, D. L., Wehr, P., Harms, P. D., and Strasser, D. I. (2002). Use of exemplar surveys to reveal implicit types of intelligence. *Personality and Social Psychology Bulletin*, 28(8), 1051–62.

Paxton, J. M., Ungar, L., and Greene, J. D. (2012). Reflection and reasoning in moral judgment. *Cognitive Science*, 36(1), 163–77.

Schwartz, S. H. (2012). An overview of the Schwartz theory of basic values. *Online Readings in Psychology and Culture*, 2(1), Article 11. Downloaded from https://core.ac.uk/download/pdf/10687025.pdf

Staudinger, U. M. (2019). The distinction between personal and general wisdom: How far have we come? In R. J. Sternberg and J. Glück, eds., *The Cambridge Handbook of Wisdom.* Cambridge University Press, pp. 182–201.

Sternberg, R. J. (1998). A balance theory of wisdom. *Review of General Psychology*, 2(4), 347–65.

(2015). Epilogue: why is ethical behavior challenging? A model of ethical reasoning. In R. J. Sternberg and S. T. Fiske, eds., *Ethical Challenges in the Behavioral and Brain Sciences.* Cambridge University Press, pp. 219–26.

Sternberg, R. J. and Glück, J. (2022). *Wisdom: The Psychology of Wise Thoughts, Words, and Deeds.* Cambridge University Press.

Webster, J. D. (2010). Wisdom and positive psychosocial values in young adulthood. *Journal of Adult Development,* 17(2), 70–80.

Weststrate, N. M., Ferrari, M., and Ardelt, M. (2016). The many faces of wisdom: an investigation of cultural-historical wisdom exemplars reveals practical, philosophical, and benevolent prototypes. *Personality and Social Psychology Bulletin,* 42(5), 662–76.

CHAPTER 9

Wisdom, Personality, and Well-Being*

Monika Ardelt and Stephen Pridgen

9.1 Introduction

Is wisdom a state, comparable to a momentary feeling of happiness when one sees an old friend or has a delicious meal, or a more enduring trait-like personality quality, such as being an introvert or an extrovert? The answer to this question depends on how wisdom is defined and assessed. Wise advice, wise reasoning, and wise decision making depend on a person's specific wisdom-related knowledge and expertise, and might easily change from one context or situation to the next (Grossmann, 2017; Grossmann et al., 2019; Santos et al., 2017). However, if wisdom is defined as a personality quality, then it is likely to be relatively stable, at least in the short term (Ardelt, 2003, 2016), without precluding the possibility of change in the long term.

This does not mean that a person with a wise personality will always act wisely, just as a person with an introverted personality might sometimes be quite outgoing among a small group of friends or in professional settings (Cain, 2012). Yet, on average, an individual with a wise personality is expected to behave in a way that is consistent with definitions of personal wisdom across situations and over time (cf. Chapter 5). Specifically, when confronted with hardship, life crises, or circumstances that do not have a clear course of action, people with a wise personality are more likely to act wisely than those who lack this quality (Ardelt, 2005; Plews-Ogan et al., 2012).

Consider the life stories of two men, Charles Howard and John Palmer,[1] who participated in the Longitudinal Study of Adult Development (Ardelt & Vaillant, 2009). The two men belonged to a study cohort of 268 Harvard college sophomores who were selected from the graduating classes of 1940–1944. All of the selected men had a satisfactory freshman academic record and no history of physical or mental illness. As students, the men were studied by an interdisciplinary team of internists, psychiatrists, psychologists, and anthropologists, and the students' parents were interviewed to obtain the family's social and medical history. Subsequently, mail questionnaires were sent to the men repeatedly over the course of their lives, and qualitative in-depth interviews were conducted when the men were approximately 25, 30, 50, 65, and 85 years old (Vaillant, 1977, 1993, 2002, 2012).

Mr. Charles Howard was born in 1921 to a stockbroker father and a homemaker mother who was also active in social service work. While growing up and then throughout his life,

* We are very grateful to George E. Vaillant for access to the two case studies. The case study comparison was supported by a previous grant from the John T. Templeton Foundation. Many thanks are due to Judith Glück, Robert J. Sternberg, Rasee R. Bhoola, and Gabriel A. Kaul-Ardelt for helpful comments and suggestions on an earlier draft of this chapter.
[1] All names are pseudonyms, and some of the demographic information has been altered to protect the men's identity.

Mr. Howard had a warm and loving relationship with his close-knit extended family and especially his father, his mother, and his sister, who was three years younger than him. Although the family was wealthy and owned three houses, his father had started out with nothing and worked his way up the social ladder. Yet Mr. Howard's father was not distant, but made sure that he spent time with his family. At the age of 19, Mr. Howard said of his father, "We do everything together, practically" and of his family, "We all get along beautifully together." Mr. Howard's mother described her 20-year-old son as "very affectionate, sensitive but with a great deal of courage and determination." This positive family environment was repeated in Mr. Howard's own family when he married at the age of 22 and later had three children. In mail questionnaires that he completed between the ages of 25 and 49, he always wrote very positively about his wife and children, making clear that he was very fond of them.

Mr. Howard worked hard in a variety of jobs throughout his life, and found meaning in whatever he did. Work was not seen as a necessity to pay for other needs, but as meaningful in itself. At the age of 25, he wrote in a questionnaire:

> The monetary end interests me but little. . . . My work means the full enjoyment of life, my children and my wife. It means the fulfillment of man's desire to better himself and those about him. My work means living life and not working at it.

In his thirties and forties, Mr. Howard worked in various jobs in industry and business, climbing the corporate ladder. Although he considered these jobs interesting and lucrative, he was not really satisfied with this work because, as he wrote in a questionnaire at the age of 43:

> I feel I am making so little contribution to the world. Too little time is spent helping people and too much time spent on relative trivia. I realize my community activity has helped a few. Keeping our business or company going and prospering will give people jobs and security. But it's all so confining. I feel wasted and unused.

At the age of 48, Mr. Howard left his company job and bought and ran two small businesses. However, this career move did not benefit his marriage. At the age of 52, after 30 years of marriage, his wife divorced him. Even though the divorce was hard on him, he did not have any bad feelings toward his wife, and he understood the reasons why she wanted to leave him. In fact, he was very happy that she ended up marrying one of his close friends. At the age of 54, Mr. Howard wrote in a questionnaire:

> Very amicable divorce after a long period of unhappiness for her and same for me. We just wanted different lifestyles. I guess I exhausted her. Her drinking and jealousy were real problems for me. As for me, I guess I didn't love her enough. She is a wonderful person but so negative with everything. I saw life as beautiful and joyous and was terribly active with children and people. She wanted a comfy home life with trips with a few close friends. When her best friend committed suicide, she wanted to marry her husband who was one of my dear friends. As they are perfectly suited, I was most happy. They are to be married in three weeks and I couldn't be more pleased for them. They are two very nice people who have found happiness together.

Of course, Mr. Howard's contentment with his ex-wife's new marriage was not completely selfless. He realized that his love for her had waned and that he was attracted to other women. In the same questionnaire, he mentioned two younger women with whom he fell in love. At the age of 56, he married the widow of his business partner who had committed suicide a year earlier. In the questionnaire of this year, he wrote:

> [She] and her children had only me to turn to in their tragedy. Also, she was now my business partner in our two companies. We were together constantly. She loved me very deeply [as] I soon discovered. . . . We decided there was no point in waiting. She is a true love. The children needed me very badly. . . . It has been perfect for me. No one has ever healed me with such love. And in return I have come to love her completely. We have been enormously happy.

Mr. Howard's second wife was not only his marriage partner but also his partner in the many businesses that he pursued during the second half of his life. Even after "retirement" at the age of 64, he and his wife continued to engage in several business activities and served as volunteers in various positions. At the age of 80, Mr. Howard wrote, "I love my wife more! She is totally loving to me." His wife expressed the same sentiments. When Mr. Howard was 82 years old, his wife was asked by an interviewer how her relationship to her husband had changed over time. She answered, "Well, it's just gotten more so, stronger, definitely stronger." To the question asking what the best things were about being in this marriage, she responded, "Oh heavens, where to begin? Just about everything. I can't think of anything that hasn't been positive about being in this relationship."

Now compare the life story of Mr. Howard with that of Mr. Palmer. Mr. John Palmer was born in 1923 to a middle-class family. His father was a technician and his mother was a homemaker. He had one sister, who was five years younger than him. Unlike Mr. Howard, Mr. Palmer did not have a close relationship with his family. At the age of 18, he said, "I really don't think I know either of my parents very well. Father is kind of quiet and has never had much to say to me, but I know he thinks a heck of a lot of me and is proud of me." About his mother he said, "I can talk to her better than I can to my father, but even at that I don't feel too close to her." His relationship with his sister was also quite distant. He said, "I treat her sarcastically and I used to tease her. Now as we have grown older we have grown apart a little." In addition, he reported that all the members of his family suffered from "mood swings." Similarly, Mr. Palmer's mother described her son as "a moody person and I think he enjoys his moodiness."

At Harvard, Mr. Palmer suffered from social insecurities, anxiety, and low self-esteem, because he felt that he did not quite belong to the Harvard community as a scholarship student from a middle-class family. After graduating, he worked as an architect for several companies in New York until his retirement at the age of 67. It appears, however, that he did not obtain much satisfaction from his career. When asked at the age of 47 to rate in a questionnaire his career over the past two decades compared with his college classmates, he reported that he felt "less" satisfaction in terms of achievement on the job and enjoyment on the job, "less" success and achievement on the job in the eyes of others, and "less" benefit or service to others in the course of the job.

At the age of 27, Mr. Palmer married a fellow architectural student who was of higher social standing than he was. His wife also had a sizeable trust fund and stocks for investment, so that their income, particularly in the early years, was considerably supplemented by his wife's dividend income. Yet after only three years of marriage, Mr. Palmer sought help for unsatisfactory sexual relations with his wife and a lack of warmth in the relationship. The marriage remained childless, and the marital problems continued over the years. At the age of 41, Mr. Palmer revealed in a questionnaire that his wife had been diagnosed with a serious mental illness and had spent over a year in a psychiatric hospital four years earlier. He wrote:

> With the help of my own psychiatrist I have long since gotten rid of my own guilt feelings about [my wife's] problems and also any feeling that [my wife] is responsible for what is happening to her. However, living with her day-to-day is exasperating and frustrating. . . . Realistically I think the

marriage is finished but I can't as yet face the idea of breaking up, especially because I seem to be the only one she can trust, but also because I am lonely and somewhat afraid myself. No matter how hollow a marriage may be, it still gives one a home and a place in society.

The marriage continued to deteriorate. During a qualitative interview at the age of 47, Mr. Palmer admitted that he had had two extramarital affairs, but he still did not want to divorce his wife, because, as the interviewer noted:

> … with old age coming on and having his heart flutter he saw himself being old and alone with no money, and he pointed out to me [the interviewer] that [his wife] did have money. He said "The thing about marriage, it gives me a place" and that despite "even some hatred, it's easier to suffer with [his wife] than without her." … He said he perceived divorce as an excruciating expense and damned difficult.

A couple of months later, Mr. Palmer's wife died of lung cancer, which most likely allowed him to inherit his wife's assets. After her death, he dated several women his own age, because "they were so grateful for any attention that you paid them," but he was able to resist the many women who wanted to tie him down in another marriage, as he remarked in an interview at age 52. However, at the age of 62, Mr. Palmer remarried a wealthy widow of relatively high social standing whom he had known for 33 years.

The marriage appeared to give him social and financial security, and he judged this to be the happiest period of his life in subsequent questionnaires. Yet, in an interview at the age of 74, he revealed that he and his wife began fighting as soon as they got married. He also stated that his biggest worry over the past year was "the underlying meaning of life," and minor worries were that they were not entertaining enough, because he still had social aspirations. Even at the age of 74, Mr. Palmer was concerned about his social standing. His insecurities also continued, and he did not seem to be capable of sexual intimacy with his new wife.

9.2   Wisdom as a Personality Quality

For Socrates (469–399 BCE) and the ancient Greek philosophers, the goal of philosophy was not just to think deeply about life, but also to become aware of one's unconscious beliefs and values and consciously create new habits of thinking, feeling, and acting to become a wiser person and live a fulfilling and flourishing life (Evans, 2013). Hence, philosophy was perceived not just as an intellectual endeavor but also as a practice. **Theoretical wisdom (*sophia*)**, which is an understanding of timeless, universal truths, is attained through contemplation. However, these insights only contribute to a good and flourishing life if they lead to **practical wisdom (*phronesis*)**, which is a deep and valuable understanding and practice of how one *should* live and conduct oneself (Curnow, 1999; Schwartz & Sharpe, 2019; Swartwood & Tiberius, 2019). Practicing practical wisdom requires the strengthening of rational thinking to control one's impulses so that one can live a wise and virtuous life.

Mr. Howard's practical wisdom became evident when he was asked in a questionnaire at the age of 74 to share his wisdom, rules of life, or "pearls" that he had gathered during his lifetime that might be valuable to the next generation. He wrote:

> No one listens but here goes. Be less concerned about yourself. Relax and enjoy life as it comes to you. Don't be so serious about the big problems of life. Get the damned facts on anything and don't go off on emotion. Try to like and love people as they are. You sure can't change them! Accept us all as we

are. You can't be expected to like and love everyone or even many, but that's no reason not to be pleasant. Giving of oneself may not be appreciated, but it will sure make you happier and a nicer person to be around. Achievement is all in fashion, but if you can achieve the above, the world will be a better place for us all.

These are great words of wisdom, but much easier said than done. However, Mr. Howard appeared to have lived according to his own maxims. He had discovered one of the paradoxical truths – that caring about the well-being of others rather than exclusively about oneself leads to a happy life. Contrast this with the answer given by Mr. Palmer who, when asked at the age of 74 whether he could give an example of some wisdom he had acquired as he grew older, wrote, "I am a fatalist, resulting from experience and observation." This response signifies the powerlessness that the Harvard-educated, financially well-off Mr. Palmer felt to get what he wanted throughout most of his life. Whereas Mr. Howard was striving to be a better person for the greater good, Mr. Palmer was disappointed that he was unable to bend the world to his liking. Mr. Palmer exemplified the first two Noble Truths the Buddha taught – that life is suffering, because we desire something we do not have and become miserable if we do not get it or, if we do get it, we soon desire something else, continuing the cycle of suffering (Armstrong, 2001; Ñanamoli, 2001).

Following the ancient Greeks, Fischer (2015, p. 73) described wisdom as "knowledge of the fundamental truths in the domain of living well." If this kind of knowledge helps people to live wisely, it will affect their personality by developing wise personality qualities. However, if the knowledge remains theoretical, they might be able to reason wisely or to give wise advice, but it will not change them personally (Ardelt, 2004). As Blanchard-Fields and Norris (1995, p. 105) emphasized, "wisdom is not simply one aspect of knowledge, but knowledge is only one aspect of wisdom."

One can have wisdom-related knowledge without having a wise personality, as was illustrated by Mr. Palmer when he described the qualities of a wise man as "Perspective, sense of the larger context of life, realization that there are two sides to everything, nothing is black and white. Patience. Sense of the irony of life." This description covers lifespan contextualism, value relativism, and a recognition of uncertainty, which are elements of general wisdom-related knowledge (Baltes & Smith, 2008; Baltes & Staudinger, 2000). However, this wisdom-related knowledge did not help Mr. Palmer to live a good and flourishing life. According to Moody (1986, p. 142), "one can *have* theoretical knowledge without any corresponding transformation of one's personal being. But one cannot 'have' wisdom without *being* wise" (emphasis in original). Therefore it makes sense that having wisdom refers to specific personality qualities that are relatively stable(Glück et al., 2013, 2019; Jeste et al., 2010; Lee et al., 2020; Staudinger & Kessler, 2009; Sternberg, 1998).

We present three conceptualizations of a wise personality – wisdom as an integrative personality, as optimal personality development, and as a self-transcendent personality. These three conceptualizations are not mutually exclusive, but emphasize different aspects of a wise personality.

9.2.1 *Wisdom as an Integrative Personality*

Many wisdom researchers define wisdom as an integration of cognitive, reflective, and benevolent personality qualities (Ardelt & Oh, 2010). After reviewing the scientific wisdom literature, Meeks and Jeste (2009) concluded that wisdom is most often described as a combination of (1) prosocial attitudes/behaviors, (2) social decision making/pragmatic knowledge of life, (3) emotional homeostasis, (4) reflection/self-understanding, (5) value relativism/tolerance, and (6) acknowledging and dealing with uncertainty/ambiguity. Although the emphasis on these wisdom qualities might differ according to culture, with Western cultures focusing more on the cognitive, analytic aspects of wisdom, and Eastern cultures synthesizing both cognitive and non-cognitive wisdom components (Takahashi & Overton, 2005), a substantial overlap exists in depictions of wise individuals. For example, similar to Western conceptions of a wise person, a wise Sharia judge in Islam is described as being knowledgeable, understanding, compassionate, virtuous, patient, and humble (Woerner-Powell & Edmondson, 2019), and a wise leader in Indian Vedanta philosophy tends to be characterized as insightful, practical, compassionate, virtuous, mindful, and humble (Tahora et al., 2019).

The **Three-Dimensional Wisdom Model (3D-WM)**, consisting of cognitive, reflective, and compassionate dimensions, tries to integrate the essential qualities that are necessary but also sufficient for a person to be considered wise (Ardelt, 1997, 2003, 2004). All other qualities of a wise person, such as virtue, humility, patience, humor, and coping skills, are considered predictors, correlates, or effects of three-dimensional wisdom. This relatively parsimonious model originated in research by Clayton and Birren (1980), and is compatible with many wisdom definitions across cultures (Ardelt et al., 2020; Weststrate et al., 2019; Yang & Intezari, 2019). Compared with the review of the wisdom literature conducted by Meeks and Jeste (2009), the cognitive dimension of the 3D-WM encompasses pragmatic knowledge of life, value relativism/ tolerance, and acknowledging and dealing with uncertainty/ambiguity. The reflective dimension includes emotional homeostasis and reflection/self-understanding, and the compassionate dimension incorporates prosocial attitudes and behavior.

The deeper insight, knowledge, and understanding of the intrapersonal and interpersonal aspects of life of the cognitive wisdom dimension are obtained through the process of perspective taking, self-reflection, and self-examination that defines the reflective wisdom dimension. Perceiving phenomena, events, and oneself from multiple perspectives leads to a reduction in self-centeredness, subjectivity, and projections (the tendency to blame other people or circumstances for one's own shortcomings). The process enables deeper insight into reality, including acceptance of the positive and negative aspects of human nature, the inherent limits of knowledge, and life's unpredictability and uncertainty. It also increases understanding and tolerance of others, resulting in the sympathetic and compassionate love that describes the compassionate wisdom dimension. The 3D-WM can be assessed by the Three-Dimensional Wisdom Scale (3D-WS, Ardelt, 2003) or cognitive, reflective, and compassionate items from existing scales or ratings (Ardelt, 1997).

In the Longitudinal Study of Adult Development, three-dimensional wisdom at midlife (around the age of 50 years) was measured mainly by the *absence* of cognitive, reflective, and compassionate personality qualities selected from the Lazare–Klerman–Armor Personality Inventory (Lazare et al., 1966). Three-dimensional wisdom in old age (around the age of 80 years) was assessed as the *presence* of cognitive, reflective, and compassionate personality qualities selected from the Gallup Wellsprings of a Positive Life Survey (Ardelt et al., 2018; Isaacowitz et al., 2003). Mr. Howard scored in the top 5 percent of three-dimensional wisdom at midlife, and had the highest three-dimensional wisdom score in old age. By contrast, Mr. Palmer scored in the bottom 10 percent of three-dimensional wisdom at midlife, and had the second lowest three-dimensional wisdom score in old age.

9.2.2 *Wisdom as Optimal Personality Development*

If wisdom is understood to be a lifelong developmental process, the focus is on the processes through which people evolve emotionally and socially to grow wiser. Erik Erikson's stage theory (Erikson, 1963, 1982) is an example of psychosocial development toward wisdom. According to this theory, psychosocial growth takes place through the resolution of eight age-appropriate developmental tasks. During midlife, the seventh psychosocial task is to overcome self-absorption and develop generativity. A generative person cares about the success and well-being of younger generations beyond their own children and grandchildren, often through personal mentorships and teaching, but also by promoting environmental or social policies that benefit younger generations.

The eighth psychosocial task of old age consists of the tension between ego integrity and despair. To achieve ego integrity, older adults need to accept their past life course as a whole, including failures, missed opportunities, and disappointments, and to come to terms with the many losses that accompany old age without succumbing to despair over the inalterability of the past, the physical frailties of an aging body, and the nearing of death. The virtue that arises if this psychosocial task is resolved successfully is wisdom, which Erikson (1964, p. 133) defined as "detached concern with life itself in the face of death itself."

Similar to Erikson's model of psychosocial development, Webster's *H.E.R.O.(E.) model of wisdom* focuses on wisdom as optimal personality development based on life experiences. The model is assessed by Webster's *Self-Assessed Wisdom Scale (SAWS)* (Webster, 2003, 2007), and portrays a wise person as an individual who has *H*umor, has *E*xperienced critical (i.e., difficult, morally challenging, and/or profound) life events, engages in self-*R*eflection and life review, is *O*pen to all kinds of experiences, and regulates negative *E*motions. As expected, the SAWS was positively correlated with generativity and ego integrity.

Although ego integrity was not assessed in the Longitudinal Study of Adult Development, two independent staff members judged whether the men had achieved generativity at midlife based on the men's qualitative interviews up to the age of 47. Of the two men, only Mr. Howard was rated as having achieved generativity at midlife. When asked, at the age of 58, what he would leave as a "legacy" or most lasting accomplishment from his career, Mr. Howard wrote,

> I feel I will have or have accomplished the following:
>
> 1. Salvaged several floundering companies and kept them going.
> 2. Established several small companies and kept them going.
> 3. Taught a lot of men and women economics and business administration, and helped them along in their careers.
> 4. Helped bring up and get started in life five children and a good number of foster children.
> 5. Started a number of local land trusts, which have preserved a great deal of land for future generations to enjoy.
> 6. Have had some influence in helping many others in seeing the other person's point of view, tolerance, and understanding.

Points 3–5 of Mr. Howard' six legacies clearly depicted his generativity, and even the remaining three points might have had generative elements if the companies that he salvaged or founded were passed on to the next generation, and his mediation skills improved interactions between members of different generations. Mr. Howard's care for younger generations was evident not only through his professional and private mentorship of young people, but also through the establishment of local land trusts, which preserved nature for future generations. By contrast, at the age of 56, Mr. Palmer stated that his "legacy" or most lasting accomplishment from his career was "Years of hard work and loyalty to the company." This self-referential answer lacked any concern for future generations.

Although both Mr. Howard and Mr. Palmer experienced critical life events and reflected on their lives, only Mr. Howard appeared to have reached ego integrity and approached life with humor as gauged by the questionnaire entries. He fully accepted and embraced his life, and grew more open to experiences with age. By contrast, Mr. Palmer always had the nagging feeling that life was unfair to him. He became fatalistic and less open to experiences with age, and was unable to regulate his emotions, as evidenced by his lifelong struggle with social insecurity and anxiety.

9.2.3   Wisdom as a Self-Transcendent Personality

One aspect of wisdom is self-transcendence, which entails both liberation from self-centered concerns and the development of a unitive or cosmic consciousness that dissolves the boundaries between self and others (Aldwin et al., 2019). This conceptualization of wisdom as self-transcendence (Levenson, 2009; Levenson & Aldwin, 2013), assessed by the *Adult Self-Transcendence Inventory (ASTI)* (Levenson et al., 2005), derived from the review of Western and Eastern wisdom philosophies by Curnow (1999).

The development of self-transcendence occurs in four stages and starts with the question "Who am I?" (Aldwin et al., 2019; Levenson & Aldwin, 2013). During the first stage, the sense of self is tied to a person's social roles, relationships, achievements, beliefs, thoughts, and feelings, and is strictly separated from "the other." During the second stage, individuals realize that social roles, relationships, achievements, beliefs, thoughts, and feelings are not fixed and stable but transient and changing, which results in a detachment from external definitions of the self. During the third stage, a dissolution of separate "inner selves" occurs, with all aspects of the self, including negative and problematic aspects, integrated into a unified self that encompasses the whole person. The acknowledgement of all positive and negative aspects of the self opens the path to an understanding and acceptance of our common humanity – that all humans struggle with conflicting inner selves. This shift from a self-centered to an observer stance dissolves the boundaries between self and other, and leads to self-transcendence and a unitive consciousness during the fourth stage. The developmental process toward self-transcendence is recursive rather than linear, and is supported by self-reflective examination practices such as meditation, contemplation, and journal writing. These foster self-knowledge and self-insight and weaken self-centered emotional reactions that constrain and limit the self, such as fear, anxiety, shame, anger, hatred, jealousy, lust, and greed, allowing a liberated (or "freer") form of consciousness to emerge.

As a consequence of this process, people with a self-transcendent personality are less concerned about their own individual successes than with the promotion of the greater good. For example, when asked in a questionnaire at the age of 76 what he was most proud of, and for what he wanted to be remembered, Mr. Howard answered:

> I don't give a damn if I'm remembered for anything. I've enjoyed my life and had a hell of a good time. I'm more proud of those times I've helped others. No fanfare or trawlers needed.

At the age of 74, Mr. Palmer replied to the same question:

> Receiving a Harvard scholarship, coming east while gradually ridding myself of family prejudices and obsolete ideas (while still loving them and admiring their good qualities), achieving a certain amount of acceptance as a Johnny-come-lately, as an easterner.

Whereas Mr. Palmer was proud of his personal achievements and his acceptance into high society, Mr. Howard's answer shows that he did not care at all about personal accolades. He had transcended self-centered concerns in favor of other-centered accomplishments.

9.3 Evidence for Wisdom as a Personality Quality

If wisdom can be conceptualized as an integrative personality, as optimal personality development, or as a self-transcendent personality that is relatively stable in the short term across different contexts and situations, assessments of these wise personality qualities should consistently correlate with other measures of personality. Moreover, if a wise personality results in a fulfilling and flourishing life, it should correlate with measures of psychological and subjective well-being. This section will test these hypotheses.

9.3.1 Wisdom and the Big Five Personality Traits

The most widely used classification of personality is the **Five Factor Model (FFM) of personality**, which sorts a diverse set of personality facets into five overarching "Big Five" personality traits. These are emotional stability (the opposite of neuroticism), openness to new experiences, agreeableness, conscientiousness, and extraversion (Costa & McCrae, 1992; Goldberg, 1993; McCrae & Costa, 1997; McCrae & John, 1992). Individuals with a wise personality would be expected to be more emotionally stable, rather than neurotic (i.e., anxious, hostile, depressed, self-conscious, impulsive, and vulnerable), because they are able to regulate their emotions and know how to deal with crises and obstacles in their life (Ardelt, 2005; Plews-Ogan et al., 2012). Openness to experiences has been proposed as a predictor of wisdom (Ardelt et al., 2018; Glück et al., 2013, 2019; Helson & Srivastava, 2002; Staudinger & Kunzmann, 2005; Wink & Staudinger, 2016), as growth in wisdom requires a willingness to change and to be open-minded rather than closed-minded. The prosocial and compassionate aspects of wisdom suggest that a wise person would be agreeable (i.e., forgiving, straightforward, altruistic, compliant, modest, and tender-minded) rather than antagonistic. The discipline and effort required to develop wisdom through self-reflection and self-examination would necessitate a personality that is conscientious, self-disciplined, deliberate, and dependable, rather than heedless, careless, or negligent. The personality facets of extraversion include "warmth" and "sociable," which might correlate positively with the compassionate quality of a wise person, but the extraversion facets of "excitement-seeking" and "assertiveness" might be counter-indicative of wisdom. Therefore extraversion might be unrelated or have a less strong positive correlation with a wise personality.

Figure 9.1 shows the bivariate correlations between different measures of wisdom and the Big Five personality traits. As expected, wisdom, defined as integrative or self-transcendent personality qualities and assessed by the 3D-WS and the ASTI, respectively, was consistently and moderately positively correlated with emotional stability, openness to experiences,

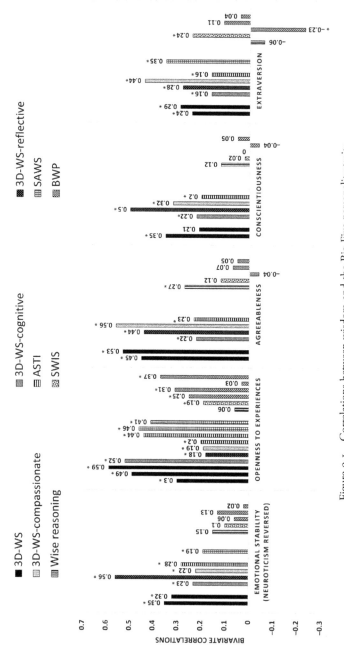

Figure 9.1 Correlations between wisdom and the Big Five personality traits

Note: * $p < 0.05$. 3D-WS, Three-Dimensional Wisdom Scale; ASTI, Adult Self-Transcendence Inventory; SAWS, Self-Assessed Wisdom Scale; SWIS, Situated Wise Reasoning Scale; BWP, Berlin Wisdom Paradigm. All correlations $r > 0.15$ are statistically significant at $p < 0.05$ except for the correlation between the 3D-WS and conscientiousness at 0.21 due to the small sample size ($n = 72$–74).

144

agreeableness, conscientiousness, and extraversion in diverse samples of high-school principals (Chima, 2014), military officers (Zacher et al., 2015), and the general population (Glück et al., 2013; Levenson et al., 2005). One study of college students only correlated the three dimensions of the 3D-WS with the five personality traits (Neff et al., 2007). In accordance with theoretical reasoning, this study revealed that the cognitive wisdom dimension was most strongly correlated with openness to experiences, the reflective wisdom dimension was most strongly correlated with emotional stability and conscientiousness, and the compassionate wisdom dimension was most strongly correlated with agreeableness and extraversion. It was not surprising that wisdom, conceptualized as optimal personality development and measured by the SAWS, was most strongly associated with openness to experiences – a personality quality that is one factor of the SAWS (Glück et al., 2013). However, the SAWS was also positively correlated with emotional stability and extraversion, while agreeableness and conscientiousness were not included in the study (Webster et al., 2014).

By contrast, wisdom measures that do not assess wisdom as a personality quality, such as wise reasoning and wisdom-related knowledge (see Chapter 6), would not be expected to be consistently correlated with the Big Five personality traits. This is exactly what was found. Wise reasoning, assessed as a rating measure, was significantly related to greater agreeableness only (Grossmann et al., 2013). However, wise reasoning, measured by the *Situated Wise Reasoning Scale* (SWIS), correlated positively with openness to experiences and extraversion but not with agreeableness, emotional stability, or conscientiousness (Brienza et al., 2018). Similarly, wisdom-related knowledge, assessed by ratings of the Berlin Wisdom Paradigm (BWP), was positively associated with openness to experiences in three studies (Glück et al., 2013; Pasupathi & Staudinger, 2001; Staudinger et al., 1998), and negatively associated with extraversion in one study (Staudinger et al., 1998), but unrelated to all five personality traits in the sample of military officers (Zacher et al., 2015). Except for the relatively consistent correlation between the BWP and openness to experiences, measures of wise reasoning and wisdom-related knowledge were either uncorrelated or inconsistently correlated with the Big Five personality traits.

The personalities of the men in the Longitudinal Study of Adult Development were first rated by the clinical study staff when the men were 21 years old. These personality assessments were later weighed and factor analyzed to conform to Costa and McCrae's Big Five personality traits (Soldz & Vaillant, 1999). The original Big Five personality traits were measured when the men were around 70 years of age.

At the age of 21, Mr. Howard and Mr. Palmer received similar personality ratings on openness to experiences and agreeableness. Mr. Howard was rated at the median on openness and in the top 25 percent on agreeableness, and Mr. Palmer was rated in the top 40 percent on openness and the top 30 percent on agreeableness. However, the men were markedly different in terms of emotional stability, conscientiousness, and extraversion. Mr. Howard was rated in the top 10 percent and Mr. Palmer in the bottom 10 percent on emotional stability and conscientiousness. Interestingly, Mr. Howard received the second lowest rating on extraversion, while Mr. Palmer was rated in the top 10 percent on this personality characteristic.

Around the age of 70, Mr. Howard's score on emotional stability was still in the top 10 percent. His relative scores on agreeableness (top 35 percent) and conscientiousness (top 25 percent) were slightly lower than at age 21, but his extraversion score increased dramatically from the second lowest in young adulthood to the top 15 percent, and he had the highest score on openness to experiences. By contrast, around age 70, Mr. Palmer scored in the bottom 5 percent on emotional stability, in the bottom 25 percent on agreeableness, in the bottom 15 percent on conscientiousness and extraversion, and in the bottom 35 percent on openness. Mr. Howard became more outgoing and open to new experiences from age 21 to age 70, relative to his study peers, due to his interests in others and developing self-transcendence. However, Mr. Palmer was less agreeable and open to new experiences and more introverted in old age than in young adulthood, and his scores on emotional stability and conscientiousness remained low. While primarily concerned about his own social standing and success, Mr. Palmer's interest in the wider social world seemed to have shrunk and this, paradoxically, might have prevented his acceptance into the desired social circles.

9.3.2   Wisdom and Well-Being

Based on the ancient and modern wisdom literature from both the East and the West, one of the hallmarks of wisdom is knowing how to live a good and flourishing life, which leads to *eudaimonia,* or **psychological well-being** (Ardelt, 2019; Curnow, 1999; Kekes, 1995; Swartwood & Tiberius, 2019). Similarly, Ryff (1989) argued that successful human development results in psychological well-being, consisting of self-acceptance, positive relationships with others, environmental mastery, purpose in life, a sense of autonomy, and an orientation toward further personal growth, rather than **subjective well-being**, such as feelings of happiness and satisfaction. Yet, empirically, indicators of psychological and subjective well-being are positively correlated and appear to be intertwined (Ryff, 1989; Ryff & Keyes, 1995).

Although some have cautioned that "it takes extraordinary effort and most likely pain to progress on the road toward wisdom or personality growth" (Staudinger & Kunzmann, 2005, p. 326), and that the greater insight that wisdom entails might come with the realization that life involves suffering, wise teachers, such as the Buddha, also taught a way out of suffering (Armstrong, 2001; Ñanamoli, 2001). Even if "ignorance is bliss" in the short term, in the long term a deeper understanding of life and the human condition and the development of compassion will help wise individuals to cope with the vicissitudes of life – including change, adversity, loss, and mortality – with equanimity and calmness rather than anxiety and despair. This will have the effect of preserving both psychological and subjective well-being.

Hence, if wisdom is the apex of successful human development that results in a flourishing life, measures of wisdom would be expected to correlate with greater psychological and subjective well-being. However, this is only the case if wisdom is assessed as a personality quality. In several studies, measures of wisdom as an integrative or self-transcendent personality or as optimal personality development were consistently positively correlated with indicators of psychological well-being (i.e., self-acceptance, positive relationships with others, mastery, purpose in life, autonomy, and orientation toward personal growth) and subjective well-being (i.e., general well-being, life satisfaction, happiness, positive emotions/affect and the absence of negative emotions/affect, depressive symptoms, and alienation). These significant correlations were found both cross-sectionally (for a review, see Ardelt, 2019) and, in a study with the 3D-WS, also longitudinally (Ardelt, 2016). By contrast, wisdom assessed as general and personal wisdom-related knowledge or wise reasoning was either uncorrelated or inconsistently correlated with indicators of psychological and subjective well-being (Glück et al., 2013; Grossmann et al., 2013; Kunzmann & Baltes, 2003; Mickler & Staudinger, 2008; Staudinger et al., 1997). Hence, possession of wisdom-related knowledge does not necessarily lead to well-being and a flourishing life.

Mr. Howard's most striking characteristic was his positive personality disposition throughout his life. He consistently declared himself "very happy" in his responses to questionnaires, except during the year when his wife divorced him. For example, when he was asked at the age of 76 to rate the best and worst periods of his life on a scale of 1 to 10, he rated his whole life as a "10," and commented:

> I have been greatly blessed. I had an incredibly happy childhood, school years, college years and career. I loved my own business. I love my two and three children and both wives. Why I have been so lucky, I do not know. At times I feel there must be something wrong with me. My friends seem to have so much unhappiness and so many problems. Sure, my father was an alcoholic but I loved him and stuck with him and helped get him with AA. I'm sure I could drum up some problems but I guess I forgot them.

Two years later, he wrote in a questionnaire, "Every period in my life has been happy. . . . I've loved my life. I'm only sad when I hurt somebody or make them unhappy."

By contrast, Mr. Palmer's lifelong quest for higher economic and social standing and acceptance into high society caused him much mental anguish and prevented his development toward self-transcendence. He suffered from many psychosomatic and mental health problems, and his life appears to have lacked a deeper meaning. He often attributed his setbacks, such as difficulties in his job or his wife's mental illness, to "bad luck" and saw himself as the victim. His anxiety and depression, which were prevalent during his college years, remained with him throughout his life, although Mr. Palmer was in regular psychiatric therapy from the age of 31, and received antidepressive medication from the age of 63 and probably until his death at the age of 82. He was also drinking alcohol on a daily basis throughout his adult life, maybe in an attempt to self-medicate. At the age of 80, Mr. Palmer scored in the bottom 5 percent on a measure of subjective well-being, whereas Mr. Howard had the highest possible score (Ardelt et al., 2018).

9.4   Wise Personality, Wise Behavior, and Wise Personality Development

Unless individuals are completely wise – that is, unless they have overcome all self-centeredness and self-serving biases, impulses, and motivations, which often unconsciously guide a person's behavior (Staudinger, 2019) – it is unlikely that they will always act and behave wisely. Yet even a person with underdeveloped wise personality qualities might sometimes behave in a wise way, although the underlying motivation for this behavior might be self-centered and self-serving – for example, attempting to make a good impression on others rather than acting out of compassion and good-will. Therefore, although Mr. Howard possessed wise personality qualities whereas these qualities were underdeveloped in the case of Mr. Palmer, this did not mean that Mr. Palmer never acted wisely or made a wise decision, or that all of Mr. Howard's actions and decision were wise. For example, Mr. Palmer engaged in altruistic volunteer activities in midlife that brought him much more pleasure and satisfaction than his private and professional life. After interviewing Mr. Palmer at the age of 52, the interviewer noted:

> [Mr. Palmer] said his greatest interest . . . was that he had become president of the Home for the Aged, and that he was amazed at the amount of energy he was able to put into that and how creative he felt, especially in the last eight months. . . . He felt that he genuinely had been able to help the residents gain a better quality of life.

Although Mr. Palmer might have liked the social prestige that came with such a position, this other-centered work clearly made him happier than his pursuits of higher economic and social standing ever could. Yet he did not seem to realize this, and he never gave up his economic and social ambitions, even though they exacerbated his pervasive feelings of anxiety, insecurity, and depression.

It is also true that Mr. Howard sometimes acted unwisely. When asked in a questionnaire at the age of 76 what he most regretted in his life, he wrote:

> My only true regret[s] are the times I have hurt someone. I have spoken too hastily or been too much of a smart ass. I struggled hard with my first wife's alcoholism but I guess I may have been partly responsible. . . . Also, I think my sense of humor hurts some. I just can't get so serious about life.

Mr. Howard was able to be self-critical and admit his own shortcomings, while still being at peace with who he was. This is another indication of his growth toward self-transcendence. By accepting both the positive and negative aspects of his personality, he also appeared to have developed compassion and tolerance toward the imperfections of others. Moreover, and in contrast to Mr. Palmer, Mr. Howard learned from his failures and weaknesses. At the age of 51, he admitted, "Due to my own selfishness I'm sure, my relations with my wife have not been all that great." A year later, he had a "very amiable divorce" from his wife and was very happy when she married one of his dear friends. He still felt that she was a wonderful person, but he had been unable to love her enough due to their different lifestyles, which might have contributed to her alcoholism. At the age of 50, Mr. Howard wrote in a questionnaire:

> I feel a marked change has come over me [between the ages of 40 and 50]. I have learned to be more kind, have more empathy. I have learned to be tolerant. I have a much better understanding of life, its meaning and purposes.

By becoming more compassionate, patient, understanding, tolerant, and other-centered, Mr. Howard was able to grow wiser. This demonstrates that wisdom can develop and change with age, similar to changes in personality over long periods of time (Ardelt, 2000; Roberts et al., 2006). Individuals might grow in wisdom when confronted with crises and hardship in life (Glück & Bluck, 2013; Glück et al., 2019; Plews-Ogan et al., 2012), a process that is known as stress-related or posttraumatic growth (Park et al., 1996; Tedeschi & Calhoun, 1996). It might not have been a coincidence that the "marked change" Mr. Howard referred to happened during a time of marital crisis. In fact, the first shift toward other-centeredness occurred when he was in his twenties and his father developed a drinking problem. At the age of 50, he reported in a questionnaire that between the ages of 20 and 30:

> I became a father, which is a sobering enough experience. My father's alcoholism gave me a better insight into the true values of life. I changed in a short space of time from a spoiled S.O.B. to one with a good deal of responsibility. I learned humility and how to work hard and to dedicate myself to others. I learned to love.

At the age of 61, he stated in a questionnaire:

> I guess the alcoholism of my father had the greatest single impact on my life. I'm sure I was spoiled and immature up to that time. But I sure grew up in a hurry. I never turned my back on him. I just tried to get him to AA and on his feet. It taught me patience, the value of love, the meaning of frustration. You plug along with a sense of humor and do the best you can.

Mr. Howard started to transcend his self-centeredness and understand the true meaning of love through his father's alcoholism. This shift toward greater other-centeredness, compassionate love, kindness, tolerance, and understanding appeared to have continued throughout his life, with another acceleration during the time of marital distress.

However, crises and hardships do not automatically result in greater wisdom (Ardelt, 1998; Glück & Bluck, 2013; Glück et al., 2019). Mr. Palmer did not grow wiser as a result of his personal and marital difficulties, although he sought help and guidance through psychiatric therapy throughout his life, starting at the age of 31 at the advice of the study psychiatrist. Yet, even after many years of therapy, Mr. Palmer failed to overcome his self-centeredness and develop a wise personality. At the age of 47, he mentioned in an interview that he had enjoyed seeing his psychiatrist, but his psychiatrist had gotten bored and impatient with him and felt that he could not do anything more for him.

Crises and hardships are not the only ways to increase wisdom. A supportive childhood environment appears to be a good foundation for the development of competence in adolescence, which is positively related to emotional stability in early adulthood, generativity in midlife, and wisdom in old age (Ardelt et al., 2018). Mr. Howard's childhood environment was rated as thoroughly positive by the study staff, whereas Mr. Palmer's childhood environment was rated as non-nurturing. Moreover, individuals can purposefully attempt to grow wiser through the practice of meditation (Levenson et al., 2005; Williams et al., 2016), contemplation (Aldwin et al., 2019), or mindfulness (Beaumont, 2011; Sharma & Dewangan, 2017; Whitehead et al., 2020). It is also possible that schools and university classes can promote wise personality qualities through their curriculum and through assignments that ask students to practice various forms of wise living and to reflect on their experiences through journal writing (Ardelt, 2020; Bruya & Ardelt, 2018a, 2018b, 2018c; Ferrari & Kim, 2019; Ferrari & Potworowski, 2008; Miller, 2005; Rooney et al., 2021; Sternberg & Hagen, 2019; Sternberg et al., 2008).

Positive events, such as parenthood, might also contribute to wise personality qualities (Glück & Bluck, 2013; Glück et al., 2019). For example, when Mr. Howard was asked, during an interview at the age of 79, what he had learned from his children, he replied without hesitation:

> Oh my gosh. An infinite amount. Much, much more than they've learned from me, I'm sure. Children show you different aspects of life, different aspects of human nature. They're fascinating. You don't always have to like them, of course. I've learned so much from them – their problems, their hopes, their dreams. They keep me up to date, they keep me young. I'm infinitely grateful to them for keeping me on the positive side of life.

Mr. Howard's children strengthened the reflective dimension of wisdom by showing him different aspects of life and human nature, which likely deepened his understanding of life and increased his tolerance, empathy, and compassion. By contrast, Mr. Palmer and his first wife could not have any children, which contributed to his marital problems and might have precluded an opportunity to reduce self-centeredness and practice generativity through being concerned about the next generation (Vaillant, 2002; Westermeyer, 2004). Of course, parenthood is not a prerequisite for generativity. However, there is no indication that Mr. Palmer engaged in any generative activities, such as mentoring younger architects or contributing to the well-being of future generations.

9.5   Concluding Remarks

Wisdom is key to successful adult human development and a flourishing, happy, and satisfying life that benefits oneself, others, and the larger community. Although we are not born wise, a benevolent and supportive childhood appears to be a good foundation for fostering wisdom (Ardelt et al., 2018). However, a nurturing childhood is neither necessary nor sufficient for the acquisition of wisdom. Growth in wisdom occurs through the practice of reflection and self-reflection, which provides deeper insight into the intrapersonal and interpersonal aspects of human existence, reduces self-centeredness, and increases sympathy and compassion for others. If wisdom is to have a consistent positive influence on daily life, it needs to become part of a person's personality that manifests in behavioral tendencies and correlates with other positive personality characteristics, such as emotional stability, openness to experiences, agreeableness, conscientiousness, warmth, and sociability. Yet the notion of a wise personality is an "ideal type" in the sense used by Max Weber (Weber, 1980), and not many individuals, if any, might be considered completely wise. However, we can determine how close people come to this "ideal type" by assessing to what extent they have developed wise personality qualities.

After reading through Mr. Howard's questionnaires and interview transcripts, a cynic might object that he is "too good to be true." In fact, after a face-to-face interview with him at the age of 79, the interviewer wrote in her "reflections":

> Reading through Mr. Howard's file before I met him, I had found him quite tedious. In every questionnaire, exclamation points cheered his enthusiasm for his good fortune in leading such a wonderful life. In her 1983 interview, [the interviewer] described him as the "master of suppression," which seemed a fair assessment. . . .
>
>   But in fact, my experience with him was delightful. From the moment I stepped out of the car into those sunny gardens, I found him to be interesting and interested, gracious, charming, engaged. . . . Though he didn't really claim it for himself with words, he had a sort of mystical/spiritual energy which gave him a sort of "in but not of this world" detachment. I believe he actually experiences his life with the exclamation points he uses to describe it. He drinks (to use one of the Study's favorite expressions) a lot of sweet lemonade.

Both Mr. Howard and Mr. Palmer were highly intelligent, highly educated, and financially successful. In fact, Mr. Palmer was one of five men who had the highest IQ scores in the study in young adulthood, whereas Mr. Howard scored only in the top 55 percent. The major differences between the two men were their emotional upbringing, and the contrast between Mr. Howard's loving, giving, and generous attitude toward others and Mr. Palmer's concern for his own well-being and social and economic standing. Whereas Mr. Howard saw life as beautiful and appeared genuinely happy throughout most of his life, Mr. Palmer experienced lifelong feelings of anxiety, depression, and insecurity. Paradoxically, it was Mr. Howard's concern for others rather than Mr. Palmer's self-concern that led to growth in wisdom and greater personal well-being.

9.6   Comprehension and Discussion Questions

(1)   Think about a person who is very knowledgeable. What are the characteristics that make this person knowledgeable? Think about a person who is wise. What are the characteristics that make this person wise? What are the major differences between the characteristics of a knowledgeable person and a wise person?

(2)   Compare and contrast the lives of Mr. Howard and Mr. Palmer. How did Mr. Howard's life exemplify practical wisdom? What could Mr. Palmer have done to lead a more flourishing life?

(3)   Why might psychiatric therapy not have helped Mr. Palmer to alleviate his anxiety and depression? What might have prevented Mr. Palmer from experiencing contentment and growth in wisdom?

(4)   In what ways do practical wisdom and a wise personality contribute to human flourishing and a good life?

(5)   Do you believe that prosocial behavior and compassion are integral aspects of wisdom? Explain why you do or do not believe this.

(6)   Do you believe that wisdom is a quality of old age or do you think that individuals have the ability to be wise earlier in life? Explain why you do or do not believe this.

(7)   What is the importance of humor in life? Create one scenario that illustrates the concept of approaching life with humor, and one scenario without humor. Compare and contrast the two scenarios. What are some ways that we can incorporate humor into our lives?

9.7   Investigations

Monika Ardelt developed the Three-Dimensional Wisdom Model (3D-WM) and the Three-Dimensional Wisdom Scale (3D-WS) to study the predictors, correlates, and effects of three-dimensional wisdom across the adult life course, and how wisdom contributes to a flourishing life, aging well, and dying well. Recently, she has become interested in organizational wisdom.

Stephen Pridgen's research has focused on the areas of wisdom development over the life course, and the practical use of wisdom to challenge anti-intellectualism worldviews. He is currently investigating the application of wisdom-based teaching and learning strategies within organizational structures and the classroom.

9.8   Practical Applications

Not everyone is gifted with wise personality qualities and a wisdom-fostering environment early in life in the way that Mr. Howard seems to have been. Yet it appears that the ancient Greeks, Buddha, Confucius, Lao-Tzu, and spiritual mystics were correct – one can become wiser through practice (Ardelt, 2010; Evans, 2013). There are many practices that develop the cognitive, reflective, and compassionate dimensions of wisdom and foster self-transcendence, including meditation (Levenson et al., 2005; Williams et al., 2016), contemplative prayer (Aldwin et al., 2019; Bourgeault, 2004), and mindfulness (Beaumont, 2011; Sharma & Dewangan, 2017; Whitehead et al., 2020). However, it is also important that schools and universities try to foster the development of wisdom rather than focusing solely on the intellectual development of their students (Ardelt, 2020; Bruya & Ardelt, 2018c; Ferrari & Kim, 2019; Ferrari & Potworowski, 2008; Miller, 2005; Rooney et al., 2021; Sternberg & Hagen, 2019). An increasing number of schools and universities are acknowledging that wisdom is needed to promote the common good and the well-being of all, although implementation challenges remain (e.g., Grunwald & LaMontagne, 2021).

Glossary

Five Factor Model (FFM) of personality a model based on the "Big Five" personality traits, namely neuroticism, openness to new experiences, agreeableness, conscientiousness, and extraversion.

practical wisdom (*phronesis*) a deep and valuable understanding of how one *should* live and conduct oneself in order to live a good life.

psychological well-being a state characterized by self-acceptance, positive relationships with others, environmental mastery, purpose in life, a sense of autonomy, and an orientation toward further personal growth.

subjective well-being a state of general well-being that is characterized by the presence of life satisfaction, happiness, and positive emotions/affect, and the absence of negative emotions/affect, depressive symptoms, and alienation.

theoretical wisdom (*sophia*) an understanding of timeless, universal truths about life that is attained through contemplation.

Three-Dimensional Wisdom Model (3D-WM) a model that defines wisdom as the integration of cognitive, reflective, and compassionate dimensions.

REFERENCES

Aldwin, C. M., Igarashi, H., and Levenson, M. R. (2019). Wisdom as self-transcendence. In R. J. Sternberg and J. Glück, eds., *The Cambridge Handbook of Wisdom*. Cambridge University Press, pp. 122–43.

Ardelt, M. (1997). Wisdom and life satisfaction in old age. *The Journals of Gerontology, Series B: Psychological Sciences and Social Sciences*, 52B(1), P15–27.

(1998). Social crisis and individual growth: the long-term effects of the Great Depression. *Journal of Aging Studies*, 12(3), 291–314.

(2000). Still stable after all these years? Personality stability theory revisited. *Social Psychology Quarterly, Special Millennium Issue on The State of Sociological Social Psychology*, 63(4), 392–405.

(2003). Empirical assessment of a three-dimensional wisdom scale. *Research on Aging*, 25(3), 275–324.

(2004). Wisdom as expert knowledge system: a critical review of a contemporary operationalization of an ancient concept. *Human Development*, 47(5), 257–85.

(2005). How wise people cope with crises and obstacles in life. *ReVision: A Journal of Consciousness and Transformation*, 28(1), 7–19.

(2010). Age, experience, and the beginning of wisdom. In D. Dannefer and C. Phillipson, eds., *The SAGE Handbook of Social Gerontology*. Sage, pp. 306–16.

(2016). Disentangling the relations between wisdom and different types of well-being in old age: findings from a short-term longitudinal study. *Journal of Happiness Studies*, 17(5), 1963–84.

(2019). Wisdom and well-being. In R. J. Sternberg and J. Glück, eds., *The Cambridge Handbook of Wisdom*. Cambridge University Press, pp. 602–25.

(2020). Can wisdom and psychosocial growth be learned in university courses? *The Journal of Moral Education*, 49(9), 30–45.

Ardelt, M. and Oh, H. (2010). Wisdom: definition, assessment, and relation to successful cognitive and emotional aging. In C. Depp and D. Jeste, eds., *Successful Cognitive and Emotional Aging*. American Psychiatric Publishing, Inc., pp. 87–113.

Ardelt, M. and Vaillant, G. E. (2009). "*The Presence and Absence of Wisdom in Everyday Life: Evidence from Two Longitudinal Case Studies.*" The Gerontological Society of America Annual Meetings, Atlanta, GA, November 2009.

Ardelt, M., Gerlach, K. R., and Vaillant, G. E. (2018). Early and midlife predictors of wisdom and subjective well-being in old age. *The Journals of Gerontology: Series B, Psychological Sciences and Social Sciences*, 73(8), 1514–25.

Ardelt, M., Ferrari, M., and Shi, W. (2020). Implicit wisdom theories from around the world and their implications for wise business and management. In B. Schwartz, C. Bernacchio, C. González-Cantón, and A. Robson, eds., *Handbook of Practical Wisdom in Business and Management*. Springer, pp. 1–30.

Armstrong, K. (2001). *Buddha*. Penguin Group.

Baltes, P. B. and Smith, J. (2008). The fascination of wisdom: its nature, ontogeny, and function. *Perspectives on Psychological Science*, 3(1), 56–64.

Baltes, P. B. and Staudinger, U. M. (2000). Wisdom: a metaheuristic (pragmatic) to orchestrate mind and virtue toward excellence. *American Psychologist*, 55(1), 122–36.

Beaumont, S. L. (2011). Identity styles and wisdom during emerging adulthood: relationships with mindfulness and savoring. *Identity: An International Journal of Theory and Research*, 11(2), 155–80.

Blanchard-Fields, F. and Norris, L. (1995). The development of wisdom. In M. A. Kimble, S. H. McFadden, J. W. Ellor, and J. J. Seeber, eds., *Aging, Spirituality, and Religion: A Handbook*. Fortress Press, pp. 102–18.

Bourgeault, C. (2004). *Centering Prayer and Inner Awakening*. Cowley Publications.

Brienza, J. P., Kung, F. Y. H., Santos, H. C., Bobocel, D. R., and Grossmann, I. (2018). Wisdom, bias, and balance: toward a process-sensitive measurement of wisdom-related cognition. *Journal of Personality and Social Psychology*, 115(6), 1093–126.

Bruya, B. and Ardelt, M. (2018a). Fostering wisdom in the classroom, Part 1: A general theory of wisdom pedagogy. *Teaching Philosophy*, 41(3), 239–53.

(2018b). Fostering wisdom in the classroom, Part 2: A curriculum. *Teaching Philosophy*, 41(4), 349–80.

(2018c). Wisdom can be taught: a proof-of-concept study for fostering wisdom in the classroom. *Learning and Instruction*, 58, 106–14.

Cain, S. (2012). *Quiet: The Power of Introverts in a World That Can't Stop Talking*. Crown Publishers.

Chima, A. S. (2014). *The contribution of wisdom, cognitive intelligence, emotional intelligence, and Big Five personality traits of high school principals to student achievement*. Dissertation, Sofia University, Palo Alto, CA.

Clayton, V. P. and Birren, J. E. (1980). The development of wisdom across the life span: a re-examination of an ancient topic. In P. B. Baltes and O. G. Brim, Jr., eds., *Life-Span Development and Behavior*, Vol. 3. Academic Press, pp. 103–35.

Costa, P. T. and McCrae, R. R. (1992). *Revised NEO Personality Inventory (NEO-PI-R) and NEO Five-Factor Inventory (NEO-FFI) Professional Manual*. Psychological Assessment Resources.

Curnow, T. (1999). *Wisdom, Intuition, and Ethics*. Ashgate Publishing.

Erikson, E. H. (1963). *Childhood and Society*. W. W. Norton & Co.

(1964). *Insight and Responsibility: Lectures on the Ethical Implications of Psychoanalytic Insight*. W. W. Norton & Co.

(1982). *The Life Cycle Completed: A Review*. W. W. Norton & Co.

Evans, J. (2013). *Philosophy for life and other dangerous situations: Ancient philosophy for modern problems*. New World Library.

Ferrari, M. and Kim, J. (2019). Educating for wisdom. In R. J. Sternberg and J. Glück, eds., *The Cambridge Handbook of Wisdom*. Cambridge University Press, pp. 347–71.

Ferrari, M. and Potworowski, G., eds. (2008). *Teaching for Wisdom: Cross-Cultural Perspectives on Fostering Wisdom*. Springer.

Fischer, A. (2015). Wisdom – the answer to all the questions really worth asking. *International Journal of Humanities and Social Science*, 5(9), 73–83.

Glück, J. and Bluck, S. (2013). The MORE life experience model: a theory of the development of wisdom. In M. Ferrari and N. Weststrate, eds., *The Scientific Study of Personal Wisdom: From Contemplative Traditions to Neuroscience*. Springer, pp. 75–97.

Glück, J., König, S., Naschenweng, K. et al. (2013). How to measure wisdom: content, reliability, and validity of five measures. *Frontiers in Psychology*, 4, Article 405.

Glück, J., Bluck, S., and Weststrate, N. M. (2019). More on the MORE Life Experience Model: what we have learned (so far). *The Journal of Value Inquiry*, 53(6), 349–70.

Goldberg, L. R. (1993). The structure of phenotypic personality traits. *American Psychologist*, 48(1), 26–34.

Grossmann, I. (2017). Wisdom in context. *Perspectives on Psychological Science*, 12(2), 233–57.

Grossmann, I., Na, J., Varnum, M. E. W., Kitayama, S., and Nisbett, R. E. (2013). A route to well-being: intelligence versus wise reasoning. *Journal of Experimental Psychology: General*, 142(3), 944–53.

Grossmann, I., Kung, F. Y. H., and Santos, H. C. (2019). Wisdom as state versus trait. In J. Glück and R. J. Sternberg, eds., *The Cambridge Handbook of Wisdom*. Cambridge University Press, pp. 249–74.

Grunwald, S. and LaMontagne, L. (2021). The state of mindfulness at top U.S. public universities: a brief review and lessons learned. In S. K. Dhiman, ed., *The Routledge Companion to Mindfulness at Work*. Routledge, pp. 331–53.

Helson, R. and Srivastava, S. (2002). Creative and wise people: similarities, differences, and how they develop. *Personality and Social Psychology Bulletin*, 28(10), 1430–40.

Isaacowitz, D. M., Vaillant, G. E., and Seligman, M. E. P. (2003). Strengths and satisfaction across the adult lifespan. *The International Journal of Aging and Human Development*, 57(2), 181–201.

Jeste, D. V., Ardelt, M., Blazer, D. et al. (2010). Expert consensus on characteristics of wisdom: a Delphi method study. *The Gerontologist*, 50(5), 668–80.

Kekes, J. (1995). *Moral Wisdom and Good Lives*. Cornell University Press.

Kunzmann, U. and Baltes, P. B. (2003). Wisdom-related knowledge: affective, motivational, and interpersonal correlates. *Personality and Social Psychology Bulletin*, 29(9), 1104–19.

Lazare, A., Klerman, G. L., and Armor, D. J. (1966). Oral, obsessive, and hysterical personality patterns: an investigation of psychoanalytic concepts by means of factor analysis. *Archives of General Psychiatry*, 14(6), 624–30.

Lee, E. E., Bangen, K. J., Avanzino, J. A. et al. (2020). Outcomes of randomized clinical trials of interventions to enhance social, emotional, and spiritual components of wisdom: a systematic review and meta-analysis. *JAMA Psychiatry*, 77(9), 925–35.

Levenson, M. R. (2009). Gender and wisdom: the roles of compassion and moral development. *Research in Human Development*, 6(1), 45–59.

Levenson, M. R., and Aldwin, C. (2013). The transpersonal in personal wisdom. In M. Ferrari and N. M. Weststrate, eds., *The Scientific Study of Personal Wisdom: From Contemplative Traditions to Neuroscience*. Springer, pp. 213–28.

Levenson, M. R., Jennings, P. A., Aldwin, C. M., and Shiraishi, R. W. (2005). Self-transcendence: conceptualization and measurement. *International Journal of Aging and Human Development*, 60(2), 127–43.

McCrae, R. R. and Costa, P. T., Jr. (1997). Personality trait structure as a human universal. *American Psychologist*, 52(5), 509–16.

McCrae, R. R. and John, O. P. (1992). An introduction to the five-factor model and its applications. *Journal of Personality*, 60(2), 175–215.

Meeks, T. W. and Jeste, D. V. (2009). Neurobiology of wisdom: a literature overview. *Archives of General Psychiatry*, 66(4), 355–65.

Mickler, C. and Staudinger, U. M. (2008). Personal wisdom: validation and age-related differences of a performance measure. *Psychology and Aging*, 23(4), 787–99.

Miller, J. P. (2005). *Educating for Wisdom and Compassion: Creating Conditions for Timeless Learning*. Corwin Press.

Moody, H. R. (1986). Late life learning in the information society. In D. A. Peterson, J. E. Thornton, and J. E. Birren, eds., *Education and Aging*. Prentice-Hall, pp. 122–48.

Ñanamoli, B. (2001). *The Life of the Buddha. According to the Pali Canon*. BPS Pariyatti Editions.

Neff, K. D., Rude, S. S., and Kirkpatrick, K. L. (2007). An examination of self-compassion in relation to positive psychological functioning and personality traits. *Journal of Research in Personality*, 41(4), 908–16.

Park, C. L., Cohen, L. H., and Murch, R. L. (1996). Assessment and prediction of stress-related growth. *Journal of Personality*, 64(1), 71–105.

Pasupathi, M. and Staudinger, U. M. (2001). Do advanced moral reasoners also show wisdom? Linking moral reasoning and wisdom-related knowledge and judgement. *International Journal of Behavioral Development*, 25(5), 401–15.

Plews-Ogan, M., Owens, J. E., and May, N. (2012). *Choosing Wisdom: Strategies and Inspiration for Growing Through Life-Changing Difficulties*. Templeton Press.

Roberts, B. W., Walton, K. E., and Viechtbauer, W. (2006). Patterns of mean-level change in personality traits across the life course: a meta-analysis of longitudinal studies. *Psychological Bulletin*, 132(1), 1–25.

Rooney, D., Kupers, W., Pauleen, D., and Zhuravleva, E. (2021). A developmental model for educating wise leaders: the role of mindfulness and habitus in creating time for embodying wisdom. *Journal of Business Ethics*, 170(3), 181–94.

Ryff, C. D. (1989). Happiness is everything, or is it? Explorations on the meaning of psychological well-being. *Journal of Personality and Social Psychology*, 57(6), 1069–81.

Ryff, C. D. and Keyes, C. L. M. (1995). The structure of psychological well-being revisited. *Journal of Personality and Social Psychology*, 69(4), 719–27.

Santos, H. C., Huynh, A. C., and Grossmann, I. (2017). Wisdom in a complex world: A situated account of wise reasoning and its development. *Social and Personality Psychology Compass*, 11(10), Article e12341.

Schwartz, B. and Sharpe, K. E. (2019). Practical wisdom: what Aristotle might add to psychology. In J. Glück and R. J. Sternberg, eds., *The Cambridge Handbook of Wisdom*. Cambridge University Press, pp. 226–48.

Sharma, A. and Dewangan, R. L. (2017). Can wisdom be fostered: time to test the model of wisdom. *Cogent Psychology*, 4(1), Article 1381456.

Soldz, S. and Vaillant, G. E. (1999). The Big Five personality traits and the life course: a 45-year longitudinal study. *Journal of Research in Personality*, 33(2), 208–32.

Staudinger, U. M. (2019). The distinction between personal and general wisdom: how far have we come? In J. Glück and R. J. Sternberg, eds., *The Cambridge Handbook of Wisdom*. Cambridge University Press, pp. 182–201.

Staudinger, U. M. and Kessler, E.-M. (2009). Adjustment and growth: two trajectories of positive personality development across adulthood. In M. C. Smith, ed., *Handbook of Research on Adult Learning and Development*. Routledge, pp. 241–68.

Staudinger, U. M. and Kunzmann, U. (2005). Positive adult personality development: adjustment and/or growth? *European Psychologist*, 10(4), 320–29.

Staudinger, U. M., Lopez, D. F., and Baltes, P. B. (1997). The psychometric location of wisdom-related performance: intelligence, personality, and more? *Personality and Social Psychology Bulletin*, 23(11), 1200–14.

Staudinger, U. M., Maciel, A. G., Smith, J., and Baltes, P. B. (1998). What predicts wisdom-related performance? A first look at personality, intelligence, and facilitative experiential contexts. *European Journal of Personality*, 12(1), 1–17.

Sternberg, R. J. (1998). A balance theory of wisdom. *Review of General Psychology*, 2(4), 347–65.

Sternberg, R. J. and Hagen, E. S. (2019). Teaching for wisdom. In R. J. Sternberg and J. Glück, eds., *The Cambridge Handbook of Wisdom*. Cambridge University Press, pp. 372–406.

Sternberg, R. J., Jarvin, L., and Reznitskaya, A. (2008). Teaching for wisdom through history: infusing wise thinking skills in the school curriculum. In M. Ferrari and G. Potworowski, eds., *Teaching for Wisdom: Cross-Cultural Perspectives on Fostering Wisdom*. Springer, pp. 37–57.

Swartwood, J. and Tiberius, V. (2019). Philosophical foundations of wisdom. In J. Glück and R. J. Sternberg, eds., *The Cambridge Handbook of Wisdom*. Cambridge University Press, pp. 10–39.

Tahora, S., Shah, S., and Rooney, D. (2019). Vedanta philosophy's contribution to wisdom development for leadership: grounding Indian practical wisdom in higher knowledge and purpose. In R. J. Sternberg, H. C. Nusbaum, and J. Glück, eds., *Applying Wisdom to Contemporary World Problems*. Palgrave Macmillan, pp. 309–36.

Takahashi, M. and Overton, W. F. (2005). Cultural foundations of wisdom: an integrated developmental approach. In R. J. Sternberg and J. Jordan, eds., *A Handbook of Wisdom: Psychological Perspectives*. Cambridge University Press, pp. 32–60.

Tedeschi, R. G. and Calhoun, L. G. (1996). The Posttraumatic Growth Inventory: measuring the positive legacy of trauma. *Journal of Traumatic Stress*, 9(3), 455–71.

Vaillant, G. E. (1977). *Adaptation to Life*. Little, Brown and Company.

  (1993). *The Wisdom of the Ego*. Harvard University Press.

  (2002). *Aging Well: Surprising Guideposts to a Happier Life from the Landmark Harvard Study of Adult Development*. Little, Brown and Company.

  (2012). *Triumphs of Experience: The Men of the Harvard Grant Study*. Belknap Press.

Weber, M. (1980). *Wirtschaft und Gesellschaft: Grundriss der verstehenden Soziologie [Economy and Society: An Outline of Interpretive Sociology]*, 5th revised ed. Mohr.

Webster, J. D. (2003). An exploratory analysis of a self-assessed wisdom scale. *Journal of Adult Development*, 10(1), 13–22.

  (2007). Measuring the character strength of wisdom. *International Journal of Aging and Human Development*, 65(2), 163–83.

Webster, J. D., Westerhof, G. J., and Bohlmeijer, E. T. (2014). Wisdom and mental health across the lifespan. *The Journals of Gerontology: Series B, Psychological Sciences and Social Sciences*, 69(2), 209–18.

Westermeyer, J. F. (2004). Predictors and characteristics of Erikson's life cycle model among men: a 32-year longitudinal study. *The International Journal of Aging and Human Development*, 58(1), 29–48.

Weststrate, N. M., Bluck, S., and Glück, J. (2019). Wisdom of the crowd: exploring people's conceptions of wisdom. In J. Glück and R. J. Sternberg , eds., *The Cambridge Handbook of Wisdom*. Cambridge University Press, pp. 97–121.

Whitehead, R., Bates, G., and Elphinstone, B. (2020). Growing by letting go: nonattachment and mindfulness as qualities of advanced psychological development. *Journal of Adult Development*, 27(1), 12–22.

Williams, P. B., Mangelsdorf, H. H., Kontra, C., Nusbaum, H. C., and Hoeckner, B. (2016). The relationship between mental and somatic practices and wisdom. *PLoS ONE*, 11(2), Article e0149369.

Wink, P. and Staudinger, U. M. (2016). Wisdom and psychosocial functioning in later life. *Journal of Personality*, 84(3), 306–18.

Woerner-Powell, T. and Edmondson, R. (2019). Practical wisdom and Islam: reimagining Islamic law, from the local to the global. In R. J. Sternberg, H. C. Nusbaum, and J. Glück, eds., *Applying Wisdom to Contemporary World Problems*. Palgrave Macmillan, pp. 201–36.

Yang, S.-y. and Intezari, A. (2019). Non-western lay conceptions of wisdom. In J. Glück and R. J. Sternberg, eds., *The Cambridge Handbook of Wisdom*. Cambridge University Press, pp. 429–52.

Zacher, H., McKenna, B., Rooney, D., and Gold, S. (2015). Wisdom in the military context. *Military Psychology*, 27(3), 142–54.

CHAPTER 10

The Wisdom in Emotions[1]

Ute Kunzmann

10.1 Introduction

Wisdom is a human characteristic that many – researchers and laypeople alike – have considered a resource for well-being and growth (e.g., Baltes & Smith, 1990; Clayton & Birren, 1980; Erikson, 1959; Labouvie-Vief, 1990; Sternberg, 1990, 1998). The notion is thus that wisdom has beneficial effects for the person who is wise as well as for the people who may turn to the wise individual for advice and support. Although different researchers have proposed different definitions of wisdom (e.g., Ardelt, 2004; Baltes & Smith, 1990; Grossmann, 2017; Staudinger & Glück, 2011; Sternberg, 1998; see Chapter 4), at a more abstract level of analysis, these definitions have a common core. More specifically, wisdom is different from other human strengths in that it facilitates a holistic and integrative attitude toward life and all the phenomena we may encounter as human beings. Importantly, wisdom does not mean that one does not have problems or difficulties, because these are simply part of life. Rather, what constitutes wisdom is the attitude toward difficulties. According to many definitions of wisdom, a wise person does not see a problem in isolation, but acknowledges that the causes and consequences of life problems are typically complex, and that one problem rarely occurs in isolation. A wise person does not usually take sides, but considers different points of view – for example, when mediating a conflict between two people or two groups. This does not mean that there are not also situations in which a wise person takes a stand – for example, in response to the violation of human rights. However, the attitude of a wise person is one that seeks to balance and reconcile opposing stances. Finally, a wise person is aware that they cannot know and control everything, and that in fact they often can control very little (Ardelt, 2004; Baltes & Smith, 1990; Staudinger & Glück, 2011; Sternberg, 1998).

Together, these core features make a wise person someone who thinks things through, who can see behind the obvious, who humbly acknowledges the limits of their knowledge, and who can see what is important in the midst of uncertainty. This often results in highly balanced judgements and advice that focuses on the good of each individual, or what has been called the "common good" (Sternberg, 1998).

The situations in which we long for a wise counselor rather than a counselor who is an expert in a particular field are typically those in which we are dealing with a very difficult problem – a problem for which there seems to be no clear right or wrong solution. Often it is even difficult to grasp the problem fully, and we do not understand why we, of all people, need to experience the

---

[1] Portions of this chapter draw on ideas expressed in Kunzmann, U. and Glück, J. (2019). Wisdom and emotion. In R. J. Sternberg and J. Glück, eds., *The Cambridge Handbook of Wisdom*. Cambridge University Press, pp. 575–601.

problem and not someone else. It challenges our long-held beliefs about who we are. Simply put, the problem is existential. Prototypical examples of existential problems include accepting the end of a romantic relationship, resolving an entrenched conflict among friends, learning that a person to whom you feel close is suffering from a terminal illness and will soon die, or being betrayed by a close friend whom you have always trusted.

Obviously, what such situations or problems have in common is that they are highly emotional, potentially eliciting a wide range of negative emotions such as fear, sadness, and despair, and also sometimes anger, frustration, guilt, shame, and embarrassment. The list of emotions that we can experience in difficult situations is long. Some researchers argue that negative emotions, whatever they may be, can mislead and interfere with rational thinking just when we need it most – when we are faced with a difficult problem. In fact, at first glance, negative emotions, which often narrow the view to one or a few aspects of a problem, may seem at odds with wise judgment or advice, which is definitely not one-sided, but balanced and well thought out. Why do we have negative emotions, if they are only harmful and lead us astray? As we shall see, emotions – whether they are positive or negative – are very useful in many situations. When we experience them ourselves, they can give us important clues about the causes of a problem and what the problem means to us. If we can identify negative emotions correctly in another person, they can help us to better understand and support that person.

Seeing emotions in this light, how do you think a wise person deals with their emotions? How can they use their emotions without being overwhelmed by them? To begin to address these and related questions, we shall first define the terms **emotion** and **emotional competence**. We shall then discuss the role that emotions and emotional competence play in current psychological models of wisdom. Finally, we shall discuss research on emotions as correlates of individual differences in wisdom-related knowledge. What this chapter is trying to convey is that wisdom has a lot to do with whether we are open to our emotions and how we deal with them, because there is wisdom in emotions. In other words, emotions are part of our human nature, and as such they are part of wisdom.

10.2   The Wisdom in Emotions

Emotions such as joy, fear, anger, or sadness are fast and short-lived reactions to events that are important to our personal goals and well-being. Emotional reactions can be observed at various levels, and involve certain cognitive appraisals, specific action tendencies, patterns of physiological activity, configurations of facial expressions, and inner feelings (e.g., Ekman, 1999; Frijda et al., 1989; Levenson, 2000). Functional approaches to emotion assume that negative emotions evolved during evolution because they offer adaptive solutions to specific imbalances between the individual and the environment (e.g., Lazarus, 1991; Levenson, 2000). For example, sadness facilitates goal disengagement in the face of irreversible loss, and it signals to the self and others the need for social support and comfort. By contrast, anger facilitates sticking to one's goals in the face of obstacles, and it signals to the self and others the need for control and self-assertion. Seen in this way, negative emotions are an inherent part of human life and they contribute to long-term well-being rather than hinder it. Certainly, negative emotions may be unpleasant, but they signal to the individual that there is something wrong, and they motivate cognitive and behavioral processes that help to regain a balance between the person and the environment.

In this respect, it is important to keep in mind that discrete emotions such as sadness, fear, or anger are short-lived phenomena that are coupled with specific situations. It is only if such emotions become chronic, decoupled from concrete situations, and thus generalized, that they can become dysfunctional – for example, leading to the onset of physical and mental illness (Kunzmann & Wrosch, 2018; Kunzmann et al., 2019). Thus longer-term and more generalized emotional traits such as depression or generalized anxiety need to be differentiated from specific short-term responses to circumscribed emotion elicitors.

As an example of this difference, imagine a student who is one week away from an important exam and who definitely feels a moderate level of anxiety at the thought of it. The exam is important, and the fear helps him to prepare and study well. After the exam, the fear disappears or is replaced by feelings of relaxation and perhaps pride if the exam went well. But what if the anxiety persists and the student worries about all sorts of study-related things, even things that other students would see as a positive challenge? Then we would be talking about generalized and chronic anxiety, which is probably not helpful and in fact causes harm.

According to functional approaches to emotions, similar arguments hold true for positive emotions, which are not only pleasant but also adaptive. Certainly, in contrast to negative emotions, positive emotions occur in situations that are safe and that typically do not require a specific course of action, such as preparing very well for an important exam that you anxiously await, as in the above example. However, past theoretical and empirical work strongly suggests that positive emotions broaden people's momentary thought–action repertoires, which in turn help to build their long-term resources. More specifically, Fredrickson states in her broaden-and-build theory of positive emotions that "joy produces the urge to play, interest, the urge to explore, contentment, the urge to savor and integrate, and love, a combination of many of these urges" (Fredrickson & Branigan, 2001, p. 144). Over time and as a product of recurrent play, exploration, and integration, positive emotions have the effect of building a person's social, physical, and personal resources (e.g., recurrent exploration increases a person's knowledge base; see also Fredrickson, 1998, 2001). Empirical evidence consistently suggests that people who experience positive emotions will more often process information in new, creative, and integrative ways (Isen, 1999), and are more likely to help other people in need (Isen, 1987) and contribute resources to the self and others (Kunzmann et al., 2005).

Although both positive and negative emotions are often our best allies, helping us to respond effectively to the opportunities and difficulties that we encounter, in many situations it is necessary to regulate our spontaneous action impulses so that they will not hurt us or others, or become chronic and decoupled from concrete and immediate causes. For example, in many societies it is considered inappropriate to experience or express anger about one's professor's behavior in their presence, or pride in one's own achievement in the presence of others who have failed, or to experience recurrent episodes of intense fear although the actual threat no longer exists. As these examples illustrate, the ability to regulate positive and negative emotions is one central aspect of emotional competence (e.g., Salovey et al., 2004).

At an abstract level of analysis, emotional competence can be understood as the ability to "work" with our own and others' emotions in ways that help us to make progress toward our immediate and longer-term goals and maximize our own and others' well-being. At least three different types or components of emotional competence can be differentiated. We have already thought of a first component, emotion regulation – that is, the ability to regulate emotions so that the emotions fit situational affordances and facilitate our goals. We often down-regulate our negative emotions in social contexts (e.g., perhaps we do not want to show our anger toward a professor, or we do not want to appear anxious in an exam). However, emotion regulation can also refer to up-regulating negative emotions (e.g., when we want to put someone in their place and therefore show our anger, or we want to better understand our negative feelings and therefore trace them). Finally, it is important to keep in mind that not only negative but also positive emotions are regulated (e.g., when we want to motivate others and therefore express our anticipation of a joint activity particularly strongly, or share another person's pride about their success).

In order to regulate our emotions successfully, we can resort to quite different strategies. For example, we can focus our attention on specific aspects of the situation, we can try to think about the situation in a new way (e.g., by looking at the situation from a neutral point of view), or we can try to change a situation or avoid it altogether (e.g., by avoiding a person when a conflict with them is imminent). Some of these strategies are easier to implement than others. For example, distraction typically requires fewer cognitive resources than the elaborate reassessment of a difficult situation. However, strategies that are easy to implement are often less sustainable and thus less effective in the long run (Sheppes et al., 2014). Thus emotion-regulation strategies have benefits and costs, and whether or not they best serve our goals depends on whether their use is context-sensitive and flexible.

A second component of emotional competence is emotional understanding. There are many definitions of emotional understanding in the literature (e.g., Castro et al., 2016), but researchers agree that emotional understanding in adults requires knowledge about the nature of emotions, including their causes, temporal dynamics, and consequences. Some researchers have also highlighted the fact that emotional understanding can refer to how well we understand our own emotions, how well we understand emotions in a specific other (e.g., a friend, parent, or teacher), and how well we understand emotions in the general population (e.g., someone we do not know). A person who knows a lot about emotions is aware, for example, that even the most intense grief can pass (they have knowledge about the temporal dynamics of emotions). This person knows that one feels fear if one is exposed to a threat (they have knowledge about the causes of emotions), that fear shows itself in certain wrinkles in the face and certain body gestures (they have knowledge about the outward signs of emotions), and that fear is associated with escape impulses (they have knowledge about the behavioral consequences of emotions). All of these examples demonstrate that knowledge about emotions is multifaceted and can be very helpful in concrete situations for understanding oneself or others better.

A third component of emotional competence is empathy – that is, the ability to accurately infer others' emotions and share their feelings. The ability to infer another's emotions accurately has been labeled "empathic accuracy," and is the cognitive component of empathy. It is closely related to fluid and crystallized cognitive abilities, including processing speed, logical thinking, and verbal fluency (Kunzmann et al., 2018). The sharing of another's feelings has been labeled "emotional congruence," and is the affective component of empathy. Sharing another person's feelings (e.g., their sadness or guilt) can help us to understand the other person even better, and closeness can develop. However, it is important to keep in mind that these are not our own feelings, but rather those of the other person, so that the shared feelings do not become too strong. When shared emotions (e.g., sadness, fear, or anger) become very strong, it is quite likely that we will become preoccupied with regulating our own emotions and will no longer be able to devote ourselves to the other. Because it is so hard to find the right level of emotional congruence, some have described it as a double-edged sword that is only helpful if coupled with sympathy – that is, a feeling of warmth and compassion toward the other person. In an advice-giving situation, all of these components – empathic accuracy, emotional congruence, and sympathy – typically interact with and facilitate each other. As a result, a person in need feels that they are taken seriously and accepted, and realizes that they are not alone, but they have an adviser who understands them intellectually, accepts them emotionally, and is there for them.

The three dimensions of emotional competence – emotion regulation, emotional understanding, and empathy coupled with sympathy – have been thought to facilitate individual and social well-being across the entire lifespan, including old and very old age (e.g., Carstensen et al., 1999; Kunzmann & Wrosch, 2017; Labouvie-Vief, 2003). Given the increasing number of theoretical and empirical studies that support the idea that emotions and emotional competence are major contributors to developmental growth, the question arises as to which aspects of emotion and emotional competence may be typical of wisdom. In Section 10.3 we shall discuss the existing definitions of wisdom and explore which aspects of emotion and emotional competence have been considered to be elements of wisdom.

10.3   Emotions in Wisdom

There have been two ways of studying wisdom in psychological research (e.g., Ardelt, 2004; Glück, 2015; Baltes & Kunzmann, 2004; Staudinger & Glück, 2011; see Chapters 4 and 6). One approach has been to focus on the personality traits of wise individuals. This work is grounded in research in social and personality psychology (e.g., Ardelt, 2003; Erikson, 1959; Webster, 2003; Wink & Helson, 1997). A second approach has been to define wisdom as a body of highly developed knowledge and reasoning skills. This line of work has conceptualized wisdom in the context of models of intelligence and cognitive functioning (e.g., Baltes & Staudinger, 2000; Grossmann., 2017; Sternberg, 1998). The first approach has considered emotions and emotional competence to be elements of wisdom (i.e., part of the wise personality). The second approach views emotions and emotional competence as closely linked to wisdom-related reasoning and knowledge (e.g., as resources for the acquisition of wisdom-related knowledge). We shall discuss both approaches.

10.3.1   Personality-Based Approaches to Wisdom: Two Representative Examples

10.3.1.1   The Three-Dimensional Wisdom Model

Consistent with the idea that wisdom entails integration and a holistic attitude toward life, Monika Ardelt has defined wisdom as the integration of reflective, cognitive, and affective characteristics (e.g., Ardelt, 2003; see Chapters 4 and 9). Ardelt views the reflective dimension as a prerequisite for the acquisition of the cognitive and emotional elements during development. According to Ardelt, reflection primarily refers to a person's willingness and ability to overcome subjectivity by looking at phenomena and events from different perspectives. Seen in this light, a person who has the potential to become wise one day is someone who is very interested in all aspects of life, especially why people experience themselves in the way that they do and why they behave the way they do. It is someone who asks a lot of "why" questions and can see the aspects that are not obvious to everyone.

What would be a good example of such a reflective attitude? Imagine that you hear about two friends who are having a terrible argument about how one of them is always late and even often leaves the other stranded. A pragmatic – not to say superficial – attitude to this problem might be to think that the unreliable friend is the culprit, and to advise the other person to find another friend. A more reflective approach would be to first find out the reasons for the unreliability, to bear in mind that the seemingly innocent friend may also have a stake in the situation, and to consider whether the friendship can be sustained – in other words, to work out how the needs of both individuals might best be met. Thus a reflective attitude entails first looking beyond the obvious and thinking extensively about the reasons that may lie behind the experience and behavior of the people involved.

Ardelt defines the cognitive element of wisdom as a person's ability to understand life – that is, to comprehend the significance and deeper meaning of life experiences, of course without neglecting the highly subjective nature of any search for meaning, as the deeper meaning of a particular life experience can vary for different individuals. This component of wisdom refers to the depth and breadth of the individuals' knowledge. It is difficult to determine the domain to which this knowledge refers, but it includes knowledge about human emotions, motives, strengths, and weaknesses. This type of knowledge can be very concrete and specific, or abstract and generalized; it encompasses knowledge about facts as well as knowledge about how to apply knowledge and give advice to others. A counselor with high levels of wisdom-related knowledge will also have a wealth of experience. With this combination of knowledge and experience they are well placed to classify the problems of a person seeking advice. It is important that their knowledge and wealth of experience relate not to specialized knowledge (such as would be acquired through reading or academic study) but rather to life itself – its meaning and conduct.

According to Ardelt, the affective component of wisdom refers primarily to how we relate emotionally to others. She posits that a wise person relates to others with compassion and empathy rather than with indifference or even with negative emotions. Thus the emotional elements that Ardelt included in her model are the absence of negative emotions (see Chapter 9) and the presence of sympathy and compassion. Although wisdom does entail sympathy and compassion, the idea that wisdom excludes certain negative and perhaps positive emotions may require important qualifications. More specifically, and as discussed above, emotions (both positive and negative) are part of life. As long as a wise person is alive, they will experience emotions. Even "enlightened" people, in the Buddhist sense, experience emotions (e.g., Kramer, 2007). From this point of view, it is important not to reduce wisdom to "vicarious" emotions.

Wise individuals have their own history and therefore their own emotions. How would they be able to have knowledge about emotions if they could not experience any emotions themselves? As Ardelt and many other wisdom researchers have postulated, the wise person has deep knowledge about human nature, and this includes emotions. A critical question, of course, is how wise individuals deal with their emotions and regulate them. We can assume that wise people are particularly good at acknowledging their emotions and then letting them go again, so that the emotions do not become chronic and decoupled from the relevant situations. We shall now take a closer look at a definition of wisdom in which the ability to regulate emotions is rightly considered to be a central component.

10.3.1.2   The HERO(E) Model of Wisdom

Webster (2003, 2007) introduced a definition of the wise personality. Based on his review of the literature, he defined wisdom as "the competence in, intention to, and application of critical life experiences to facilitate the optimal development of self and others" (Webster, 2007, p. 164). In contrast to Ardelt (2003), who identified three dimensions of the wise personality, Webster (2003, 2007) stated that his literature review suggested that the wise personality has five dimensions, namely critical life experience, reminiscence and reflectiveness, openness, emotion regulation, and humor (see Chapter 4).

At first sight, what Webster has labeled as emotion regulation refers to how individuals manage and deal with their own and others' emotions when confronted with emotionally charged events. However, a closer look at how Webster defines emotion regulation suggests that he is not referring to emotion regulation per se and as defined by emotion researchers (e.g., Gross, 2015), but rather to emotional sensitivity, emotional understanding, and the ability to use the information inherent in emotions. He writes: "The emotional dimension of wisdom involves an exquisite sensitivity to the gross distinctions, subtle nuances, and complex blends of the full range of human affect. Recognizing, embracing, and employing emotions in a constructive way is a benchmark of wisdom" (Webster, 2003, p. 14). Consistent with this definition, the items that measure emotion regulation cover a range of emotional competencies, including the ability to recognize one's own emotional state accurately, and the tendency to empathize with others without becoming overwhelmed by one's own negative feelings.

The second emotional dimension in Webster's wisdom model is humor. As the author observed, not all forms of humor are typical of wisdom – examples of this include sarcasm and caustic humor. However, humor can reflect the ability to distance oneself from certain point of views, the recognition of irony, and the ability not to take oneself too seriously. In this sense, Webster views humor as resulting from cognitive flexibility, playfulness, and an openness to ideas, and in addition he points out that humor can be used to strengthen emotional bonds with others, and thus to reach out to others and contribute to their short-term happiness as well as their longer-term development and well-being (e.g., Webster, 2003, p. 15).

Thus, according to Webster, the wise personality is sensitive to emotions, and recognizes, embraces, and uses emotions in constructive ways to facilitate other people's well-being and contribute to their development. Webster's general approach to identifying the emotional aspects of the wise personality is extremely useful. However, his ideas about emotion regulation are somewhat vague, and his definition of emotion regulation does not align with established definitions of this term (e.g., Gross, 2015). In addition, it is not entirely clear why he focused on humor as a positive emotion, but did not consider other positive emotions that could be characteristic of the wise personality (e.g., curiosity, gratitude, and serenity).

10.3.2 *Summary and Conclusions: Emotions in Personality-Based Approaches to Wisdom*

As highlighted by the two definitions of the wise personality introduced by Ardelt and Webster, researchers who support this school of thought agree that the wise personality possesses a range of distinct, highly desirable traits. However, the two definitions have focused on slightly different components of the wise personality, making it difficult to draw firm conclusions about its exact nature and structure. Importantly, for the purposes of this discussion, according to both definitions, wisdom has cognitive, reflective, and emotional elements. With regard to the emotional elements, there is a consensus that wise individuals are empathic toward others and exhibit compassion and sympathy when giving advice. In addition, although only hinted at in Ardelt's wisdom model, there seems to be agreement that the wise individual has a comprehensive understanding of emotions, and can use them in constructive ways. According to Webster, humor is particularly significant because it can facilitate bonding, self-distancing, and creativity.

Crucially, it is apparent that the theoretical ideas about the emotional traits of wise individuals have remained relatively abstract and vague. For example, based on what the authors who support this approach have written, it is difficult to understand how the wise personality reacts to concrete emotionally laden events, regulates their own and other people's emotions, or uses knowledge about emotions during judgment and decision-making processes or when giving advice to others. In part, this vagueness is due to the trait approach to defining the wise personality and the associated global nature of self-report questionnaires. For example, items such as "If I see people in need, I try to help them in one way or another" or "I am good at identifying subtle emotions within myself" assess participants' beliefs about the degree to which general traits and competencies are typical of them (i.e., apply to them in most situations for most of the time). Such items do not relate to situation-specific behaviors or states, and thus do not address how people specifically deal with emotionally challenging situations, express and regulate their emotions, or use their emotions during advice-giving and decision-making processes (see Chapter 6).

10.4 Emotions and Emotional Competencies as Correlates of Wisdom

A growing number of empirical studies have addressed a range of person-related characteristics as antecedents, concomitants, and consequences of wisdom. Thus, in much of this work, emotions and emotional competencies are not regarded as elements of wisdom, but rather as person characteristics that contribute to (or hinder) wisdom (see also Chapter 11).

10.4.1 Emotional Antecedents and Correlates of Wisdom: The Berlin Wisdom Model

In the Berlin Wisdom Model, wisdom has been defined as expert knowledge about the fundamental pragmatics of life (Baltes & Smith, 1990; Baltes & Staudinger, 2000; see Chapter 4). To assess wisdom that is based on performance rather than self- or other reports, study participants read short vignettes about difficult life problems (e.g., "Someone receives a phone call from a good friend who says that he cannot go on anymore and wants to commit suicide.") and then think aloud about what one could think and do in such situations. The test takers' responses are recorded, and after the test session the audiotapes are transcribed by research assistants. The written texts can then be coded by trained raters according to the degree to which they match several criteria that the researchers have identified as defining elements of wisdom. For example, to rate the criterion "relativism," the raters have to find out whether the test takers demonstrate in their answer that they are tolerant of the values of others and can view the situation from their perspective, even if these values differ from their own. To rate a second criterion, "management of uncertainty," the raters evaluate whether the test takers are aware that they do not know everything, but that they can find the best possible way of dealing with a problem despite the uncertainty. A third criterion is "lifespan contextualism," for which raters evaluate whether the test takers can grasp the complexity of a life problem, and thus not consider it in isolation. This paradigm was the first to assess wisdom-related knowledge that is performance based, and it is still influential, given how many researchers in this tradition have adopted modified versions of it (e.g., Grossmann, 2017; Mickler & Staudinger, 2008).

How does wisdom-related knowledge relate to emotions and emotional competencies? In other words, do individuals who differ in their level of wisdom-related knowledge also differ in their affective experiences or in the way in which they recognize, regulate, and use emotions (e.g., when being confronted with a challenging stressor, or when giving advice to someone in need)? These issues have not yet been extensively studied. However, there is some evidence that wisdom-related knowledge does indeed have an impact on emotional well-being and the way in which we interact emotionally with others.

To this end, several studies have suggested that individuals with high levels of wisdom-related knowledge are more emotionally stable (i.e., less neurotic in the psychometric sense) than individuals with low levels of wisdom-related knowledge (e.g., Staudinger et al., 1997; Wink & Staudinger, 2016). In addition, wisdom-related knowledge has been shown to be positively associated with certain positive feelings, particularly interest, curiosity, and inspiration (e.g., Kunzmann & Baltes, 2003). Finally, people with high levels of wisdom-related knowledge typically report that they are compassionate, interested in other people's thoughts and feelings, and willing to help others to develop themselves (e.g., Kunzmann & Baltes, 2003; Staudinger et al., 2017; Wink & Staudinger, 2016). Further research is needed that is more process oriented and that observes individuals with high levels of wisdom-related knowledge in concrete situations. How do they react emotionally to stressors? How do they deal with their own and other people's emotions in situations where they are experiencing emotional arousal? To what extent do they take into account their own emotions and those of the other person in their decision making?

10.4.2 Emotional Antecedents and Correlates of Wisdom: The MORE Life Experience Model

The MORE Life Experience Model (Glück & Bluck, 2013) is a theoretical account of how wisdom develops. In short, it proposes that life challenges – experiences that overthrow a person's worldviews, which include many negative events but also positive ones, such as having one's first child – are the main catalysts that can foster the development of wisdom (see Chapter 11). However, not everyone who goes through such challenges grows wiser. For example, the experience of going through a difficult divorce may teach some people that no one should be trusted, and the experience of serious illness may lead some people to optimize their life with respect to their own needs without consideration of others. According to the MORE Life Experience Model, only individuals who have the following four intrapersonal resources are likely to gain wisdom-relevant insights from life challenges (e.g., Glück & Bluck, 2013). The first resource is the ability to manage uncertainty and uncontrollability. This includes not only an awareness of the highly limited amount of control that people have over their lives, but also the ability to deal with uncontrollability constructively. The second resource is openness to new ideas and viewpoints, which includes a high level of tolerance of diverging perspectives. The third resource is reflectivity, which is a willingness and ability to think about complex things in a complex way, and typically includes self-critical reflection. The fourth and fifth resources, which most relevant to the current topic, refer to emotional competencies, namely emotion regulation and empathy.

Thus the MORE Life Experience Model considers similar emotional competencies to the two personality-based models of wisdom discussed earlier. However, in contrast to those two models, these emotional competencies are not viewed as wisdom elements but rather as predictors of wisdom. A test of these alternative views would clearly require **longitudinal** studies, in which each person is examined several times over a period of many years with regard to their wisdom-related strengths. In the context of such studies, one could, for example, examine whether emotional competencies in adolescence predict wisdom-related knowledge in middle adulthood, or whether emotional competencies and wisdom-related knowledge develop in parallel. To date, empirical studies of the associations among variables inherent in or related to wisdom have been **cross-sectional** – that is, individuals take part in one session during which all wisdom-related variables are assessed.

One such cross-sectional study, conducted by Judith Glück and her colleagues (Glück et al., 2018), is particularly interesting because the authors assessed wisdom by means of self-report and performance-based measures. The performance-based measure was based on the Berlin Wisdom Model, and the self-report measures were based on the models of wisdom offered by Ardelt (2003) and Webster (2007), and described earlier in this chapter. In addition, the authors assessed emotional resources via standardized self-report scales as well as open-ended measures. The findings suggested that, independent of whether self-report or performance-based measures were used, the two emotional resources – emotion regulation and empathy – were positively associated with the wisdom measures.

Given that Ardelt's and Webster's wisdom measures include items that assess emotional competencies, these positive relationships may not be surprising, and may be partly due to conceptual overlap between the wisdom measures and emotional measures. However, the positive associations between wisdom and emotional measures were also evident in the analyses of (1) a self-report wisdom measure that does not include emotional competencies and (2) the Berlin Wisdom Model measure that focuses on wisdom-related knowledge. Thus the evidence strongly supports the theoretical idea that wisdom is more than knowledge, but may best be conceptualized as the integration of cognition and emotion. Further research will be necessary to elucidate how wise people achieve this integration in concrete situational contexts.

A first step in this direction has been made by Igor Grossmann and his colleagues (Grossmann et al., 2016), who used a daily-diary approach to study the extent to which wise reasoning is coupled with certain emotional resources when individuals are confronted with daily stressors. Over a period of 9 days, participants completed online assessments each morning in which they were asked to recall a stressful situation from the previous day. They were guided through a detailed reconstruction of the circumstances of the event and their thoughts and feelings during the event, including thoughts that can be considered to be wisdom related because they reflect intellectual humility (i.e., an awareness of uncertainty and the limits of one's knowledge), self-transcendence (i.e., a distanced attitude), and perspective taking/a search for compromise (i.e., the willingness to adopt different perspectives and integrate them) in the situation.

A major finding of this study was that when the study participants reported higher levels of wise reasoning than they did on average, they also reported a greater diversity of affective feelings and greater use of adaptive emotion regulatory strategies. These findings are of major significance because they focused on the covariation between cognitive and emotional processes within individuals as they experienced different types of stressors in their daily life, whereas previous studies, such as the one conducted by Glück et al. (2018), assessed the covariation between cognitive and emotional traits across individuals.

10.4.3   Summary and Conclusions: Emotions as Correlates of Wisdom-Related Knowledge

A small but growing number of studies confirms that wisdom as knowledge and reasoning is positively related to emotional stability, certain positive emotions, emotion regulation, and a compassionate attitude toward other people. It should be noted that previous research has largely conceptualized emotional processes and outcomes at a trait level. To date, only one study has tested cognitive and emotional processes in concrete situations (Grossmann et al., 2016).

10.5 General Conclusions and Directions for Future Research

As discussed above, researchers in the field of personality research have conceptualized wisdom as a resource or personal characteristic that encourages the experiencing of certain emotions (e.g., humor, sympathy, and compassionate love), discourages the experiencing of other emotions (e.g., anger, hostility, and rage), and involves certain emotional competencies (e.g., emotion regulatory skills and emotional understanding) (e.g., Ardelt, 2003; Webster, 2003). Researchers in the field of intelligence research have focused on the cognitive processes that are typical of wisdom, and have viewed emotions and emotional competencies as factors that can both foster and hinder wisdom-related thoughts and knowledge.

There is clearly a need for further research that addresses the emotional aspects of wisdom more comprehensively and systematically. In this way, functional approaches to emotion could serve as a useful background for wisdom research, because these approaches can distinguish between different types of emotions (e.g., sadness, anger, fear, joy). Thus functional approaches go beyond models of emotion that have merely viewed emotions as being either pleasant or unpleasant, and so not provided an ideal starting point for theoretical ideas about the arguably complex emotional experiences and expressions of wise individuals, and how those experiences and expressions are balanced.

With regard to emotional competencies, contemporary standards in emotion research suggest that one should consider at least three sets of abilities, each of which is itself multidimensional, namely emotion regulation, emotional understanding, and empathy. Although a range of existing models of wisdom clearly suggest that these competencies are involved in wisdom, the models differ in the exact number and definitions of emotional competencies considered. In addition, all of the models of wisdom that have been reviewed in this chapter encompass somewhat abstract and vague ideas about how wise individuals apply their emotional competencies in concrete situations, and how these emotional competencies interact with their cognitive and reflective abilities.

Many exciting questions remain for future research. One of them is whether wise people actually welcome all of the emotions that can be experienced in a concrete situation. Proponents of functional emotion theories would certainly agree with this idea, because from their point of view every emotion has a meaning, and no emotion is dysfunctional per se, because they provide us with important information and can motivate adaptive behavior. At the same time, according to wisdom theories, wise people would not be likely to lose themselves in their emotions, so that short-term feelings (e.g., anger or dislike) would not turn into chronic or extreme feelings (e.g., hatred or aggressiveness). Through this process of being permeable to emotions – of being open to them without becoming attached to them – wise people may use the information inherent in their emotions in the best possible way for their own good and that of other people. This, of course, requires a repertoire of efficient strategies of emotion regulation, which wise individuals can implement flexibly and in accordance with situational demands.

Seen in this light, the idea that emotion and cognition are antagonists can be safely shelved. Emotions can serve as an important basis for decision making, and this is true not only in situational contexts that require immediate action or that are ill-defined, but also in all situational contexts in which individuals deal with existential problems and questions related to the meaning and conduct of life. At the same time, emotions often need to be regulated. This requires the flexible use of emotion-regulation strategies – a process that can be highly cognitively demanding, as can the processes of recognizing emotions in the self and others, understanding emotions, and using emotions in decision-making processes (e.g., Gross, 2015; Kunzmann et al., 2018; Salovey et al., 2004).

However, with regard to wisdom research the question remains to what extent emotions and emotional competencies actually belong to the core of wisdom, or instead are factors that are not themselves part of wisdom and are merely closely linked to it. This intriguing question cannot be answered by previous studies with their cross-sectional and correlative research designs. Instead we need longitudinal research (e.g., studying whether early emotional competencies predict later wisdom-related knowledge), intervention research (e.g., studying whether emotional competency training has an impact on how wise people can think about life problems), or experimental research (e.g., studying whether the activation of wisdom-related knowledge can cause people to react differently to emotional stimuli to the way they react in the absence of activation). At a conceptual level, I have argued in this chapter that emotions and emotional competencies are inherent in wisdom, as are certain cognitions and knowledge contents. Why should such a useful part of human nature not be a core element of wisdom? If wisdom is among the highest virtues, and if it is truly integrative and holistic, then it does not exclude one faculty of the mind.

Thus, if you had a major problem that you were stuck with, would you turn to a person with a lot of life experience and knowledge but without special emotional competencies, or would you turn to someone who has both life experience and knowledge, and is emotionally responsive and very emotionally competent? In this chapter, I have argued that a wise adviser is particularly reflective, experienced, and knowledgeable, and at the same time pays attention to your feelings, shows feelings him- or herself, can regulate his or her feelings, and considers your feelings when giving you advice.

10.6 Comprehension and Discussion Questions

(1) What emotional competencies were mentioned in this chapter? Describe them again in your own words.

(2) Describe in your own words the two wisdom models proposed by Ardelt and Webster. Then discuss the similarities and differences between these two models. In your view, is one model more useful than the other? Give reasons for your answer.

(3) Can a person be very wise and yet often experience strong and prolonged negative emotions? Give reasons for your answer.

(4) In your view, what are the emotional competencies available to a wise person? Are there also emotional competencies that are completely atypical of a wise person? Give reasons for both your answers.

(5) Gather arguments for and against the position that emotions and emotional competencies are correlates of wisdom, but not elements of wisdom.

(6) Think about what resources a person needs in order to become wise over the course of a lifetime. How important do you think emotional competencies are?

10.7 Investigations

Ute Kunzmann is a lifespan development psychologist who studies social, emotional, and cognitive development from adolescence up to very old age. Her research interests include age differences in emotional competencies such as emotion regulation and empathy, processes of successful development, and the psychology of wisdom. With regard to the psychology of wisdom, her main interests are the measurement of wisdom in psychological research, the interplay of cognitive and emotional qualities in wisdom, and the translation of wisdom as knowledge into wisdom as action.

10.8 Practical Applications

Ute Kunzmann's wisdom research has practical relevance to the application of wisdom in daily life and in concrete counseling situations. The insights into how wise people give advice, and which emotional competencies they use during the advice-giving process, can be directly translated into interventions to make counseling fruitful, by adopting a holistic and integrative approach that is characteristic of wisdom.

Glossary

cross-sectional referring to a study design in which the participants are tested only once – that is, all variables are assessed at one point in time. This design allows the analysis of correlations among wisdom-related knowledge, and can thus be used to test the idea that people who score high (or low) on some wisdom components (e.g., knowledge) also score high (or low) on other wisdom components (e.g., emotional competencies).

emotion any fast, short-lived reaction to events that are important to our personal goals and well-being. Positive emotions are experienced in situations that are safe, whereas negative emotions occur in situations in which there is an imbalance between the individual and the environment. Functional approaches to emotion emphasize the adaptive value of emotions, because they help to regain a balance between the individual and the environment, and to build resources in the longer term.

emotional competence the ability to work with our own and others' emotions. At least three different components of emotional competence have been identified. The first component is emotion regulation – that is, the ability to regulate emotions so that they fit situational affordances and facilitate personal goals. The second component is emotional understanding – that is, knowledge about emotions, including their causes, temporal dynamics, and consequences. The third component is empathy – that is, the ability to infer other people's emotions accurately, share their emotions, and feel sympathy.

longitudinal referring to a study design in which the participants are tested several times – that is, all variables are assessed at multiple points in time. The retesting intervals can range from very short (e.g., in daily-diary studies) to very long (e.g., in long-term longitudinal studies that can last for one or two decades). This design allows the analysis of the temporal order of wisdom components, and is better suited to addressing the question of whether some competencies (e.g., emotional competencies) are precursors of others (e.g., cognitive competencies).

wisdom a multidimensional concept that has several distinct components. Wisdom models differ in the number and exact nature of these components. Wisdom as studied in the field of personality research includes cognitive, reflective, and emotional components.

REFERENCES

Ardelt, M. (2003). Empirical assessment of a three-dimensional wisdom scale. *Research on Aging*, 25(3), 275–324.

(2004). Wisdom as expert knowledge system: a critical review of a contemporary operationalization of an ancient concept. *Human Development*, 47(5), 257–85.

Baltes, P. B. and Kunzmann, U. (2004). The two faces of wisdom: wisdom as a general theory of knowledge and judgment about excellence in mind and virtue vs. wisdom as everyday realization in people and products. *Human Development*, 47(5), 290–99.

Baltes, P. B. and Smith, J. (1990). The psychology of wisdom and its ontogenesis. In R. J. Sternberg, ed., *Wisdom: Its Nature, Origins, and Development*. Cambridge University Press, pp. 87–120.

Baltes, P. B. and Staudinger, U. M. (2000). Wisdom: a metaheuristic (pragmatic) to orchestrate mind and virtue toward excellence. *American Psychologist*, 55(1), 122–36.

Carstensen, L. L., Isaacowitz, D. M., and Charles, S. T. (1999). Taking time seriously: a theory of socioemotional selectivity. *American Psychologist*, 54(3), 165–81.

Castro, V.L., Cheng, Y., Halberstadt, A.G., and Grühn, D. (2016). EUReKA! A conceptual model of emotion understanding. *Emotion Review*, 8(3), 258–68.

Clayton, V. P. and Birren, J. E. (1980). The development of wisdom across the life span: a re-examination of an ancient topic. In P. B. Baltes and O. G. Brim, Jr., eds., *Life-Span Development and Behavior*, Vol. 3. Academic Press, pp. 103–35.

Ekman, P. (1999). Basic emotions. In T. Dalgleish and M. J. Power, eds., *Handbook of Cognition and Emotion*. John Wiley & Sons Ltd, pp. 45–60.

Erikson, E. H. (1959). *Identity and the Life Cycle*. International University Press.

Fredrickson, B. L. (1998). What good are positive emotions? *Review of General Psychology*, 2(3), 300–19.

(2001). The role of positive emotions in positive psychology: the broaden-and build theory of positive emotions. *American Psychologist*, 56(3), 218–26.

Fredrickson, B. L. and Branigan, C. A. (2001). Positive emotions. In T. J. Mayne and G. A. Bonnano, eds., *Emotion: Current Issues and Future Developments*. Guilford Press, pp. 123–51.

Frijda, N. H., Kuipers, P., and ter Schure, E. (1989). Relations among emotion, appraisal, and emotional action readiness. *Journal of Personality and Social Psychology*, 57(2), 212–28.

Glück, J. (2015). Wisdom, psychology of. In Wright, J., ed., *International Encyclopedia of Social and Behavioral Sciences*, 2nd ed. Vol. 25. Elsevier, pp. 590–97.

Glück, J. and Bluck, S. (2013). The MORE Life Experience Model: a theory of the development of personal wisdom. In M. Ferrari and N. Weststrate, eds., *The Scientific Study of Personal Wisdom*. Springer, pp. 75–98.

Glück, J., Bluck, S., and Weststrate, N. M. (2018). More on the MORE Life Experience Model: what we have learned (so far). *Journal of Value Inquiry*, 53(6), 349–70.

Gross, J. J. (2015). Emotion regulation: current status and future prospects. *Psychological Inquiry*, 26(1), 1–26.

Grossmann, I. (2017). Wisdom in context. *Perspectives on Psychological Science*, 12(2), 233–57.

Grossmann, I., Gerlach, T. M., and Denissen, J. J. (2016). Wise reasoning in the face of everyday life challenges. *Social Psychological and Personality Science*, 7(7), 611–22.

Isen, A. M. (1987). Positive affect, cognitive processes, and social behavior. *Advances in Experimental Social Psychology*, 20, 203–53.

(1999). Positive affect. In T. Dalgleish and M. Power, eds., *Handbook of Emotion and Cognition*. Erlbaum, pp. 521–39.

Kramer, G. (2007). *Insight Dialogue: The Interpersonal Path to Freedom*. Shambhala Publications.

Kunzmann, U. and Baltes, P. B. (2003). Wisdom-related knowledge: affective, motivational, and interpersonal correlates. *Personality and Social Psychology Bulletin*, 29(9), 1104–19.

Kunzmann, U. and Wrosch, C. (2017). Emotional development in old age. In Pachana, N., ed., *Encyclopedia of Geropsychology*. Springer, pp. 752–62.

(2018). Comment: The emotion–health link: perspectives from a lifespan theory of discrete emotions. *Emotion Review*, 10(1), 59–61.

Kunzmann, U., Stange, A., and Jordan, J. (2005). Positive affectivity and lifestyle in adulthood: do you do what you feel? *Personality and Social Psychology Bulletin*, 31(4), 574–88.

Kunzmann, U., Wieck, C., and Dietzel, C. (2018). Empathic accuracy: age differences from adolescence into middle adulthood. *Cognition and Emotion*, 32(8), 1611–24.

Kunzmann, U., Schilling, O., Wrosch, C. et al. (2019). Negative emotions and chronic physical illness: a lifespan developmental perspective. *Health Psychology*, 38(11), 949–59.

Labouvie-Vief, G. (1990). Wisdom as integrated thought: historical and developmental perspectives. In R. J. Sternberg, ed., *Wisdom: Its Nature, Origins, and Development*. Cambridge University Press, pp. 52–83.

(2003). Dynamic integration: affect, cognition, and the self in adulthood. *Current Directions in Psychological Science*, 12(6), 201–6.

Lazarus, R. S. (1991). *Emotion and Adaptation*. Oxford University Press.

Levenson, R. W. (2000). Expressive, physiological, and subjective changes in emotion across adulthood. In S. H. Qualls and N. Abeles, eds., *Psychology and the Aging Revolution: How We Adapt to Longer Life*. American Psychological Association, pp. 123–40.

Mickler, C. and Staudinger, U. M. (2008). Personal wisdom: validation and age-related differences of a performance measure. *Psychology and Aging*, 23(4), 787–99.

Salovey, P., Kokkonen, M., Lopes, P. N., and Mayer, J.D. (2004). Emotional intelligence: what do we know? In A. S. R. Manstead, N. H. Frijda, and A. H. Fischer, eds., *Feelings and Emotions: The Amsterdam Symposium*. Cambridge University Press, pp. 319–38.

Sheppes, G., Scheibe, S., Suri, G. et al. (2014). Emotion regulation choice: a conceptual framework and supporting evidence. *Journal of Experimental Psychology: General*, 143(1), 163–81.

Staudinger, U. M. and Glück, J. (2011). Psychological wisdom research: commonalities and differences in a growing field. *Annual Review of Psychology*, 62(1), 215–41.

Staudinger, U. M., Lopez, D. F., and Baltes, P. B. (1997). The psychometric location of wisdom-related performance: intelligence, personality, and more? *Personality and Social Psychology Bulletin*, 23(11), 1200–14.

Sternberg, R. J., ed. (1990). *Wisdom: Its Nature, Origins, and Development*. Cambridge University Press.

(1998). A balance theory of wisdom. *Review of General Psychology*, 2(4), 347–65.

(2001). Why schools should teach for wisdom: the balance theory of wisdom in educational settings. *Educational Psychologist*, 36(4), 227–45.

Webster, J. D. (2003). An exploratory analysis of a self-assessed wisdom scale. *Journal of Adult Development*, 10(1), 13–22.

(2007). Measuring the character strength of wisdom. *The International Journal of Aging and Human Development*, 65(2), 163–83.

Wink, P. and Helson, R. (1997). Practical and transcendent wisdom: their nature and some longitudinal findings. *Journal of Adult Development*, 4(1), 1–15.

Wink, P. and Staudinger, U. M. (2016). Wisdom and psychosocial functioning in later life. *Journal of Personality*, 84(3), 306–18.

PART III

The Modifiability of Wisdom

CHAPTER 11

The Development of Wisdom[1]

Judith Glück

11.1   A Little Interview Project

Box 11.1 Interviewing a wise person about where wisdom comes from.

Who is the wisest person you know personally? Ask this person where they think their wisdom comes from. Did they gain insights from specific life experiences? Did they learn wisdom from other people? What else in their life story contributed to their wisdom? Are there certain life phases from which they think they particularly learned and grew? As you read this chapter, think about which of the developmental influences that are discussed apply to "your" wise person. The path to wisdom is highly individual, so it is unlikely that all of the influences mentioned will apply to every wise person.

Why do some people become incredibly wise in the course of their life – the mentors we turn to when we are struggling, and the models of how to live a life that is good for themselves and everyone around them – while so many other people do not quite get there? Most people manage to live largely satisfactory and happy lives, but few people develop extraordinary levels of wisdom. Where does wisdom come from? This chapter describes a broad developmental framework for wisdom, then focuses more specifically on how people gain wisdom from life experiences, and finally takes a look at the empirical evidence for relationships between age and wisdom.

11.2   A Broad Developmental Framework for Many Individual Pathways to Wisdom

Wise people are not born wise. They may be born with some qualities that make it easier for them to gain wisdom, but for the most part, wisdom is learned from life. The interesting question is, then, why some people learn things from life that make them wiser, while other people may go through very similar experiences without gaining any wisdom.

To understand which factors may contribute to the development of wisdom, let us first draw on the Berlin Wisdom Model proposed by the late Paul Baltes and his colleagues (Baltes & Smith, 1990; Baltes & Staudinger, 2000). As discussed in Chapter 4, the Berlin Wisdom Model defines wisdom as expert knowledge about the "fundamental pragmatics of human life" – that is, being an expert about the big questions of our existence. Baltes and his colleagues used the term "expert knowledge" for good reasons. At the time when they first proposed the Berlin Wisdom Model,

---

[1] Portions of this chapter draw on ideas expressed in Sternberg, R. J. and Glück, J. (2022). *Wisdom: The Psychology of Wise Thoughts, Words, and Deeds*. Cambridge University Press.

many researchers were studying **expert knowledge** in domains ranging from chess to mathematics, and from music to sports. The question underlying their studies was why and how some people develop extremely high levels of performance in a particular domain. The main factor that those studies identified was called "deliberate practice" – that is, purposeful, focused training in the domain, working especially on those parts that are particularly difficult. If you are learning to play a musical instrument, for example, you may develop a certain level of skill by just playing when you feel like it, for as long as you like, and focusing on those pieces that you find easy and enjoyable to play. To become an expert, however, you need to practice a lot more, and you need to focus much of your practice on precisely those pieces that you find difficult to play. Many researchers cite the "10,000 hour rule" (e.g., Ericsson, 2008), which asserts that to become an expert in a field, you need to invest about 10.000 hours of deliberate practice (note that this is a rule of thumb more than an actual rule – the main point is that it is a *lot* of time to invest in one activity!). However, practice is not the only requirement. First of all, you need a lot of motivation and determination to invest so much time in a type of practice that tends to be little fun. Then you need an environment that supports your ambitious goals. You need a good teacher who will show you how to best develop your skill. And so on. In any domain that you look at, many people develop a certain basic skill level, but few people become true experts.

Baltes and Smith (1990) applied the theory of expert knowledge to wisdom, and proposed a broad framework of factors that contribute to the development of wisdom. Importantly, they emphasized that there is no one single path to wisdom – very wise individuals differ considerably in the experiences they have had and the way they learned from them. However, it is very likely that at least some of the factors in the model have contributed to every wise person's development. They proposed three types of factors that foster the development of wisdom – person characteristics, factors that generally foster the development of expertise, and experiential contexts that facilitate the development of wisdom.

11.2.1   Person Characteristics

Baltes and Smith argued that certain personal qualities may make it easier for a person to become wiser over time. For example, a certain level of **intelligence** is definitely helpful and probably even necessary for the development of wisdom (see Chapter 7). A person needs to be able to grasp the complexity of a difficult situation and consider the various different aspects of it, as well as to reflect on experiences in depth and gain insights from them. Baltes and Smith also argued that **creativity** – the ability to think outside the box and come up with unusual but useful solutions to problems – helps people to develop wisdom (see Chapter 7). **Openness to experience** is a personality characteristic that has often been related to wisdom (see Chapter 9). People with high levels of openness to experience are motivated to try out new activities, curious about cultures and worldviews that differ from their own, willing to critically reflect on their own behavior, and attentive to their own and others' feelings, all of which should help them to gain a broad range of insights and knowledge about life. Importantly, none of these qualities by itself is sufficient for wisdom. There are people who are highly intelligent or highly creative or highly open, but not particularly wise. It seems likely that a certain constellation of personal qualities, combined with the other factors in the model, is needed. It is also important to mention that each quality has a complex developmental background of its own. All of them have a certain innate component – both intelligence and personality have been shown to be partly heritable. However, a nurturing childhood environment can foster qualities such as intelligence, creativity, and openness independent of a person's genetic makeup.

11.2.2   *Factors that Generally Foster the Development of Expertise*

Expertise research has identified a number of factors that contribute to the acquisition of expert knowledge in any domain. The first factor is, obviously, **life experience**. If you don't have the opportunity to play chess, your chances of becoming a chess expert are zero. With respect to wisdom, we probably all get our share of life experiences that could teach us something about life, but some people just have more such opportunities – because they are interested in other people's experiences as well as their own, because they are more open to new experiences and therefore more things happen in their life, or sometimes just because more things happen to happen in their life. The second factor is having a **mentor** or trainer. If you have a wise family member or friend, consider yourself lucky! A lot of wisdom can be gained from observing wise individuals as they deal with life matters. In fact, having known a wise person may enable people to "channel" that person's wisdom in difficult situations, simply by imagining themselves discussing the situation with that person (Staudinger & Baltes, 1996). The third important factor, as discussed above, concerns **motivation**. Not everyone is equally interested in questions of life. Some people may be interested in mathematics, information technology, or music. People on the pathway toward wisdom are often driven by a deep curiosity about life (Ardelt, 2003). They want to understand themselves, other people, and the world, not because they want to be able to manipulate others or to earn a lot of money, but simply because they are fascinated by the "big questions" of our existence.

11.2.3   *Experiential Contexts that Facilitate the Development of Wisdom*

This type of factor concerns contexts and situations that provide people with either a particularly large number of or particularly good opportunities for developing wisdom. For example, professional or social roles that involve advice giving or mentorship, such as being a pastor, judge, or teacher, can provide people with many insights into life, people, and themselves. Many people feel that being a parent has taught them a lot of lessons and given them many insights. Another important contextual factor is the place and time in which a person lives. Cultural contexts and historical periods have important influences both on the experiences that we have and on the insights that we gain from them. It is an interesting question whether the time we are living in right now, with global crises such as the COVID-19 pandemic, climate change, and global inequalities will have a positive effect on the wisdom of individuals, communities, and nations. Chapters 13 to 15 of this book discuss how wisdom may be implemented on a larger scale than just within individuals.

Having distinguished between the three types of factors, it is important to point out that in real life they are closely interrelated. To actually gain wisdom from the experiences that certain contexts provide, a person probably needs (1) a certain mindset, as described by the general person characteristics, (2) some of the expertise-conducive factors, such as a wise mentor, and (3) a certain amount of life challenges to enable them to actually develop and apply wisdom-related insights.

11.3   A Little Interview Study (Continued)

Box 11.2 Applying Baltes and Smith's three developmental factors to the interview.

How do the three factors identified by Baltes and Smith (1990) – person characteristics, expertise-fostering factors, and relevant experiential contexts – apply to the wise person you interviewed? Can you identify any personal characteristics that may have helped them to gain wisdom? Were some of the expertise-specific factors present in their life? Did certain experiential contexts contribute to their wisdom?

Box 11.2 asks you to apply Baltes and Smith's three developmental factors to your interview project.

11.4   A Psychological Theory of the Development of Wisdom from Experiences

Baltes and Smith's framework describes many factors that play a role in how people develop wisdom-related expertise. However, it does not explain *how* exactly individuals learn from experiences. Which ways of dealing with and thinking about experiences can help people to grow wiser? My colleague Susan Bluck and I drew on research from the fields of lifespan psychology, wisdom, and stress-related growth to develop a model of how people gain wisdom from life challenges. It is called the MORE Life Experience Model (Glück & Bluck, 2013; Glück et al., 2019a), although the name is somewhat paradoxical because the main point of the model is that more life experience in itself does not make people wiser. It is the way in which we think about the things that happen to us that can teach us wise insights. MORE stands for four types of psychological resources that help people to become wiser from experiences: **m**anaging uncertainty and uncontrollability, **o**penness, **r**eflectivity, and **e**motional sensitivity and emotion regulation.

   The MORE Life Experience Model proposes that while people on the way to wisdom are more or less constantly learning, certain types of experiences are particularly likely to foster new insights into life. Many people think that wisdom requires suffering – that in order to become truly wise, a person has to endure severe hardship. Our research does not support this idea. As mentioned earlier, many people feel that becoming a parent was (1) one of the best things in their life and (2) gave them many new insights – about what is really important in life, about unconditional love, and even (in some cases) about their own limitations (e.g., when it comes to functioning without sleep). Therefore we believe that the main characteristic of wisdom-fostering experiences is not that they are negative, but that they change a person's life or at least a person's views about life. It is certainly true that negative events – ranging from a global pandemic to a personal cancer diagnosis, and from losing a job to losing a partner – can fundamentally shatter our worldviews. However, highly positive events, such as the birth of one's child or grandchild or winning the lottery, can also give one a completely new outlook on life, as can more emotionally mixed or neutral experiences, such as moving to another country or changing job. Any experience that challenges a person's views on life has the potential to open up new experiences, perspectives, and worldviews.

We all encounter such challenges, but not everyone grows wiser from losing a job or having a baby. Most people have found ways to maintain a certain level of well-being in their life and are able to return to that level of well-being even after difficult challenges. They find ways to adjust their way of living to new circumstances, and then continue living their life. Ursula Staudinger and Ute Kunzmann have called this way of adapting to challenges the "adjustment pathway" (Staudinger & Kunzmann, 2005). Other people, however, take what Staudinger and Kunzmann call the "growth pathway." When they encounter a challenge, they actively try to learn from it. They think deeply about what this experience means to them and what they can take away from it. They try to integrate the event into the way they think about life in general. For example, if a person on the adjustment pathway gets divorced, they might want to protect themselves from some not-so-pleasant insights into themselves that the experience might bring. They may turn to people who love them and care about them for comfort, and they may focus on getting over the negative feelings quickly. A person on the growth pathway who gets divorced would want to understand how it happened – what went wrong, what their own role was in the course of events, and whether they and their partner could have avoided the divorce if they had done things differently. Some of these reflections may be painful, as they might tell the person something about their less positive sides. However, the reflections clearly also have the potential to teach them important insights into themselves and other people. Clearly, people who take the growth pathway are more likely to do just that – grow – as they explore the meaning of their experiences in depth. Of course, people can alternate between the pathways throughout the course of their life, or they may choose the growth pathway as they reflect on some events but prefer the adjustment pathway for others. However, most people seem to have one preferred or dominant pathway. There is also a timeline involved. In the midst of the emotional turmoil of divorce proceedings, few people will be willing or able to explore their own mistakes in depth. However, once the event is essentially over, the question is whether we just try to move on and forget, or whether we look back and explore. In a study in which Nic Weststrate and I analyzed how more wise and less wise people looked back on difficult experiences from their life (Weststrate & Glück, 2017), we found that people who showed a focus on adjustment (i.e., they emphasized that the experience had been bad, but now it was over) tended to be happier than people who did not focus on adjustment. However, people who showed a focus on growth by exploring the experience in depth turned out to be wiser than people who did not focus on growth.

Box 11.3 shows a segment from an interview that we conducted in that study. Ms. Y was nominated as wise to our project team. When the interviewer asked her to select a difficult event from her life, she told the story of the birth of her first child, who was born with a severe brain disorder. Maybe you would like to read Ms. Y's narrative and mark the places where you see aspects of wisdom in it. After that we are going to use her story to illustrate the components of the MORE Life Experience Model. Ms. Y is not showing all of the components in this segment of her interview, but she does show a considerable number of them. (The interview was conducted in German and then translated into English.)

11.4.1 *Managing Uncertainty and Uncontrollability*

The "M" component of the MORE Life Experience Model describes how people on the pathway to wisdom deal with the uncertainty and uncontrollability of our existence. Generally, most people feel that they are largely in control over what happens in their life. They think that if they

---

Box 11.3 A story from a life-challenge interview: Ms. Y talks about her life with her handicapped daughter.

I often say that my oldest child is just my greatest teacher. When it comes to our everyday life, to how we go through life … she lives differently, she needs more time. She needs time for many things. And so, I think about how we often rush through things, how we go crazy about things that really aren't that important. So, as I observe her and have the chance to live alongside her, I'm in a continuous learning process. She is giving me a totally new perspective on life. This has changed a lot in me, in my relationship to my husband, in our family, in everything. I continuously get to reflect on what really matters in life or what's important in life; so many things lose importance as I observe how she lives. I think about why some things are so important to me and whether they really are so important.

[Interviewer: How did you feel at the time, after your daughter was born?]

That's complicated. On the one hand, I was like wrapped in cotton wool. I didn't really have very intense feelings, maybe because I was breastfeeding and the hormones absorbed some of the shock. But there was a feeling of hopelessness, of having no way out, of being massively overburdened. At the same time, there already was some hope, and I could actually feel a really strong will growing inside me, I felt a lot of strength. [cries] I'm sorry, it still makes me cry when I think about those days, it was so intense.

[…] I definitely don't want to judge how other people deal with having a handicapped child. I know what an extreme challenge it is and that everyone copes with it differently, doing their best the way they can.

I'm working as a life coach. And what's really important to me is, well, acceptance, that [the clients] are the way they are and that that's okay. That I'm trying not to judge, I'm not evaluating them. And that there is some kind of love. That may sound a bit romantic or silly, but trying to look at a person with love, at what they are.

[My daughter]'s 16 now, and that age naturally brings new issues into our life, and … and I'm still feeling that there is an experience in my life that is sanding me, sanding, sanding me like a pebble in a creek – more and more the edges are rounded and life is just pulling me through the sand. … The beginning was hard, and there still are things that are just hard. The hardest part was certainly the insight, or the acceptance: this is how it is. Because we didn't expect anything like this to happen, it was just something that came into our life out of nowhere.

[Interviewer: Would you say that you learned something from the experience?]

I've grown up, really grown up, in a positive sense. I've lost many fears. I've really begun to have trust in life. That's strange, because I often see the exact opposite happening – that people lose trust when they are confronted with a handicapped life. But I just know that nothing can happen to us – everything has already happened! And I'm continuing to learn.

[Interviewer: How do you feel about this experience now?]

Well, the first thing that comes to my mind is that I'm feeling grateful, that I just … well, grateful that I was confronted with this, this challenge. It probably sounds strange, but I'm really grateful that I got a chance to live through this, to master this, to still be mastering it continuously.

---

don't drink and drive, they won't have an accident – they do not consider the small but definite possibility that some other drunk driver may crash into their car. In other words, people tend to overestimate the amount of control they have over what happens in their life, and this feeling of control goes along with emotional stability and well-being (e.g., Harris, 1996; Taylor & Brown, 1988). However, wise individuals have learned from life that our control is limited – that bad things can and do happen. As Ms. Y says at the end of the interview, she did not expect her child to have brain damage. She was expecting to have a healthy baby, and then bad news hit her out of nowhere. However, as she observes, learning the hard way that bad things can happen at any time has not made her anxious about the next thing that may come along. On the contrary, she feels that "nothing can happen" to her and her family – after all, "everything has already happened." Of course, she does not literally mean that nothing else is ever going to happen to them. What she means is that she knows she will be able to deal with whatever happens. Her experience has given her trust in her own strength and in life itself. According to the MORE Life Experience Model, people on the path toward wisdom are fully aware of the uncertainty and uncontrollability of their future, but they are not afraid, because they have also acquired trust in their own ability to handle whatever happens. At the same time, they are not just passively waiting for what happens next – they are fully willing and able to take control in those situations that they can change. As in Reinhold Niebuhr's famous "serenity prayer," wise individuals have "the serenity to accept the things [they] cannot change, the courage to change the things [they] can, and the wisdom to know the difference" (Ardelt, 2005; Glück & Bluck, 2013).

11.4.2 Openness

Individuals on the pathway to wisdom share one basic personality characteristic – they are highly open to new experiences, new ideas, and new ways of thinking. Consider the way Ms. Y talks about the experience of living with her daughter. She does not just say that she has gained two or three specific insights. She says that she is constantly learning – that her experience is changing all the time as her daughter grows older and life confronts her with new experiences. And she seems to enjoy this constant learning. Many people find it difficult to accept that our lives will never stay the same, and they try to ensure that their life is as stable as possible. People on the growth pathway view change as an opportunity for learning.

Openness also implies that people on the path to wisdom do not judge other people for being different from themselves. They feel that they can learn a lot from others who see things differently. Ms. Y says that she definitely does not want to judge how people deal with their handicapped children. She understands that people are different because they have different personalities and different backgrounds and upbringings, and not because some people are "good" and others are "bad." In her practice, she tries to look at everyone with love, accepting them as they are.

11.4.3 Reflectivity

One remarkable feature of Ms. Y's narrative is that she seems to be thinking a lot about her experiences, and drawing insights and meaning from them. Seeing her daughter go through life makes her think about how people tend to rush, pursuing relatively unimportant goals without ever stopping and wondering how important those goals really are. Thus the experience of her daughter being slower than other people prompts her to take a much broader view on what she and other people usually do. Individuals on the path to wisdom try to understand experiences in depth, whether it is something that happened to them or something that happened to a friend or even just something they saw on TV.

Many people like simple explanations for complex issues, which is one reason why a lot of people like populist politicians. When the COVID-19 pandemic began, many people were deeply upset and scared, and some of them preferred politicians like Donald Trump, who essentially told them it was no worse than the flu and would disappear in a few weeks, over politicians who told the uncomfortable truth that there was (at that time) no effective cure or vaccine. However, problems that require wisdom – be they a pandemic, the global threat of climate change, or the breakdown of someone's marriage – tend to be highly complex (involving many different perspectives and interests), highly uncertain, and may not even be clearly defined. There is no simple solution, and probably not even an optimal solution, for such problems – any solution will require trade-offs and compromises. People on the path to wisdom are undaunted by the complexity of such problems. They ask many questions, try to take different perspectives, and are wary of any "quick fix" that will only lead to superficial short-term improvements. In other words, wise individuals are able to think about complex problems in all their complexity.

Thinking about matters in depth also involves questioning oneself. As mentioned earlier, individuals on the pathway to wisdom are willing and able to take a critical look at their own role in how, for example, a conflict came about. As described earlier, they are likely to engage in exploratory reflection (Weststrate & Glück, 2017). As they learn more about themselves, they also learn more about their own biases and blind spots. For example, they may learn that they can be quite wrong when they think they know exactly how someone else feels. This insight may bring them to the conclusion that it is important to listen to people with a truly open mind. Another example of an insight reported by the participants in our study was that the things that we are most critical about in other people may be the things that we don't like in ourselves. Such insights can help us to become less self-focused in the way we interact with other people.

11.4.4   Emotional Sensitivity

The MORE Life Experience Model should actually be named the MOREE Life Experience Model, because the "E" resource consists of two interrelated components, but that doesn't sound quite so good! The first of the two E components is emotional sensitivity. It describes the extent to which people pay attention to their own emotions, taking them seriously and regarding them as potentially important information. Some people are taught from early on to essentially ignore their own feelings, or at least not to show them to other people. People on the wisdom pathway may not necessarily show every feeling they experience. However, they will acknowledge their own feelings and try to understand them even if they are unwanted, complicated, or ambivalent, because they know that feelings can tell them a lot about situations and about themselves (Kunzmann & Glück, 2019; see also Chapter 10). People on the pathway to wisdom are willing to look into negative emotions. For example, Ms. Y cried when she was talking about the intense first phase of her daughter's life.

In a very interesting study, King et al. (2000) interviewed parents about the time when they first found out that their newborn baby had Down syndrome. They found that parents who acknowledged the emotional turmoil and despair of those early days showed more growth and learning from the experience. All of those parents were happy with their current life situation, and many said they were grateful for the experience, but they did remember that the beginning had been tough. If a person says about such an experience that they never had any doubts that everything was going to be fine, the chances are high that they have never really explored the emotional depths of the experience.

Of course, emotional sensitivity does not apply only to one's own feelings. Wise individuals know a lot about specific other people and about people in general, which enables them to be excellent listeners and advice givers. People on the path to wisdom will take other people's emotions seriously. They know that it makes no sense to tell people that they shouldn't feel the way they feel – feelings are feelings, and they are part of who we are. Importantly, people on the path to wisdom are not just willing and able to understand and share the feelings of others, but they also care about other people's well-being and want to alleviate others' emotional suffering. Some people may be good at knowing how others feel, but use this knowledge for their own purposes – to manipulate or exploit others. Wise individuals care about the needs of others and, more broadly, about a common good, as we have discussed in Chapters 4 and 8 (see also Sternberg, 2019).

Most of us are empathic and compassionate toward people to whom we are close, people we like, or people whom we regard as similar to us. Wise people's concern for others extends beyond those groups. Wise individuals even try to understand the feelings of people with whom they have a serious conflict. They care about the welfare and well-being of people everywhere, people whom they will never meet personally. They also care about the welfare of animals and about the natural resources of our world (Glück et al., 2019b).

To summarize the component of emotional sensitivity, wise individuals are attentive to feelings – their own feelings and those of other people. Paying attention to emotions fosters the development of wisdom because emotions can provide us with insights into ourselves and other people. Importantly, however, being attentive to feelings in itself does not make a person wise. You probably know people who pay a lot of attention to feelings, especially their own, and basically follow their feelings in everything they do. These people are not necessarily wise! Wise individuals know that feelings are real inner states of a person, but that they do not necessarily reflect an objective reality. For example, a person may be extremely jealous of their partner for reasons in their own past that have nothing to do with their partner's actual behavior. Someone else may get angry very easily because they tend to interpret remarks or behaviors as insults that are not even directed at them. People on the path to wisdom know that acknowledging and accepting their own feelings does not necessarily mean acting on them. Although they take feelings seriously, they have also learned to regulate them as each situation requires.

11.4.5 Emotion Regulation

The second part of the "E" component in the MORE Life Experience Model is **emotion regulation**. Developmentally, although the foundations of our ability to empathize with others are innate (de Waal, 2010), our ability to regulate our own and others' feelings is acquired over time as we learn to identify and deal with those feelings in ourselves and others. Both wisdom researchers (see Chapter 10) and people outside academia (see Chapter 3) believe that equanimity and peace of mind are highly typical of wise individuals. Although they will show a caring and empathic attitude toward people in distress, they will also remain calm and take a broad, balanced view of the situation. In other words, wise people are able to "take a step back," or not even to "step in" in the first place, even in emotionally challenging situations. Ms. Y is not directly talking about emotion regulation in the interview segment in Box 11.3, but you can imagine from the way she describes being "sanded" by life like a pebble in a river that she probably does not get worked up about small problems anymore, and that she is probably able to remain calm even in the face of large problems.

Importantly, regulating emotions wisely does not mean ignoring or suppressing unwanted or inappropriate feelings (see Chapter 10). Wise individuals acknowledge and accept their own and others' feelings – as one participant said, "They are feelings, they can't be wrong, they are just there." However, wise individuals know that in many situations it is neither wise nor helpful to act out one's feelings. If someone's way of talking to you drives you crazy, is that their fault or yours? They may be unable to read your emotions, but you are responsible for how you react to their behavior. A wise person would be able to communicate the problem to the person in a friendly, constructive, and perhaps even humorous way.

11.5   Wisdom and Age

How do you think wisdom is related to age? Box 11.4 shows an empty graph with age as the horizontal axis and wisdom as the vertical axis (with 100 percent representing the maximum possible wisdom and 0 representing no wisdom at all). Imagine a representative sample of, say, 30 to 50 people, each of whom will be represented by a dot indicating the combination of their age and their wisdom. Draw 30 to 50 dots (or more if you like) that show how you believe wisdom will be distributed over the life course.

Figure 11.1 shows different possible patterns that you may have drawn. Panel A suggests an almost perfectly linear relationship between age and wisdom – older people are generally wiser than young people, which suggests that everyone becomes wiser as they grow older. Panel B still suggests a linear relationship, but a far weaker one – on average, people in their eighties are wiser than people in their twenties, but there is much more variation within each age group, and overlap between the groups. Panel C suggests that there is no relationship at all – people at the age of 20 years are no more or less likely to be wise than people at the age of 80 years. Panel D suggests a "triangular" rather than linear pattern – people at the age of 20 years are generally low in wisdom, while people at the age of 80 years cover the whole possible spectrum of wisdom. In other words, wise people are generally old, but not all older people are wise.

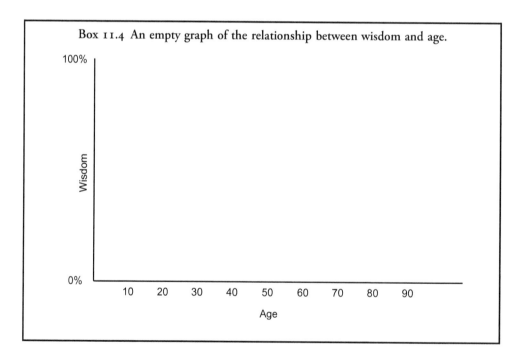

Box 11.4 An empty graph of the relationship between wisdom and age.

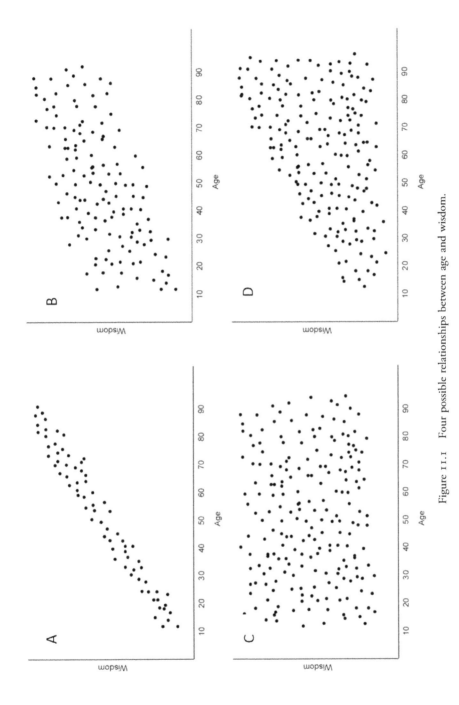

Figure 11.1   Four possible relationships between age and wisdom.

Now what is the right answer? How is wisdom related to age? Given what we have discussed in this chapter, you probably did not draw a strong linear relationship like the one in Panel A in Figure 11.1. If wisdom is a special kind of expert knowledge that requires certain ways of thinking about experience, then it is quite obvious that not everyone would acquire this kind of expertise. (Also, most of us probably know older people who are not particularly wise.) On the other hand, a complete lack of relationship, as in Panel C of Figure 11.1, also seems improbable. After all, in order to gain wisdom-fostering insights from life-changing experiences, people need to have had a number of such experiences, and that is statistically more likely for an 80-year-old person than for a 20-year-old. Therefore Figures B and D seem like the most plausible candidates.

Empirical studies of the relationship between wisdom and age show once again that what one finds out about wisdom depends, to some extent, on how one measures wisdom. However, in recent studies, one pattern seems to be emerging across at least three different wisdom measures. Figure 11.2 shows somewhat simplified results for (a) the Berlin Wisdom Model (combining data from Pasupathi et al., 2001, and Staudinger, 1999) and (b) the Self-Assessed Wisdom Scale (based on Webster et al., 2014). Similar findings were also reported for the Three-Dimensional Wisdom Scale by Ardelt et al. (2018). As you can see in Figure 11.2, none of the drawings in Figure 11.1 got it quite right. Scores in the Berlin Wisdom Model increase steeply and quite linearly between the ages of approximately 15 years and 20 years, during late adolescence and into young adulthood (Pasupathi et al., 2001). After that, there is a broad range of scores at any age, but the scores are somewhat lower above the age of about 60 years than below that age. For the Self-Assessed Wisdom Scale, no data from adolescents are available (generally, the figure shows that the distribution of study participants over the age range was rather uneven, with many young participants around 20 years of age, and few between 20 and 40 years of age), but the pattern of lower scores above the age of about 60 years looks very similar. Ardelt et al. (2018) reported a similar pattern with lower scores above the age of about 60 years, especially for participants with little formal education.

These findings do not quite fit with what we discussed earlier in this chapter. If wisdom is gained from experience, why would there be lower scores from a certain age onward? These lower scores are also somewhat inconsistent with the views of most people. As reviewed in Chapter 3, there are a number of studies in which people were asked to name very wise persons – either individuals they knew personally or public figures. The results of those studies show that most "wisdom nominees" were in the second half of life, and many were well over 60 years old (Weststrate et al., 2019; see also Chapter 3). There are several possible explanations for these findings, namely age-related declines in basic wisdom components, differences between wisdom measures, positivity biases in old age, cohort effects, and differences between wisdom measures and real-life situations that require wisdom.

11.5.1 Age-Related Declines in Basic Wisdom Components

First, the classic popular notion of the relationship between age and wisdom may be rather outdated. The idea that wisdom is characteristic of very old people probably dates back to a time when few people lived beyond about 70 years of age. Research suggests that there are good reasons why very old people may have difficulty with measures such as the Berlin Wisdom Model. Some components of wisdom decrease with age in the general population. For example, most people become less open to new experiences and less able to think in very complex ways as they age, because a certain amount of decline in **working memory** is very common in old age (Hertzog,

Berlin Wisdom Paradigm

Self-Assessed Wisdom Scale

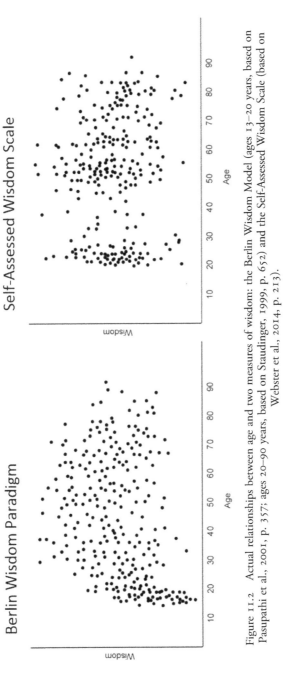

Figure 11.2 Actual relationships between age and two measures of wisdom: the Berlin Wisdom Model (ages 13–20 years, based on Pasupathi et al., 2001, p. 357; ages 20–90 years, based on Staudinger, 1999, p. 652) and the Self-Assessed Wisdom Scale (based on Webster et al., 2014, p. 213).

2020). To give a very wise response to a problem from the Berlin Wisdom Model, one needs to be able to see the problem from many different perspectives. The mild declines in working memory that we often see in very old people were rare in earlier times simply because most people did not reach an advanced age, and those who did were exceptionally healthy.

11.5.2   Differences between Wisdom Measures

Second, it is important to note that relationships with age vary by wisdom measure. As we discussed in Chapter 6, different measures of wisdom focus on different aspects of wisdom. Lower levels of wisdom after the age of about 60 years were found for three measures, but different patterns have been found for other measures. No age-related differences across adulthood were found for the Adult Self-Transcendence Inventory, and the self-transcendence component of that measure actually increases with age (Glück et al., 2013; Glück, 2019). Another study found that wise reasoning about how political and intergroup conflicts might evolve was positively related to age well into the participants' nineties (Grossmann et al., 2010).

If a measure of wisdom emphasizes openness or complex thinking, it will show a decline in old age. In fact, the decline from the age of about 60 years onward is particularly pronounced for the Openness subscale of the Self-Assessed Wisdom Scale (Webster et al., 2014) and the cognitive component of the Three-Dimensional Wisdom Scale (Ardelt et al., 2018). Other components of wisdom, such as a willingness to compromise and to accept one's own limitations, tend to increase with age in the general population. Measures of wisdom that focus on these aspects will show higher scores for older participants. In short, different aspects of wisdom have different relationships with age in the general population, and the age relationships for any measure of wisdom will depend on the wisdom aspects that the measure emphasizes.

11.5.3   Positivity Biases in Old Age

One reason why people in advanced old age may score lower in some measures of wisdom than younger people is that many old people tend to focus on the positive aspects of life, and to ignore or try to avoid negative information or emotionally challenging situations. Put briefly, socio-emotional selectivity theory (Carstensen et al., 2003) posits that as people feel that their remaining lifetime is becoming more and more limited, they tend to focus on the positive things in life and maximize their well-being. In other words, as they do not know how many days they have left, they try to enjoy each day as much as possible. This makes a lot of sense but is not necessarily conducive to wisdom, which involves engaging oneself with the sad, scary, and difficult aspects of life. Therefore people in advanced old age might score lower in wisdom measures such as the Berlin Wisdom Model, which involve thinking and talking about difficult life challenges, than people in the earlier phases of old age.

11.5.4   Cohort Effects

The three explanations we have just considered all assumed that the folk conception that wisdom peaks in very old age may be wrong. However, there are also reasons why current empirical studies may give a somewhat inaccurate picture. The first of these reasons concerns **cohort effects**. The large majority of the findings on the relationships between wisdom and age were obtained from so-called cross-sectional studies. For example, the dots in the left-hand panel of Figure 11.2 represent data that were collected between 1995 and 2000. The participants in those studies covered a wide age range – that is, they were born at very different times and therefore had very different life histories. Therefore we do not know how wise the 80-year-olds in the figure were when they were 40 years old. At the age of 80 years they were somewhat less wise, on average, than the 40-year-olds in the figure, so we could conclude that their wisdom had declined. However, it is possible that they had been even less wise when they were 40 years old, and had grown in wisdom since then, or that they were just as wise at 40 years of age and their wisdom remained stable.

People who were about 80 years old in 2000 were born around 1920. The participants in the Berlin study were German, so anyone born around 1920 was born right after World War One and came of age during the Nazi regime (1933–1945) and World War Two (1939–1945). Their upbringing and early experiences were certainly very different from those of people born around 1960 and growing up in the 1970s! Generally speaking, we cannot conclude that comparisons of different age groups, such as those shown in Figure 11.2, are accurate representations of individual changes over time. We would need long-term longitudinal studies, which follow the same individuals over decades, to find out how wisdom develops individually (two individual stories from one such long-term study are presented in Chapter 9, but wisdom was not directly measured during most of that study). A recent analysis of the long-term development of empathy (Oh et al., 2020) found a very interesting result. While cross-sectional studies suggest that empathy decreases as people grow older, the longitudinal data analyzed in that study suggest that it actually increases. In cross-sectional analyses, the increase in empathy within individuals was completely masked by the fact that the later in the twentieth century people were born, the higher was their average level of empathy. At least in Western societies, empathy has become much more valued over the past few decades. For that reason, an 80-year-old whose empathy has been steadily increasing may still show a lower level of empathy than a 40-year-old. The same might be true for wisdom. Wisdom-related qualities such as perspective taking, intellectual humility, or openness to new ideas may be far more highly valued now than they were a century ago.

11.5.5 Differences between Wisdom Measures and Real-Life Situations that Require Wisdom

There is one more reason why studies which show that wisdom peaks in late middle age may not capture the whole truth about wisdom. It is that measures of wisdom are not perfectly representative of wisdom in real life. As discussed in Chapter 6, describing oneself as highly wise in a self-report wisdom scale or giving a highly wise response to a problem from the Berlin Wisdom Model does not necessarily require precisely the same qualities as acting wisely in a difficult, emotionally challenging real-life situation. For example, responding wisely to a problem from the Berlin Wisdom Model, such as "A 15-year-old girl wants to move out of her family home immediately," requires a lot of cognitive resources. To obtain a high score, a participant needs to discuss many different perspectives and possibilities concerning the problem. In real life, a person faced with their neighbor's angry 15-year-old teenager and the teenager's crying mother and yelling father may need somewhat different qualities. To calm the family down and get them to sit around her kitchen table, she may rely on emotion-regulation capacities that she has learned and automatized earlier in life. She may know a lot about the family already, so she does not need much working memory to process many details. Her personal relationships to each family member may be an important foundation for working with them in a wise way, which obviously cannot be captured by standardized wisdom measures. As she is looking back on the experiences of a long life, she may have a clearer view of what is really important than would younger people. In short, real-life wisdom may be less affected by age than are measures of wisdom.

To summarize, we actually know relatively little about the general relationship between wisdom and age. Although there is a lot of heterogeneity between studies, there seems to be converging evidence that individual "peaks" of wisdom are most often reached around the age of 60 years. As people enter advanced old age, they may lose some of their wisdom. Generally, as wisdom is a rare quality, the most interesting question may not be how it develops on average, but which factors contribute to its development in an individual. It is probably more important to understand how and why high levels of wisdom emerge in some people, as discussed in Section 11.2 of this chapter. If we gain a better understanding of the factors that contribute to individual wisdom development, we may be able to find ways to teach wisdom in schools and to emphasize wisdom in parenting.

11.6   Comprehension and Discussion Questions

(1)   Summarize, in your own words, the most important psychological and situational resources that help people to grow wiser.
(2)   Think about the resources you have identified in your answer to Question 1. If our goal is to make people wiser, could there be ways to foster some of these resources (a) through parenting, (b) in schools and other educational contexts, and (c) in wisdom interventions for adults? Choose one resource and outline some ways in which it could be fostered.
(3)   Go back to the wise person you interviewed for Box 11.1. Ask them to tell you the story of a challenging experience they have had in their life. Can you identify some of the MORE resources in the way they talk about that experience?
(4)   Think about a recent difficult event (such as a conflict) from your own life, and how you dealt with it. Could you have handled that event better if you had used the MORE resources? Or did you use some of them anyway?
(5)   What are the most important insights you have gained from your own life experiences? What would the developmental trajectory of your own wisdom look like?

11.7   Investigations

Judith Glück's main topic of research is wisdom psychology. Having been trained in psychometrics, she has a strong interest in developing new ways to measure wisdom. She is also interested in the development of wisdom through an interplay of life experiences and internal and external resources, factors that influence wisdom in professional contexts, ways to foster wisdom through interventions and through changes in structures and systems, the relationship between wisdom and morality, and people's conceptions of wisdom in different cultures.

11.8   Practical Applications

Judith Glück's work is relevant to many areas of everyday life. Ways to foster the development and manifestation of wisdom seem very important for today's world. Although research on measuring wisdom may seem less directly relevant than applied research, we need to provide the best tools for measuring wisdom if we want to study the factors that influence whether people grow toward wisdom and display wisdom in their everyday lives.

Glossary

cohort effects the effects that occur in studies when people of one age group differ from those in another age group not because of their age, but because of common influences in their life history.

creativity the ability to create something – such as an idea, an object, or a theory – that is new and original, but also valuable and useful in that it fulfills a purpose or solves a problem.

emotion regulation people's ability to exert control over their own emotional state. Emotion regulation can involve seeking out or avoiding certain situations, reinterpreting situations, suppressing or hiding certain emotions, or consciously focusing on experiencing certain emotions.

expert knowledge the body of broad and deep knowledge and skills that people develop when they engage in training or education and extensive deliberate practice in a specific field.

intelligence there are a number of different definitions of intelligence. One definition is that it comprises the mental abilities that people need in order to deal with novel problems, including verbal skill, logical reasoning, mathematical and spatial abilities, and memory. Other definitions put more emphasis on also including people's accumulated knowledge and skills.

mentor a person who acts as an adviser or coach for people who are less experienced or advanced, providing expertise, professional knowledge, and support.

motivation the reason why people (or animals) initiate, continue, or stop a certain activity at a particular time. Motivations can range from physiological needs, such as hunger or fatigue, to psychological needs, such as a desire to understand life.

openness to experience a personality characteristic that is found in people who are not afraid of novelty and change, who are curious about cultures and worldviews that differ from their own, and who are eager to learn new things and gain new insights.

working memory the cognitive system that enables us to hold a limited amount of information in our mind for a limited amount of time. Working memory is needed, for example, when we try to remember an address or when we memorize a list of words or numbers.

REFERENCES

Ardelt, M. (2003). Empirical assessment of a Three-Dimensional Wisdom Scale. *Research on Aging*, 25(3), 275–324.

(2005). How wise people cope with crises and obstacles in life. *ReVision: A Journal of Consciousness and Transformation*, 28(1), 7–19.

Ardelt, M., Pridgen, S., and Nutter-Pridgen, K. L. (2018). The relation between age and three-dimensional wisdom: variations by wisdom dimensions and education. *The Journals of Gerontology, Series B: Psychological Sciences and Social Sciences*, 73(8), 1339–49.

Baltes, P. B. and Smith, J. (1990). Toward a psychology of wisdom and its ontogenesis. In R. J. Sternberg, ed., *Wisdom: Its Nature, Origins, and Development*. Cambridge University Press, pp. 87–120.

Baltes, P. B. and Staudinger, U. M. (2000). Wisdom: a metaheuristic (pragmatic) to orchestrate mind and virtue toward excellence. *American Psychologist*, 55(1), 122–36.

Carstensen, L. L., Fung, H. H., and Charles, S. T. (2003). Socioemotional selectivity theory and the regulation of emotion in the second half of life. *Motivation and Emotion*, 27(2), 103–23.

De Waal, F. (2010). *The Age of Empathy: Nature's Lessons for a Kinder Society*. Broadway Books.

Ericsson, K. A. (2008). Deliberate practice and acquisition of expert performance: a general overview. *Academic Emergency Medicine*, 15(11), 988–94.

Glück, J. (2019). The development of wisdom during adulthood. In R. J. Sternberg and J. Glück, eds., *The Cambridge Handbook of Wisdom*. Cambridge University Press, pp. 323–46.

Glück, J. and Bluck, S. (2013). The MORE Life Experience Model: a theory of the development of personal wisdom. In M. Ferrari and N. M. Weststrate, eds., *The Scientific Study of Personal Wisdom*. Springer, pp. 75–98.

Glück, J., König, S., Naschenweng, K. et al. (2013). How to measure wisdom: content, reliability, and validity of five measures. *Frontiers in Psychology*, 4, article 405.

Glück, J., Bluck, S., and Weststrate, N. M. (2019a). More on the MORE Life Experience Model: what we have learned (so far). *The Journal of Value Inquiry*, 53(3), 349–70.

Glück, J., Gussnig, B., and Schrottenbacher, S. M. (2019b). Wisdom and value orientations: just a projection of our own beliefs? *Journal of Personality*, 88(4), 833–55.

Grossmann, I., Na, J., Varnum, M. E. W. et al. (2010). Reasoning about social conflicts improves into old age. *Proceedings of the National Academy of Sciences of the United States of America*, 107(16), 7246–50.

Harris, P. (1996). Sufficient grounds for optimism? The relationship between perceived controllability and optimistic bias. *Journal of Social and Clinical Psychology*, 15(1), 9–52.

Hertzog, C. (2020). Intelligence in adulthood. In R. Sternberg, ed., *The Cambridge Handbook of Intelligence*. Cambridge University Press, pp. 181–204.

King, L. A., Scollon, C. K., Ramsey, C., and Williams, T. (2000). Stories of life transition: subjective well-being and ego development in parents of children with Down syndrome. *Journal of Research in Personality*, 34(4), 509–36.

Kunzmann, U. and Glück, J. (2019). Wisdom and emotion. In R. J. Sternberg and J. Glück, eds., *The Cambridge Handbook of Wisdom*. Cambridge University Press, pp. 575–601.

Oh, J., Chopik, W. J., Konrath, S., and Grimm, K. J. (2020). Longitudinal changes in empathy across the life span in six samples of human development. *Social Psychological and Personality Science*, 11(2), 244–53.

Pasupathi, M., Staudinger, U. M., and Baltes, M. M. (2001). Seeds of wisdom: adolescents' knowledge and judgement about difficult life problems. *Developmental Psychology*, 37(3), 351–61.

Staudinger, U. M. (1999). Older and wiser? Integrating results on the relationship between age and wisdom-related performance. *International Journal of Behavioral Development*, 23(3), 641–64.

Staudinger, U. M. and Baltes, P. B. (1996). Interactive minds: a facilitative setting for wisdom-related performances? *Journal of Personality and Social Psychology*, 71(4), 746–62.

Staudinger, U. M. and Kunzmann, U. (2005). Positive adult personality development. *European Psychologist*, 10(4), 320–29.

Sternberg, R. J. (2019). Why people often prefer wise guys to guys who are wise: an augmented balance theory of the production and reception of wisdom. In R. J. Sternberg and J. Glück, eds., *The Cambridge Handbook of Wisdom*. Cambridge University Press, pp. 162–81.

Taylor, S. E. and Brown, J. D. (1988). Illusion and well-being: a social psychological perspective on mental health. *Psychological Bulletin*, 103(2), 193–210.

Webster, J. D., Westerhof, G. J., and Bohlmeijer, E. T. (2014). Wisdom and mental health across the lifespan. *The Journals of Gerontology, Series B: Psychological Sciences and Social Sciences*, 69(2), 209–18.

Weststrate, N. M. and Glück, J. (2017). Hard-earned wisdom: exploratory processing of difficult life experience is positively associated with wisdom. *Developmental Psychology*, 53(4), 800–14.

Weststrate, N. M., Bluck, S., and Glück, J. (2019). Wisdom of the crowd: exploring people's conceptions of wisdom. In R. J. Sternberg and J. Glück, eds., *The Cambridge Handbook of Wisdom*. Cambridge University Press, pp. 97–121.

CHAPTER 12

Interventions for Developing Wisdom[1]

Michel Ferrari, Juensung J. Kim, and Stephanie Morris

12.1 Development and Teaching for Wisdom

> In the schools of antiquity philosophers aspired to impart wisdom, in modern colleges our
> humbler aim is to teach subjects. The drop from the divine wisdom, which was the goal of the
> ancients, to text-book knowledge of subjects, which is achieved by the moderns, marks an
> educational failure, sustained through the ages.
>
> Whitehead (1929/1967, p. 29)

Wisdom is defined in many different ways, but scientists generally agree with Grimm (2014), who says that wisdom is knowledge of how to live the best life – for yourself and others, now and into the far future (see Chapter 4). When asked what exactly that means, many people will point to specific exemplars, some of which are culturally iconic, such as Jesus or the Buddha, and some of which are personally known, such as a family member, mentor, or friend.

However, let's be honest – people continue to debate who is wise, how to live the best life, and how to teach people to do so. Anyone who claims to have the final answer does not deserve to be taken seriously. So let us say up front that we do not have the final answer about how to teach for wisdom. However, we hope that this chapter helps to point to and synthesize a few interesting current directions on how to help the next generation to gain some wisdom through their education.

12.2 Teaching for Wisdom in Schools

Learning can happen in many places. We learn informally from our families (through story-telling, advice, and observation) or from personal exploration, and through non-formal educational opportunities provided by religion or therapy (Commission of the European Communities, 2000; Coombs & Ahmed, 1974). Although all three kinds of learning are important for gaining wisdom, this chapter will focus on formal public education that is designed to cultivate wisdom.

There are ancient examples of curricula designed to educate for wisdom all around the world. Consider three of the most well known. According to Diogenes Laertius (180–240 CE), the education of Roman Stoic philosophers (literally, "lovers of wisdom") – from slaves to emperors – included three interconnected aspects: (1) patterns in nature that justify thinking and acting in a certain way (metaphysics), (2) how best to think and act in particular circumstances (ethics), and

[1] Acknowledgments: Work on this manuscript was supported by the Templeton Religion Trust and the University of Oklahoma Grant 311678 (to MF).

(3) analysis of how best to think and act (logic). Perhaps the most famous example is the Roman Stoic School of Epictetus in Nicopolis. The conversations of Epictetus with students and visitors were written down by Arrian and later circulated as the *Discourses*. A classical neo-Confucian education, canonized by Zhu Xi (1130–1200), included practicing the arts, and mastering classical Confucian texts about humane and virtuous character. A Buddhist education, most famously in Indian Buddhist monastic universities such as Nalanda (*c.* 500–1200 CE),[2] included debates about Buddhist concepts, and trained the mind to be tranquil and focused, before directing attention to deeper reality and social harmony.

These three ancient traditions focused on developing students in ways that are still championed in teaching for wisdom today, through training in critical thinking, character education, and mindfulness. We believe that integrating them is essential to fully teaching for wisdom.

12.2.1 Wisdom Connections

What general principles underlie these ancient programs? We believe that they are the same ones that are needed to become a balanced, fully functioning person. To better articulate what this requires, we build on the work of Jack Miller, according to whom six connections underpin **holistic education**, namely *lived body–mind connection, earth connection. soul connection, community connection, thoughtful connection*, and *subject connection* (Miller, 2007).

We further group these six connections into inner and outer expressions of being, feeling, and thinking (see Figure 12.1), and consider them integral to becoming a wise, fully functioning person:

(1) Inner being (Miller's lived body–mind connection) involves the connection to one's body, understands the body as the medium through which we connect to the world and its beauty, and so it must stay healthy and be listened to. Too many students experience a disconnect between mind and body.

(2) Outer being (Miller's earth connection) involves one's connection to the physical environment that sustains the body. Education should encourage students to see their relationship to the Earth and its processes, and beyond to the "big history" of the cosmos and our relationship to it (Christian et al., 2014).

(3) Inner feeling (Miller's soul connection) involves one's connection to one's own emotional processing, teaching that one's feelings must be listened to, accounted for, and balanced.

(4) Outer feeling (Miller's community connection) involves understanding that we are part of a community of other people who have valid experiences of the world that may differ from our own but that are no less interesting or important, and who must sometimes be informed or persuaded.

(5) Inner thinking (Miller's thoughtful connection) involves a mindful connection to effective forms of critical reasoning, teaching that the human mind is a powerful tool that (like any tool) requires skill to use properly. It is also a connection to the psychological conditions that allow for skilled thinking, **openness to experience**, and **reflection**. The linear, analytic (rational, logical) thinking favored by today's schools must be complemented by and integrated with intuitive, creative thinking (through imagination and metaphor).

---

[2] The contemporary Naropa University in Colorado (named for the eleventh-century Buddhist sage Naropa, an abbot of Nalanda) was founded in 1974 by the Tibetan Buddhist teacher Chögyam Trungpa in a similar spirit to Nalanda.

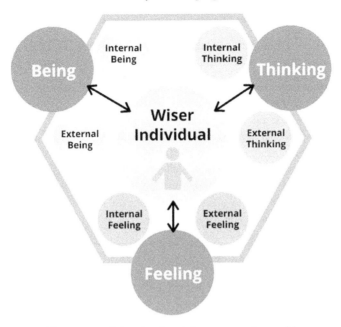

Figure 12.1   Educating for wisdom: summative model.
Adapted from Miller's six connections of holistic education (Miller, 2007)

(6)   Outer thinking (Miller's subject connection) involves connection to complex problems, understanding that they are not usually as simple as they initially appear, and that there are many approaches to solving them. It also includes a deep and systemic understanding of how different subject areas relate to each other.

These six connections integrate and harmonize several common scientific approaches to wisdom (see Chapter 4) and others that are rarely considered, such as indigenous wisdom (Narvaez, 2014; Turner et al., 2000). Ideally, we can imagine an education for wisdom that leads to students who are physically confident, emotionally sensitive, and critically informed about issues that extend beyond themselves to their social and even physical environment – people who emulate the sages of antiquity. Realistically, teaching for wisdom will not consistently produce exemplary sages like Confucius, Socrates or the Buddha, any more than the mathematics curriculum will consistently produce exemplars like Fermat or Fourier.

In this, we can learn from Confucianism. The goal of a classical Confucian education was not necessarily to produce a supremely wise sage (*shengren*, 聖人) – that is, a perfected human being with penetrating insight and universal benevolence – but rather to produce lesser stages of sagehood, students who were: cultivated/noble (*junzi*, 君子), superior (*xianzhe* 賢者), or scholarly (*shi* 士) (Kim, 1992). This point was also made by Karami and Ghahremani (2016) in relation to Iranian understanding of wisdom. Rather than failing if it does not produce a sage every time, an education for wisdom has succeeded if students are wiser than they might have been without it – that is, if they are more fully functioning human beings who are better connected in the six ways described earlier.

12.2.2   *How to Foster the Six Wisdom Connections*

Porter (2016) provides a summary of methods used to teach for character education that we believe also applies to teaching for the above-mentioned six wisdom connections:

(1)   crafting an educational environment
(2)   discussing exemplars (who show these ideas in action)
(3)   teaching strategies to emulate exemplars (e.g., journaling)
(4)   direct instruction in concepts related to these six wisdom connections, and the good life in general (e.g., mindfulness)
(5)   "therapeutic intervention" to cultivate students' self-image, self-efficacy, attributions, etc. that impact their motivation to develop wisdom; this is no small task, and is sometimes perhaps beyond the scope of teachers, requiring the intervention of other school personnel, such as school psychologists and social workers.[3]

These five aspects of educating for wisdom are not mutually exclusive and must be combined, with a different emphasis for different learners.

- For preschool children, when intuitive learning is strongest (and learning can best be achieved through play and direct imitation), educating for wisdom should emphasize well-crafted educational environments in which they can learn these six connections through exploration of the world around them.
- For elementary school children, educating for wisdom can refer to exemplars combined with explicit instruction in specific concepts, within the standard curriculum.
- As they begin to think about their own identity, high-school students can be encouraged to reflect on exemplars and wise people they know personally, and to test strategies for emulating them.
- College students can debate what it means to be wise in pursuit of a particular career and way of life. As emerging adults, and later as lifelong learners, these students can be encouraged to take full control of their own development through self-examination of their beliefs, articulation of their values, deliberate self-development, self-reflection, and perspective taking that strives for a common good (Bruya & Ardelt, 2018a). After college, the most interested and talented can study further with teachers who have devoted themselves to particular wisdom traditions.

Therapeutic intervention to recalibrate students' self-image and engage them in the learning process happens at all levels.

12.2.3   *Examples of Teaching for Wisdom Connections in Schools Today*

Some alternative schools explicitly claim to be "wisdom schools." For example, Waldorf schools[4] established by Rudolph Steiner – who developed and taught a path of "spiritual research" he

---

[3] Linden and colleagues (Arnold & Linden, 2022) have developed a "wisdom therapy" based on the Berlin Wisdom Model that helps to reframe bitter life experiences by adopting different roles and perspectives about unsolvable life problems. However, any therapeutic intervention that fosters wisdom-related knowledge and resources can help to develop wisdom, hopefully, even from traumatic life experiences (Blevins & Tedeschi, 2022).

[4] www.waldorfeducation.org/waldorf-education

called anthroposophy (or human wisdom) – have been operating for over 100 years. Likewise, the "Living Wisdom School,"[5] in California, was inspired by similar schools in India established by the Hindu monk, yogi, and guru Parmahansa Yogananda (1893–1952). These alternative schools for wisdom typically champion some form of wisdom from the Indian subcontinent (i.e., a Hindu, Buddhist, or Jain understanding of wisdom). However, their claims about how to teach for wisdom are echoed in mainstream public education efforts to teach for wisdom connections mentioned earlier, and these will be the focus of our chapter.

Some wisdom education in mainstream schools is considered to be a special case of character education. For example, Kristjánsson (2014, 2015) proposed an "Aristotelian character education" that teaches for **practical wisdom** (in Greek, *phronesis*), integrating intellectual and ethical virtue (important to Greco-Roman philosophical education), in contrast to the typical character education in schools, which is often organized around an ethical "virtue of the month" (Berkowitz & Bier, 2004). For the ancient Greeks, virtue was synonymous with excellence – intellectual virtues are excellent ways to think, and ethical virtues are excellent ways to act. For Kristjánsson, fully developing practical wisdom involves more than habitual character traits and skills. It involves direct instruction in concepts implicated in what a good life requires – a "blueprint for flourishing" (in Greek, *eudaimonia*).

Some scholars have attempted to develop curricula specifically to teach for wisdom, and have evaluated their efficacy. It is to these that we shall now turn.

12.2.4 Teaching for Wisdom Connections in K-12: Philosophy for Children

Matthew Lipman (1923–2010) developed Philosophy for Children,[6,7] a curriculum designed for children aged 4–18 years, and modeled on Plato's Socratic dialogues, to provide teachers with curriculum manuals that explain how to use the **Socratic method** in the classroom for each chapter of his novels, along with lesson plans that explain the story and discussion questions about the story characters that encourage students to explain their actions. Materials in the primary years (grades K–4) are designed to help students develop their language skills, while in the junior and intermediate grades (grades 5 and 6) students begin to develop both "formal" and "informal" logic skills, with "philosophical specialization" increasing in the upper grades and throughout high school (Lipman, 1976, 2003; Lipman et al., 1980). For example, *Harry Stottlemeier's[8] Discovery*, Lipman's junior and intermediate novel, is about how a young student accidentally discovers how logic works. By reversing one of his sentences, he realizes that he has made it false (Lipman 1974). Importantly, this novel integrates many fundamental concepts in language arts and mathematics.

The goal of Philosophy for Children is for children to create a community of inquiry where students can ask more questions, construct better arguments, engage in reasoned discussion, and generally promote cognitive improvement and self-confidence: Typically, the teacher and students gather in a circle to read something (a book, poem, or article) or watch video clips.

Originally piloted in a low-income, inner-city, mostly African-American school in New Jersey, Philosophy for Children has grown into an international educational movement. At the Institute for the Advancement of Philosophy for Children (IAPC) in New Jersey, Lipman's followers

---

[5] https://livingwisdom.org/school/   [6] Philosophy for Children (www.p4c.com)
[7] See Institute for the Advancement of Philosophy for Children (http://cehs.montclair.edu/academic/iapc/index.shtml)
[8] A play on Aristotle.

continue to educate teachers who want to learn this method. A recent program in the UK (Gorard et al., 2015) found that disadvantaged students particularly benefited from this method. For example, students with behavioral problems learned to control their behavior and reason through problems (see also the BBC documentary on the use of this method; Lipman, 1990).

Philosophy for Children has been explicitly adapted to teach Islamic wisdom at an international secondary school in Malaysia. Like Philosophy for Children, the Hikmah[9] Program aims to develop critical, creative, and ethical thinking, and finding meaning in experience, but incorporates an Islamic worldview by having students reflect on Qur'anic verses, the actions of the Prophet Mohammed, and local Malaysian traditions through teaching material written for this purpose for primary school students. A qualitative study found that students enjoyed the classes more, were more knowledgeable about Islamic concepts, and improved their thinking and their confidence compared with students in traditional classes (Hashim et al., 2014) .

12.2.5   Teaching for Wisdom in University: "Philosophies of Life" Course

Brian Bruya and Monika Ardelt adapted an introductory-level "Philosophies of Life" course to teach for wisdom, and examined the difference between a standard course delivery (control condition) and two wisdom-fostering curricula – one with more traditional exercises and exams, and a second curriculum that encouraged self-reflection and development of a personal philosophy of life (Bruya & Ardelt, 2018b). Interestingly, students in the control curriculum lost wisdom by the end of the term (maybe due to stress), no change was observed for the first experimental curriculum, and students in the second experimental curriculum increased their wisdom slightly. For this reason, we shall focus on the second wisdom curriculum.

Inspired by Philosophy for Children, Bruya and Ardelt considered it essential to craft an educational environment in which the class became a "community of inquiry" debating the significance of classic narrative or didactic texts in the light of their core values and beliefs about metaphysics; society and politics, psychology, ethics, aesthetics, and self-cultivation (Bruya & Ardelt, 2018b). Drawing on three ancient wisdom texts and their associated traditions – Stoicism (Marcus Aurelius' *Meditations*), Confucianism (*Analects of Confucius*) and Buddhism (Buddha's *Dhammapada*) – students debated the importance of key concepts from each tradition (e.g., Logos [discourse], ren [benevolence], and dukka [suffering/dissatisfaction], respectively) and their relevance to their own emerging life philosophy. In addition to these philosophical readings, they used journal exercises to better understand and test the value of these concepts. Students also debated moral dilemmas (e.g., if someone's fiancé became an invalid before the wedding, should they still get married?) and justified their positions on them.

12.2.6   Educating for Wisdom in Other University Curricula

Philosophies of Life specifically claims to educate for wisdom, but the question arises as to whether any other courses can also educate for wisdom connections. Ardelt (2020) examined changes in wisdom and psychosocial growth in service-learning classes, and found that students in the control courses lost wisdom by the end of the semester, whereas students enrolled in the **service learning** courses showed an increase in both wisdom (as assessed by Ardelt's three-

[9] "Hikmah" is the Arabic word for wisdom.

dimensional wisdom scale) and psychological well-being. Ardelt also investigated changes in purpose in life, sense of **mastery**, orientation toward growth, and self-acceptance, but found little significant difference at the end of the semester. These findings are in line with the ideas of Brown (2004), who found that undergraduate education had led students to develop wisdom.

Some educational programs not specifically billed as educating for wisdom are designed to achieve outcomes that were mentioned earlier in relation to educating for wisdom connections, including connections to students' lived environment that extend beyond the concepts and strategies discussed by Bruya and Ardelt or Philosophy for Children. For example, Education for Sustainable Development (https://en.unesco.org/themes/education-sustainable-development) is a UNESCO initiative that teaches for a sustainable future through lesson plans that require students to do assignments that mirror real-world issues such as global citizenship, environmental challenges, and sustainable infrastructure. However, a recent survey shows that these ideas are still not widely integrated into public education worldwide (UNESCO, 2021).

12.3 Augmenting Education for Wisdom

12.3.1 Education for Mindfulness

Mindfulness has been essential to efforts to educate for wisdom in alternative "wisdom schools", as well as in the Buddhist tradition explored in Philosophies for Life. Sharma and Dewangan (2017) used mindfulness, narrative simulation, and journaling to develop wisdom in a university leadership course. They found that although students in this program became more aware of their emotions and habits, they showed no significant change in wisdom (as assessed by Ardelt's scale) over the 18 weeks of the intervention. (Unfortunately, this study did not contain a control group.)

Mindfulness has also been used in more nuanced ways in many other **educational settings** (Schonert-Reichl & Reiber, 2016). For example, MindUP™, developed by the Goldie Hawn Foundation, uses mindfulness and other social, emotional, and attentional self-regulatory strategies and skills to cultivate student well-being and emotional balance. Research shows that this program improves self-reported empathy, optimism, emotional control, focused attention, and collaboration in class (Schonert-Reichl et al., 2015). Rechtschaffen (2014) has identified four types of mindfulness lessons, namely embodiment, focused attention, heartfulness, and interconnection. *Embodiment* is the language of the body. When students learn the language of the body, they can focus their attention on sensory phenomena (such as breath or movement), cultivating internal physical connections. *Heartfulness* is developed by students understanding the affective language of their body and learning to regulate their emotion, cultivating internal feeling connections. *Interconnection* occurs when students develop awareness of their heart, mind, and body, cultivating inner feeling connections, and also when they imagine increased compassion, forgiveness, and gratitude in their lives, cultivating outer feeling connections. Simple practices derived from mindfulness-based interventions help students to develop the necessary skills in each of these four areas – a sort of imagined **behavioral experiment** as described next.

12.3.2 Behavioral Experiments

Much as the ancient philosophers engaged in "spiritual exercises" in order to grow in wisdom, curricula and assignments can make use of what are known as "behavioral experiments" in psychotherapy. For example, the *Oxford Guide to Behavioural Experiments in Cognitive Therapy* (Bennett-Levy et al., 2004) describes examples of homework that is sometimes given to help develop cognitive strategies for coping with day-to-day anxiety, depression, and low self-esteem. For instance, a fear of making mistakes may be "experimentally tested" by asking students to keep a journal of other people's mistakes, and to note whether or not this made them like or respect that person any less. Here, too, embodiment exercises can help students to assess their avoidance of emotions –strengthening inner physical and inner feeling connections, and encouraging greater outer feeling connections with their community through greater emotional engagement with others. Although teachers should be cautious about using these clinical techniques outside of a therapeutic context, Philosophies for Life and many other character education or positive education programs invite students to engage in behavioral experiments (e.g., exploring dukkha in their own life). Our point is that existing programs to teach for wisdom can refine these efforts (and highlight potential risks for students) by enabling an understanding of how behavioral experiments are used in clinical settings with more vulnerable populations.

12.3.3   *Practical Challenges*

These are just a few examples of the kinds of programs and practices which are already in place and that can be used to teach for wisdom, and how to improve them by bringing in research finding on mindfulness and behavioral experiments. Used together, they target all six wisdom connections. Nevertheless, some readers may wonder whether teachers, especially those who have very rigid views about education, would ever agree to implement these practices. The simple answer, we think, is that this curriculum can accommodate a range of teaching philosophies, since it is teachers themselves, or school systems, that will determine the exemplars, concepts, and strategies that they feel are integral to living a good life. The goal of educating for wisdom should not be to provide answers, but rather to provide students with the flexible imagination and critical reasoning skills necessary to think about difficult questions. In all cases, students need to become mindful of the value of these concepts and see them work in action through behavioral experiments. Thus all educators, in principle, should endorse these six connections and some version of these wisdom curricula, if delivered in an effective way, while at the same time being alert to individual differences or vulnerabilities that can undermine the pedagogic aim of activities that supposedly teach for wisdom.

For example, journaling activities can sometimes cause problems. Sin and colleagues found that "best possible selves" journaling increased positive feeling for up to 6 months, but "count your blessings" journaling became less effective if it was practiced more than once a week (Sin et al., 2011; see also Bono & Froh, 2009). These researchers also found that that unhappy students actually felt worse immediately after writing a gratitude letter (although if they expected to benefit from this exercise, they felt a little better 3 weeks later). These findings clearly demonstrate that programs designed to cultivate wisdom need to carefully scaffold their activities, and perhaps aim to cultivate practical wisdom (i.e., *phronesis*, cf. Kristjánsson, 2014, 2015) as a "master virtue" that coordinates all the others (Schwartz & Sharpe, 2006).

Admittedly, regardless of one's teaching philosophy, this ideal is difficult to achieve. Modern educational environments often stress evaluation based on competitive standardized testing of individual subjects more than cooperation between learners, and even between subjects. This may work against students developing the flexible, interconnected base of skills that would facilitate wisdom education. To address this, improved teacher training is required, and this will be considered next.

12.4   Institutional Support to Better Teach for Wisdom

12.4.1   The Wisdom of Teachers

One of the few empirical studies of teachers' wisdom (Marchand, 1998) found that teachers are no wiser than anyone else. This is not surprising, since teacher training and the daily life of a mainstream school teacher are not oriented toward developing wisdom. Teachers' identities and experiences shape their pedagogical strategies (Kosnik et al., 2016), and teachers can best deliver the lessons expected of them when they have mastered both the pedagogical content and how to teach it (Shulman, 1986). According to Shulman, pedagogical content knowledge makes instruction more flexible, by using a wide range of metaphors, examples, phrasings, and demonstrations that build students' knowledge and skills – what Shulman (2004) called the **wisdom of practice**. As teachers experiment along with their students, the classroom becomes a living laboratory where teachers "experiment with truth" of their pedagogical practices to apply them in new and potentially more effective ways. However, some teachers do not see themselves as tasked with educating for wisdom, while others lack pedagogical content knowledge about how to do so – nor are all teacher-candidates equally wise (Ferrari & Guthrie, 2014).

According to the Prosocial Classroom Model of Jennings and Greenberg (2009), deficits in teacher social–emotional competence and well-being can lead to burnout that affects classroom relationships, classroom management, and climate. Therefore they emphasize the importance of cultivating teacher and student social–emotional competence and well-being through improved relationships, classroom management, and social–emotional learning.

In a longitudinal study of graduates from a teacher certification program at the Ontario Institute for Studies in Education, Kosnik and colleagues explored how to better prepare student teachers for the challenges of their early years of teaching (Kosnik et al., 2009). They found that new teachers struggled with program planning and developing a vision of teaching that encouraged broad, long-range strategizing to achieve particular goals effectively and flexibly. These goals could include supporting their own and students' mental health.

New teacher training is particularly needed for school programs that emphasize contemplative education and mindfulness (for a review, see Emerson et al., 2017). At the University of Toronto's Ontario Institute for Studies in Education (OISE), Geoffrey Soloway and his colleagues developed a program for teachers in OISE's initial Teacher Education Program, called Mindfulness-Based Wellness Education (MBWE) (Soloway, 2016), in the context of a course on "Stress and Burnout." It included instruction in how to integrate mindfulness into the classroom and into the participants' own lives through "reflection in action" to cultivate greater inner and outer feeling connections.

As in Bruya and Ardelt's Philosophies for Life class, they were asked to write weekly reflections on various aspects of wellness that helped teacher candidates to increase their self-knowledge and gain insight into their deeply held values and beliefs, as well as their emotional responses in the classroom. In particular, teacher candidates were taught to become mindful of their experience of failure with acceptance and self-compassion, not as a final assessment but as a "teachable moment" for their own practice. The class also encouraged teacher candidates to reflect on their identity – that is, how they wanted to be perceived and how they perceived themselves – in the classroom and in their professional identity as a teacher. Soloway interviewed 23 teacher candidates in the MBWE program over three consecutive semesters, and found that these practices had a profound effect both on their classroom practices and on their professional identity as teachers (Soloway et al., 2010).

This is consistent with findings from Taiwan. When interviewed, educators who were wisdom nominees cited eight factors that help to develop wisdom, namely work experiences, life experiences, social interactions, observations, family teachings, professional development, religion, and reading considered necessary but not sufficient for wisdom (Chen et al., 2011, 2014). They also identified four core components of wisdom, namely intrapsychic integration, actions in service of problem solving and ideal implementation, positive results, and feedback and adjustments. Importantly, experience was found to be necessary, but not sufficient, for wisdom, which suggests that expecting teachers to develop wisdom "in the field" without support is unrealistic, and perhaps unfair.

12.4.2   Assessment

Beyond teacher education, we also need to adapt student assessment to measure for wisdom. The Kaleidoscope Project at Tufts University offered prospective students the option of completing an admission test based on the **WICS model** (WICS is an acronym for Wisdom [analytic, creative, and practical], Intelligence and Creativity, Synthesized) in addition to the Scholastic Aptitude Test/American College Test (SAT/ACT). One wisdom-related item asked students to write about how to transform a high-school passion into a project that would benefit society (an external feeling connection); such items might be adapted to assess all six wisdom connections. Kaleidoscope test performance predicted students' engagement in student life and their academic performance in their first year of university more accurately than did SAT/ACT alone (Sternberg, 2012).

Although wisdom is difficult to evaluate directly, we can assess students' understanding of concepts related to the six wisdom connections, and design assignments to cultivate skills associated with these (perspective taking, integrative thinking styles, reasoning ability, reflectiveness, etc.). Commensurate with dynamic assessment, students' mistakes can reveal which connections have not yet been made. New technology-rich learning environments seem especially promising for dynamic assessment of these six connections in person-centered ways (Hu et al., 2017; Jang et al., 2017; Shute et al., 2016).

Of course, efforts to assess these six connections may not be welcomed by all teachers, especially those with a very traditional conception of what it means to be a teacher. In this regard, the most important avenue for cultivating teaching for wisdom may require changes to educational policy.

12.4.3   Policy

Policy can orient teacher education and assessment and by extension all six wisdom connections into the broader educational system. The approach taken by the Garrison Institute to promoting contemplative education and mindfulness training can be extended to teaching for wisdom. Since its founding in 2003, the Garrison Institute has provided a collaborative hub for those pursuing high-quality, evidence-based research in this area. In 2005, it published a survey that mapped the field, identified emerging practices, and provided a preliminary theoretical framework (Garrison Institute, 2005). This was called the CARE (Cultivating Awareness and Resilience in Education) program. It offered a teacher training curriculum based on current research on the neuroscience of emotion that introduces emotion skills instruction to promote understanding, recognize and regulate emotion, and promote empathy and compassion through caring practice and mindful listening. Although the Garrison Institute focuses primarily on elementary and secondary school education, the Association for Contemplative Mind in Higher Education (ACMHE) advocates for contemplative practice in higher education, to encourage new forms of inquiry and imaginative thinking, and educate citizens who will actively support a more just and compassionate society. We suggest that a similar institute is needed to promote education for wisdom.

12.5 Conclusion

Educating for wisdom means teaching to promote a deep understanding of what is important for a meaningful life for oneself and others, how to achieve such a life, and where people currently stand in relation to such a life (Grimm, 2014. Expanding on the work of Jack Miller (Miller, 2007, 2012), we propose that six wisdom connections need to be cultivated in order to enable students to thrive physically, emotionally, and intellectually. We believed that this approach can be adapted to conservative and liberal teaching philosophies, both of which seek to cultivate some degree of balance between personal flourishing and civic engagement.

However, teaching for wisdom not only needs a curriculum that cultivates these six connections, but also requires the appropriate teacher training, relevant assessment tools, and other institutional infrastructure mandated by educational policies. Far from being utopian, we believe that teaching for wisdom is a realistic goal for public education. In this chapter we have suggested a few programs that seem promising (e.g., Philosophy for Children, Philosophies for Life, Education for Sustainable Development), but we invite others to place their favorite programs within this frame, or to expand and improve upon the frame itself. Indeed, we hope that this chapter can be a catalyst for a more wide-ranging discussion about (1) how to help schools and the school system to teach for wisdom, and (2) how to find ways to overcome the practical obstacles to making teaching for wisdom integral both to teachers' identity and to educational policy.

12.6 Comprehension and Discussion Questions

(1) What does it mean to successfully teach for wisdom? How will these students be different from those who have received a typical education? (This chapter provides some suggestions, but include your own thoughts on the topic as well.)

(2) What are some factors that can help teachers to develop wisdom? Have you had a wise teacher? What do you think made them wise?

(3) Are there any students whom teachers should avoid teaching for wisdom in a typical classroom setting (e.g., people who have had traumatic life experiences). Should they be taught in this way, or do they need clinical support to develop wisdom?

(4) Are wisdom education programs more likely to be successful in early education, or at university level? In other words, are elementary students better able to develop the six wisdom connections, because they are young and still developing? Or are university students better candidates, because they are capable of more abstract thinking and personal reflection?

(5) Is it really the place of mainstream schools to be teaching for wisdom, or is this something that requires alternative educational schools, or maybe clinical therapy? Suggest some arguments both for and against these ideas.

12.7   Investigations

Michel Ferrari directs the Wisdom and Identity Lab, which explores personal wisdom as an ideal aspiration of personal development in typical and atypical populations in different countries around the world, including people of different ages and people with autism. Among recent major projects, the Lab has led an international study exploring the relationship between wisdom, motivation, and virtue in younger and older adults of different faith traditions in Canada and South Korea. Our most recent project is a government-funded investigation into how wisdom helps new immigrants and refugees to acclimate to life in Canada.

Juensung J. Kim is a PhD candidate at the Ontario Institute for Studies in Education at the University of Toronto. His research focuses on investigating tools, practices, and experiences that facilitate intentional self-transformation, particularly the cultivation of wisdom and self-transcendence. Currently, he is conducting exploratory research on the influence of esoteric spiritual practices on wisdom.

Stephanie Morris is a PhD student at the Ontario Institute for Studies in Education at the University of Toronto. Her research focuses on investigating how interacting with narratives and storytelling can influence the cultivation of wisdom and creation of identity. Currently, she is conducting research on teachers' personal wisdom and well-being.

12.8   Practical Applications

Our research contributes to a broader understanding of the role of wisdom in the pursuit of a good life in many contexts. We study the influence of wisdom on post-traumatic growth, immigrant and refugee well-being, and student mental health, as well as the aspiration to cultivation of wisdom. Focusing on participants' lived experience, our mixed-methods approach integrates statistical and narrative analysis from self-report questionnaires and face-to-face interviews. These data help to develop and evaluate programs, predominantly in schools, that support efforts to develop wisdom in pursuit of a good life.

Glossary

behavioral experiments deliberate efforts to document people's own actions and the actions of others, in order to enable them to better understand themselves and their relationship to others.

educational settings education can occur in three different settings: formal education in mainstream schools (e.g., specific curriculums), informal education (e.g., familial stories or personal exploration), and non-formal education (e.g., religion or therapy).

holistic education a form of alternative education in which the generation of an integrated and personally meaningful understanding is the goal of education.

mastery a personal understanding of what one can and cannot control, both within oneself and externally.

mindfulness an idea based on Buddhist practices, that refers to a state or skill of being attentive to one's present feelings, sensations, and surroundings.

openness to experience the possession of high levels of tolerance for ways of life that differ from one's own. In personality psychology, openness to experience is considered to have six facets or dimensions, namely active imagination, aesthetic sensitivity, attentiveness to inner feelings, preference for variety, intellectual curiosity, and challenging authority. People high in openness like to seek out new experiences and engage in self-examination.

practical wisdom wisdom that is involved in making judgements about what to do in specific concrete circumstances.

reflection the process of contemplating a specific experience in order to gain a better understanding of the event itself, as well as its impact on oneself and those around one.

service learning a form of education in which learning takes place through an experiential cycle of action and reflection. It enables students to gain a deeper understanding of civic responsibilities by engaging in actions of community service that integrate personal and communal meaning, and it results in a strengthening of the wider community.

Socratic method a method of teaching in which the instructor focuses on providing students with questions, not answers, in order to foster their critical thinking skills.

WICS model a model of wisdom proposed by Sternberg (2003); WICS is an acronym for Wisdom, Intelligence, and Creativity, Synthesized.

wisdom of practice wisdom that people develop as they become intuitive experts, able to discern how best to teach particular students, under particular circumstances.

REFERENCES

Ardelt, M. (2020). Can wisdom and psychosocial growth be learned in university courses? *Journal of Moral Education*, 49(1), 30–45.

Arnold, C. and Linden, M. (2022). Wisdom therapy in overcoming trauma and burdens of life. In M. Munroe and M. Ferrari, eds., *Post-Traumatic Growth to Psychological Well-Being: Coping Wisely with Adversity*. Springer.

Bennett-Levy, J., Butler, G., Fennell, M. et al. (2004). *The Oxford Guide to Behavioural Experiments in Cognitive Therapy*. Oxford University Press.

Berkowitz, M. W. and Bier, M. C. (2004). Research-based character education. *The Annals of the American Academy of Political and Social Science*, 591(1), 72–85.

Blevins, C. L. and Tedeschi, R. G. (2022). Posttraumatic growth and wisdom: processes and clinical applications. In M. Munroe and M. Ferrari, eds., *Post-Traumatic Growth to Psychological Well-Being: Coping Wisely with Adversity*. Springer.

Bono, G. and Froh, J. (2009). Gratitude in school: benefits to students and schools. In R. Gilman, E. S. Huebner, and M. J. Furlong, eds., *Handbook of Positive Psychology in Schools*. Routledge, pp. 77–88.

Brown, S. C. (2004). Learning across the campus: how college facilitates the development of wisdom. *Journal of College Student Development*, 45(2), 134–48.

Bruya, B. and Ardelt, M. (2018a). Fostering wisdom in the classroom, Part 1. A general theory of wisdom pedagogy. *Teaching Philosophy*, 41(3), 239–53.

(2018b). Wisdom can be taught: a proof-of-concept study for fostering wisdom in the classroom. *Learning and Instruction*, 58, 106–14.

Chen, L. M., Wu, P. J., Cheng, Y. Y., and Hsueh, H. I. (2011). A qualitative inquiry of wisdom development: educators' perspectives. *The International Journal of Aging and Human Development*, 72(3), 171–87.

Chen, L. M., Cheng, Y. Y., Wu, P. J., and Hsueh, H. I. (2014). Educators' implicit perspectives on wisdom: a comparison between interpersonal and intrapersonal perspectives. *International Journal of Psychology*, 49(6), 425–33.

Christian, D., Brown, C. S., and Benjamin, C. (2014). *Big History: Between Nothing and Everything*. McGraw Hill Education.

Commission of the European Communities (2000). *A Memorandum on Lifelong Learning*. Commission of the European Communities.

Coombs, P. and Ahmed, M. (1974). *Attacking Rural Poverty: How Nonformal Education Can Help*. Johns Hopkins Press.

Emerson, L. M., Leyland, A., Hudson, K. et al. (2017). Teaching mindfulness to teachers: a systematic review and narrative synthesis. *Mindfulness*, 8(5), 1136–49.

Ferrari, M. and Guthrie, C. E. (2014). Positive education and teaching for wisdom. In A. C. Parks and S. M. Schueller, eds., *The Wiley-Blackwell Handbook of Positive Psychological Interventions*. Wiley-Blackwell, pp. 213–31.

Garrison Institute (2005). *Contemplation and Education. A Survey of Programs Using Contemplative Techniques in K-12 Educational Settings: A Mapping Report*. Garrison Institute.

Gorard, S., Siddiqui, N., and Huat See, B. (2015). *Philosophy for Children: Evaluation Report and Executive Summary*. The Education Endowment Foundation.

Grimm, S. R. (2014). Wisdom. *Australasian Journal of Philosophy*, 93(1), 139–54.

Hashim, R., Hussein, S., and Imran, A.M. (2014). Ḥikmah (wisdom) pedagogy and students' thinking and reasoning abilities. *Intellectual Discourse*, 22(2), 119–38.

Hu, C. S., Ferrari, M., Wang, Q., and Woodruff, E. (2017). Thin-slice measurement of wisdom. *Frontiers in Psychology*, 8, Article 1378.

Jang, E.E., Lajoie, S.P., Wagner, M. et al. (2017). Person-oriented approaches to profiling learners in technology-rich learning environments for ecological learner modeling. *Journal of Educational Computing Research*, 55(4), 552–97.

Jennings, P. A. and Greenberg, M. T. (2009). The prosocial classroom: teacher social and emotional competence in relation to student and classroom outcomes. *Review of Educational Research*, 79(1), 491–525.

Karami, S. and Ghahremani, M. (2016). Toward an Iranian conception of giftedness. *Gifted and Talented International*, 31(1), 4–18.

Kim, S. (1992). The sage in Chinese tradition: wisdom and virtue personified. *Inter-Religio*, 22, 61–68.

Kosnik, C., Beck, C., Cleovoulou, Y., and Fletcher, T. (2009). Improving teacher education through longitudinal research: how studying our graduates led us to give priority to program planning and vision for teaching. *Studying Teacher Education*, 5(2), 163–75.

Kosnik, C., Dharamshi, P., Menna, L., Miyata, C., and Cleovoulou, Y. (2016). You teach who you are: the experiences and pedagogies of literacy/English teacher educators who have a critical stance. In J. Lampert and B. Burnett, eds., *Teacher Education for High Poverty Schools*. Springer, pp. 135–51.

Kristjánsson, K. (2014). Phronesis and moral education: treading beyond the truisms. *School Field*, 12(2), 151–71.

  (2015). *Aristotelian Character Education*. Routledge.

Linden, M., Baumann, K., Lieberei, B., Lorenz, C., and Rotter, M. (2011). Treatment of posttraumatic embitterment disorder with cognitive behaviour therapy based on wisdom psychology and hedonia strategies. *Psychotherapy and Psychosomatics*, 80(4), 199–205.

Lipman, M. (1974). *Harry Stottlemeier's Discovery*. Institute for the Advancement of Philosophy for Children.

  (1976). Philosophy for children. *Metaphilosophy*, 7(1) 17–33.

  (1990). *Socrates for 6-Year-Olds*. BBC documentary (retrieved from https://www.youtube.com/watch?v=fp5lB3YVnlE).

  (2003). *Thinking in Education*, 2nd ed. Cambridge University Press.

Lipman, M., Sharp, A., and Oscanyon, F. (1980). *Philosophy in the Classroom*, 2nd ed. Temple University Press.

Marchand, H. (1998). Wisdom: a case of high level of human performance concerning the contextual and pragmatic features of everyday functioning. In A. C. Quelhas and F. Pereira, eds., *Cognition and Context*. Instituto Superior de Psicologia Aplicada, pp. 367–80.

Miller, J. P. (2007). *The Holistic Curriculum*. University of Toronto Press.

(2012). Contemplative practices in teacher education: what I have learned. In J. Groen, J. Graham, and D. Coholic, eds., *Spirituality in Education and Social Work: An Interdisciplinary Dialogue*. Wilfred Laurier University Press.

Narvaez, D. (2014). *Neurobiology and the Development of Human Morality: Evolution, Culture and Wisdom*. W. W. Norton & Company.

Porter, S. (2016). A therapeutic approach to virtue formation in the classroom. In J. Baehr, ed., *Intellectual Virtues and Education: Essays in Applied Virtue Epistemology*. Routledge, pp. 221–39.

Rechtschaffen, D. (2014). *The Ways of Mindful Education: Cultivating Well-Being in Teachers and Students*. W. W. Norton & Company.

Schonert-Reichl, K.A. and Reiber, R. (2016). *Mindfulness in Education*. Springer.

Schonert-Reichl, K. A., Oberle, E., Lawlor, M. S. et al. (2015). Enhancing cognitive and social–emotional development through a simple-to-administer mindfulness-based school program for elementary school children: a randomized controlled trial. *Developmental Psychology*, 51(1), 52–66.

Schwartz, B. and Sharpe, K. E. (2006). Practical wisdom: Aristotle meets positive psychology. *Journal of Happiness Studies*, 7(3), 377–95.

Sharma, A. and Dewangan, R. L. (2017). Can wisdom be fostered: time to test the model of wisdom. *Cogent Psychology*, 4(1), Article 1381456.

Shulman, L. S. (1986). Those who understand: knowledge growth in teaching. *Educational Researcher*, 15(2), 4–14.

(2004). The wisdom of practice: managing complexity in medicine and teaching. In S. M. Wilson, ed., *The Wisdom of Practice: Essays on Teaching, Learning, and Learning to Teach*. Jossey-Bass, pp. 251–71.

Shute, V., Leighton, J. P., Jang, E. E., and Chu, M.-W. (2016) Advances in the science of assessment. *Educational Assessment*, 21(1), 34–59.

Sin, N. L., Della Porta, M. D., and Lyubomirsky, S. (2011). Tailoring positive psychology interventions to treat depressed individuals. In S. I. Donaldson, M. Csikszentmihalyi, and J. Nakamura, eds., *Applied Positive Psychology: Improving Everyday Life, Health, Schools, Work, And Society*. Routledge, pp. 79–96.

Soloway, G. B. (2016). Preparing teacher candidates for the present: investigating the value of mindfulness-training in teacher education. In K. A. Schonert-Reichl and R. W. Roeser, eds., *Handbook of Mindfulness in Education: Integrating Theory and Research into Practice*. Springer-Verlag, pp. 191–205.

Soloway, G. B., Poulin, A., and Mackenzie, C. S. (2010). Preparing new teachers for the full catastrophe of the 21st century classroom: integrating mindfulness training into initial teacher education. In A. Cohan and A. Honigsfeld, eds., *Breaking the Mold of Pre-Service and In-Service Teacher Education*. Rowman & Littlefield Education, pp. 219–27.

Sternberg, R. J. (2003). *Wisdom, Intelligence, and Creativity Synthesized*. Cambridge University Press.

Turner, N.J., Boelscher, M., and Ignace, R. (2000). Traditional ecological knowledge and wisdom of aboriginal peoples in British Columbia. *Ecological Applications*, 10(5), 1275–87.

UNESCO (2021). *Learn for Our Planet: A Global Review of How Environmental Issues are Integrated in Education*. UNESCO.

Whitehead, A. N. (1929/1967). *The Aims of Education and Other Essays*. Free Press.

PART IV

Wisdom in the World

CHAPTER 13

Wisdom in the Professions

Barry Schwartz and Kenneth E. Sharpe

13.1 Introduction

Professionals – such as doctors, nurses, lawyers, judges, teachers, and social workers – are indispensable to our modern society. They have important skills, and they aim to use those skills in the service of others. They keep us healthy, help us to navigate disputes, negotiate complexity and crisis, and help us develop skills of our own. Writing about the promise and problems of professionalism in modern America, William Sullivan pointed out the religious origin of the term "profession": "It derives from the act of commitment, the declaration to enter into a distinct way of life, as in the profession of monastic vows. It was, at least in theory, a response to the belief that one had received a 'call,' not an action imposed by economic or other necessity. Profession entailed a commitment to embody the virtues needed to realize the community's highest purposes" (Sullivan, 1995, p. 12). To be deemed to act "professionally" is high praise in any situation – one of the most damning epithets that can be hurled at politicians, financiers, and athletes by their critics is the charge of being "unprofessional."

What does it take to be a respected professional? It takes more than just learning a good set of rules and following them. Experienced professionals know that rules can only take them so far. Rules might be useful guides, but they are not subtle and nuanced enough to tell professionals how to make the important decisions at the heart of their work – decisions that demand the balancing of competing considerations and the constant interpretation of the specifics of a context. Doing that not only requires wisdom, but a very particular kind of wisdom. It demands wisdom that is practical. Wisdom must be practical because professionals are asking themselves "What am I to do, right here and right now, with this student, client, or patient who is in front of me, awaiting my advice?"

Professionals earn a living (sometimes a very good one) from the work that they do. They are frequently afforded status and respect in their community. They often wield power as a result of their income and their prestige in their community. However, their critical marker as "professionals" is that they aim to be excellent in serving others. Making money, gaining glory, and wielding power are not the aims of their profession. In fact these rewards, if not reined in, can be a threat that undermines the central aim of service – teachers educating their students, doctors, nurses, and other medical practitioners caring for the well-being of their patients, judges meting out justice, lawyers counseling and advocating for clients, police even-handedly enforcing laws and protecting the safety and well-being of their community, soldiers serving in the defense of their nation, or financial advisers guiding their clients toward long-term financial stability. Thus professionals are motivated primarily not by the prospect of some financial reward or status gain, but rather by the desire to do what being a good teacher or a good doctor, or a good whatever, demands.

In this chapter, we shall look more carefully at the choice-making capacities and motivations that professionals need. We shall see that it takes good judgment – indeed wisdom – to make good decisions, and that rules, even good ones, fall short. And we shall see that financial incentives and the prospect of gains in status or power are poor motivational substitutes for doing the right thing simply *because* it is the right thing.

13.2   Practical Wisdom: What Can Judges Teach Us?

Writing 2,300 years ago, the Greek philosopher Aristotle argued in the *Nicomachean Ethics* that **practical wisdom**, which he called *phronesis*, was a necessary attribute of all the key citizens of his time – statespeople, navigators, doctors, builders, and legislators (Aristotle, 1999). He surely would have included all of today's professionals. Three of the aspects of practical wisdom that he directed us to look at are these: (1) that the practitioner knows and aims to deliver the service that their profession demands; (2) that the practitioner has the practical knowledge and skills (not just the academic or theoretical knowledge) to make the appropriate choices to serve their public; and (3) that the practitioner is motivated to do the right thing for the right reasons, and feels the right way about it.

The reason why practical wisdom is needed is that, in real-life choice making, no one size fits all. Context is crucial. Exceptions to rules or standard operating procedures are often required. The decisions that professionals make about how to serve others occur in conditions that are complex, uncertain, ambiguous, or contradictory, and where good and ethical purposes are often in tension with each other and need to be balanced. Practical wisdom is what enables professionals to negotiate the varied circumstances that they encounter as they practice their professions.

In this chapter, we shall emphasize two components of practical wisdom. The first component is the *skill* to size up a situation, to understand it, and to choose well. Important here are the capacities for **perception** (to listen and observe well), for **reflection**, and for **deliberation**. The second component is the *will*, the *character traits* – the habits and dispositions – that motivate one to act. Motivating behaviors are not financial incentives or threats of punishment, but rather they are virtues such as courage, patience, self-control, empathy, and anger at wrongdoing. Because of these virtues of character, practically wise professionals want to do the right thing, even when no one is watching and no threat is looming.

Consider Judge Lois Forer. "Michael's case appeared routine," explained Judge Forer (Forer, 1992). When Michael was brought before the Criminal Division of Philadelphia's Court of Common Pleas, he was a typical offender – young, black, and male, a high-school dropout without a job. The trial itself was a run-of-the-mill event. Michael had held up a taxi driver while brandishing a gun, and had taken $50. He was caught and tried. There was no doubt that Michael was guilty, but Forer needed to mete out punishment. She turned to the state's sentencing guidelines. They recommended a minimum sentence of 24 months. The law seemed clear, but then Forer looked at the particular circumstances. The gun that Michael had brandished was a toy gun. Furthermore, this was his first offense:

> Although he had dropped out of school to marry his pregnant girlfriend, Michael later obtained a high school equivalency diploma. He had been steadily employed, earning enough to send his daughter to parochial school—a considerable sacrifice for him and his wife. Shortly before the holdup, Michael had lost his job. Despondent because he could not support his family, he went out on a Saturday night, had more than a few drinks, and then robbed the taxi. (Forer, 1992, pp. 12–18)

Judge Forer thought that the 24-month sentence was disproportionate. However, the sentencing guidelines allowed a judge to deviate from the prescribed sentence only if she wrote an opinion explaining the reasons. "I decided to deviate from the guidelines," she explained, sentencing Michael to eleven and a half months in the county jail and permitting him to work outside the prison during the day to support his family:

> I also imposed a sentence of two years' probation following his imprisonment conditioned upon repayment of the $50. My rationale for the lesser penalty, outlined in my lengthy opinion, was that this was a first offense, no one was harmed, Michael acted under the pressures of unemployment and need, and he seemed truly contrite. He had never committed a violent act and posed no danger to the public. A sentence of close to a year seemed adequate to convince Michael of the seriousness of his crime. (Forer, 1992, pp. 12–18)

Forer was clearly aiming at justice and fairness in Michael's case. From the perspective of practical wisdom, here are some things to note about Judge Forer's decision making.

Deliberating about difficult choices is at the heart of what a judge – and all professionals – do. Being able to deliberate well about choices, said Aristotle, was a central capacity of a practically wise person. It was what enabled good judgment in complex and uncertain circumstances where a simple rule or principle was not enough. This was the case with Michael. Forer needed to interpret the general rules to fit Michael's particular circumstances, and only then craft an appropriate punishment. She needed to know whether and how to make an exception. Wisdom is at the heart of what we expect of judges – the ability to exercise judgment. And judicial wisdom is profoundly practical. Forer could not do her work well without it.

Finding a just punishment for Michael demanded that Forer reflect on the details of his case and other cases like it. And she had to work out how to balance legitimate but competing aims of the American court system – retribution, deterrence, and rehabilitation – in Michael's particular case. It was right that his punishment should fit the crime and that the community be protected from any danger he might pose. However, it was also right that Michael be rehabilitated so that he would not commit another offense upon release. And it was important that his sentence should cause minimal harm to his wife and child, and to his chances of being reintegrated into the community. To balance rightly in Michael's particular case, Forer also had to reflect on the kind of person he was, as inferred from his history and past actions. She had to reflect on whether he was the kind of person who would continue to steal in the future (a continued danger to others). And to do this, she also had to understand his particular context, his immediate circumstances (the nature of his family life and relationships, his just having lost his job, and his severe worries about how to feed his family). Figuring out who he was and understanding his life situation would help her to deliberate about how likely it was that he would be a threat in the future.

In making her decision, Judge Forer was guided by rules – the laws specifying the appropriate punishment for a given crime. However, rules were not enough. Because context, circumstances, and the effect of the penalties on the accused are often complex, ambiguous, and uncertain, judges frequently need to exercise discretion.

For Judge Forer to deliberate well in Michael's case, so that she could balance the famous scales of justice and mete out the appropriate sentence, she needed a capacity for noticing – that is, perception. The ability to imagine well is an important element of noticing – perceiving through imagination what has not yet happened, and so what is not yet available to the senses. Judge Forer had to be skillful at imagining how Michael was likely to act with his family and the community in the future. To interpret the law in Michael's case, she also needed to create an accurate narrative that made sense of his actions and his intentions in the light of his character and circumstances – his stable family and work history, the job crisis he was going through, the nature of the crime and choice of weapon, and the harm done – to enable her to imagine as accurately as she possibly could what would be the likely outcomes from the various sentences she was considering. To notice what was most important about Michael's motives and future actions, she had to draw on her own past experience by interpreting the similarities and differences he shared with other alleged perpetrators she had judged.

According to Aristotle, "in matters concerning action and questions of what is beneficial, the agent must consider on each different occasion what the situation demands, just as in medicine and in navigation" (Aristotle, 1999, book 2, ch. 2 [1104a]). "A man of practical wisdom," he argued, "[must] take cognizance of particulars." Particular facts are the "starting points," and, in order to deliberate well, "one must have perception of particular facts" (Aristotle, 1999, book 6, ch. 11 [1143a–1143b]). Every day in court, Judge Forer had to sort through a deluge of information about the lives of the defendants and the nature of their misdeeds. Determining motives, parceling out responsibility, understanding how this crime was different from or similar to others, and determining the future danger to the community all required her to have an ability to select what was significant from a lot of background noise. These tasks demanded an ability to see the nuance – the gray – of a particular situation, and not simply the black and white of the rules that distinguished legal from illegal.

One kind of imaginative perception that was important for Forer and is particularly important for professionals in general is empathy. Empathy involves both cognitive skill (the ability to imagine the situation as it is perceived by another) and emotional skill (the capacity to understand what another person is feeling). To find the right sentence, Forer needed empathy so that she could put herself in Michael's shoes and imagine the likely consequences of letting him work outside of prison during the day. She asked herself the following questions: Was this an irrational crime? Was there wanton cruelty? Is this a hostile person? Can this person control himself?

Emotional skill is critical in another way. Reading the facial expressions, body language, and tone of voice of another person alerts us that something may be wrong and that we need to make choices about how to respond. Our own feelings of anger, guilt, compassion, or shame signal to us the need to pay special attention to what is happening. This may sound obvious, but all too often the rules that govern our lives are aimed at removing emotion from our decision making. The rules are in fact teaching us not to trust the signals we send ourselves. There is good reason to be suspicious of our emotions. They can certainly lead us astray. The error, Aristotle might say, is to focus on eliminating emotions from decisions, rather than schooling them.

Astute perception about Michael's character and circumstances and clear deliberation about how to balance the competing ends of justice were critical capacities that enabled Forer to exercise good judgment in this case. However, they were not enough. She had to move from thought to action. She had to be able to *do* the right thing, not just to *think* the right thing. What motivations did she need to act wisely? This might all seem straightforward – she was motivated by the very purpose of her profession, her deep commitment to justice and fairness and the rule of law. And acting might seem straightforward – all she had to do was write down her judgment and submit it to the appropriate authorities. However, it was not that easy.

Forer was under tremendous pressure to do something else. In the early 1980s, prosecutors and legislators were rapidly rolling out new get-tough-on-crime laws. When Forer sentenced Michael, she knew that there were two standards that could be applied. There were the state's sentencing guidelines, which gave her the discretion she used, but there was also a new 1982 statute that required a mandatory minimum of five years for a serious offense committed in or near a public transportation facility. Making punishments mandatory took discretion – that is, judgment – away from the judges. The statute, said Forer, violated "the fundamental Anglo-American legal principles of individualized sentencing and proportionality of the penalty to the crime." Mandatory sentencing laws, Forer concluded, wring the judgment out of judging. They create a justice system "that operates like a computer—crime in, points tallied, sentence out—utterly disregarding the differences among the human beings involved" (Forer, 1992, p. 17) .

For Forer to use her judgment under these circumstances required courage. She needed it again two years later. By then, Michael had fully complied with her sentence. He had successfully completed his term of imprisonment and probation. He had paid restitution to the taxi driver. He had returned to his family and obtained steady employment. He had not been rearrested. However, the prosecutor had insisted on appealing Forer's sentence, and he won his appeal. Pennsylvania Supreme Court required Forer to re-sentence Michael to a five-year minimum sentence and put him back into jail. Forer said:

> I was faced with a legal and moral dilemma. As a judge, I had sworn to uphold the law. ... Yet five years' imprisonment was grossly disproportionate to the offense. The usual grounds for imprisonment are retribution, deterrence, and rehabilitation. Michael had paid his retribution by a short term of imprisonment and by making restitution to the victims. He had been effectively deterred from committing future crimes. And by any measurable standard he had been rehabilitated. There was no social or criminological justification for sending him back to prison. Given the choice between defying a court order or my conscience, I decided to leave the bench where I had sat for sixteen years. That didn't help Michael, of course; he was resentenced by another judge to serve the balance of the five years: four years and fifteen days. Faced with this prospect, he disappeared. (Forer, 1992, p. 17)

13.3 What Practical Wisdom Is: Lessons from Judge Forer

Judge Lois Forer made a wise decision in sentencing Michael. What components of wisdom can we extract from her decision? The components of wisdom are listed in Table 13.1.

(1) A wise person knows the **proper aims (*telos*)** of the activity in which they are engaged. They want to do the right thing to achieve these aims.

(2) A wise person is perceptive, knowing how to read a specific context.

Table 13.1 *Components of practical wisdom*

(1) Having proper aims
(2) Perceptiveness
(3) Improvisation
(4) Ability to balance competing good aims
(5) Perspective taking and empathy
(6) Good listening
(7) Ability to balance empathy and detachment
(8) Emotional intelligence: making emotion an ally of reason
(9) Experience: we learn to be wise by making unwise decisions and learning from our mistakes.

(3)   A wise person is capable of **improvisation**, finding novel solutions to the novel problems they face every day.

(4)   A wise person knows how to achieve a balance among good but sometimes conflicting aims as they face a decision (e.g., deterrence, public safety, and rehabilitation in the case of Michael).

(5)   A wise person knows how to take the **perspective** of another to serve that person's interests – to see the situation as the other person does and thus to understand how the other person feels.

(6)   A wise person is a **good listener**, able to learn deeply from the testimony of others.

(7)   A wise person knows how to balance empathy with detachment, so that they can step back from the needs and desires of those they serve and balance these with what is legal, right, and fair (see Chapter 10).

(8)   A wise person knows how to make emotion an ally of reason – to rely on emotion to signal what a situation calls for, and to inform judgment without distorting it. Often, they can intuit the right thing to do, which enables them to act quickly when timing matters.

(9)   A wise person is an experienced person. Practical wisdom is a craft, and craftspeople are trained by having relevant experiences, making mistakes, and learning from those mistakes. People learn how to be brave, said Aristotle, by doing brave things. People learn to be wise by doing wise things – and learning how to do better when they fail.

13.4   Wise Medicine

Like judges, doctors and nurses need practical wisdom to navigate the often difficult choices they make to serve their patients' healthcare needs in situations that are frequently uncertain, contradictory, and ambiguous. Doctors, nurses, and other medical professionals have a public purpose that is to care for those who are ill, to alleviate their pain and suffering, to promote their physical and psychological health, and, when possible, to cure them. Central to medical practice is the technical knowledge and expertise of medicine (what Aristotle called *techne*), and we rightly praise remarkable, even dazzling advances in both diagnosis and treatment.

Unfortunately, medicine is in a quandary. Despite remarkable advances in both diagnosis and treatment, there is a growing discontent with health care, both among patients and among clinicians themselves. There is a sense that medicine, despite amazing advances, has in some ways lost its footing. What is critical for doctors and nurses, aside from the technical expertise that they deploy, is the practical wisdom necessary to make everyday decisions in messy situations where technical expertise will not do the job. Medicine is about the health of people, and human beings are not objects but choosers. Freedom and preferences are important. Medicine is about quality of life and not just quantity of life. Increasingly, in the developed world, medicine is about managing chronic conditions (e.g., heart disease, arthritis, hypertension) rather than curing acute diseases. And management of chronic conditions often requires cooperation from the choosing patient (e.g., losing weight, taking more exercise, quitting smoking, using less salt). How does an effective physician enlist the patient as a partner in the pursuit of better health? Empathy and **good listening** are more likely to be helpful here than knowing how to thread a catheter or read an EEG.

Take the common yet profound problem of delivering bad news to a seriously ill patient and caring for that patient when medical treatments can no longer provide a cure. Jerome Groopman, a cancer specialist, faced Maxine, his 30-year-old patient (Groopman, 2002). He had to tell her that the lump in her breast was malignant, and that the cancer had already spread to her spine and liver. As she sat across the desk from him, accompanied by her parents and her fiancé, Groopman had to tell her that she would probably be dead within two years. How was he to approach this?

On the one hand, the canons of medical ethics told him that he had to tell her the truth. On the other hand, there are many different ways to tell the truth – and many different truths. What Groopman said, and how he said it, might determine whether Maxine's last months of life would be full of hopelessness and misery, or whether she would have the strength to go through rigorous treatment with some measure of optimism.

The aim of a professional medical practitioner is to deliver bad news in a way that encourages the patient to pursue the best care possible. The professional should give the news in a way that is honest, respects the patient's dignity, and also encourages the patient to have the hope and resilience to follow a treatment plan and to accept what cannot be controlled. It would be nice if doctors like Groopman could merely follow a simple rule, such as "Always tell patients the truth." However, important as rules may be as scaffolds, they are not enough. That is what Groopman had learned through earlier experiences. In one case, he was brutally honest with a patient who ended up living in abject misery for a further four years. In reaction to that experience, Groopman held back the truth from another patient, intubating him, supporting him on a respirator in the ICU, and giving him numerous blood transfusions. Groopman never asked this patient what he wanted. He stayed alive for more than a week on the respirator, with a catheter in his heart, tubes in his throat, and unable to speak to his family and friends who had come to his bedside.

The problem here was not that Groopman did not want to do the right thing. The problem was that the choices he and his patients, with his help, had to make were context dependent – there was no clear rule for him to follow. The patients he cared for were different people with different preferences with regard to what they wanted to know and when, and how they wanted to hear it. The choices to be made were not simply technical. The outcomes were uncertain, and the patients needed to figure out which risks to incur.

In his conversation with Maxine, Groopman began by reviewing the facts – the size and location of the original tumor, and the evidence of spread. However, before complete hopelessness set in, he advised Maxine that the cancer should be treated aggressively. "You stand a strong chance of remission," he told her.

When Maxine's mother responded by asking "So that means she'll be OK?," Groopman realized that he had to backtrack. He had to make clear that remission was not cure. Treatment might make the current metastatic deposits go away, but they would almost certainly come back, in other places. Treatment would be palliative.

So what did "palliative" mean? He went on to say "We can knock out the cancer with drugs. Your bones and liver can heal. You can go back to living a normal life. And when the cancer returns, we'll work to knock it down again. Meanwhile, new treatments may emerge from research that are far more effective than our current ones. So, at the very least, we're buying time."

Now what? Groopman had presented a best-case scenario, and their eyes were welling up with tears, but he had to present a worst-case scenario, too. He had to let Maxine know that a point might be reached at which treatments would no longer be effective. He had to say this both because he owed his patient an honest assessment and because she would probably face decisions about when to stop therapy that she should think about while she was still well enough to do so coherently.

Therefore Groopman presented the worst-case scenario as well. Maxine appeared to be satisfied with his explanation. She didn't seem to want to know any more. Throughout this painful conversation, Groopman was aware that it was not just what he said that mattered, but how he said it. If he hesitated for too long before answering a bleak question, no matter how encouraging he was, they would think he was holding something back. If he was too upbeat in describing the most positive scenario, they would leave the office with unrealistic hopes. For Groopman to pull this off, both form and content had to be just right.

In writing about his delicate dance of a conversation with Maxine, and his earlier clumsy attempts with other terminally ill patients, Groopman made clear how hard it is to get these conversations right, and how inadequate current medical education is in training professionals to do these conversations well. Success is never guaranteed. All one can hope for is that by wanting to do the right thing, and learning from doing the wrong thing, one can get closer and closer to hitting the mark.

13.5   Wisdom and Choice Making for Doctors and Judges

The kind of choices that professionals like Dr. Groopman and Judge Forer have to make if they are to practice well cannot simply be made by applying technical skills or following rules or standard operating procedures. The specifics of the choices faced by Dr. Groopman in his conversation with Maxine were very different from the choices that Judge Forer faced in handing down a sentence, but there are important commonalities, too, and these are shared across virtually all professions. What Forer and Groopman needed, and indeed what most professionals need, are the attributes of practical wisdom that we outlined earlier – commitment to doing the right thing, ability to improvise, perceptiveness, perspective taking, empathy, and ability to balance worthwhile but competing objectives.

In talking with Maxine and her family, Groopman had to balance being honest with being kind. He had learned from past mistakes that Maxine and her family would need some hope. He had to weigh Maxine's preferences against what medical professionals think is generally best in a case like hers. The medical literature refers to weighing the patient's preferences as respect for patient *autonomy* – the patient's freedom of choice. The older and recently more criticized tradition of "the physician knows best" is referred to as *doctor beneficence*, or *paternalism*. The waters swirling around a patient's autonomy and a doctor's paternalism need constant navigation.

Before professionals like Judge Forer and Dr. Groopman can make the subtle judgments necessary for them to make a wise decision about a case, they need to be able to see the case clearly. The starting point might be the general knowledge the judge has about the infraction and the law, or the doctor's skilled diagnosis of and standard treatments for this kind of cancer. However, the decision as to which law or treatment to administer will depend on the particularities of the defendant or the patient, the context in which they are living, and the imagining of the yet unseen consequences of a particular course of action. Such good choice making, according to the philosopher Martha Nussbaum, depends on the "priority of the particular" (Nussbaum, 1990).

A wise professional needs to know how much information is too much information. At the meeting with Maxine, her fiancé asked Groopman, "What are the exact odds for a remission . . . I mean, how many patients like Maxine stay in remission and for how long, on average?" Groopman noticed that Maxine looked sharply at her fiancé and said, "Dr. Groopman said that there is every reason to think I'll go into remission. What more do we need to know now?" She then turned to Groopman, her face full of uncertainty. "I sense[d]," remembers Groopman, "that she preferred neither the extreme of ignorance nor the extreme of excruciating detail, but some middle ground."

13.6 Practical Wisdom in Other Work Contexts

We have illustrated the importance of practical wisdom in judging and healthcare. Is there something special about these professions? In the two examples we described, the stakes are extremely high – freedom and incarceration, and life and death – so in that sense the answer is yes. However, in virtually all work settings that involve interactions with other human beings, practical wisdom is valuable – maybe even essential – if those interactions are to go well.

13.6.1 Practical Wisdom in Law

It might seem at first that no profession could be further from the practical wisdom we expect judges and doctors to exercise than the profession of lawyering. Lawyers are often depicted as being little more than hired guns for their clients – the client wants a particular outcome, and the lawyer is paid to get it. The so-called zealous advocacy of such hired-gun lawyers is antithetical to the practical wisdom that judges bring to their practice. However, although this characterization is sometimes true, it misses the extraordinary practical wisdom that many lawyers need – and exercise – to do their work well.

All lawyers are supposed to be zealous advocates, fighting for what a client wants. However, they are also supposed to be wise counsellors, advising, urging, or nudging a client to think differently about what is in his or her best interests. So when should you advocate for what the client wants and when should you counsel the client to want something different?

The stereotypical view of the lawyer-as-advocate is "the client proposes, the lawyer disposes." The client hires the lawyer as an advocate to defend their interests, or as a counselor to advise them. What role the lawyer plays is up to the client. And if the client wants an advocate, then the lawyer's choice is simple – either represent the client zealously or decline the case. However, it is frequently not this simple. The client's objectives may be unclear, or even in conflict. The client may be impetuous. The client may not be clear about the long-term consequences of the case. Or the short-term and long-term consequences may be in conflict – as in many divorce cases, where getting even or getting money may destroy the ongoing relationship needed to share in the upbringing of the children in future years.

Mather et al. (2001) argue that a good divorce lawyer is both an advocate *and* a counselor. The lawyer helps clients to come to terms with the divorce and plan for a new life, and does this as part of the job. They are constantly navigating the rocky shoals between advocacy and counseling as part of the same commitment to helping the client. And it is their practical wisdom that allows them to steer this delicate course.

Mather et al. (2001) suggest that the media and popular culture depict the divorce attorney as the "Rambo" lawyer "who files every conceivable motion, seeks everything and more from the opposing side, refuses to cooperate in settlement, and argues vigorously and bitterly in a long, drawn-out trial" (Mather et al., 2001, p.114). However, few of the lawyers whom Mather and colleagues interviewed in their work fitted this stereotype. They educated their clients about what it was reasonable to expect, they balanced advocacy with education, and they counseled their clients to think about their long-term interests.

In addition, wise lawyers need to be both empathic and detached, and to balance these two competing virtues. They must be empathic enough to understand what their client is thinking and feeling, and detached enough to distance themselves from unreasonable client demands so that they can educate their client about what is reasonable (Kronman, 1993).

13.6.2   Practical Wisdom in Policing

Police are meant to keep citizens safe and preserve public order. When they are called to a disturbance, they have a set of standard operating procedures to rely on. However, the extraordinary complexities of particular contexts also demand that they be given some discretion to figure out which problems to prioritize (e.g., a mentally ill teenager talking to herself on a street corner, a child jumping a subway turnstile, a dark-skinned young man walking on a white suburban street, a man selling loose cigarettes without a license) and how to act in those situations. This involves working out how to balance their mandate to minimize the use of force and the legitimate concerns for their own safety and that of others in a particular situation. And these situations are complicated by the emotions and implicit biases that officers inevitably bring to their work (e.g., Eberhardt, 2019). Body cameras and prohibitions on chokeholds are rules that offer important checks and restraints, but no amount of standard operating procedures will be sufficient to answer the context-specific questions that police officers face all the time. How dangerous is this particular disturbance? Is confrontation called for? Can the threat be de-escalated by conciliation rather than confrontation? Police often have to act quickly, the stakes can be high, and they do not usually know the parties involved, so mistakes can easily be made. However, mistakes are even more likely to occur if police ignore the particulars of a given situation and treat all such disturbances alike. Thus if they are to make good decisions, police officers need practical wisdom – the skills of listening well, noticing, empathizing, reflection, and deliberation, and the character traits of courage, honesty, patience, perseverance, and fidelity to the goals of service, to name just a few (Delattre, 1996; Kennedy, 2011; Sparrow et al., 1990) .

13.6.3   Practical Wisdom in Cutting and Styling Hair

It is not just police and lawyers who need the wisdom to counsel. Such wisdom is needed by almost anyone who works on another's behalf. Take the hairdressers who Mike Rose studied in his book, *The Mind at Work* (Rose, 2004). Rose found that they were constantly serving clients who came in with a picture clipped from a beauty magazine and told the stylist, "This is the look I want – cut my hair like this." A stylist could just do the cut, take the money, and tell the customer that she got exactly what she asked for. But the good stylist knows that what a customer thinks she wants is often not what she really wants. The "look" in that picture will frequently not be the "look" on this particular customer. Rose found that most of the stylists he studied wanted to do a good job, and those who succeeded knew that the job was not just about perfectly executing the cut that had been requested. It is a challenge, explained one stylist, because you "don't assume you know what they want, because *they* may not know what they want" (Rose, 2004, p. 43).

The hairdressers' technical expertise and their experience of styling hair gives them some of the knowledge they need. They know how the face and bone structure and the condition of the hair – its density, texture, and wave pattern – will change the look in the client's favorite picture. They also know, or quickly find out, some basic things about their client, such as how she manages her hair between visits – or doesn't. However, good hairdressers will not just let the client choose for herself, nor will they simply tell her what is best and do it. Good hairdressers have the skill to help the client to figure out what she really wants. They know how to listen to the client – to hear what she is thinking and feeling. They know how to ask questions to help the client to decide what she wants. The conversations are a delicate interplay of talking and listening, and of subtle interpretations – almost an improvised dance by which each partner steers the other in the right direction. Being a good hair stylist requires the wisdom to be a good counselor.

13.6.4 *Practical Wisdom in Working in Retail*

Consider the job of a retail clerk in a shopping mall store. This clerk's supervisor instructs him to sell as much as he can, as fast as he can. He is also to convince the customer that the high-end computer is the right choice, no matter what the customer intends to use it for. He is to convince the customer to buy three storage bins rather than two, because "we all know how junk tends to accumulate." This is one view of the task of retail salespeople. Now imagine a different view: "Everyone who comes into the store has a problem. I'm the expert. I know what we have and what it can do. My job is to help the customer solve his problem, even if it means selling cheaper goods – indeed, even if it means selling nothing ('I think the computer you already have will meet your needs; you just have to clean out your hard drive and install a new operating system.')." Wise salesclerks will diagnose the customer's problem and craft a solution that is right for that customer. Imagine how much more satisfying working in retail might be if employees saw their jobs as solving dozens of small problems in a way that made customers' lives better each and every day. Of course, as we shall discuss below, there are risks involved in being such a salesperson. The customer might be satisfied, but the salesperson might lose his job! For wisdom to be nurtured and deployed, organizations must be structured to allow people, and even encourage them, to do the right thing.

Our point here is a simple one. Countless times every day, across a vast array of different occupations, which require very different levels of training and skill, it is practical wisdom, and not just technical skill or detailed "standard operating procedures," that can make the difference between success and failure – between a satisfied customer, client, patient, student, or citizen and a frustrated, dissatisfied one. The need for practical wisdom is pervasive.

Professionals become practically wise as they learn to aim at the appropriate purposes of their practices, gain the ability to balance competing objectives, develop the know-how to counsel and to help clients make decisions that are appropriate to them in their specific circumstances, gain the perception skills needed to notice and discern what is relevant in a particular case, and develop the habits and character traits that motivate them to want to do the right thing. Being practically wise is not easy. No one is born wise, but we can all become wise, with the right encouragement, experience, and feedback.

13.7 Threats to Practical Wisdom in the Professions

The aim of this chapter so far has been to provide you with an understanding of the role that practical wisdom plays in a variety of different occupations, professional and otherwise. "Practical wisdom" is our term – and Aristotle's term – for a large collection of skills and virtues. As we have discussed, to be wise is to be perceptive, to be a good listener, to be flexible and able to improvise, to be empathetic, to be reflective, and to be able to balance competing objectives. To be wise is to be honest, compassionate, and fair. To be wise is to be humble enough to keep learning from experience – both one's own and that of other people. To be wise is to know whether, when, and how to deviate from the rules – the standard operating procedures. And, critically, attributes such as these are not merely "nice" to have. They do not merely turn good practitioners into great ones. They are *essential* if one is to minister the sick, educate the young, advise those with legal challenges, or sit in judgment on the actions of others, but they are also needed in many other occupations – for example, if one is to cut people's hair or work in retail. Taken together, these attributes comprise what we might call the skills that make up practical wisdom. However, they are only a part of what wisdom demands.

Just as important is what we might call will. The doctor must *want* to cure the sick, because that is what good doctors do. The teacher must *want* to educate the young, because that is what good teachers do. The lawyer must *want* to advise and advocate, because that is what good lawyers do. In other words, wise practitioners want to do the right thing *because* it is the right thing – not because they will get a bonus or promotion for doing the right thing, and not because they will get fired or demoted for doing the wrong thing. The desire to do one's work well is baked into what it means to be wise.

However, there are two serious contemporary problems for the professions in the USA. Increasingly, the major institutions in which most professionals practice – schools, medical institutions, and law firms – have substituted a set of rigid rules to be followed for the skill and judgment that practitioners need. As a result, practitioners are denied the opportunity to develop or deploy these skills. We might say that we are now living in the midst of a "war on skill." In addition, these institutions design systems that seek to influence professional decision making with either overweening punishments for straying from standardized rules and procedures, or a reliance on incentives to induce practitioners to follow the rules. We might call this a "war on will." Underlying the logic of these developments is the belief that rewards, punishments, and rules can be substitutes for good judgment and good purpose in shaping choices.

We have described this "war on wisdom" in detail elsewhere (Schwartz & Sharpe, 2010). Here we shall illustrate it with examples from one profession, namely teaching, and one institution, namely public schools.

13.7.1   How Educational Institutions Undermine the Wisdom of Teachers

When schools throughout the USA embraced standardized, heavily scripted curricula tied directly to high-stakes standardized tests, the aim was to improve education through "scientific" management. "High stakes" means that schools and teachers are rewarded (with more money) or punished (by having funds denied, schools closed, or staff dismissed or reassigned) based on student test performance. Most states have such systems, and the No Child Left Behind Act of 2001 required all states to administer standardized reading and math tests in third and eighth grade, and risk losing federal funding if students consistently failed to meet the standards. Standardized tests led to standardized, scripted curricula. If schools and teachers would be rated, funded, or paid based on student test performance, it made sense to mandate that teachers use materials explicitly designed so that students could pass the tests. In fact, novice teachers – quite reasonably – often appreciated the scripts. If they and their students were to be judged by test scores, here was a set of routines that promised to make their students better test takers.

Many educators who valued guidelines and innovative curriculum materials that helped teachers to learn about content, pedagogy, and the different ways in which students learned were critical of the new rules requiring that all teachers use these rigid curriculum materials. They warned against a one-size-fits-all pedagogy shaped by rules and incentivized by punishments or rewards (e.g., Kohn, 1993; Koretz, 2017). Teachers needed to have the autonomy to develop the practical wisdom to adapt the curriculum to the needs of the particular students in their classes and in their communities. However, this was rarely an option. Most schools simply purchased standardized materials from private vendors, complete with texts, lesson plans, and lockstep scripts, along with the standardized tests coordinated with these materials (Steinberg, 1999, p. 1):

> On "Day 53," Ms. Jabbari joined all the other kindergarten teachers in the Chicago system in teaching the letter *b* to her students. The binder she used identified the section of the Iowa Test of Basic Skills to which that day's lesson plan corresponded and provided step-by-step questions and conversation starters.
> **Script for Day: 053**
> TITLE: Reading and enjoying literature/words with "b"
> TEXT: *The Bath*
> LECTURE: Assemble students on the rug or reading area ... Give students a warning about the dangers of hot water. ... Say, "Listen very quietly as I read the story." ... Say, "Think of other pictures that make the same sound as the sound bath begins with."
>
> Her students sat cross-legged on a corner rug. The children's book *The Bath* was not available, so Ms. Jabbari chose *Jesse Bear, What Will You Wear?* But no matter. She still began with the script, reminding them: "It's always safe to have an adult around when you take your bath."

Supporters of lockstep curricula and high-stakes standardized tests were not out to undermine the wisdom, creativity, and energy of good teachers. The scripted curricula and tests were aimed at improving the performance of weak teachers in failing schools. If lesson plans were tied to tests, teachers' scripts would tell them what to do to get the students ready. If students still failed, the teachers could be "held accountable." In some systems, teachers' annual evaluations, and even their pay, were based on their students' performance on standardized tests, and the scripted curricula were written to prepare students to pass these tests. Equality would seemingly be achieved (i.e., no child would be left behind) by using the same script, thus giving the same education to all students. However, this also meant that all teachers, whether they were novice or expert, or weak or strong, would be required to follow the standardized system for all students, weak or strong.

Teachers on the front lines often point to the considerations that are left out of the teach-to-test paradigm. Tests are only one indicator of student learning, and there are many other causes of poor performance on tests apart from poor teaching – for example, poorly funded urban schools, students from poor or immigrant backgrounds with few resources at home and sometimes little or no English, overcrowded classrooms with not enough teachers, poor facilities, lack of books and equipment, and students with learning problems or other disabilities.

Beyond all these problems, one of the chief criticisms made by many teachers is that the system within which they are forced to work is dumbing down their teaching. It is deskilling them. It is not allowing them – or teaching them – the judgment they need to provide good teaching. They are encouraged, says education scholar Linda Darling-Hammond, "to present material that [is] beyond the grasp of some and below the grasp of others, to sacrifice students' internal motivations and interests in the cause of 'covering the curriculum,' and to forgo the *teachable moment,* when students [are] ready and eager to learn, because it [happens] to fall outside of the prescribed sequence of activities" (Darling-Hammond, 1997, p. 79). Sooner or later, turning out kids who can turn out the right answers the way you turn out screws, or hubcaps, comes to seem like normal practice. Worse, it comes to seem like best practice (Darling-Hammond, 1997).

It is not just the skill of teachers that is being undermined, but also their motivation – their will. Mrs. Dewey teaches third grade at Beck Elementary School in Texas (Booher-Jennings, 2005, 2007). Many of the students are economically disadvantaged, and most are Hispanic – longtime residents of Texas as well as first-, second-, and third-generation immigrants. The principal wants to raise the test scores, and so do the teachers. Scores on these high-stakes tests are the metric of evaluation under the Texas Accountability System. Since 1992, Beck Elementary has been performing adequately, but only adequately. The state rates it "acceptable," but the administration and most of the teachers are anxious to achieve the more prestigious "recognized" status, which requires that more than 80 percent of the students pass the state tests. The system is, in the words of administrators, "data driven," and there is only one kind of data that ensures officially sanctioned success – scores on a standardized test. All third-grade students must pass the reading test to move on to fourth grade. The teachers regularly administer "practice" tests throughout the year. The goal is to get 80 percent of the students to pass the test, moving the school from "acceptable" to "recognized" status.

Mrs. Dewey, a 20-year veteran, listens as a consultant hired by the district explains how to use the data from practice tests:

> Using the data, you can identify and focus on the kids who are close to passing. The bubble kids. And focus on the kids that count—the ones that show up after October won't count toward the school's test scores this year. Because you don't have enough special education students to disaggregate scores for that group, don't worry about them either. (Booher-Jennings, 2007, p. 757)

To make this concept tangible for teachers, the consultant passes out markers in three colors – green, yellow, and red. Mrs. Dewey hears someone mutter, "What is this? The traffic light theory of education?"

> Take out your classes' latest benchmark scores and divide your students into three groups. Color the "safe cases," or kids who will definitely pass, green. Now, here's the most important part: identify the kids who are "suitable cases for treatment." Those are the ones who can pass with a little extra help. Color them yellow. Then, color the kids who have no chance of passing this year and the kids that don't count—the "hopeless cases"—red. You should focus your attention on the yellow kids, the bubble kids. They'll give you the biggest return on your investment. (Booher-Jennings, 2007, p. 757)

Mrs. Dewey stares blankly into the hallway. Focus on the bubble kids. Tutor only these students. Pay more attention to them in class. This is what most of her colleagues have been doing, and test scores have gone up. The community is proud, and the principal has been anointed one of the most promising educational leaders in the state. At every faculty meeting the principal presents a "league table," ranking teachers by the percentage of their students who have passed the latest benchmark test. And the table makes perfect fodder for faculty-room gossip: "Did you see who was at the bottom of the table this month?"

Mrs. Dewey has made compromises, both large and small, throughout her career. Every educator who's in it for the long haul must. But this institutionalized policy of educational triage weighs heavily and hurts more. Should she really focus only on Brittney, Julian, Shennell, Tiffany, George, and Marlena—the so-called bubble kids—to the exclusion of the other seventeen students in her class? Should Mrs. Dewey refuse to tutor Anthony, a persistent and eager little boy with no chance of passing the state test this year, so that she can spend time with students who have a better shot at passing? What should she tell Celine, a precocious student, whose mother wants Mrs. Dewey to review her entry for an essay contest? Celine will certainly pass the state test, so can Mrs. Dewey afford the time? What about the five students who moved into the school in the middle of the year? Since they don't count toward the school's scores, should Mrs. Dewey worry about their performance at all? (Booher-Jennings, 2007, p. 757)

In her angrier moments, Mrs. Dewey pledges to ignore this test-centered approach and to teach as she always has – the best way she knows how. Yet, if she does ignore it, she risks being denounced as a traitor to the school's effort to increase scores. This is what stings the most.

Importantly, it is not just that these *particular* incentives are demoralizing for Mrs. Dewey. The danger is that these incentives can undermine other, better motives to do the right thing. Teachers like Mrs. Dewey spend their day figuring out how much time to spend with each student and how to tailor what they teach to each student's particular strengths and weaknesses. They are continually balancing conflicting aims – to treat all students equally, to give the struggling students more time, and to energize and inspire the gifted students. Making these choices well demands practical wisdom. Along comes the incentive to increase the school's test scores, and the scripts to follow to do so, and all the nuance and subtlety of Mrs. Dewey's moment-by-moment decisions fly out of the window. Some might say that the problem in this Texas school is not the use of incentives, but the use of "dumb" incentives. Smarter incentives will get us what we want, but what "smarter" incentive can replace judgment in making sensitive choices in a complex and changing context like a classroom (see Schwartz & Sharpe, 2010; Schwartz & Wrzesniewski, 2019)?

13.8 Conclusion

What is true of teachers in schools is also true of professionals in other institutions. Psychology shows us that it is a fact that you can change people's behavior either by brandishing sticks or by dangling carrots in front of their noses. We can "motivate" lawyers by offering bonuses when they win their cases. We can motivate prosecutors by rewarding them for the number of convictions they chalk up, or police for the number of arrests made or tickets issued. The leaders of commercial companies can win massive bonuses if the company's stock price goes up. The use of incentives like these is all around us – arguably, it is the way the world works. However, if these incentives come to dominate professional choice making, they will destroy the professions. Lawyers will cut ethical corners, doing whatever it takes to win. Teachers will teach their students how to take the tests so that the students get higher scores, but the students will not learn how to think, reflect, deliberate, and use their judgement. CEOs and corporate boards can raise the price of a stock – and stockholder profits – by trading away long-term success for impressive short-term numbers while eroding the trust and health of their clients, their employees, their communities, and the environment. Any incentive scheme can be gamed, except one – the desire to do the right thing precisely and only because it is the right thing.

Practical wisdom is a combination of skill and will, but of a different kind to the skill and will needed for riding a bike. The skill and will that constitute practical wisdom are **moral skill** and **moral will.** Unlike bike riding, the core activities of doctors, lawyers, teachers, and most if not all other professionals are morally significant acts. They have effects on the well-being of other people who come to professionals in need of their services. Wise people are good people, if not in all aspects of their life, at least in the discharge of their profession (Schwartz and Sharpe, 2010, pp. 177–228).

Rules and incentives will never disappear from institutions such as schools, hospitals, medical organizations, law firms, and police forces. No organization can run without them. However, when they dominate professional practice, they threaten to squeeze out the good judgment and motivation that is the heartbeat of professional life, especially when the goals that they pursue run counter to the goals they *should* pursue. A central challenge for those concerned about protecting and nurturing practical wisdom in the professions is to work out how to design the curriculum of professional schools and the organization and management of professional institutions so as to protect and nurture the practical wisdom of current and future practitioners.

13.9   Comprehension and Discussion Questions

(1)   Among the wisdom skills that professionals need to do their work well are the capacity for *perception, empathy, reflection,* and *deliberation.* From your reading or your own experience with professionals, give a concrete example of why each of these is important in the everyday decisions that a professional has to make.

(2)   Among the character traits or habits that professionals need to be motivated to choose well in their work with clients, patients, or students are *courage, patience, self-control, empathy, anger at wrongdoing, loyalty,* and *caring.* From your reading or your own experience with professionals, give a concrete example of why each of these is important in the everyday decisions that a professional has to make.

(3)   In figuring out how to balance autonomy and paternalism, how, if at all, should a professional consider factors such as the culture the patient comes from, their gender, their class, and their race?

(4)   When you have to make a moral judgment, people commonly say "Forget your feelings, be objective" or "Don't let your feelings interfere with your judgment" or "Be rational, don't be emotional." Why does such advice limit good decision making by professionals? Give at least one example.

(5)   For professionals to be able to help their clients, patients, or students make good decisions about their health or well-being they often have to balance the ethical principle "Always be honest" with the need to give their client, patient, or student hope. Why is this often difficult? What are some of the skills or character traits of practical wisdom that enable a professional to get the right balance between honesty and hope?

(6)   Professionals need to respect the freedom of choice of their clients, patients, or students (client "autonomy"), but they also want to use their expertise to service their clients', patients', or students' best interests (professional "beneficence" or paternalism). Give an example of why it is so difficult to balance these two positive aims. What are some of the skills or character traits of practical wisdom that enable a professional to get the balance right?

(7) For lawyers there is often a tension between being an advocate for a client and counselling them. Explain why this is so, by giving an example. Why is practical wisdom critically important for resolving this tension? Can you think of a similar tension in other professions or in your own life?

(8) Institutions such as schools are in a bind – they need rules, standards, common curriculum, and testing to direct the activities of teachers and students. Yet these very rules and structures can discourage or erode the practical wisdom that teachers and students need to do their work well. Explain this bind and give an example. Can you think of ways to ameliorate this tension?

(9) Teachers like Mrs. Dewey have to continually make tough decisions about how to distribute their scarce time among their students. Why is this difficult? What are the kinds of things that a good teacher needs to balance? How does the emphasis that this school system places on "bubble kids" undermine Mrs. Dewey's ability to exercise practical wisdom? Can teachers "fight back"?

(10) Professionals, like people in many other lines of work, earn money, gain power and influence, and achieve glory or prestige. Choose one of these three major human motivations with regard to work – monetary gain, power, or glory – and explain how this aim can potentially undermine the very purpose of a professional's work. Illustrate this with an example or a story.

13.10 Investigations

Barry Schwartz and Kenneth Sharpe have together conducted extensive research on the role of practical wisdom in various professions, the psychological processes that make wisdom possible, and the threats to the development and deployment of practical wisdom in modern American society. The results of their research are gathered in their book, *Practical Wisdom*. In addition, Kenneth Sharpe's recent research focuses on how to design institutions and organizations that encourage practitioners to learn practical wisdom. He has helped to design a program for such learning for college teachers and for a law school, and he is currently studying ways to encourage the learning of practical wisdom as part of the design of education in medical schools and in the palliative care service at a major hospital. Barry Schwartz, at the Haas Business School at University of California Berkeley, has explored the role of practical wisdom in all aspects of the world of business.

13.11 Practical Applications

Any organizations where professionals practice – law firms, medical organizations, schools, social service agencies, and engineering firms, to name just a few – need to structure their workplaces to encourage professionals to continually learn practical wisdom and to exercise it in their daily practice. Examples of the practical application of these principles can be found in organizations that have created a wisdom learning environment by, for example, creating safe spaces for people to learn through trial and error, encouraging good listening and noticing, reflecting together on what is working and what needs to work, deliberating together about how to do better, and encouraging ongoing coaching and mentoring.

Glossary

deliberation the thought required to tailor an action to the particular situation (patient, client, student, or customer) before you. There is no one-size-fits-all solution to the challenges that professionals confront, so deliberation is required.

good listening the ability to hear and understand what your patient, client, or student is telling you, sometimes with facial expressions and gestures rather than with words.

improvisation the ability to develop novel solutions to the novel problems one faces because each patient, client, or student is different.

moral skill and moral will moral skill is the ability to work out what a particular situation requires; moral will is the motivation to do the right thing in a situation just because it *is* the right thing. Moral skill and moral will together make up practical wisdom. They are moral because they guide actions in ways that have profound effects on other people.

perception the ability to notice often subtle aspects of the situation and the person one is confronting in an effort to find the unique solution to the unique problems that this person and situation are presenting.

perspective the ability to see a situation as the other person (patient, client, or student) sees it. A solution to a problem that might be right for you might not be right for the person whose problem you are trying to solve.

practical wisdom (*phronesis*) the combination of moral will and moral skill that inspires one to want to do the right thing and enables one to work out what is the right thing to do in the specific situation that one faces.

proper aim (*telos*) in Aristotle's view of the world, each activity had its own proper goal or aim (*telos*). This concept still applies today. For example, the aim of medicine is to cure the sick, the aim of law is to achieve justice, and the aim of education is to awaken young minds. People may earn a living and attain glory, status, or fame from their professional activities, but the pursuit of money, status, and glory are all improper aims of professional practice.

reflection unique situations require unique solutions, which in turn require one to imagine the consequences of possible actions, take the perspective of the person one is trying to serve, and balance a number of often competing goals. Deploying these skills commonly requires reflection. Actions taken also require reflection about what has worked and what has failed in the past, so that practitioners can learn through their mistakes.

REFERENCES

Aristotle (1999). *Nicomachean Ethics*, M. Ostwald, trans. Prentice Hall.

Booher-Jennings, J. (2005). Below the bubble: "educational triage" and the Texas Accountability System. *American Educational Research Journal*, 42(2), 231–68.

(2007). Rationing education in an era of accountability. *Phi Delta Kappan*, 87(10), 756–61.

Darling-Hammond, L. (1997), *The Right to Learn: A Blueprint for Creating Schools That Work*. Jossey-Bass.

Delattre, E. J., (1996), *Character and Cops: Ethics in Policing*. The AEI Press.

Eberhardt, J. (2019). *Biased*. Penguin.

Forer, L. G. (1992). Justice by numbers. *Washington Monthly*, 24(4), 12–18.

Groopman, J. (2002), Dying words. How should doctors deliver bad news? *The New Yorker*, October 28, pp. 62–70.

Kennedy, D. M. (2011). *Don't Shoot: One Man, A Street Fellowship, and the End of Violence in Inner-City America*. Bloomsbury.

Kohn, A. (1993). *Punished by Rewards: The Trouble with Gold Stars, Incentive Plans, A's, Praise, and Other Bribes*. Houghton Mifflin.

Koretz, D. (2017). *The Testing Charade*. University of Chicago Press.

Kronman, A. T. (1993). *The Lost Lawyer*. Harvard University Press.

Mather, L., McEwen, C. A., and Maiman, R. J. (2001). *Divorce Lawyers at Work: Varieties of Professionalism in Practice*. Oxford University Press.

Nussbaum, M. (1990). *Love's Knowledge: Essays on Philosophy and Literature*. Oxford University Press.

Rose, M. (2004). *The Mind at Work: Valuing the Intelligence of the American Worker*. Viking.

Schwartz, B. and Sharpe, K. (2010). *Practical Wisdom: The Right Way to do the Right Thing*. Riverhead Books.

Schwartz, B. and Wrzesniewski, A. (2019). Reconceptualizing intrinsic motivation. In K. A. Renninger and S. E. Hidi, eds., *The Cambridge Handbook of Motivation and Learning*. Cambridge University Press, pp. 373–93.

Sparrow, M. K., Moore, M. H., and Kennedy, D. M., (1990). *Beyond 911: A New Era for Policing*. Basic Books.

Steinberg, J. (1999). Teachers in Chicago schools follow script from day 001. *New York Times,* November 26; www.nytimes.com/1999/11/26/us/teachers-in-chicago-schools-follow-script-from-day-001.html

Sullivan, W. M. (1995). *Work and Integrity: The Crisis and Promise of Professionalism in America*. Harper Collins.

CHAPTER 14

Wisdom and Leadership

David Rooney and Bernard McKenna

14.1 Introduction

The ancient Greek philosophers often referred to wisdom as a way of being – that is, wisdom as a way of conducting oneself in life that is built on particular attitudes or orientations to the world and one's place in it. The ancients also maintained that wisdom is a disposition that one develops through learning, discipline, and cultivating virtuous habits. Wise leaders therefore need to have a cultivated set of dispositions, values, and ideas that lend themselves to acting wisely in the course of doing their job. Consequently, wisdom requires more than wise thoughts – it requires wise actions because it is something that you do.

Although leadership is widely researched and the leadership literature provides a great deal of theory and data, we continue to see too many unwise leaders in the world. Why is it, then, that despite having a large body of research evidence and theory that explains what excellent leadership is, leaders are not better at their jobs? This problem has not yet been solved, but we can unravel the problem using wisdom theory.

This chapter will first explain what leadership research tells us about good and bad leaders, so that we can build up a picture of excellent leadership. It will then discuss practical wisdom theory and explore how a person could become a wise leader. This includes considering what practical wisdom is as a social practice and how we think about wisdom and leadership development. Finally, the practical implications for leadership development and leader selection will be discussed.

14.2 Leadership

Because wisdom is the **embodiment** of excellent social practice, it can inform leadership theory and practice. We begin this chapter by evaluating leadership research to understand what it says about good and bad leaders. Leaders exist in every sphere of life. Some are given formal leadership roles, while others take on informal leadership roles – for example, through starting a community wildlife protection group. The word "leader" therefore refers to someone who guides or shows the way or directs us. Anyone can be a leader depending on the circumstance and the type of attributes needed – for example, a surgeon in a hospital theatre requires different leadership attributes from a negotiator settling differences between warring groups.

The three most prominent (business) leadership theories are transformational leadership, servant leadership, and authentic leadership, each of which we shall discuss in turn. Before doing so, however, it is useful to describe notable aspects of traditional, authoritarian leadership.

Traditional leaders are directive and often authoritarian. Leadership researchers typically call them command-and-control, transactional, heroic, or authoritarian leaders. Transactional leaders are so called because they direct their **followers** to do things by using rewards or punishments, depending on how well those people follow orders. Followers do not normally question or enter into any kind of dialogue with this kind of leader about his or her decisions. Although such leadership is appropriate in certain circumstances. such as crises (e.g., siege, rescue operations, trauma emergencies), it is generally considered to be ineffective, and even potentially dysfunctional. This is because it is ineffective in promoting necessary change, it makes leaders unaccountable to followers, it fails to enable experienced and qualified employees to contribute their ideas and insights to important decision making, and it makes these organizations unattractive to young, educated, and motivated potential employees.

Transformational leadership theory was the first significant attempt to move away from the traditional, invariably masculine understanding of leadership, which was characterized by charisma, forcefulness, and an authoritarian approach. In contrast, transformational leaders inspire followers to strive to become better and more fulfilled workers or followers, and to be leaders themselves. These leaders are extraverted, open, agreeable, and conscientious (Bono & Judge, 2004). Implicitly ethical, transformational leadership theory focuses on respectful and growth-oriented relationships with followers. Thus the four characteristics of transformational leadership are:

(1)   ideal influence (the leader is an excellent role model)
(2)   inspirational motivation (the leader inspires followers by providing an attractive vision for the organization's future)
(3)   individualized consideration (the leader pays personal attention to the development, well-being, and goals of followers to help them to fulfill their potential)
(4)   intellectual stimulation (the leader provides followers with meaningful challenges) (Bass & Riggio, 2006).

Authentic leaders incorporate the qualities of the transformational leader, but are distinguished particularly by their moral character. Because followers see them as legitimate leaders, they want to be led by them. Although the authentic leadership construct is still being refined and developed (Avolio et al., 2018), its original four characteristics remain relatively unaltered. That is, authentic leaders:

(1)   use balanced reasoning
(2)   maintain transparent relationships by openly sharing their thoughts and feelings
(3)   are self-aware
(4)   have a sound moral compass (Walumbwa et al., 2008).

For a person to be an authentic leader, it is vital that either their personal values align with those of the organization, or the leader modifies their organization's values.

Servant leaders are selfless leaders who serve the needs of their followers. Robert K. Greenleaf developed the original idea of servant leadership (Greenleaf, 1977) while working as a manager, so it is a theory that was initially based on his practical experience rather than on empirical research. Servant leadership theory is much harder to define than transformational leadership because Greenleaf's definition was vague, leading researchers to develop competing versions of the concept (Van Dierendonck, 2011). A range of scales that reflect different definitions have been developed to measure servant leadership (Barbuto & Wheeler, 2006; Liden et al., 2008; Reed et al., 2011; Sendjaya et al., 2008). However, to summarize, servant leaders:

(1)   have a pastoral concern for followers
(2)   are service oriented
(3)   are motivated by their spirituality (which is not necessarily religious) and a sense of having a calling
(4)   are trustworthy
(5)   have impeccable integrity
(6)   are emotional healers
(7)   empower their followers (Parris & Peachey, 2013).

Servant leadership theory is probably the most extreme theory of leadership – the leader is part priestly guide, part social worker, and part teacher – because it is so counter-intuitive to historical perceptions of what a leader should be.

It is safe to characterize leadership theory today as heavily **values** based, although we suggest that a better term is "**virtues** based." However, viewed from a wisdom perspective, it is concerning that none of these theories has much to say about how to become the kind of idealistic leader that is represented in the theories. If you studied any of those theories, it would be difficult to see what you would need to do to reach the standards of practice they describe.

Other problems also exist in less prominent leadership theories. Spiritual leadership theory, for example, has been criticized for omitting contemplation (Case et al., 2012), which raises the question of how spiritual it actually is. Furthermore, there is no evidence that increased spirituality leads to increased wisdom (Jeste et al., 2021). There are problems in mindful leadership research, too. Mindfulness theory used in business school is criticized for being superficial, and has even been called "McMindfulness" (Purser & Loy, 2013). The McMindfulness critique is also linked to a broader problem with how psychology research (mis)understands mindfulness, which is a spiritual, ethical, contemplative, and wisdom development practice. Some prominent psychologists, such as Ellen Langer (Langer, 1989; Langer et al., 1978), seem to reject any ethical, spiritual, or wisdom connotations in mindfulness theory, and Langer's scale does not measure what we traditionally understand as mindfulness, but instead measures something like general awareness.

A further and related problem is when authentic leadership theory pays insufficient regard to defining what authenticity means. Authentic leaders must, by definition, avoid any tendency to become overly self-absorbed and narcissistic (Guignon, 2004). The ancient philosophers developed practices that promote authenticity as a civic virtue rather than a private one (cf. Guignon, 2004). This has little to do with the popular contemporary understanding of authenticity as an overly self-obsessed (bordering on narcissistic) rather than civic concern. Consequently, this understanding of authenticity is inconsistent with leadership, authenticity, and wisdom theory – self-obsessed leaders are problematic in practice and in theory.

The overly rosy picture of leadership (Alvesson & Einola, 2019) that paints transformational, authentic, and servant leadership as morally heroic (Manz & Sims Jr, 1991) is under challenge (Ryömä, 2020). Critics of these theories are concerned that they almost lapse into fantasy, which can lead to three problems. First, the unreal goodness presented in them can make leadership appealing to narcissists, egotists, and highly conceited people – precisely the people that these theories would tell us to avoid. Second, the literature might wrongly convince some perhaps humbler or introverted people that they could never develop the right qualities to be a leader. If so, this would reduce the pool of available people. Third, and significantly, research indicates that they will also reduce the number of women and minority group members who take on leadership roles (Hogue & Lord, 2007; Rosette et al., 2008).

If we consider idealized models of excellent leadership, we should also examine the dark or toxic side of leadership practice. Understanding this kind of leader takes us some way toward understanding what needs to be done to get better leaders.

14.2.1 Toxic Leadership

An important recent branch of leadership research focuses on bad leaders, including narcissistic leaders (Chatterjee & Hambrick, 2007; Ouimet, 2010; Rosenthal & Pittinsky, 2006), psychopathic leaders (Boddy, 2015; Landay et al., 2019), and otherwise toxic and destructive leaders (Einarsen et al., 2007; Padilla et al., 2007; Pelletier, 2010; Schyns & Schilling, 2013; Sternberg, 2020; Thoroughgood et al., 2012). Because such leaders are manipulative and unethical, they can seriously damage the organizations that they work for and individuals within those organizations (Schyns & Schilling, 2013). It remains clear, however, that these kinds of leaders find work in leadership roles far too easily, and that those who hire them are often slow (at best) to react and remove them once it becomes clear that they hired the wrong person (Boddy et al., 2015; Landay et al., 2019; Sheehy et al., 2020; Valentine et al., 2018).

This built-in bias toward appointing extroverted, confident, competitive, grandiose, and power-focused (often male) leaders is a problem that hirers need to be aware of (Berger et al., 2020; Fahy, 2017; Oc et al., 2020b). Although clinical and sub-clinical narcissists and psychopaths are over-represented in leadership roles (and prisons) (Boddy, 2017; Schouten et al., 2012), we keep hiring them because they fit our unconscious biases about what leaders look like (Hogue & Lord, 2007). We all have unconscious or implicit biases – that is, unconscious beliefs or stereotypes that we are (by definition) not aware of. These could also be gender biases or specific culture- or ethnicity-related biases that drive our spontaneous reactions and gut feelings about people. A person's unconscious biases will have an impact on them at work, including when making decisions about whom to hire and whom not to hire, because we use these biases as ways to quickly organize how to think about the social world and groups within it. If we did not do this we would overload our brain with thinking. We all have unconscious biases – this is inevitable – but they lead us astray. Some biases such as ageism and gender bias are probably familiar to you. These and other biases, such as overconfidence bias (a person's overestimation of their capabilities), beauty bias (the belief that attractive people are more competent), and name bias (a preference for people with familiar, usually Anglo-origin names), can lead us to want to hire the wrong people. If you are aware of your biases you can be reflexive when making these choices, but you need to be determined and persistent in detecting your bias in practice. Research suggests that you need to develop awareness skills and undertake diversity skills training (in which you practice or simulate being inclusive, aware, etc.), and that you must work at these over the long term (from 7 months up to 4 years) (Bezrukova et al., 2016). Cognitive learning (in which you have to think and analyze facts and experiences in a focused way using formal concepts or models), training that is integrated or embedded (in a larger curriculum) rather than being taken as a one-off workshop, and educational training (at school and at university, rather than at work) are vital, according to a major meta-analysis (Bezrukova et al., 2016).

There is no need to assume that organizations just have to put up with bad leaders. Today there are much better ways to select people for leadership roles than has historically been the case. Screening for toxicity during the selection process by using psychometric tools (see Moshagen et al., 2018, 2020) as well as by talking frankly to previous employers are obvious starting points. However, it is important to emphasize here that bad leadership is not solely the domain of people with psychopathologies. Abusive and otherwise obnoxious leaders may not meet the full diagnostic criteria for psychopathology, but can still be deeply problematic; in fact many problematic leaders have subclinical psychopathology (Boddy, 2017; Schouten et al., 2012).

There are two important messages from this research that we should keep in mind. First, although researchers know the psychological warning signs of problem leaders, most managers do not, and second, leadership research has little to say about how to become a good leader. Practical wisdom places the process of becoming excellent – that is, learning to embody wisdom – at the center of leadership development. However, those who are ill suited to leadership, because it is a craving rather than a calling, will probably not welcome the need for participation in long-term and focused wisdom development processes. But what is wisdom?

14.3   Wisdom

The Greek word "philosophy" means love of wisdom; philosophers in ancient Greece loved wisdom so much that seeking it was, as we suggested earlier, a way of life for them. There are two important things to note about this. First, philosophy did not just involve doing philosophical analysis (as happens in modern universities). Second, ancient philosophers deliberately and systematically practiced becoming wise in order to live a philosophical life. Thus a philosophical life was explicitly a practically wise life that was lived in the routine of a typical social existence, immersed in everyday life as a virtuous citizen. Aristotle called this "practical wisdom." Our understanding of wisdom is an extension of practical wisdom, called **social practice wisdom** **(SPW)** (McKenna et al., 2009; Rooney et al., 2010). We summarize this view of practical wisdom as the pinnacle of social excellence that is focused on the greater good. Wisdom is therefore a social or civic virtue.

14.3.1   Wisdom Virtues

Aristotle outlined five intellectual virtues, namely scientific knowledge (*episteme*), applied technical knowledge (*technē*), **practical wisdom (*phronesis*)**, mental agility and judgment (*nous*), and **conceptual or contemplative wisdom (*sophia*)**. In simple terms, a leader needs to be knowledgeable generally and in their disciplinary specialization (e.g., accounting, nursing, engineering) so that they are able to make decisions based on their ability to integrate their knowledge, **ethics**, conceptual ability, judgment, and experience. This raises important questions in business. Does a CEO of a pharmaceutical company need to be qualified in pharmaceutical science, or should they rely on the second rung of experts, such as the Chief Scientific Officer or Chief Information Officer? And how much general knowledge, including understanding of the human condition and the different contexts in which people live, should they have?

Realistically, the larger and more complex the company, the more unlikely it is that the CEO will have sufficient knowledge of the technological aspects as well as expertise in the financial, marketing, and human resource management aspects. However, a high-quality CEO will need sufficient intelligence to understand sophisticated briefings by specialists so that they can properly understand the various problems that they face. Technical expertise is useful for leaders, but it is usually not the most important thing for them.

We need to turn to the other intellectual virtues to consider what else a wise leader would need. Conceptual and contemplative wisdom is crucial because it refers to perceptive and insightful ways of thinking and deciding. For example, a leader who displays *sophia* would be able to draw on general principles of fairness, justice, and honesty in making decisions, knowing that acting fairly may involve contravening some degree of honesty, in order to save embarrassment – for example, when replacing a less capable, but decent, section head with a more capable person. That is, when faced with a practical problem such as the poor performance of an organizational section, a wise leader filters their technical understanding through the prism of moral principles and the ultimate good of the organization, or sometimes of society. These moral principles and abstract beliefs are a highly developed way of governing how one thinks about things (Curnow, 2011, p. 99). Conceptual wisdom – metacognitive and contemplative faculties – matters because underlying all practical decision making is a set of beliefs and understandings held by the decision maker (Trowbridge & Ferrari, 2011, p. 91). Reassuringly, a leader's ability to contemplate a decision and metacognitive capacity are learnable. Metacognition operates at a level above cognition (hence *meta*). It is a conscious process by which people can regulate the way that they think. This happens in three ways. First, having declarative knowledge, a person has the metacognitive ability to articulate the beliefs underlying their decision or judgment. Second, a person has the ability to understand their feeling when dealing with a particular issue or type of issue – for example, they may or may not feel confident about a topic or a line of reasoning. Third, they consciously deploy cognitive strategies that they know work for them to monitor and regulate their thinking (Efklides, 2008). Contemplation is understandable as a practice, and even as a habit, of stopping to think carefully (Trowbridge & Ferrari, 2011, p. 91). Conceptual wisdom also draws on a person's ability to empathize and to feel a sense of responsibility for the environment, as well as their ability to apply moral principles in their workplace.

In addition to these intellectual virtues, Aristotle stated that a wise person needs moral virtues and the ability to work out what is right. Perhaps the most important of these moral virtues is humility, which is also positively correlated with good leadership (Collins, 2001; Oc et al., 2020a). A humble person is able to accurately assess their personal strengths and weaknesses by accepting feedback and criticism. Humble people also acknowledge their own capabilities and can feel satisfaction in that. However, they do not consider that they are entitled to privilege, special treatment, or excessive deference – that is, they lack conceit. Such a person is also much more likely to display intellectual humility by acknowledging the limits of their own knowledge and understanding, seeking out alternative viewpoints, and trying to understand the cultural, psychological, and logical reasons underlying other viewpoints. However, there are two caveats. First, not all decisions can be or need to be informed by multiple viewpoints, as swift decision making is often needed. Second, a good leader's intellectual humility will not undermine their ability to make a decision or lead them to indecision, or "paralysis by analysis." Having engaged in dialogues with diverse viewpoints, a leader must show resolve in making a judgment, must explain that judgment, and must acknowledge to those whose viewpoints were not adopted that their views are still valued. Humility of this sort is not to be confused with automatic self-deprecation. Undermining one's own knowledge by being automatically self-deprecating would not be wise.

Courage, temperance, generosity, magnanimity (avoiding gloating or hubris when things go well), truthfulness, gentleness, and agreeableness were identified by Aristotle (1984) as virtues linked to wisdom. Significantly, contemporary psychological research has confirmed many of Aristotle's claims (Glück & Bluck, 2011; Jeste & Vahia, 2008; Sternberg, 2004; Webster, 2007). Moral and ethical reasoning to find out what is right for a particular situation is a core aspect of practical wisdom, and some business people are better at it than others. Being a moral business leader is difficult. To be fair, when the economic and political environment is founded on principles of materialism, growth at any cost, self-interest, and global competitiveness, even fundamentally decent people are often forced by shareholders and "market forces" to make judgments that clearly are not guided by ethical integrity. This tells us that the developmental path to wise leadership must treat ethical reasoning as something that it is important to learn (Ditto et al., 2009).

Furthermore, it is well understood that different moral principles may be incompatible. In his book *The Crooked Timber of Humanity*, the philosopher Isaiah Berlin, who borrowed this phrase from Immanuel Kant, argues that the ideal values of a humane society cannot always coexist in a sometimes harsh world. For example, although this was not well publicized, during the COVID-19 pandemic in certain countries, such as Italy, India, and some US states, doctors made decisions not to admit some elderly or frail people to intensive-care units in order to give younger, healthier patients access because of a shortage of ICU beds. What is noteworthy is that such decision making when moral principles are incompatible will be based on the decision maker's knowledge, values, and **morals**.

Aristotle also argued that, although mental agility and judgment are deeply connected to intuition and wisdom, but that they are not formally learned. Intuition is holistic because it integrates a set of diverse cues into a spontaneous sense of right and wrong (Pretz et al., 2014, p. 454). Intuition allows the wise person to skip over the formal processes of reasoning, but to do so only because they "know" what is the right thing to do using heuristics or rules of thumb (Piętka, 2015, p. 35). Keep in mind, though, that rules of thumb might be a kind of common sense, and that an important difference between common sense and wisdom is that wisdom includes the ability to think and act post-conventionally (González, 2002), whereas common sense is defined by its adherence to conventional ideas and actions. Although common sense and intuition are useful, intuitive judgment is prone to error due to cognitive biases (Tversky & Kahneman, 1974). Clearly, intellectual humility should curb excessive confidence in one's intuitive judgment.

Importantly, then, practical wisdom is the executive function that integrates the intellectual and moral virtues. The word "executive" literally means "to carry out," but it also implies that some psychological processes underpin this process of wise executive functioning, and that these processes are integrative. However, this raises the following question: how does one "do" this executive integration to produce wise action?

14.4 Leaders Applying Rules and Laws

Invariably leaders will need to apply and enforce rules and laws. A wise leader does not simply apply "the letter of the law" with no consideration of context or the intended purpose of a rule, as this can lead to perverse outcomes. An example of a perverse outcome arising from a mindless application of the law occurred in the 2008 Christopher Ratte case. Ratte, a University of Michigan archaeology professor, bought his 7-year-old son a lemonade at a Detroit Tigers game, unaware that it contained alcohol. The state's Child Protective Services accused the father of negligence and forced the son into foster care. Bureaucrats and judicial officers acknowledged the unfairness, but claimed they had to "follow procedure" (www.npr.org/templates/story/story.php?storyId=90157342). Not one person had the courage, insight, or wisdom to say that it made no sense to rigidly apply the law in this case, despite the profoundly traumatic outcome.

By contrast, in an Australian court, when a former Australian international sportsman ended up in court yet again after a string of offences, the judge sensed that something was not right. He called the prisoner aside, saying "You need to give me something because I've got nowhere to go but incarceration. What's going on with you?" The footballer told him how he had been sexually abused at school by his religious school teachers, and how this abuse had destroyed his life, his marriage, and his business,[1] leading to depression and potential self-harm. The judge clearly displayed intuition in sensing that something was not right. He also displayed post-conventional thinking in looking for the ultimate purpose of the law he was administering – not just to punish, but also to attempt rehabilitation. Furthermore, he used creative intelligence and knowledge to find a just outcome specific to the particulars of the case.

Wise leaders display insightful or compassionate actions through discretion, tolerance, mercy, and understanding when applying rules or norms. However, as Aristotle stated, tolerance and understanding must be balanced. An excess of tolerance and consideration can cause considerable organizational harm. For example, a person's behavior might be condoned because he "has problems" or she "has always been like that." Because the role of the leader is to ensure workers' right to a safe and respectful workplace, a wise leader must confront the person about their poor behavior and require appropriate behavior. If the person reveals that they are going through a crisis or have a chronic problem, the wise leader can direct them to seek professional assistance while still requiring behavioral change.

Having described the important foundations of wisdom, we shall now move on to discuss the social practice aspects of wise leadership.

14.5   Things You Can Do

In this section we shall consider what you can do to develop yourself as an excellent leader. Although education at all levels tends to neglect components of wisdom such as self-awareness, self-transcendence, character development, contemplative skills, and reflection, there is much that you can do yourself. We can add to this list of developable wisdom components things like emotion regulation, open-mindedness and curiosity, clarity about what your values are, intellectual humility, and critical thinking. What is increasingly clear is that aspects of intellectual and moral virtue, contemplation, and ethical action can be changed with appropriate guidance. In the following paragraphs we shall outline some practical things that you can do on your own or with others.

14.5.1   Changing Behaviors

Because values are very abstract, you should try to make them more concrete. For example, the value of generosity might turn into being generous with your time for others, if being generous with your time is the most meaningful way for you to embody that value. In our classes, we would design a behavioral experiment for the student (for additional ideas, see Bennett-Levy et al., 2004)

---

[1] www.abc.net.au/news/2021-03-07/former-wallaby-tony-daly-speaks-about-sexual-abuse-rugby-union/13206412

based on being generous with their time. You can design a 2-week or longer experiment in which you attempt to do things on a daily basis which honor that value. For example, you might decide to try spending 20 minutes (uninterrupted) with an elderly relative every day, or you might spend an hour each week simply listening to what your best friend is concerned about in their life.

Simultaneously, you would keep a daily journal reporting on your experiences, including failures, feelings, and worries. Finally, you can write yourself a considered report that also links to the relevant research literature and that provides you with your personal detailed leadership development plan for the next 5 years. In creating the plan, you should also report on the results of any other relevant psychometric assessments that you have undertaken.

14.5.2   *Mindfulness*

Our students have used mindfulness meditation to find ways to calm their minds. In some classes, we simply provide calming music to assist people in letting go of the stresses they bring with them into the classroom. Your university may even have mindfulness teachers on campus. Making wise decisions and doing difficult things effectively so that you achieve wise outcomes requires mental discipline, such as being able to calm your mind so that you have more emotional control and clearer thinking.

Reflexivity is a contemplative process that involves reassessing and, if need be, changing your values and assumptions so that you can make personal changes. These changes are equivalent to growth rather than simply adjusting what you already think and do. Reflexivity, then, involves calmly inspecting your values and actions and then changing your habits where necessary. Purposeful and disciplined access to your habits of mind is possible using mindfulness meditation (see Rooney et al., 2021). It is possible to mindfully reassess basic assumptions, values, and behaviors, as we have done this with thousands of business school students, not only through mindfulness training but also through self-critique and reflection. One disciplining practice that some of our students undertake is not to touch their smartphone during the first and last hours of the day. Those who are uncomfortable with meditation could also employ daily journaling, and have a mentor or coach to help them through the process. Leadership, executive, and life coaches specialize in doing this (King, 2017; King et al., in press).

You might also visit the Ethics Unwrapped website at McCombs Business School, University of Texas, Austin, which provides an impressive array of short videos and other resources with which you can learn about the psychology of everyday ethics.[2]

14.5.3   *Wise Habits*

The processes that we have just described will begin to instill wise habits in you. These are best thought of as the habits of mind and body that you have, but may not be aware of. We can become habituated to wise ways of being if we develop wise habits of mind and body (Rooney et al., 2021). To develop wise habits you must work systematically at developing them over time. Much of this development involves psychological growth for wisdom and maturity rather than mere adjustment (cf. Glück & Bluck, 2013; Glück et al., 2018). Aristotle proposed an idealized notion of acquiring wisdom from childhood by book learning and being mentored. Of course,

---

[2] https://ethicsunwrapped.utexas.edu/

such an upbringing is highly desirable, but it does not guarantee wisdom, partly because it may never involve serious dilemmas or trauma from which we can grow and learn. Conversely, having an emotionally and physically disturbed upbringing does not preclude people from becoming wise. For example, in her book *Educated*, Sara Westover describes how, in the home of religious fanatics, she not only survived a violent and exploited childhood without education, but also went on to complete a PhD at Cambridge University (Westover, 2018).

To do this required her to think outside the repressive confines of her life as a child. This is not easy, because a child's reality is strongly framed by their parents, who in this instance prevented their children from engaging with other people, and forced them to do dangerous and physically demanding work on the farm. So powerful was this emotional and physical control that Westover was still racked by guilt and doubt despite intellectually understanding the corruption of her upbringing. Also vitally important was the love and care shown by a grandmother and some friends who helped her understand that it was safe to abandon the life she was enduring. Thus she came to a deep understanding of the complexity of human life, but it did come at enormous cost, and she needed the kindness of others to help her to freedom. A significant wisdom researcher, Jeffrey D. Webster, has shown that posttraumatic growth is positively correlated with wisdom (Webster & Deng, 2015).

14.6   Concluding Thoughts

It is one thing to develop your own wisdom, but the other side of the coin is to ask what your role is in making sure that bad leaders do not get into influential roles in business or politics. The research on toxic leaders that we have discussed tells us much that is useful in this respect. Our main point is that toxic leaders may be manipulative, charming, and grandiose, but it is other people (possibly including you) who put them in positions of power. Because such leaders overstate their accomplishments, skills, and knowledge, and because of their charm and skill at being manipulative, it is easily possible to become alert to them. Grandiosity is easy to spot because grandiose people will seem too good to be true. Very often leaders' self-confidence is so seriously misplaced and so obviously defies reality that it should sound alarm bells immediately. It takes a commitment to developing your own wisdom skills and knowledge of leadership research such as we have presented in this chapter to alert yourself to people who are too good to be true, and to trigger you to look more carefully at them as potential leaders.

It is our collective responsibility to put different and better people in place to lead us. We all need to ask ourselves why it is that so often we don't pick up on those signals. You should ask this question of yourself. One reason relates to your unconscious biases. You can work to change your unconscious biases, assumptions, beliefs, stereotypes, and other habits of mind so that you are better able to see these leaders coming.

Finally, wisdom is something in which we all have a stake, and so we all have responsibility for fostering it. We may not be especially wise ourselves, but if we are one of the people involved in selection or leadership development processes, shouldn't we be wise enough to at least inform ourselves? The informed citizen with a cultivated mind and character is after all central to the ancient concepts of wisdom and democratic leadership. If we consistently fail to do such things then there is something missing in our education and adult development. Wisdom is both an individual quality and a collective responsibility. Even if you are not able to be a wise leader you can help to create the right conditions for one to exist, and everyone will benefit from that.

14.7   Comprehension and Discussion Questions

(1) How could someone convince you that they know how to be wise, and how would you assess them?

(2) To what extent should leaders develop self-awareness and self-knowledge? Why?

(3) Do some leadership theories present leaders as too good to be true and, if so, what problems might the too-good-to-be-true situation cause?

(4) What would *you* need to work on to become a wise leader?

(5) How could leadership research address the lack of leadership diversity? Do you think that leadership theory and practice hinder or advance women and members of minority groups?

(6) How should organizations deal with psychopathic and narcissistic leaders? What problems would you anticipate when dealing with them?

14.8   Investigations

David Rooney is Honorary Professor of Management and Organization Studies at Macquarie Business School, Macquarie University. He has researched, taught, and published widely in the areas of wisdom, leadership, business ethics, corporate social responsibility, the knowledge-based economy, and creative industries. His current research focuses on leadership and wisdom development, what organizational structures and processes support employees' wisdom, and examining whether ancient wisdom practices can be incorporated into contemporary education and training.

Bernard McKenna is Honorary Associate Professor of Management at the University of Queensland Business School. He has researched, taught, and published widely in the areas of wisdom, leadership, communication, business ethics, critical studies, and research methods. He co-authored the book *Wisdom and Management in the Knowledge Economy,* and has published in major academic journals. He is particularly interested in dealing with organizational paradox and incommensurability, and has also collaborated with Iranian scholars on wisdom in Shi'a Islamic societies.

14.9   Practical Applications

This chapter has focused on practical wisdom, which is a way of acting in the world – wisdom as a social practice, if you like. Much of what wise social practitioners can do is learnt. Wise social practitioners have over time developed good mental and bodily habits that make their wise action in life consistent. When you come to this view of wisdom, the process of becoming wise seems less intimidating. If you can organize yourself to authentically answer and act on the following four questions you will make progress toward being wiser. Who are you? What do you stand for? Where are you going in life? How will you get there?

Glossary

conceptual or contemplative wisdom (sophia) the ability to think and draw conclusions by using intuitive understanding, contemplation, wise reasoning, theory, and scientific knowledge. Also called theoretical wisdom, this way of thinking about wisdom is most closely associated with Plato.

embodiment the daily enactment of a person's moral and epistemic knowledge, which is achieved after learning and understanding within a particular community. In short, the way we behave in daily practice is an embodiment of our tacit knowledge and our morals. An accountant who has a good knowledge of their profession and acts according to morals based on honesty and fairness would display certain habits and behaviors that are quite different from someone who is equally knowledgeable but immoral. In the context of ethics, embodiment is a visible display of one's morals and values through one's behavior (e.g., whether one walks past a person in distress, or stops to assist them).

ethics the ability to reason and decide about what is right and wrong, good and bad, and desirable and undesirable. In practical wisdom, an ethical thinker uses moral principles as decision-making tools with which to determine what they ought to do. Ethics helps us to solve problems in positive ways that support a flourishing world.

follower a person who is subordinate to or voluntarily takes direction from a leader. Many people are simultaneously followers (taking direction from an authority figure) and leaders (supervising people who are subject to their authority).

morals the standards of what are widely accepted as principles that guide good behavior. They prescribe how people ought to act. For example, morals may relate to welfare (not harming others), or justice, as well as preserving the beneficial aspects of social institutions such as family (broadly defined) and community to produce a common good.

practical wisdom (phronesis) the ability to integrate the intellectual and moral virtues. It is often referred to as an executive function that decides what is the wise thing to do, as well as the capacity to do it. Practical wisdom is most closely associated with Aristotle's ideas about virtue and character. The measure of practical wisdom is one's ability to do things that contribute to a flourishing world.

social practice wisdom (SPW) an extension of the concept of practical wisdom that includes influences from Eastern philosophy and contemporary social science and neuroscience research. This view of wisdom makes more explicit the role of context and social dynamics in wise behavior.

values fundamental beliefs about what people consider to be desirable. Values act as guiding principles that motivate decision making and action. They specify how a person and their goals are related. Some values are concerned with positive relationships of self to others (e.g., benevolence), which might also be viewed as "moral." Other values express self-interest (e.g., power seeking, hedonism, stimulation, self-direction). Thus values are not the same as morals. For example, a self-achievement value might sometimes conflict with values of benevolence. One's primary values are likely to determine whether a behavior is oriented toward one's own benefit and happiness or toward the greater good.

virtues good character traits; virtues are the opposite of vices (bad character traits). Virtuous people not only know what is good in a moral and ethical sense, but they also go beyond this to commit themselves to producing socially positive outcomes. A virtuous person habitually or spontaneously acts rightly because they have an embodied virtuous disposition.

REFERENCES

Alvesson, M. and Einola, K. (2019). Warning for excessive positivity: authentic leadership and other traps in leadership studies. *The Leadership Quarterly*, 30(4), 383–95.

Aristotle. (1984). *Nicomachean Ethics*, H. G. Apostle, trans. The Peripatetic Press.

Avolio, B. J., Wernsing, T., and Gardner, W. L. (2018). Revisiting the development and validation of the Authentic Leadership Questionnaire: analytical clarifications. *Journal of Management*, 44(2), 399–411.

Barbuto, J. E., Jr. and Wheeler, D. W. (2006). Scale development and construct clarification of servant leadership. *Group and Organization Management*, 31(3), 300–26.

Bass, B. M. and Riggio, R. E. (2006). *Transformational Leadership*, 2nd ed. Laurence Erlbaum Associates.

Bennett-Levy, J., Westbrook, D., Fennell, M. et al. (2004). Behavioural experiments: historical and conceptual underpinnings. In J. Bennett-Levy, G. Butler, M. Fennell et al., eds., *Oxford Guide to Behavioural Experiments in Cognitive Therapy*. Oxford University Press, pp. 1–20.

Berger, J., Osterloh, M., Rost, K., and Ehrmann, T. (2020). How to prevent leadership hubris? Comparing competitive selections, lotteries, and their combination. *The Leadership Quarterly*, 31(5), 101388.

Bezrukova, K., Spell, C. S., Perry, J. L., and Jehn, K. A. (2016). A meta-analytical integration of over 40 years of research on diversity training evaluation. *Psychological Bulletin*, 142(11), 1227–74.

Boddy, C. R. (2015). Psychopathic leadership: a case study of a corporate psychopath CEO. *Journal of Business Ethics*, 145(1), 141–56.

  (2017). *A Climate of Fear: Stone Cold Psychopaths at Work*. Clive R. Boddy.

Boddy, C. R., Mile, S. D., Sanyal, C., and Hartog, M. (2015). Extreme managers, extreme workplaces: capitalism, organizations and corporate psychopaths. *Organization*, 22(4), 530–51.

Bono, J. E. and Judge, T. A. (2004). Personality and transformational and transactional leadership: a meta-analysis. *Journal of Applied Psychology*, 89(5), 901–10.

Case, P., French, R., and Simpson, P. (2012). From *theoria* to theory: leadership without contemplation. *Organization*, 19(3), 345–61.

Chatterjee, A. and Hambrick, D. C. (2007). It's all about me: narcissistic chief executive officers and their effects on company strategy and performance. *Administrative Science Quarterly*, 52(3), 351–87.

Collins, J. (2001). *Good to Great*. Harper Collins.

Curnow, T. (2011). *Sophia* and *phronesis*: past, present, and future. *Research in Human Development*, 8(2), 95–108.

Ditto, P. H., Pizarro, D. A., and Tannenbaum, D. (2009). Motivated moral reasoning. *Psychology of Learning and Motivation*, 50, 307–38.

Efklides, A. (2008). Metacognition: defining its facets and levels of functioning in relation to self-regulation and co-regulation. *European Psychologist*, 13(4), 277–87.

Einarsen, S., Schanke-Aasland, M., and Skogstad, A. (2007). Destructive leadership behaviour: a definition and conceptual model. *Leadership Quarterly*, 18(3), 207–16.

Fahy, P. (2017). How to avoid hiring a narcissist: a toxic hire will hurt your team and your leadership credibility. *The Journal of Medical Practice Management*, 33(3), 146–9.

Glück, J. and Bluck, S. (2011). Laypeople's conceptions of wisdom and its development: cognitive and integrative views. *Journals of Gerontology, Series B: Psychological Sciences and Social Sciences*, 66(3), 321–4.

  (2013). The MORE Life Experience Model: a theory of the development of personal wisdom. In M. Ferrari and N. M. Weststrate, eds., *The Scientific Study of Personal Wisdom: From Contemplative Traditions to Neuroscience*. Springer, pp. 75–98.

Glück, J., Bluck, S., and Weststrate, N. M. (2018). More on the MORE Life Experience Model: what we have learned (so far). *The Journal of Value Inquiry*, 53(3), 349–70.

González, E. (2002). Defining a post-conventional corporate moral responsibility. *Journal of Business Ethics*, 39(1), 101-108.

Greenleaf, R. K. (1977). *Servant Leadership*. Paulist Press.

Guignon, C. B. (2004). *On Being Authentic*. Routledge.

Hogue, M. and Lord, R. G. (2007). A multilevel, complexity theory approach to understanding gender bias in leadership. *The Leadership Quarterly*, 18(4), 370–90.

Jeste, D. V. and Vahia, I. V. (2008). Comparison of the conceptualization of wisdom in ancient Indian literature with modern views: focus on the Bhagavad Gita. *Psychiatry: Interpersonal and Biological Processes*, 71(3), 197–209.

Jeste, D. V., Thomas, M. L., Liu, J. et al. (2021). Is spirituality a component of wisdom? Study of 1,786 adults using expanded San Diego Wisdom Scale (Jeste-Thomas Wisdom Index). *Journal of Psychiatric Research*, 132, 174–81.

King, E. (2017). *Developing leaders to perform in uncertainty: the mindfulness solution*. Ph.D thesis, Macquarie University, Sydney.

King, E., Norbury, K., and Rooney, D. (in press). Coaching for leadership wisdom. *Organizational Dynamics*. doi:https://doi.org/10.1016/j.orgdyn.2020.100815

Landay, K., Harms, P. D., and Credé, M. (2019). Shall we serve the dark lords? A meta-analytic review of psychopathy and leadership. *Journal of Applied Psychology*, 104(1), 183–96.

Langer, E. J. (1989). Minding matters: the consequences of mindlessness–mindfulness. *Advances in Experimental Social Psychology*, 22, 137–73.

Langer, E. J., Blank, A., and Chanowitz, B. (1978). The mindlessness of ostensibly thoughtful action: the role of "placebic" information in interpersonal interaction. *Journal of Personality and Social Psychology*, 36(6), 635–42.

Liden, R. C., Wayne, S. J., Zhao, H., and Henderson, D. (2008). Servant leadership: development of a multidimensional measure and multi-level assessment. *The Leadership Quarterly*, 19(2), 161–77.

McKenna, B., Rooney, D., and Boal, K. (2009). Wisdom principles as a meta-theoretical basis for evaluating leadership. *The Leadership Quarterly*, 20(2), 177–90.

Manz, C. C. and Sims, H. P., Jr. (1991). Superleadership: beyond the myth of heroic leadership. *Organizational Dynamics*, 19(4), 18–35.

Moshagen, M., Hilbig, B. E., and Zettler, I. (2018). The dark core of personality. *Psychological Review*, 125(5), 656–88.

Moshagen, M., Zettler, I., and Hilbig, B. E. (2020). Measuring the dark core of personality. *Psychological Assessment*, 32(2), 182–96.

Oc, B., Daniels, M. A., Diefendorff, J. M., Bashshur, M. R., and Greguras, G. J. (2020a). Humility breeds authenticity: how authentic leader humility shapes follower vulnerability and felt authenticity. *Organizational Behavior and Human Decision Processes*, 158, 112–25.

Oc, B., Netchaeva, E., and Kouchaki, M. (2020b). It's a man's world! The role of political ideology in the early stages of leader recruitment. *Organizational Behavior and Human Decision Processes*, 162, 24–41.

Ouimet, G. (2010). Dynamics of narcissistic leadership in organizations: towards an integrated research model. *Journal of Managerial Psychology*, 25(7), 713–26.

Padilla, A., Hogan, R., and Kaiser, R. B. (2007). The toxic triangle: destructive leaders, susceptible followers, and conducive environments. *The Leadership Quarterly*, 18(3), 176–94.

Parris, D. L. and Peachey, J. W. (2013). A systematic literature review of servant leadership theory in organizational contexts. *Journal of Business Ethics*, 113(3), 377–93.

Pelletier, K. L. (2010). Leader toxicity: an empirical investigation of toxic behavior and rhetoric. *Leadership*, 6(4), 373–89.

Piętka, D. (2015). The concept of intuition and its role in Plato and Aristotle. *Organon*, 47, 23–40.

Pretz, J. E., Brookings, J. B., Carlson, L. A. et al. (2014). Development and validation of a new measure of intuition: the types of intuition scale. *Journal of Behavioral Decision Making*, 27(5), 454–67.

Purser, R. E. and Loy, D. (2013). Beyond McMindfulness. *Huffington Post*, 1(7), 13.

Reed, L. L., Vidaver-Cohen, D., and Colwell, S. R. (2011). A new scale to measure executive servant leadership: development, analysis, and implications for research. *Journal of Business Ethics*, 101(3), 415–34.

Rooney, D., McKenna, B., and Liesch, P. (2010). *Wisdom and Management in the Knowledge Economy*. Routledge.

Rooney, D., Küpers, W., Pauleen, D., and Zhuravleva, E. (2021). A developmental model for educating wise leaders: the role of mindfulness and habitus in creating time for embodying wisdom. *Journal of Business Ethics*, 170(1), 181–94.

Rosenthal, S. A. and Pittinsky, T. L. (2006). Narcissistic leadership. *The Leadership Quarterly*, 17(6), 617–33.

Rosette, A. S., Leonardelli, G. J., and Phillips, K. W. (2008). The White standard: racial bias in leader categorization. *Journal of Applied Psychology*, 93(4), 758–77.

Ryömä, A. (2020). The interplay of heroic and post-heroic leadership: exploring tensions in leadership manifestations in the oscillations between onstage and offstage contexts. *Scandinavian Journal of Management*, 36(1), 101092.

Schouten, R., Silver, J., and Silver, J. (2012). *Almost A Psychopath: Do I (Or Does Someone I Know) Have a Problem with Manipulation and Lack of Empathy?* Hazelden.

Schyns, B. and Schilling, J. (2013). How bad are the effects of bad leaders? A meta-analysis of destructive leadership and its outcomes. *The Leadership Quarterly*, 24(1), 138–58.

Sendjaya, S., Sarros, J. C., and Santora, J. C. (2008). Defining and measuring servant leadership behaviour in organizations. *Journal of Management Studies*, 45(2), 402–24.

Sheehy, B., Boddy, C. R., and Murphy, B. (2020). Corporate law and corporate psychopaths. *Psychiatry, Psychology and Law*, September 10; https://www.tandfonline.com/doi/full/10.1080/13218719.2020.1795000

Sternberg, R. J. (2004). What is wisdom and how can we develop it? *The Annals of the American Academy of Political and Social Science*, 591(1), 164–74.

   (2020). Wisdom, foolishness, and toxicity in leadership: how does one know which is which? In M. Mumford and C. A. Higgs, eds., *Leader Thinking Skills: Capacities for Contemporary Leadership*. Routledge, pp. 362–81.

Thoroughgood, C. N., Padilla, A., Hunter, S. T., and Tate, B. W. (2012). The susceptible circle: a taxonomy of followers associated with destructive leadership. *The Leadership Quarterly*, 23(5), 897–917.

Trowbridge, R. H. and Ferrari, M. (2011). *Sophia* and *phronesis* in psychology, philosophy, and traditional wisdom. *Research in Human Development*, 8(2), 89–94.

Tversky, A. and Kahneman, D. (1974). Judgment under uncertainty: heuristics and biases. *Science*, 185(4157), 1124–31.

Valentine, S., Fleischman, G., and Godkin, L. (2018). Villains, victims, and verisimilitudes: an exploratory study of unethical corporate values, bullying experiences, psychopathy, and selling professionals' ethical reasoning. *Journal of Business Ethics*, 148(1), 135–54.

Van Dierendonck, D. (2011). Servant leadership: a review and synthesis. *Journal of Management*, 37(4), 1228–61.

Walumbwa, F. O., Avolio, B. J., Gardner, W. L., Wernsing, T. S., and Peterson, S. J. (2008). Authentic leadership: development and validation of a theory-based measure. *Journal of Management*, 34(1), 89–126.

Webster, J. D. (2007). Measuring the character strength of wisdom. *The International Journal of Aging and Human Development*, 65(2), 163–83.

Webster, J. D. and Deng, X. C. (2015). Paths from trauma to intrapersonal strength: worldview, posttraumatic growth and wisdom. *Journal of Loss and Trauma*, 20(3), 253–66.

Westover, T. (2018). *Educated*. Windmill Books.

CHAPTER 15

Wisdom and Social Policy

Don Ambrose

15.1 Introduction

The governing of nations has always been complex and difficult, but is becoming even more so as the world deals with large-scale problems that are not confined within national borders. The ways in which nations are governed vary considerably from one region to another (Croley, 2007; Hacker & Pierson, 2010; Levitsky & Ziblatt, 2018; Snyder, 2018). Some nations provide maximal freedom to economic actors while ensuring that government regulation has very little influence. Other nations employ more government regulation and provide their citizens with stronger social safety nets. The ways in which national governments are designed to operate determine their impact on the well-being of their citizens, including the ways in which economic resources are distributed and laws are designed and implemented.

This chapter will explore the extent to which **wisdom** guides the leaders and policymakers in governments as nations attempt to grapple with large-scale problems such as **climate change** and pollution, resource shortages, the widespread erosion of democratic governance, the growth of severe economic inequality, the harmful aspects of rapid developments in technology, and the dangers posed by global pandemics. Although there are other twenty-first-century problems, these examples provide windows into the connections between wisdom and governance.

If political leaders are wise, they will deal with these problems more effectively than if they are weak-minded and/or corrupt. Therefore this chapter will also explore some of the causes of large-scale twenty-first-century problems, and it will propose some ways in which citizens and societal leaders can inject more wisdom into **policy making** and other actions of governments.

15.2 Recognizing Wisdom and Its Absence in Social Policy Leaders

If we want leaders and policymakers to use wisdom when they are dealing with twenty-first-century problems, we must first understand what wisdom is. Those who are wise have the ability to see beyond their own needs and wants and appreciate the common good (Ambrose & Cross, 2009; Sternberg, 2017, 2018, 2020, 2021; Sternberg et al., 2019). They are able to escape the hyperindividualism that tends to saturate the economic and political systems of some societies, especially in the USA.

Hyperindividualism arises from **rational actor theory**, which has dominated mainstream economics. According to this theory, humans are extremely rational individuals who use complete information sets to make decisions for selfish purposes. Supposedly, the actions of millions of these selfish individuals come together to create a prosperous society. However, this theory has several serious flaws (Ambrose, 2011, 2012a, 2012b, 2017; Freedman, 2008; Madrick, 2014;

Quiggin, 2010; Stiglitz, 2010, 2012). Humans are not extremely rational, they seldom have access to complete information about complex issues, and they are not entirely selfish (with the exception of psychopaths, who make up a small percentage of any population). The flaws in the theory tend to create or aggravate some of our twenty-first-century problems, especially the **erosion of democracy** and the worsening of severe inequality (Ambrose, 2017; Stiglitz, 2010, 2012).

To escape the severe damage caused by these misconceptions about selfish **individualism,** we must seek out and support wise political and economic leaders. The **WICS** (wisdom, intelligence, and creativity synthesized) model of leadership (Sternberg, 2005, 2008) can help us do this. Individuals who are lacking in wisdom, intelligence, and creativity to varying degrees cannot do much in terms of generating new ideas or products or intelligently judging and refining ideas or products created by others. Other individuals may be intelligent but not very creative or wise. They can effectively judge and practically refine ideas and products, but they cannot readily create anything new and useful. And if they do come up with something that has some small impact on the world, it may cause harm due to lack of wisdom, which is in part the ability to appreciate and address the needs and wants of other stakeholders in a situation. Other individuals may be creative but not very intelligent or wise. They may be able to come up with new and useful ideas, but they cannot intelligently refine or implement them. And again, if they do achieve some sort of impact on the world, this may be harmful due to their lack of wisdom. More dangerous is the combination of creativity and intelligence without adequate wisdom. Individuals who have these characteristics can produce ideas with high potential and intelligently refine them to make them work effectively. Consequently, their ideas and products can have a large impact on the world. However, the lack of wisdom means that these ideas could potentially cause severe damage. The creatively designed, intelligently refined and implemented innovations in the financial industry that did severe damage during the economic collapse of 2008 are examples of this (see Ambrose, 2017).

15.3   A Brief Overview of Major Twenty-First-Century Problems

Major problems have plagued humanity for thousands of years. While we have solved or escaped some of these (e.g., large, predatory animals are no longer a threat to us), others have been worsening in recent decades, and new problems are emerging.

Due to global networking through new technologies, some of these worsening and emerging problems have reached massive proportions. They have been called **macroproblems** because they are international (i.e., they cannot be solved from within the borders of a single nation), interdisciplinary (i.e., they cannot be solved by experts within a single profession or field), and long-term (i.e., they took years, decades, or even centuries to emerge, and are likely to take significant amounts of time to solve) (see Ambrose & Sternberg, 2016a, 2016b). The following are examples of twenty-first-century macroproblems (for further details, see Ambrose & Sternberg, 2016a, 2016b; Lopez-Claros et al., 2020; Wiegandt, 2018).

15.3.1   *Climate Change and Environmental Devastation*

The ongoing destruction of the ecosystems that support life has been taking place for centuries. It accelerated considerably with the Industrial Revolution, but has now reached the point where disastrous events are occurring more frequently and with greater severity in the twenty-first century (Wiegandt, 2018). Just some of the damage includes severe, lengthy droughts in dry parts of the world, more frequent hurricanes and flooding in other regions, rising sea levels, massive wildfires, air that is becoming extremely unhealthy in an increasing number of locations, massive dumps of toxic chemicals and plastics, mass extinctions of animal populations, and the emergence of desperate environmental refugees in growing numbers. Climate change and environmental destruction have become so devastating that environmental scientists say we are in a new era, which they have termed the **Anthropocene** (Lewis & Maslin, 2018; Purdy, 2018). This macroproblem has the potential to destroy the environment necessary for the sustenance of life on earth.

15.3.2 Resource Shortages

The twenty-first century has brought forth a looming shortage of resources such as arable land, fresh water, minerals, and hydrocarbons (Daly & Farley, 2010; Ember et al., 2020; Friedrichs, 2013; Klare, 2012; Prior et al., 2012; Rockström et al., 2014). Consider the following example of a reaction to a resource shortage. Extraction industries, such as oil drilling, are being encouraged to take greater risks that threaten the environment. For example, highly destructive deepwater drilling, hydraulic fracturing ("fracking"), and tar-sands mining have led to widespread, long-lasting environmental destruction. The oil and gas industries have always been environmentally destructive, but these more risky extraction initiatives have exacerbated the situation. There is also a danger that this trend will increase the likelihood of international military conflict as nations compete for ownership of the resources.

15.3.3 Eroding, Disintegrating Democracies

Governments that are healthy democracies tend to be ethical enough to push much of the decision-making power down into the hands of citizens. Undemocratic, totalitarian governments are dominated by a few powerful, selfish individuals and/or groups that make and harshly enforce laws that primarily benefit themselves. Governments that are not democratic include dictatorships (where there is dominant rule by a powerful individual) and **oligarchies** (where there is dominant rule by and for a small number of extremely wealthy, powerful individuals and groups). Governments that are midway between democracy and totalitarianism reserve most of the power and benefits of government for elites, but provide some benefits and some minimal decision-making power to the masses (Ambrose, 2019; Hacker & Pierson, 2010).

Whereas democracies were emerging and growing stronger in the late twentieth and early twenty-first century, that pattern has recently been reversed. Democracies have been disintegrating while authoritarian leaders have been claiming power by using divide-and-conquer techniques to deceive the masses into supporting them (Kirchick, 2018; Mounk, 2018; Snyder, 2018). Those leaders recognize that most of the citizens in their nations would not tolerate being oppressed and exploited if they were more aware that the totalitarian regime in which they are living is the true reason for their suffering. Therefore the corrupt leaders choose a population within the nation that they can blame for the ills of the majority (see Bermeo, 2003; Fording & Schram, 2017). The selected victims are usually members of minority groups, such as people of specific minority races, ethnicities, or religions, as well as immigrants.

There are a number of other strategies that are used by totalitarian leaders and oligarchs to protect and increase their power. They take control of or eliminate voting systems so that they can ensure that the will of the people is suppressed as much as possible. They also undermine, directly attack, or take over the national and local media so that they can disseminate self-serving, deceptive **propaganda** instead of the accurate reporting that comes from objective, investigative **journalism** (Roper et al., 2016; Starkman, 2015). The propaganda enables them to drive wedges between population groups and political parties so that they can increase the power of their political operations above that of their competitors.

This set of operations tends to create **polarization**, in which followers of different belief systems move away from each other toward opposite extremes. In this way, the totalitarians or would-be totalitarians reduce any possibility of compromise on important issues (Bermeo, 2003; Galston, 2018). This polarization usually results in one side or the other becoming far more powerful and pulling the system down toward an even more toxic form of **totalitarianism** (Ambrose, 2019). Historical examples of these collapses into totalitarianism include the left-wing dominance that accompanied the rise of Communism in the Soviet Union and under Pol Pot's rule in Cambodia, and the right-wing dominance that occurred in Nazi Germany and under Pinochet's rule in Chile.

While these extreme forms of democratic disintegration have been taking place in various nations, such as Hungary, Turkey, and Brazil, supposedly powerful, long-standing democracies have also experienced significant erosion. In one notable example, the United States Supreme Court struck a serious blow to American democracy with its Citizens United decision, which gave large corporations and extremely wealthy individuals the right to undermine democracy by essentially purchasing and controlling politicians (see Hasen, 2015).

15.3.4   Severe Inequality

Economic inequality has waxed and waned over the decades. At times throughout the world, societies became more egalitarian. They still had rich, poor, and middle-class groups within their populations, but the differences were not so extreme. At other times, inequality intensified considerably as the rich captured and hoarded almost all the wealth while the poor were reduced to life-threatening desperation. We are now living in one of the most extremely unequal eras in modern history (Payne, 2017; Scheidel, 2017; Temin, 2017; Wilkinson & Pickett, 2009, 2019).

The devastating era of inequality that currently plagues us emerged from the above-mentioned undermining of democracy, and a decades-long push toward an extreme form of corporate capitalism (see Dayen, 2020; Mattli, 2019; Piketty, 2014; Stiglitz, 2012). In its moderate form, **capitalism** is a beneficial way for a society to operate its economic system. Innovation and diligent work are rewarded, and the society becomes more prosperous. However, when capitalism is pushed too far and takes an extreme form, corporate monopolies arise, tax dodging becomes commonplace, and government programs for the masses are undermined and dismantled.

In addition, severe inequality causes most of the population to suffer from chronic stress, which makes societal problems far more severe (Payne, 2017; Wilkinson & Pickett, 2009, 2019). There are damaging increases in mental illness, drug and alcohol abuse, violence, and incarceration. Furthermore, trust diminishes, educational performance suffers, and social mobility (the likelihood that children will surpass their parents' level of wealth when they become adults) is suppressed.

The chronic stress also causes mental abilities to decline in much of the population, due to the **biological grind** that it produces (Sapolsky, 2018). Along with increasing rates of heart disease and diabetes, the brain–mind system comes to operate at a lower level than it would in a more egalitarian society. According to Sapolsky, severe inequality suppresses cognitive functioning in a number of specific ways: prefrontal cortex impairment reduces executive functioning, which hinders planning, decision making, and impulse control; hippocampus suppression hinders learning and memory; and decreased connections between neurons impair thinking capacity. Of course, this seems to run counter to the Flynn effect, which indicates a long-term elevation of IQ scores (Flynn, 1987). Clarification of these conflicting findings will require more interdisciplinary research that enables the linking of insights from psychology, social epidemiology, and neuroscience.

15.3.5   *Double-Sided, Rapidly Advancing Technology*

Throughout human history, advances in technology have often generated both significant benefits and serious problems. The human penchant for creative technological development has proved to be something of a two-sided coin, with a macroproblem side and a macro-opportunity side. The mass production of steel allowed for industrial advances as well as larger-scale conflicts enabled by more sophisticated weaponry. The discovery of nuclear energy led to the production of both beneficial and harmful nuclear power plants, as well as nuclear weapons that could deter enemy nations from continuing major wars, but could also potentially destroy life on earth (Ferguson, 2011).

The emergence of **artificial intelligence (AI)** is an especially intriguing example of this phenomenon. Artificial intelligence promises to make the economy far more productive and efficient, potentially enriching societies in ways that were never conceived of before. It also brings with it some serious dangers. The combination of growing knowledge bases in artificial intelligence and the biological sciences could facilitate devastating biological warfare (Jordan et al., 2020). The confluence of these knowledge bases can simultaneously strengthen **cybersecurity** while giving cyber attackers more powerful tools (Truong et al., 2020). It promises to improve medical diagnoses considerably while also creating more opportunities for corrupt, unethical dealings in the domain of finance (Meissner, 2020). It is the unpredictable nature of this macroproblem that makes it both intriguing and threatening.

Careful investigation of the nature and dynamics of these various forms of twenty-first-century technological developments is essential if we are to protect humanity from the dangerous face of the double-sided coin. If thoughtful, purposeful attention is not given to them, one or more of these existential threats could seriously disrupt life on Earth (Ord, 2020).

15.3.6   *Pandemics*

For some time, the predominant assumption was that massive **pandemics** were a thing of the past. The increasing knowledge base and sophistication of healthcare in the late twentieth and early twenty-first centuries supposedly built an imposing barrier between humanity and deadly diseases such as the 1918 so-called "Spanish flu," which spread around the globe in multiple waves. killing tens of millions of people and infecting about a third of the world population (Spreeuwenberg et al., 2018). However, the COVID-19 pandemic recently spread around the world largely unchecked in many nations, putting to rest the notion that this was a problem of the past. Some prominent leaders and policymakers failed to contain the outbreak in its early phases, and they did not learn from the events that had unfolded during the spread of previous viruses (MacKenzie, 2020). It is essential that the prominent decision makers of the future listen carefully to medical experts and think both critically and creatively in order to make plans for staving off the next dangerous pandemic (Edwards & Lessler, 2020). This critical and creative thinking must take into account the fact that the economic interactions and widespread travel generated by twenty-first-century globalization facilitate and accelerate the international spread of these diseases (Goldin & Mariathasan, 2014).

15.4   Causes of Macroproblems

Macroproblems arise and plague us for a wide variety of reasons, far too many to address adequately here. However, there are some underlying phenomena that initiate and energize most of them. A primary cause of the rising number of macroproblems is **dogmatism**, which infects the minds of virtually all of us to some extent, but some far more than others. Dogmatism is any blend of narrow-minded, superficial, shortsighted, rigid thinking (Ambrose & Sternberg, 2012; Ambrose, Sternberg & Sriraman, 2012).

Arguably, dogmatism is the world's worst macroproblem because it causes and/or substantially fuels most of the others. People with a dogmatic mindset tend to hold unwaveringly to a particular, often simplistic, flawed belief system, regardless of any new evidence that might challenge it. When they are narrow-minded and rigid, they will reject ideas that come from beyond their usual sources. For example, if they work in a particular profession, they either cannot understand or refuse to tolerate new ideas that come from other fields. When they are excessively short-sighted, they cannot perceive any of the long-term implications that are embedded in most macroproblems. When their thinking is superficial, they do not even think about digging deeper beneath the surface of complex issues to discover what the underlying causes of a macroproblem might be.

Mass deception is another primary cause of our vulnerability to macroproblems. This is especially the case when citizens and their leaders are dogmatic. Populations become more vulnerable to mass deception when the media is not doing an effective job of investigating and rooting out corruption in government and the economy (allowing the erosion of democracy), and when electronic communication pathways are deluged with conspiracy theories (see Borel, 2018; Spinney, 2020).

Clearly, the above-mentioned lack of wisdom in the face of twenty-first-century macroproblems creates very threatening conditions for humanity to deal with in turbulent times. The question of what can be done will be discussed next.

15.5   Specific Ways to Inject More Wisdom into the Creation and Implementation of Policy

15.5.1   Emphasize Panoramic Scanning

We have already discussed the WICS model in detail. Another construct that can be helpful is **panoramic scanning**, which is the ability to see with long-range and broad-scope vision

(Ambrose, 1996, 2009). Panoramic scanners can perceive and consider the long-term implications of issues and actions, as well as the immediate ones. For example, they can remove themselves from the chains of quarterly reports in business, which encourage leaders and employees in corporations to focus only on the next few months rather than on what might take place years or decades from now. Panoramic scanners will think in the long term and design their actions accordingly. Obviously, the long-range nature of macroproblems such as climate change requires this kind of thinking.

At the college level, it is possible that careful choice of resources for students could aid the development of panoramic scanning. For example, the astronomer Martin Rees produced a compelling argument for the need for more interdisciplinary, long-range, optimistic thought and action so that humanity has a better chance of surviving in the midst of twenty-first-century existential threats (Rees, 2018). Another resource could extend students' thinking far beyond even the timeframes considered by panoramic scanners. An analysis by Marcia Bjornerud (2020), a leading geologist, illustrates how most people have a very limited view of the future and the past. She uses a metaphor that shows how humanity is trapped on the **island of now**, which represents the present, the very near future and the very recent past, with large seas separating us from the landmasses of the far future and the distant past. Her metaphor, along with other elements of her analysis, shows how we tend to ignore the well-being of future generations in order to capitalize on short-term materialistic gains.

15.5.2 Release Education from Corrupt Accountability Handcuffs

As well as contemplating the expansion and refinement of thinking at the college level, we must free K-12 education from the chains imposed by superficial accountability systems. For several decades, education in the USA and a few other developed nations has been undermined and controlled by influential, narrow-minded, sometimes even corrupt, self-appointed reformers (Berliner, 2011; Berliner & Glass, 2014; Costigan & Grey, 2015; Koretz, 2017; Ravitch, 2010, 2013). They tend to dislike public education and promote the control and punishment of teachers and students by imposing excessively mechanistic measures of achievement through **standardized testing**. If citizens and policymakers were to become more aware of the narrow-minded nature of these accountability systems, they might be able to expand their vision of educational purpose (Sternberg, 2017; Zhao, 2014). They would be better able to perceive and appreciate the outstanding examples of highly creative teaching that can be found in American schools, even in the face of the severe constraints imposed by reformers. Some of these examples can be found in an analysis by Dintersmith (2018), which described the inspiring results of a search throughout the nation for impressive teacher innovation.

15.5.3 Use a Spectrum of Human Capacities to Highlight Ethical Abilities

Metaphor is an effective tool for either confining or shifting minds. For example, Lakoff and Johnson (1980, 1999) showed how root-metaphorical **worldviews** trap most thinkers within one of four conceptual frameworks – mechanism (reality as machine-like), organicism (phenomena in the world as holistic and integrated), contextualism (focusing on contextual influences and the unpredictable emergence of novelty), or formism (emphasizing patterns of similarity).

Here is an example of the entrapment caused by these metaphors. Mechanistic thinkers emphasize precise measurement and predictability, while ignoring holistic interconnections and contextual influences. Consequently, they produce and enthusiastically embrace simplistic measures of highly complex, integrated phenomena, such as the workings of the economy and educational processes. Excessive faith in precise, often simplistic measurement, which has been called **sterile certainty** by the mathematician William Byers and the **tyranny of metrics** by the historian Jerry Muller (Byers, 2014; Muller, 2018), has led to over-reliance on gross domestic product as the measure of economic success in a society (Coyle, 2015), while also promoting blind faith in standardized testing as the measure of educational success (Sternberg, 2017, 2021). No single root metaphor is superior to the others. Thinkers do far better work in the world by navigating through the four perspectives than by locking their minds inside one of them.

Knowing the power of metaphor, we can contemplate the use of another one to expand our thinking about human abilities and thus emphasize those pertaining to ethical thought and action. The **spectrum of human capacities** (Ambrose & Ambrose, 2013) is based on a metaphor derived from the electromagnetic spectrum, which shows various forms of energy arrayed along the electromagnetic frequency continuum. ROYGBIV (the colors of the rainbow) show up as visible light in the middle of the continuum, where the human sensory apparatus can detect them. Other frequencies that are much less perceptible, but very important, include ultraviolet, infrared, gamma rays, X-rays, long radio waves, microwaves, and more.

Based on this metaphor, the spectrum of human capacities model shows superficial, narrow IQ and standardized achievement test scores as the easily visible light in the middle. These scores are visible because they are easily detected through mechanistic measurements. However, there are other abilities that are less visible because they are complex, less measurable, and often hidden from view. Here are just a few examples of the abilities beyond the precise, visible middle of the spectrum: the above-mentioned panoramic scanning; the visual-metaphorical insight used by Einstein to develop his theories of relativity; aesthetic appreciation, which lies at the core of scientific and technological innovation; intellectual humility, which prevents individuals from being dogmatically overconfident about their ideas; altruism; and the WICS model mentioned earlier.

Highly effective leaders often employ compelling metaphors to rally their followers around a common purpose. For example, Martin Luther King Jr. used powerful metaphors in his "I have a dream" speech to capture the imagination of millions and significantly expand the power of the civil rights movement (Ambrose, 2009). Intelligent, ethical leaders who perceive the ethical problems and opportunities of the twenty-first century could use something like the spectrum of human capacities to help their colleagues, employees, and followers to discover, appreciate, and develop the ethical abilities that are needed to address them. For example, they might recognize and promote individuals with intellectual humility, WICS, and panoramic scanning abilities. In another example, they might find individuals with strengths in visual-metaphorical insight and encourage them to develop metaphorical concept cartoons, which are analogous to the political cartoons that often make readers think a little more deeply about issues. In essence, the spectrum of human capacity, or other metaphors that leaders might create, can help all of us expand our vision of what is possible, and what should be done about complex problems. Such metaphors align with recommendations from Maxwell (2013), Sternberg (2005, 2017, 2018, 2020, 2021), and Wexler-Sherman et al. (1988) that educational institutions should expand perceptions of ability so that humanity can more effectively address complex issues in a turbulent world.

15.5.4 Move Away from Individualistic Materialism and Focus on Societal Needs

The harmful effects of severe **socioeconomic inequality** on the well-being of populations were described in Section 15.3.4 of this chapter. Extreme inequality also makes large numbers of people adhere to excessive **materialism** because the importance of social comparisons in their societies compels them to catch up or get ahead of neighbors, friends, and relatives who are perceived as economic competitors (Payne, 2017; Wilkinson & Pickett, 2009, 2019). In an example often used by Wilkinson and Pickett, imagine yourself pulling up to a stoplight in your new Mercedes. You feel pretty good about yourself, until a chauffeured Bentley pulls up beside you. Then you feel terrible.

Those trapped in the game of excessive materialism spend most of their lives chasing money so that they can buy the symbols of high status. They are never truly self-fulfilled. According to Gewirth (2009), **self-fulfillment** has been attained when we can look back at the path we followed and say, "Mine has been a life well lived." It's a rather intangible concept, but a very important one.

Fortunately, economist Daniel Cohen and political philosopher Michael Sandel have developed compelling arguments for the need to back away from an over-emphasis on material gain so that we can move toward bigger-picture, more ethical goals both as individuals and collectively. According to Cohen (2018), we can make the world a better place by shifting away from materialistic competition and paying more heed to the world's big problems. According to Sandel (2020), creating a more thoughtful, less materialistic vision of success could enable us to produce more humility and awareness of the common good. If socio-political leaders could embrace these visions of ethical, less materialistic self-fulfillment, they might be able to encourage their colleagues, employees, and followers to at least consider doing the same.

15.5.5 Generate and Use New Creative and Critical Thinking Strategies

While thinking about complex, twenty-first-century social policy issues it is useful to consider Maslow's comment: "I suppose it is tempting, if the only tool you have is a hammer, to treat everything as if it were a nail" (Maslow, 1966, p. 15). In order to successfully grapple with twenty-first-century ethical problems, we will need to get beyond the hammer and find or develop some additional cognitive tools.

Some of those tools were mentioned earlier in this chapter, but we can do more. There are many thinking strategies that are being used in education and business. For example, the creative problem-solving strategy was designed to help participants to clarify the nature and extent of a problem and then develop various approaches to solving it through a step-by-step process (Treffinger et al., 2006). Individuals or groups who are determined to inject more wisdom into social policy can try out these strategies.

They can also create their own strategies and test their usefulness with real-world issues. Based on many excursions into the conceptual terrain of more than 30 academic disciplines and professional fields, the author of this chapter has been borrowing concepts and turning them into new creative and critical-thinking strategies (Ambrose, unpublished research). Some of them are applicable to ethical issues. Here are brief glimpses of a few of these strategies and how they might help to strengthen wisdom in social policy analyses.

15.5.5.1 Undermining Your Own Position

Given the dogmatism and extreme polarization that plague social-policy leaders and citizens of the twenty-first century, we need ways to recognize our own biases and correct them. This strategy engages participants in exploration of the strengths and weaknesses of a position that they hold strongly on an issue or problem. After building the strongest possible argument, they reverse course and seek out evidence and arguments against their own position. After that, they use those discoveries to revise their original position, or reject it and develop a new one. The result is a clearer, stronger position on the topic, as well as more opportunity for developing compromise and collaboration with those previously perceived as enemies.

15.5.5.2 Panoramic Timeline Impact Analysis

Due to the long-term nature of twenty-first-century social-policy macroproblems, this strategy helps participants to develop the long-term, broad-scope vision that enables them to understand complex problems. It helps them to develop the panoramic scanning mentioned earlier in this chapter. To carry out the analysis, participants map a long-term issue (e.g., the evolution of capitalism, the growth of social media) onto the vertical timeline showing the years, decades, or even centuries in which the emergence and development of the issue have taken place. While carrying out research into the evolution of the issue, they map its positive effects with a line graph extending to the right of the vertical timeline, and the negative effects with a line graph extending to the left side. The more extreme these effects, the further the line stretches out away from the center timeline. When complete, the graph shows a big picture about the issue and how beneficial or harmful it has been at various times, and over the long term. Decision makers can then propose some ways in which policymakers and citizens can deal with the issue.

15.5.5.3 Moral–Legal Overlap Analysis

Many citizens and policymakers assume that laws are designed to encourage ethical awareness and moral actions. Ideally, they will be so designed. However, there are instances in which immoral actions are legal and moral actions are illegal. And many other cases fit into the gray areas between morality and immorality, and legality and illegality.

In this strategy, participants create a square figure and place actions or phenomena onto it according to their moral–legal nature. The horizontal dimension of the square represents **legality**, with extremely legal actions residing on the far right-hand side and extremely illegal actions residing on the far left-hand side. The vertical dimension of the figure represents morality, with the most positive **moral actions** at the top and the most immoral actions at the bottom. Participants must go through some intensive creative and critical thinking as well as discussion to make these placement decisions. For example, they might end up deciding that the civil-rights actions of Nelson Mandela belong in the upper-left corner of the square because his actions were deemed illegal by the corrupt, racist government of his nation, but nevertheless, he was doing work that was extremely positive in a moral sense. Meanwhile, another group might decide that the US Supreme Court Citizens United decision (mentioned earlier in this chapter) fits in the opposite, lower-right corner because it was extremely legal, designed by the Supreme Court after all, but quite immoral because it undermined democracy.

Possibly the strongest wisdom-generating aspect of this strategy is the discussion and argument it can generate. For example, while one group might decide the Supreme Court Citizens United decision was immoral, another group might conclude the opposite. The ensuing discussion promoted by the strategy could force either or both groups further into dogmatic positions, or encourage them to develop more nuanced insights into the issues. Of course, the issues that fall into the gray area somewhere near the middle of the square are the most complex and intriguing to deal with, and will probably generate the most argument. Those who use the strategy have the opportunity to understand the ideas of others more clearly, and to think more critically about the nuances of complex problems.

Here are the names of some other strategies in the collection that can strengthen awareness of social-policy issues. There isn't room in this chapter to describe them in detail, but their names provide some hints about their uses: Altruistic Analysis, Aggressive–Assertive–Passive Analysis, Macroproblem Analysis, Intellectual Spectrum Analysis, WICS Analysis, and Personal Responsibility Determination.

15.6 Concluding Thoughts

Based on an interdisciplinary analysis of twenty-first-century pressures, it became evident that humanity has to make a substantial leap upward above the predominant level of cognitive skill and ethical awareness (Ambrose & Sternberg, 2016a, 2016b). In the interdisciplinary exploration that provided the focus for these international, collaborative investigations, the situation was portrayed as humanity marching toward the massive wave of twenty-first-century **globalization**. On top of the wave were macro-opportunities such as international scientific networking and exciting new developments in technology. On the underside of the wave were macroproblems such as climate change, looming resource shortages, the erosion of democracy, and severe socioeconomic inequality, among others. It was proposed that the development of new, ethical thought processes could enable humanity to make the leap to the crest of the wave and enjoy the macro-opportunities, which could lead to unprecedented self-fulfillment for all. Without this leap, humanity would trudge forward into the "Hobbes trap," which positions billions underneath the descending wave of macroproblems where lives will be poor, nasty, brutish, and short (based on ideas generated by the pessimistic seventeenth-century philosopher, Thomas Hobbes; Hobbes, 1651/1985). While these explorations of twenty-first-century issues were probably overly optimistic, based on the backward nature of human evolution since 2016 (e.g., accelerating erosion of democracy, insufficient attention to climate change, etc.), the argument about the need for the upward leap to the crest of the wave is even more pressing in today's environment. If we are to survive and thrive, we have to get sociopolitical and economic leaders to develop ethical awareness and strengthen their capacities for wisdom.

15.7 Comprehension and Discussion Questions

(1) What are the twenty-first-century macroproblems and macro-opportunities that social policy leaders and citizens need to address?
(2) What are some of the causes of twenty-first-century macroproblems?
(3) What are some important characteristics of wise minds?
(4) How can citizens and socioeconomic-political leaders come to understand the twenty-first-century context and ensure that their decision making becomes more ethical and effective?
(5) How can we use creative and critical thinking strategies to strengthen our wisdom?

15.8 Investigations

Don Ambrose is an international leader and gatekeeper in the field of gifted studies. His scholarship involves interdisciplinary exploration that provides new perspectives on ethical creative intelligence by connecting giftedness, talent development, and creativity with relevant research and theory in diverse academic disciplines and professional fields. He has led numerous interdisciplinary collaborative projects on ethical awareness, involving eminent researchers and theorists from gifted studies, education, creativity studies, cognitive science, ethical philosophy, psychology, political science, economics, law, history, sociology, theoretical physics, and critical thinking. His other work includes the invention of wisdom-strengthening creative and critical thinking processes derived from constructs in various disciplines.

15.9 Practical Applications

There are a number of steps that can be taken to inject more of the W (wisdom) element into policymakers and citizens who are creative, or intelligent, or creative and intelligent, or even those who have fallen prey to mass deception. We can make the leaders of our institutions more aware of this dilemma and the desperate need for more wisdom. And we can give them some practical tools to use themselves, and with their employees, colleagues, and students (in the case of K-12 and college institutions).

More specifically, we can strive to make our education systems pay more attention to WICS (wisdom, intelligence, and creativity synthesized) and long-range, broad-scope vision. This would involve an expansion of our ideas about human potential and talent development. We can promote a more ethical balance between individual and societal needs. Finally, we can use some creative and critical thinking strategies that are designed to strengthen ethical awareness and expand our thinking.

Glossary

Anthropocene a new geological epoch in which the actions of humanity have been the primary influences on climate and the environment.

artificial intelligence (AI) the simulation of human intelligence in machines.

biological grind the process through which the human brain–mind system and the body are worn down and damaged over the long term due to chronic stress.

capitalism an economic system based on private ownership and minimal government regulation.

climate change large-scale changes in weather patterns and overall global warming.

cybersecurity systems designed to protect computer networks from theft of information and damage to hardware and software.

dogmatism a form of closed-mindedness generated by any blend of narrow-minded, shortsighted, superficial, rigid thinking.

erosion of democracy the disintegration of governance by and for the people, which produces a descent into totalitarianism.

globalization large-scale economic and communicative networking around the world.

individualism a political and economic belief system that magnifies the importance of the selfish individual.

Island of now a metaphor that portrays how humanity is trapped in short-range vision; the island represents the present and the near future and recent past, while the distant future and distant past are landmasses across large seas.

journalism the production and distribution of information based on the search for, and discovery of, facts that are supported by evidence.

legality the state of being in conformity with guidelines produced by legal systems.

macroproblems enormous, international problems that develop over the long term and require interdisciplinary collaboration for their solution.

mass deception the use of inaccurate, distorted messaging to trick large numbers of minds into embracing inaccurate, often unethical beliefs.

materialism a belief system that elevates material possessions above all other considerations in terms of importance.

moral actions actions that are guided by accurate knowledge, empathy, courage, and purpose so that we can do the right thing.

moral–legal overlap analysis a creative and critical thinking strategy that enables participants to determine the extent to which actions in the world are legal and moral, illegal and immoral, illegal and moral, or legal and immoral.

oligarchies systems of government in which small numbers of privileged, powerful people retain and exercise most or all of the decision-making power for their own benefit.

pandemic an infectious disease epidemic that spreads far and wide geographically and affects large numbers of people.

panoramic scanning the ability to think about issues and problems over the long term, and in broad-scope, interdisciplinary ways.

panoramic timeline impact analysis a critical thinking strategy that enables participants to analyze the positive and negative impacts of a trend or issue over years, decades, or even centuries.

polarization the ideological separation of large numbers of people in a society, leading to perception of those on the other side as profoundly ignorant and harmful.

policy making the process through which political parties or governments formulate and implement new policies to provide regulations for guidance of activities in a society.

propaganda misleading, biased information that is designed to promote a particular viewpoint or political agenda; it is usually spread through unethical media sources.

rational actor theory the dominant theory in mainstream economics, which portrays humans as highly rational individuals using near-perfect information sets for selfish purposes.

self-fulfillment the feeling of satisfaction that comes from achieving one's ambitions and hopes, which are based on long-term aspirations.

socioeconomic inequality substantial differences in the resources owned by members of a society; in its severe form, small numbers of the very rich own most of the resources, while the vast majority of people are impoverished and desperate.

spectrum of human capacities a metaphorical portrayal based on the electromagnetic spectrum, showing easily measurable as well as less detectable, highly important human abilities.

standardized testing the use of tests that are designed and assessed in the same way for all test takers in a particular population; it usually measures academic achievement.

sterile certainty a descriptor that shows how the surface of mathematics is highly visible and precise while the inner core is ambiguous, turbulent, highly complex, and aesthetically appealing.

258   DON AMBROSE

totalitarianism a dictatorial, centralized form of government that demands complete obedience from citizens.

tyranny of metrics a term used for criticism of excessive faith in precise, mechanistic measurement of important, complex phenomena such as the effectiveness of education, medical care, and economic growth.

undermining your own position a critical thinking strategy in which participants analyze the strengths and weaknesses of a position they hold on a complex, controversial issue.

WICS the ideal form of thought and action combining creativity, intelligence, and wisdom; people with this ability can create original initiatives, practically refine and implement them, and ensure that they are ethically positive.

wisdom the ability and willingness to guide one's actions through knowledge, deep understanding, fairness, altruism, and the disposition to transcend the self in order to work for the greater good.

worldviews four very different metaphorical perspectives on reality, including mechanism (reality as machine-like), organicism (emphasizing holism and integration), contextualism (focusing on contextual influences and the unpredictable emergence of novelty), and formism (highlighting patterns of similarity in diverse phenomena).

REFERENCES

Ambrose, D. (1996). Panoramic scanning: essential element of higher-order thought. *Roeper Review*, 18(4), 280–84.

(2009). *Expanding Visions of Creative Intelligence: An Interdisciplinary Exploration*. Hampton Press.

(2011). Dysmorphic capitalism and the aberrant development of creative intelligence. In E. N. Shelton, ed., *Capitalism in Business, Politics and Society*. Nova Science Publishers, pp. 119–30.

(2012a). Dogmatic neoclassical economics and neoliberal ideology suppressing talent development in mathematics: implications for teacher education. In L. J. Jacobsen, J. Mistele, and B. Sriraman, eds., *Mathematics Teacher Education in the Public Interest: Equity and Social Justice*. Information Age, pp. 83–97.

(2012b). The not-so-invisible hand of economics and its impact on conceptions and manifestations of high ability. In D. Ambrose, R. J. Sternberg, and B. Sriraman eds., *Confronting Dogmatism in Gifted Education*. Routledge, pp. 97–114.

(2017). Interdisciplinary invigoration of creativity studies. *Journal of Creative Behavior*, 51(4), 348–51.

(2019). The erosion of democracy: can we muster enough wisdom to stop it? In R. J. Sternberg, J. Glueck, and H. Nussbaum, eds., *Applying Wisdom to Contemporary World Problems*. Palgrave Macmillan, pp. 21–50.

Ambrose, D. and Ambrose, V. K. (2013). Adult lost prizes, missing aspirations, a 21st-century education, and self-fulfillment. *International Journal for Talent Development and Creativity*, 1(1), 75–86.

Ambrose, D. and Cross, T. L., eds. (2009). *Morality, Ethics, and Gifted Minds*. Springer Science.

Ambrose, D. and Sternberg, R. J., eds. (2012). *How Dogmatic Beliefs Harm Creativity and Higher-Level Thinking*. Routledge.

(2016a). *Creative Intelligence in the 21st Century: Grappling with Enormous Problems and Huge Opportunities*. Sense Publishers.

(2016b). *Giftedness and Talent in the 21st Century: Adapting to the Turbulence of Globalization*. Sense Publishers.

Ambrose, D., Sternberg, R. J., and Sriraman, B., eds. (2012). *Confronting Dogmatism in Gifted Education*. Routledge.

Berliner, D. C. (2011). Rational responses to high stakes testing: the case of curriculum narrowing and the harm that follows. *Cambridge Journal of Education*, 41(3), 287–302.

Berliner, D. C. and Glass, G. V. (2014). *50 Myths and Lies That Threaten America's Public Schools: The Real Crisis in Education.* Teachers College Press.

Bermeo, N. (2003). *Ordinary People in Extraordinary Times.* Princeton University Press.

Bjornerud, M. (2020). *Timefulness: How Thinking Like a Geologist Can Help Save the World.* Princeton University Press.

Borel, B. (2018). Clicks, lies and videotape. *Scientific American*, 319(4), 38–43.

Byers, W. (2014). *Deep Thinking: What Mathematics Can Teach Us About the Mind.* World Scientific.

Cohen, D. (2018). *The Infinite Desire for Growth*, M. Todd, trans. Princeton University Press.

Costigan, A. T. and Grey, L., eds. (2015). *Demythologizing Educational Reforms: Responses to the Political and Corporate Takeover of Education.* Routledge.

Coyle, D. (2015). *GDP: A Brief but Affectionate History.* Princeton University Press.

Croley, S. P. (2007). *Regulation and Public Interests: The Possibility of Good Regulatory Government.* Princeton University Press.

Daly, H. E. and Farley, J. (2010). *Ecological Economics: Principles and Applications*, 2nd ed. Island Press.

Dayen, D. (2020). *Monopolized: Life in the Age of Corporate Power.* The New Press.

DeBoom, M. J. (2021). Climate necropolitics: ecological civilization and the distributive geographies of extractive violence in the Anthropocene. *Annals of the American Association of Geographers*, 111(3), 900–12.

Dintersmith, T. (2018). *What School Could Be: Insights and Inspiration from Teachers Across America.* Princeton University Press.

Edwards, J. K. and Lessler, J. (2020). What now? Epidemiology in the wake of a pandemic. *American Journal of Epidemiology*, 190(1), 17–20.

Ember, C. R., Ringen, E. J., Dunnington, J., and Pitek, E. (2020). Resource stress and subsistence diversification across societies. *Nature Sustainability*, 3(9), 737–45.

Ferguson, C. D. (2011). *Nuclear Energy: What Everyone Needs to Know.* Oxford University Press.

Flynn, J. R. (1987). Massive IQ gains in 14 nations: what IQ tests really measure. *Psychological Bulletin*, 101(2), 171–91.

Fording, R. C. and Schram, S. F. (2017). The cognitive and emotional sources of Trump support: the case of low-information voters. *New Political Science*, 39(4), 670–686.

Freedman, C. F. (2008). *Chicago Fundamentalism: Ideology and Methodology in Economics.* World Scientific.

Friedrichs, J. (2013). *The Future Is Not What It Used to Be: Climate Change and Energy Scarcity.* MIT Press.

Galston, W. A. (2018). *Anti-Pluralism: The Populist Threat to Liberal Democracy.* Yale University Press.

Gewirth, A. (2009). *Self-Fulfillment.* Princeton University Press.

Goldin, I. and Mariathasan, M. (2014). *The Butterfly Defect: How Globalization Creates Systemic Risks, and What to Do About It.* Princeton University Press.

Hacker, J. S. and Pierson, P. (2010). *Winner-Take-All Politics: How Washington Made the Rich Richer – And Turned Its Back on The Middle Class.* Simon & Schuster.

Hasen, R. L. (2015). *Plutocrats United: Campaign Money, the Supreme Court, and the Distortion of American Elections.* Yale University Press.

Hobbes, T. (1651/1985). *Leviathan.* Penguin.

Jordan, S. B., Fenn, S. L., and Shannon, B. B. (2020). Transparency as threat at the intersection of artificial intelligence and cyberbiosecurity. *Computer*, 53(10), 59–68.

Kirchick, J. (2018). *The End of Europe: Dictators, Demagogues, and the Coming Dark Age.* Yale University Press.

Klare, M. T. (2012). *The Race for What's Left: The Global Scramble for the World's Last Resources.* Metropolitan Books.

Koretz, D. (2017). *The Testing Charade: Pretending to Make Schools Better.* University of Chicago Press.

Lakoff, G. and Johnson, M. (1980). *Metaphors We Live By.* University of Chicago Press.

  (1999). *Philosophy in the Flesh: The Embodied Mind and Its Challenge to Western Thought.* Basic Books.

Levitsky, S. and Ziblatt, D. (2018). *How Democracies Die.* Crown.

Lewis, S. L. and Maslin, M. A. (2018). *The Human Planet: How We Created the Anthropocene.* Yale University Press.

Lopez-Claros, A., Dahl, A. L., and Groff, M. (2020). *Global Governance and the Emergence of Global Institutions for the 21st Century*. Cambridge University Press.

MacKenzie, D. (2020). *COVID-19: The Pandemic That Never Should Have Happened and How to Stop the Next One*. Hachette.

Madrick, J. (2014). *Seven Bad Ideas: How Mainstream Economists Have Damaged America and the World*. Alfred A. Knopf.

Maslow, A. H. (1966). *The Psychology of Science: A Reconnaissance*. Harper & Row.

Mattli, W. (2019). *Darkness by Design: The Hidden Power in Global Capital Markets*. Princeton University Press.

Maxwell, N; (2013) From knowledge to wisdom: assessment and prospects after three decades. *Integral Review*, 9(2) 76–112.

Meissner, G. (2020). Artificial intelligence: consciousness and conscience. *AI & SOCIETY*, 35(1), 225–35.

Mounk, Y. (2018). *The People vs. Democracy: Why Our Freedom is in Danger and How to Save It*. Harvard University Press.

Muller, J. Z. (2018). *The Tyranny of Metrics*. Princeton University Press.

Ord, T. (2020). *The Precipice: Existential Risk and the Future of Humanity*. Hachette.

Payne, K. (2017). *The Broken Ladder: How Inequality Affects the Way we Think, Live, and Die*. Viking.

Piketty, T. (2014). *Capital in the Twenty-First Century*. Harvard University Press.

Prior, T., Giurco, D., Mudd, G., Mason, L., and Behrisch, J. (2012). Global transformations, social metabolism and the dynamics of socio-environmental conflicts. *Global Environmental Change*, 22(3), 577–87.

Purdy, J. (2018). *After Nature: A Politics for the Anthropocene*. Harvard University Press.

Quiggin, J. (2010). *Zombie Economics: How Dead Ideas Still Walk Among Us*. Princeton University Press.

Ravitch, D. (2010). *The Death and Life of the Great American School System: How Testing and Choice are Undermining Education*. Basic Books.

   (2013). *Reign of Error: The Hoax of the Privatization Movement and the Danger to America's Public Schools*. Knopf Publishing Group.

Rees, M. (2018). *On the Future: Prospects for Humanity*. Princeton University Press.

Rockström, J., Falkenmark, M., Allan, T. et al. (2014). The unfolding water drama in the Anthropocene: towards a resilience-based perspective on water for global sustainability. *Ecohydrology*, 7(5), 1249–61.

Roper, J., Ganesh, S., and Zorn, T. E. (2016). Doubt, delay, and discourse: skeptics' strategies to politicize climate change. *Science Communication*, 38(6), 776–99.

Sandel, M. J. (2020). *The Tyranny of Merit: What's Become of the Common Good?* Farrar, Straus and Giroux.

Sapolsky, R. M. (2018). The health-wealth gap. *Scientific American*, 319(5), 63–7.

Scheidel, W. (2017). *The Great Leveler: Violence and the History of Inequality from the Stone Age to the Twenty-First Century*. Princeton University Press.

Snyder, T. (2018). *The Road to Unfreedom: Russia, Europe, America*. Tim Duggan Books.

Spinney, L. (2020). The shared past that wasn't: how Facebook, fake news and friends are altering memories and changing history. *Scientific American*, 29(4), 50–55.

Spreeuwenberg, P., Kroneman , M., and Paget, J. (2018). Reassessing the global mortality burden of the 1918 influenza pandemic. *American Journal of Epidemiology*. 187(12), 2561–7.

Starkman, D. (2015). *The Watchdog That Didn't Bark: The Financial Crisis and the Disappearance of Investigative Journalism*. Columbia University Press.

Sternberg, R. J. (2005). WICS: a model of giftedness in leadership. *Roeper Review*, 28(1), 37–44.

   (2008). The WICS approach to leadership: stories of leadership and the structures and processes that support them. *The Leadership Quarterly*, 19(3), 360–71.

   (2017). ACCEL: a new model for identifying the gifted. *Roeper Review*, 39(3), 152–69.

   (2018). Speculations on the role of successful intelligence in solving contemporary world problems. *Journal of Intelligence*, 6(1), 4.

   (2020). Transformational giftedness: rethinking our paradigm for gifted education. *Roeper Review*, 42(4), 230–40.

   (2021). *Adaptive Intelligence*. Cambridge University Press.

Sternberg, R. J., Nusbaum, H. C. and Glück, J. (2019). *Applying Wisdom to Contemporary World Problems.* Palgrave Macmillan.

Stiglitz, J. E. (2010). *Freefall: America, Free Markets, and the Sinking of the World Economy.* W. W. Norton & Company.

(2012). *The Price of Inequality: How Today's Divided Society Endangers Our Future.* W. W. Norton & Company.

Temin, P. (2017). *The Vanishing Middle Class: Prejudice and Power in a Dual Economy.* MIT Press.

Treffinger, D. J., Isaksen, S. G., and Stead-Dorval, K. B. (2006). *Creative Problem Solving: An Introduction*, 4th ed. Prufrock Press.

Truong, T. C., Diep, Q. B., and Zelinka, I. (2020). Artificial intelligence in the cyber domain: offense and defense. *Symmetry*, 12(3), 410.

Wexler-Sherman, C., Gardner, H., and Feldman, D. H. (1988) A pluralistic view of early assessment: the project spectrum approach. *Theory Into Practice*, 27(1), 77–83.

Wiegandt, K., ed. (2018). *A Sustainable Future: 12 Key Areas of Global Concern.* Haus Publishing.

Wilkinson, R. G. and Pickett, K. (2009). *The Spirit Level: Why More Equal Societies Almost Always Do Better.* Allen Lane.

(2019). *The Inner Level: How More Equal Societies Reduce Stress, Restore Sanity and Improve Everyone's Well-Being.* Penguin.

Zhao, Y. (2014). *Who's Afraid of the Big Bad Dragon? Why China has the Best (and Worst) Education System in the World.* Jossey-Bass.

Index

naive realism, objectivity illusion and, 79–80
naivety, 26–27
narcissistic leadership, 233–34
narratives of wisdom, 3, 49–52
natural kind characteristic, wisdom and, 70–71
Navalny, Alexei, 3
negative creativity, 7–8
negative emotions, 158–60, 179–84
Nicomachean Ethics (Aristotle), 212
nomination procedures, in real-life studies, 38–39
non-wisdom, categories of, 9–10
Norris, L., 139
Nosek, B. A., 124

objectivity illusion, mismeasurement of wisdom, 79–80
oligarchies, 247
Ontario Institute for Studies in Education (OISE), 201–2
open-ended wisdom problem, 94
openness to experience
    development of wisdom and, 176–77
    HERO(E) wisdom model, 162–63
    MORE Life Experience Model, 165–66, 181
    wisdom and, 143–46
optimal personality development, wisdom as, 141–42
optimism, unrealistic optimism, 10–11
outer feeling, 194
outer thinking, wisdom and, 194–95
Oxford Guide to Behavioural Experiments in Cognitive Therapy (Bennett-Levy), 199–200

pandemics, macroproblems, 249–50
panoramic scanning, 250–51
panoramic timeline impact analysis, 254
parenthood, wise personality development and, 149
particularism, 26
Pasupathi, M., 120
Paxton, J. M., 121–22
Pearson's correlation coefficient, 74–75
pedagogy, undermining of teachers' wisdom and, 222–25
perception, practical wisdom and, 212–15
performance measures of wisdom, 93–98
    limitations of, 98–99
    MORE Life Experience Model, 166
    wise and unwise responses, 95–96
personal characteristics, development of wisdom and, 176–77
personality-based approaches to wisdom
    emotions in, 163–64
    examples of, 161–64
    HERO(E) wisdom model, 162–63
    three-dimensional wisdom model, 161–62
personality traits
    Ardelt's three-dimensional model of wisdom, 56–57
    future research issues, 167–68
    wisdom and, 28, 135–50
    wise personality development, 147–49
    personally known wisdom exemplars, 42–43
persons
    Four Ps framework for creativity and, 108
    6P framework of wisdom and, 63–64

perspective
    conflict resolution and, 96–97
    practical wisdom, 215–16
Phan, L. V., 59
philosophy
    for children, 197–98
    practical wisdom, 21–29
    wisdom and, 18–21, 234–36
Philosophy for Children (Lipman), 197–98
polarization, social policy and, 247
policing, practical wisdom in, 220
policy, wisdom and, 202–3
policy making, wisdom and, 245
political polarization, common good *vs.*, 4–5
polyhedron model of wisdom, 58–59
positive creativity, 7–8
positive emotions, 159–60
positive events, wise personality development and, 149
positive mindset, wisdom and, 41–42
positivity bias, age and, 188
post-conventional morality, 119–20
practical wisdom *(phronesis)*
    applications of, 49
    character virtues and, 21–22
    components, 215–16
    defined, 138–39
    deliberation, 212–15
    in divorce law, 219–20
    hairstyling, 220–21
    interdisciplinary approach to, 16–18
    judges and, 212–15
    measurement of, 27–29
    perception and, 212–15
    philosophical foundations of, 15–16
    philosophical puzzles about, 21–29
    policing, 220
    in retail, 221
    teaching of, 200–1
    threats in professions to, 221–25
    in work contexts, 219–21
practice, wisdom of, 201–2
preconventional morality, 119–20
prescriptive ideal
    how one ought to live, 18
    wisdom as, 17–18
prescriptive reasons and truths, 15–16
Pridgen, Stephen, 135–50
problems, 6P framework of wisdom and, 62–63
procedural knowledge, Berlin Wisdom Model, 94–95
processes
    Four Ps framework for creativity and, 108
    6P framework of wisdom and, 64
products
    Four Ps framework for creativity and, 108
    6P framework of wisdom and, 64–65
professions, wisdom and, 47, 211–26. *See also* doctors; judges; medicine
    choice making and, 218–19
    threats to, 221–25
propaganda, journalism *vs.*, 247
proper aims *(telos)*, practical wisdom, 215–16

For EU product safety concerns, contact us at Calle de José Abascal, 56–1º,
28003 Madrid, Spain or eugpsr@cambridge.org.

www.ingramcontent.com/pod-product-compliance
Ingram Content Group UK Ltd.
Pitfield, Milton Keynes, MK11 3LW, UK
UKHW030903150625
459647UK00022B/2835